Praise for *Cloud Native Transformation*

Cloud native is the latest checkpoint in software development that abstracts away entire data centers while encoding best practices into platforms such as Kubernetes. Unfortunately, rubbing some Kubernetes on neglected software and an undisciplined engineering philosophy isn't going to solve your problems. The ability to leverage this technology shift requires a cultural one as well.

—*Kelsey Hightower, Developer advocate, Google Cloud*

The patterns provide invaluable information on how to think about cloud native development the right way—and valuable context for understanding why there is more than technology to a cloud native transformation.

—*Kyle Brown, IBM Fellow and CTO, IBM Cloud Architecture;*
Pattern Languages of Programs 2018 Program Chair

Pini, Jamie, and Michelle have been some of the earliest and most insightful advocates for Cloud Native architectures. Their engagement from the earliest days of the Cloud Native Computing Foundation was enormously helpful for the growth and adoption of cloud native in Europe and around the world. This book is a great opportunity to leverage their expertise.

—*Dan Kohn, Executive Director, Cloud Native*
Computing Foundation

I haven't seen storytelling paired with such an extensive and detailed pattern library before. It's a really compelling combination, doing a terrific job of illustrating the patterns themselves and showing how they fit together. It's also a lot of fun to read.

—*Adrian Cockcroft, Cloud architect and engineer*

This book is a storehouse of practical knowledge about how to achieve a cloud native transformation. From high-level strategic considerations and leadership issues down to the details of testing, integration, and delivery approaches, every choice is presented as a pattern—detailed as to its advantages and disadvantages, the relevant contextual issues, and its place in the bigger picture alongside the other patterns described. Helping you put this knowledge together to address the needs of your own organization are carefully considered case studies as well as a wealth of strategic, management, and psychological insight to help you assemble the elements you'll need to get to your goal and alert you to the pitfalls along the way. Essential reading for anyone looking to embark on a cloud native transformation.

—Andy Wilson, Director of Technical Culture, Oliver Wyman Digital

Cloud Native Transformation
Practical Patterns for Innovation

Pini Reznik, Jamie Dobson, and Michelle Gienow

Beijing · Boston · Farnham · Sebastopol · Tokyo

Cloud Native Transformation

by Pini Reznik, Jamie Dobson, and Michelle Gienow

Published by O'Reilly Media, Inc., 1005 Gravenstein Highway North, Sebastopol, CA 95472.

O'Reilly books may be purchased for educational, business, or sales promotional use. Online editions are also available for most titles (*http://oreilly.com*). For more information, contact our corporate/institutional sales department: 800-998-9938 or corporate@oreilly.com.

Editors: Michele Cronin and Chris Guzikowski	**Indexer:** Judy McConville
Production Editor: Nan Barber	**Interior Designer:** David Futato
Copyeditor: Jasmine Kwytin	**Cover Designer:** Karen Montgomery
Proofreader: Kim Wimpsett	**Illustrator:** Rebecca Demarest

November 2019:   First Edition

Revision History for the First Edition

2019-12-03:   First Release

See *http://oreilly.com/catalog/errata.csp?isbn=9781492048909* for release details.

978-1-492-04890-9

[LSI]

Table of Contents

Foreword

A few years ago, I was in Amsterdam for Dockercon Europe and met a very enthusiastic British guy with a northern accent, Jamie Dobson. He seemed to be running a company in Holland, but it wasn't at all clear what they did. A bit later that company became Container Solutions and expanded to London, and I kept running into Jamie, Pini Reznik, and Adrian Mouat (and eventually Anne Currie) at other conferences. Then the Container Solutions crew came up with this crazy idea to run a conference in a dockside warehouse in Amsterdam, one that mixed software with a kind of Burning Man vibe. It was called Software Circus.

Outside there was a 30-foot-tall fire-breathing robot called Kevin[1] and a whole pig roasted on a spit for lunch. I was the opening keynote speaker, although I had no idea who would come and what they would want to hear about. Over 400 people turned up, and I improvised the talk with no slides, told stories, got suggestions from the audience, and the projected Twitter feed became an effective crowdsourced substitute for a presentation. Afterward, Kelsey Hightower, who was giving the keynote on the second day, told me he hadn't ever previously thought of doing a talk with no slides, but he was now inspired to have a go. Kelsey then famously gave an entire talk on container scheduling while displaying himself playing Tetris. It was one of the more memorable conferences I've attended, but there were no videos of the talks; you had to have been there!

The people at Container Solutions think differently, don't play it safe, and seem to have a lot of fun along the way. They've worked on some very interesting projects over the years, and this is an unusual book; it's a collection of stories and a pattern library. The stories are entertaining and illustrate the same common patterns I've seen around the world, as companies struggle to adopt DevOps, product-based teams, microservices, continuous delivery, containers, and serverless. The pattern library is best approached as a cross-indexed random access collection. You could do

---

1 Because Kevin is an entirely inappropriate name for a fire-breathing robot that folds up into a 10-foot cube.

a linear full table scan by reading it through, but it's better to pick an interesting starting point and walk the graph by following the cross-references to related patterns. The individual patterns contain a lot of great detailed advice and aren't afraid to be opinionated. I agree with most of the opinions and find that they reflect the real-world experience that is often written out of books that play it safe with generic answers.

From my experience I'd like to provide three core ideas that this book illustrates in detail. First, most of the customers I meet think they have a technology adoption problem, when in reality they have an org-chart problem. The most successful orgs are made up of many small independent business teams communicating via clear APIs. If that's your org chart, you will inevitably build a microservices architecture, a trick known as the Reverse Conway Maneuver.

Second, the single most important metric for executives to focus on is time-to-value, which can be instrumented most easily as committing to deploy latency for each team. Many companies can't innovate because they can't get out of their own way, and short time-to-value (target less than a day) releases pent-up innovation from your teams. Third, there is far too much time spent in analysis paralysis, discussing technology variations and arguing about how best to architect solutions.

The patterns in this book will be a helpful influence to center these arguments, speed up architectural decisions while reducing the risk of making a wrong choice, and ultimately create more commonality as the patterns that work replace low-value architectural divergence. The stories remind me of Gene Kim's books *The Phoenix Project* and *The Unicorn Project*, but I haven't seen storytelling paired with such an extensive and detailed pattern library before. It's a really compelling combination, doing a terrific job of illustrating the patterns themselves and showing how they fit together. It's also a lot of fun to read.

— Adrian Cockcroft
Cloud architect and engineer
November 2019

Preface

Five years ago, Pini Reznik and Jamie Dobson founded Container Solutions, a professional services firm that helps early adopter companies figure out the best ways to make use of the emerging cloud computing paradigm. Jamie had been working with many companies to promote Agile development practices, and Pini was the one to identify containers as something that would change the world of software development. Containers were pretty new, and a powerful way to develop and deliver software in standalone, platform-agnostic packages—more lightweight than virtual machines and infinitely more portable. They decided to work together, forming a company dedicated to helping enterprises to harness this powerful new technology.

In 2014, companies moving to containerized applications were using Apache Mesos for cluster management, since it was the only tool capable of scheduling containers at that point. Skipping ahead a few years, Mesos has become outdated, and so now these companies want to move to Kubernetes, which they absolutely should do. But they are coming to us again for help in doing it. This repeat business is flattering but led us to a moment of realization.

Three years ago, when we helped these companies move to Mesos, it was a jump. Now they are coming to us to help them jump again, this time to K8s—meaning that they didn't build in innovation capabilities so they would be ready and able to evolve to the next step whenever it came. They were still operating under the old mindset of "Buy a major tool and install it; the process is disruptive for a few weeks but then you're good again for the next five or ten years."

Don't get us wrong, it isn't trivial to migrate from Mesos to Kubernetes if you're running 100+ microservices and using continuous integration/continuous delivery (CI/CD) with configuration management pretty heavily specialized for Mesos. But moving to a new way of managing the containerized apps you're already running should not feel like another major jump. It should feel more like a reasonably straightforward step. To us the process was fairly obvious: get the new platform in place, do some test migrations. You don't need to do everything all at once, or move all the services together—you have time. Start experimenting with simple stateless services and meanwhile learn about K8s in the process. You'll get there. What was self-evident to us, however, was not so obvious to our clients, who were still of the old mindset that adopting new tooling should be a one-and-done move.

And that was our "a-ha!" moment of realization: our job is no longer simply guiding clients onto the cloud, helping them choose and adopt the best tools and technologies for their migration. Our true job now is to help them achieve complete digital transformation—not just adopting new tech, but also evolving a completely new way of thinking. Because technology is only getting faster and faster. Being cloud native means delivering a distributed system of microservices that are constantly iterated and newly deployed every day, if not many times each day. Now we are changing everything in every part of the organization all the time, and all at the same time, which is a completely different way of thinking. You will always be doing this, innovating and moving to the next thing, and the next. Innovation now needs to be simply another piece of your workflow—one that is built right in.

We didn't invent this. We didn't even invent how to do it. We decided to write this book to describe how to do it, to map the cloud native trail that we and other early adopters uncovered before this way of working even really had a name. Patterns are the most effective way we see for doing it. However, if you're looking for a book of highly technical software design patterns, this is not the book for you.

On the other hand, if you're a middle manager, a project leader, or maybe even an executive-level decision maker seriously contemplating cloud native for your company, then this is the book you've been waiting for.

There are many very good technical pattern books out there that can tell you the ten best ways to Terraform a Kubernetes cluster. We are here to explain what Kubernetes is, how it fits into cloud native, and why you need it in the first place. You don't have to build the system, just understand it.

These are high-level patterns for strategy and risk reduction to guide decision making as you transition your organization and culture to this new way of thinking and working. We hope engineers will read this book too, because they are key to helping their companies execute a transformation and then excel at delivering afterward via optimized processes on their new cloud native platform. After reading this book, they can hand it to their managers and say, "This is what we need to do."

About This Book

At first we started writing a fairly straightforward and academic book: here are some patterns, here is how this all works.

Eventually, though, it became clear that many, if not most, of the problems we see arising during real-world transformations have little to do with the technology itself. The tech and tools are concrete—you can wrap your head around infrastructure, even if it's virtual—as well as fairly well supported. Instead, culture, process, and the other human-centered changes are, we have observed, the most difficult aspect of a transformation. Many migrations stumble, or even fail, by making common mistakes rooted in cognitive bias. Patterns can help them avoid these pitfalls.

And so we decided to present this book in a more human-centered way, through telling the story of a typical transformation. The tale is drawn from actual projects we have worked on with client enterprises, though we will not be naming names, to tell the story of a typical enterprise as it undertakes a cloud migration—including failures along the way.

We created a fictional company called WealthGrid to represent this "typical enterprise," which is very similar to the companies taking a serious look at going cloud native now that the tech is entering the early edge of mainstream adoption. Wealth-Grid's transformation story is presented as a series of interludes with informational chapters in between. The first five chapters describe essential cloud native background knowledge and concepts and then introduce tools, approaches, and strategies for working with both the tech and the patterns. We provide our own cloud native Maturity Matrix tool for helping you figure out your company's current situation and select your cloud native destination. The first half of the book ends with WealthGrid's crisis moment: why, after trying so hard and investing so much, is their attempted cloud native transformation simply not succeeding?

The second half of the book brings us to the patterns themselves, organized into chapters for strategy, organization/culture, development/process, and infrastructure. After that comes our favorite part: we demonstrate a successful cloud native transformation path for a typical company, told in patterns. Basically this is the story of what WealthGrid *should* have done.

Patterns are revealed in context as the narrative unfolds, along with biases that commonly arise in these situations to slow down or even derail an initiative. We show you how to use some of these biases in a positive way, to nudge things forward, while also avoiding common mistakes. By the end, a full pattern language is established. The story functions as a transformation design that can be used as a solid starting point for a real-world cloud native initiative by a small or mid-size company.

The transformation design (and, spoiler alert, happy ending for WealthGrid) is followed by a chapter where we break out common transformation pitfalls and challenges and show you how to avoid them. The second half of the book concludes with two real-world cloud native transformation case studies, illustrated by patterns. Starling Bank's founding CTO Greg Hawkins describes how he and his team built a cloud native challenger bank in a year, and Senior Cloud Platform Strategist Daniel Eichten tells us how he helped lead Adidas, the second largest sports apparel manufacturer and retailer in the world, through the IT jungle and onto the cloud.

All of this is rooted in our own experience, not from any kind of formal research (and, realistically, this is such new knowledge that formal research doesn't really exist yet). These are our opinions and observations, and as such not offered as any kind of definitive Ten Commandments of cloud native.

Our hope is that showing, rather than simply telling, how all of these complicated pieces fit together makes it easier to grasp how a functional and efficient cloud native system is made. Committing to a full organizational transformation is anxiety-provoking because you are stepping off the known path into a completely new world up there in the clouds. Patterns give us a series of small steps to follow along this new path, so as to slowly and gradually shift in the right direction. And the story of those who went before you, facing some challenges commonly found along the way but still successfully completing the journey, lends the confidence that you can do it too.

More importantly, though, you will learn that you can also use everything you learn from this book to do it again and again. We aren't trying to teach you how to "do" cloud native. We are trying to teach you how to become a responsive and adaptive organization, able to move fast to whatever comes next—without breaking things.

Latest Pattern Developments

New cloud native patterns are emerging constantly. To continue sharing them and extending the cloud native pattern language we have established here, please visit www.CNpatterns.org.

This is where to find the latest pattern developments, but also an online community for discussing and creating new patterns. We are inviting people from across the industry, thought leaders and influencers but most importantly everyday engineers and managers—those out there working elbows-deep in cloud native code and architecture—to contribute and participate. Hope to see you there!

Conventions Used in This Book

The following typographical conventions are used in this book:

This element signifies a tip or suggestion.

 This element signifies a general note.

 This element indicates a warning or caution.

O'Reilly Online Learning

 For more than 40 years, *O'Reilly Media* has provided technology and business training, knowledge, and insight to help companies succeed.

Our unique network of experts and innovators share their knowledge and expertise through books, articles, conferences, and our online learning platform. O'Reilly's online learning platform gives you on-demand access to live training courses, in-depth learning paths, interactive coding environments, and a vast collection of text and video from O'Reilly and 200+ other publishers. For more information, please visit *http://oreilly.com*.

How to Contact Us

Please address comments and questions concerning this book to the publisher:

O'Reilly Media, Inc.
1005 Gravenstein Highway North
Sebastopol, CA 95472
800-998-9938 (in the United States or Canada)
707-829-0515 (international or local)
707-829-0104 (fax)

We have a web page for this book, where we list errata, examples, and any additional information. You can access this page at https://oreil.ly/cloud-nat-tr.

Email *bookquestions@oreilly.com* to comment or ask technical questions about this book.

For more information about our books, courses, conferences, and news, see our website at *http://www.oreilly.com*.

Find us on Facebook: http://facebook.com/oreilly

Follow us on Twitter: http://twitter.com/oreillymedia

Watch us on YouTube: http://www.youtube.com/oreillymedia

Acknowledgments

The authors have many people to thank for helping this book happen.

First, the whole Container Solutions team has contributed to us actually bringing this book into being. We would especially like to shout out to the engineers who contributed their knowledge and experience to the creation of these patterns and all the concepts surrounding them. The CS design team worked both creatively and proficiently to deliver the drawings and diagrams that bring this material to life, and so extra special thanks go to Svitlana Chunyayeva, Mickey Houlder, and Wijnand Lustof. Heather Joslyn's expert editing and Productive Feedback as the chapters emerged improved the text immensely.

We would also like to thank the editorial and production staff at O'Reilly, including Christopher Guzikowski for his willingness to take a chance on our slightly radical storytelling approach to pattern design. Particular thanks go to Michele Cronin, whose deft guidance helped this book take shape—she always knows just when to offer encouragement (and chocolate).

Additional thanks to the many people who generously gave their time and insight to make the book better. Anne Currie, who was there from the beginning, gets special credit for inspiring a lively tone throughout. Adrian Mouat, for his honest and conscientious review and comments throughout the project, which significantly helped the authors clarify and improve the material. Hans Wegener, who shepherded and then helped create Pini's first PLoP (Pattern Languages of Programs) conference paper on cloud native patterns, which was the genesis for this book. As well as Kyle Brown, who as head of the PLoP organizing committee encouraged Pini to improve and refine the paper and continue investing time into patterns. We also thank Kyle for serving as a technical reviewer and especially for lending his particular expertise in reviewing and revising the patterns.

Jamie would like to thank all of Container Solutions' earliest customers who were willing to take risks with new ideas, new technologies, and, back then, a new company. They are Henk Kolk, of ING Bank; Max Schöfmann, then of HolidayCheck; and

Ken Owens, then of Cisco. Without you, Container Solutions wouldn't be here, and this book wouldn't have been written. Thanks to the team at Container Solutions who continue to amaze on a daily basis with their utterly insane appetite for experimentation and learning. To Adrian Mouat, for his friendship for the last 17 years and his continued compassionate and critical support. To Andrew Hesketh, Ian Ravenscroft, and Andrew Clark simply for putting up with Jamie. To Andrea Dobson, Jamie's wife, and constant source of love, compassion, and honesty. Finally, and most importantly, Jamie would like to thank Pini, his partner for half a decade, and Michelle, without whom this book would never have been started let alone finished.

Pini would like to thank his wife, Sarit, for her unwavering support over the past 20 years. She had to listen for endless hours about patterns and encouraged him to invest many evenings and weekends into writing this book, all while trying to build Container Solutions into the amazing company it has become. He would also like to thank Sarit for being the best mom for our daughter, Shachar, and son, Yonatan, who always give us the inspiration to become the best possible role models we could ever be.

Michelle would like to thank her family, and especially her sons, Jack and Cole, for enduring all the evenings and weekends she disappeared into her office to work on this book. She is grateful to her husband, Jeff, for his support throughout the project and patience in listening to endless talk about cloud native in general and patterns in particular. She would like to thank Sally Neustadt for providing invaluable encouragement and insight in non-work areas of life, all of which also flowed into this project. Most of all, Michelle would like to thank her mother, Marlene Gienow, for teaching by example the value of hard work, persistence, and a glass of wine at the end of a productive day.

And, finally, thanks is due to all the other countless folks who contributed their support and ideas to this project. We may not have had room to include your names here, but we are grateful to you nonetheless!

Prologue: Evolve or Else

Cloud native is more than just a technology or tool set. It is a philosophical approach for building applications that take full advantage of cloud computing. This new paradigm requires not only embracing new technology, but also a new way of working—which makes going cloud native an extensive undertaking. The payoff is immense, but in order to reach it an organization must evolve not just its tech stack but also its culture and processes.

The story of WealthGrid, a typical enterprise undergoing a cloud native transformation, illustrates this process from start to finish. First, we will look at the factors inspiring WealthGrid's decision to pursue a cloud migration. Then, as we follow WealthGrid's migration path, we will witness the problems it encounters along the way—ones that are commonly experienced during the transformation in companies both large and small. Ultimately, we will see how to use patterns to overcome—or even better, prevent—those problems.

Welcome to WealthGrid!

Meet the organizational protagonist of our cloud native transformation tale: Wealth-Grid, a mid-size financial services company. WealthGrid is a fictional composite of real-world companies we have worked with over the past few years, when we were called in as consultants to facilitate new cloud migrations—or to rescue failing ones. We created this composite in part because we must maintain our clients' confidentiality, but also so we can illustrate the most common problems companies encounter. Thankfully, no single transformation initiative is likely to endure *all* of these troubles, but nearly all initiatives will encounter at least some of them.

WealthGrid's organizational chart looks a lot like most mid-size companies: functional and top-down. In other words, it's your traditional business setup, with the C-suite and board at the top followed by other senior management, middle managers (including project and/or program managers), department heads, and so on, down the line. Structurally the company is divided into traditional departments like IT, marketing, finance, human resources, and operations based on functional role in the organization. There are specific standards, policies, and practices to govern how things work as well as every decision the business makes. Among themselves, teams may have taken on some Agile methods (like Scrum), but WealthGrid itself is fundamentally a classic hierarchical organization following a Waterfall software development approach (from here on out we will shorten this to "Waterfall hierarchy").

Overall, WealthGrid is quite rigid in what each specific department is designed, and permitted, to do for the company. Formal and well-documented channels exist to facilitate communication between them. Since each department specializes in its specific area of responsibility, there are numerous handoffs between the many engineering teams working on any given project; project managers are in charge of coordinating between them. Though the company's hierarchical structure and highly structured communication protocols may sound inflexible and maybe even intimidating, they do confer advantages. At WealthGrid, the chain of command—whether short or long—is always crystal clear. Every team's function is explicit, and their responsibilities are clearly spelled out, which means they are optimized for proficient productivity.

Sure, this model might hinder creativity and experimentation, but WealthGrid has been around for a long time and this is the way it's always worked. It takes a lot of managers to keep a well-oiled machine like this one, with so many people and projects to keep track of, running smoothly. Or at least as smoothly as possible.

Sound familiar? Though many companies have taken some steps toward more agile management practices, most mid-size and larger enterprises still function as hierarchies using a Waterfall software development approach. WealthGrid could be almost any company, anywhere. It is presented as a financial company because that industry is particularly representative of the pressures facing many sectors. Competition is high in the financial sector, driving the existential need to evolve and keep pace. Meanwhile, it is populated by a wide variety of companies with strikingly different levels of technological savviness. No matter what your business, though, you are likely facing some, if not all, of the same market pressures.

WealthGrid could be just like your organization: a business in the real world, mid-size or even larger. Not a giant technology company, but big enough to have a real IT department with engineers. And, although yours may not be a software company, you still need to deliver software—as must almost every business these days.

WealthGrid is a well-established company with a good reputation. It's been successful for years, decades even. It delivers solid products and services, and its internal culture is positive and healthy. People enjoy working at WealthGrid. They have competition, of course, but it's not much to worry about—the players are all familiar and competing within a stable and steady market. Thus WealthGrid is financially healthy, with reasonable (though not huge) profit margins. Overall, it's a good company, with a good market. It's good to be WealthGrid.

Until one day…

A Stranger Comes to Town

All great literature is one of two stories; a man goes on a journey or a stranger comes to town.

—Leo Tolstoy

This is the story of how a stranger suddenly appears in WealthGrid's nice, comfortable world—and changes everything.

Not a literal stranger, of course, but a brand-new competitor suddenly entering the financial services market. Someone completely unanticipated, completely different from traditional competitors, and very dangerous. There are three types of strangers who might, so to speak, come to WealthGrid's town.

- **The Upstart.** The first possible stranger is a company like Starling Bank. Starling is a brash newcomer, a UK-based contender bank that launched in 2014 and essentially built an entirely functional bank in a single year. Starling, which is mobile-only (no physical locations, nor even a web-based interface) has grown steadily, adding business accounts with full mobile functionality and seamless integration of services. The bank is approaching half a million customers, most of them young. It's very efficient and very effective. Starling is not big yet but it's growing very, very fast. And, at the time of writing, there are 26 other challenger banks just like this in Europe alone, with a high likelihood of more on the way.

- **The Rogue Giant.** The second potential stranger is a bit more familiar: Amazon acquired a banking license in 2018. No one knows what the company is going to do with it—it's not saying—and there is much speculation that Amazon will be entering the retail banking market. Studies show that, if it does jump in, Amazon could quickly become the third largest bank in the United States, eventually drawing an estimated 70 million customers.

- **The Reinvented Competitor.** The third possible stranger is, in a way, even more well known: a traditional competitor, but one that is rapidly reinventing itself. For WealthGrid this means a traditional bank that is investing heavily to modernize both its technologies and the products and services it offers. Someone like

ING from the Netherlands—a bank that these days doesn't call itself a bank, but a tech company with a banking license.[1]

All three of these strangers are cloud native entities. Starling Bank was born in the cloud and optimized from the start to take advantage of the velocity and inherent scalability that cloud native confers. Amazon is literally one of the inventors of significant cloud native technologies, and ING is well on its way to transforming itself from a traditional bank to a fully optimized cloud-based operation.

Why should WealthGrid worry about any one of these, though? After all, the company has done a pretty good job building its functionality, keeping up with customer demand for online and mobile banking features. What do any of these "new" strangers offer WealthGrid's customers that it does not already also provide?

Stranger Danger

The danger at this point is still somewhat subtle. WealthGrid is a profitable company, and so much of its annual earnings go to shareholders. Some might go back into the company to invest in innovation and research, but if so, it's a tiny portion of profits. The problem is that WealthGrid's technology growth has been pretty much a straight line: the value it is building for its customers is growing, yes, but in a linear way. This is exactly what a company like WealthGrid likes. Linear also means predictable and stable. It's easy to do long-term planning with linear growth. It has worked well for decades, why stop now?

If you are a traditional company, however, and a competitor using cloud native technology advantages comes into your sector, that competitor's growth is not going to be a nice, straight line. It's going to be a steep exponential curve. Figure P-1 shows the comparative growth for a traditional company versus a disruptive newcomer who enters the market later, but with a cloud native advantage.

---

1 ING CEO Ralph Hamers during a video interview with British financial affairs publication *The Banker* (*http://bit.ly/2KNy8xj*) in August 2017.

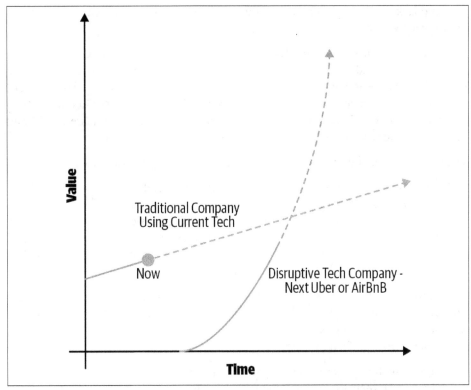

Figure P-1. Traditional linear enterprise growth curve versus the exponential growth curve a disruptive new competitor using cloud native technology will bring

At first the stranger is brand new and very small, taking only a tiny portion of your market. It's easy to feel complacent. Do not be fooled: they are still genuine—and serious—competition!

It is understandable that you and your usual competitors, the traditional vendors in a given market, may not be too worried at first. After all, you still own the majority of the market. But those newcomers will be growing exponentially. They, after all, don't carry baggage from decades of previous development and so are able to operate at a significantly lower cost. Worse, once they do demonstrate (even a little) growth, they will also have access to more or less unlimited investment funding. And they will take this money and plow it right back into ever more technological advancement, driving their growth curve ever steeper and ever higher.

So how are these newcomers so successful so fast? The main reason they are able to so quickly establish themselves in your market is because they deliver faster and more frequently using modern technologies. They have a rapid cycle of building function- ality, delivering it to the market, getting immediate customer feedback and, based on that feedback, delivering even more feature innovations and improvements. They can do this very, very quickly.

Some of these high-performing development capabilities are also used by companies following Agile and Lean practices, and those are definitely a good start. Cloud native, however, was born to take full advantage of cloud computing. For example, Agile teams may do continuous integration, but typically still deliver in one- or two-week sprint cycles. Cloud native teams add continuous delivery to create CI/CD and the ability to do new releases every day, or even multiple times each day.

The technology enabling this serious competitive advantage? Cloud native.

So these newcomers are on public clouds like Amazon Web Services, Google Cloud, or Microsoft Azure, taking advantage of the ever-more powerful services integrated with these platforms. They have optimized their architecture for microservices and containers, and use Kubernetes to orchestrate everything. Those technologies and tools and cloud-centric processes allow companies to move very fast and deliver functionality every day … or even many times a day.

Worse, they aren't entering to compete with you wherever you happen to be right now. Instead they enter the market with a serious head start, thanks to their superior technical position. They use customer feedback to iterate quickly on new features, and then get them in front of users *fast*.

No matter which stranger comes to your town—they may not be there yet, but they are definitely on their way—they will be jumping in way, way ahead. The simple truth is, once they do, you will not be able to catch up. They are going to leave you behind in your own market. You have to start now, before this competitor shows up. Because they are coming—and this way, you can be ready for them.

(If you wait until they are already here, you'll have to contend with the exponential growth curve we showed you in Figure P-1. If this disruptive stranger is already in your town, it very well may be too late for you to catch them!)

At this point you may be thinking, *This won't happen to me. Our sector is completely different, we aren't high tech, disruptors would never bother with us.* And we don't blame you; nobody likes hearing that their world is about to be upended. But think about the taxi business—global in scope, granular in implementation. Who could have imagined the disruption of such a widespread, low-tech industry? Yet Uber and Lyft, using a ridesharing model made possible by cloud technology, have done just that. Airbnb did the same thing in the hotel industry. And in both cases, once these new companies entered, the speed of change in the market was very dramatic.

Cereal Killer

Maybe you're still thinking you'll be OK, that your sector just isn't compatible with that kind of disruption. So another aspect to consider: What would happen to your business if Amazon suddenly bought your biggest competitor? Or even a small one, and then used their serious technological advantages to turbocharge that competitor? No matter what sector they may elect to enter, Amazon brings a massive innovative advantage in IT that traditional companies cannot replicate.

Case in point: in 2017, Amazon made an unprecedented move into the US retail grocery market by purchasing the Whole Foods chain of stores. On the surface, this was an utterly counterintuitive thing for Amazon to do. Supermarkets—you can't find a business more basic than that. They are everywhere, and everyone needs them, but profit margins are historically razor thin. Markets are very much fragmented by region, and studies have consistently shown that food is the one thing the vast majority of shoppers prefer to buy in person rather than order online.

Nonetheless, Amazon is now actively building its presence in the retail grocery world. The company has announced rapid expansion plans, including opening new checkout-free grocery stores in a dozen cities across the United States by the end of 2020.[2] Suddenly there is a serious challenger in a very stable, even stodgy, and low-margin industry that never saw it coming.

Amazon (along with other tech behemoths like Google and Facebook) created the cloud revolution in the first place to serve their online business needs. Now they are completing the cycle by moving into analog infrastructure, which is easy to do, and very available to them: the company has announced that one possible expansion route could be for it to buy up bankrupt supermarket and other retail chains that failed to compete and move new Amazon-run food stores right into that ready-made infrastructure.[3]

Amazon may not be in your market right now. But when it does come, it will be instant. And the competition may well be lethal.

You Say You Want an Evolution

This story is happening in the world right now. Even if WealthGrid is hypothetical, all three of these strangers actually exist.

---

2 Here is a good overview (*http://bit.ly/2OcyZd1*) of how and why Amazon got into the grocery business and their plans for the future.

3 Amazon exploring bankrupt or vacant retail infrastructure (*https://aol.it/35quL7l*) to house new brick-and-mortar Amazon Fresh and Amazon Go stores.

Companies are beginning to wake up to the existential threat. They are responding slowly, though, in part because of the lingering belief that cloud native is only accessible to giant tech companies. That belief was true just a few years ago, but now it's seriously misguided. Tiny young companies like Starling are starting small in the cloud and making it work for them. ING, an old-guard financial company, recognizes the existential threat and is seriously working to reinvent its legacy systems. Cloud technologies are maturing and becoming mainstream, and any company can "do" cloud native these days.

Like so many others out there, WealthGrid is a healthy company. It has been successful for years; it delivers a good product, and people enjoy working there. Truly it has done nothing wrong. Inevitably, however, its environment is changing. It is time to evolve, or risk extinction.

In nature, the only reason species ever adapt is to gain a benefit (survival being a pretty major benefit). If there is no benefit to gain, they simply won't change: evolution, after all, is a costly process. This works exactly the same way in the business world. If a company is not exposed to pressure, it also will never adapt.

The catalyst or pressure may not be there yet, but the very high likelihood is that it is coming to your industry. How do you know when just such a disruptive stranger will come to your market?

The answer is, you don't.

Which Evolutionary Stage Are *You* In?

In our experience it takes two to three years to truly undergo a cloud native shift and adjust to this new way of working. After that, it takes five more years to truly internalize the change—you can't succeed in an entirely new paradigm like cloud native without understanding the tools as well as how to transform your organization so it can best apply them.

Smart companies recognize that technology is always advancing, and they strive to innovate right along with it. Those that fail to adapt will fail, period. Some companies, even entire industries, will disappear. This is all part of the evolutionary process, and it will not destroy the world—it will build a better one. Cars did not destroy the world when they replaced horses; they just changed it. People switched from riding horses to driving cars. It's all thanks to technology that we now have things that even kings couldn't afford, or even imagine, 200 years ago.

This may all sound terribly dire, but it's really not. In crisis lies opportunity. If WealthGrid wakes up in time to the stranger's impending arrival and takes steps to adapt, it will emerge a stronger, more resilient and innovative company.

Change is inevitable, and the fittest species respond and adapt accordingly. Let's watch as WealthGrid gives it a shot.

CHAPTER 1

What Is Cloud Native?

Cloud native is more than a tool set. It is a complete architecture, a philosophical approach for building applications that take full advantage of cloud computing. It is also complex, both conceptually and in practice.

In this chapter we will take a look at the major components of a cloud native system —the five principles—and how they work together. Understanding these core concepts helps newcomers see how the true value of cloud native lies in harnessing the ecosystem of extraordinarily sophisticated services now available to all enterprises, not just the tech giants.

Cloud Native Is Not "The Cloud"

Though the terms are often confused, cloud computing and cloud native are two entirely separate entities.

Cloud computing—often referred to simply as "the cloud"—is the on-demand delivery of infrastructure (hardware/servers), storage, databases, and all kinds of application services via the internet. Frequently these are delivered by a cloud services platform like Amazon Web Services, Google Cloud, or Microsoft Azure, with metered pricing so you pay only for the resources you actually consume.

Cloud native is an architecture for assembling all of the above cloud-based components in a way that is optimized for the cloud environment. *It's not about the servers, but the services.* So cloud native is also an organizational *destination*: the current goal for enterprises looking to modernize their infrastructure and process, and even organizational culture, carefully choosing the cloud technologies that best fit their specific case (at least, the goal for now—eventually, even quite soon, cloud native will be replaced by another paradigm that once again completely changes our way of doing things).

There! That was easy.

Perhaps too easy, actually. After all, there are innumerable paths for reaching your cloud native migration destination. Identifying, provisioning, and then deploying the just-right combination of services to best take advantage of this new, rapidly evolving world among the clouds can take very different forms, depending on the needs of a particular organization. It's easy to get lost.

For enterprises ready to undertake their own cloud migration, staying on track means focusing on the architecture: understanding and prioritizing design before jumping into full-on implementation and deployment.

Over the course of five years spent guiding enterprises onto the cloud, Container Solutions engineers have learned a thing or two (or three) about helping each company find its own optimal route. We are most definitely not prescribing any "top-down" one-size-fits-all solution. We have by now, however, through observation and experience, collected enough data to identify some landmarks necessary for mapping that route.

Developing a cloud native pattern language is the next step in drawing a useful, and reusable, roadmap. A shared language for identifying common contexts and discussing tools, techniques, and methods is essential for developers to be able to discuss, learn, and apply the best practices in cloud native—even as they continue emerging.

But first let's take a quick, basic look at how cloud native works.

A Cloud Native Primer

Let's begin with the closest thing to an official definition for "cloud native":

> Cloud native computing uses an open source software stack to deploy applications as microservices, packaging each part into its own container, and dynamically orchestrating those containers to optimize resource utilization.

This comes from the Cloud Native Computing Foundation (CNCF), the entity that oversees and coordinates the emergence of open source technologies that support cloud native software development. CNCF emphasizes open source technologies, but there are also important cloud native tools offered by commercial providers.

Essentially, cloud native is the name of a particular approach to designing, building, and running computer applications. The architecture rests upon Infrastructure-as-a-Service, combined with new operational tools and services like continuous integration, container engines, and orchestrators. The objective, usually, is to improve speed. Companies of all sizes now see strategic advantage in being able to move quickly and get to market fast—putting a new idea into production within days or even hours, instead of months.

In fact, most enterprises migrating to cloud native these days cite velocity as their primary motive.

How Do I Know Cloud Native When I See It?

The fundamentals of cloud native are most often described as container packaging, dynamic management, and a modular distributed architecture.

We, however, believe cloud native is actually about adopting five architectural principles (which is hard) plus two cultural ones (which is even harder):

- **Containerization:** Encapsulating applications together with their dependencies/operating environment, all in a single package. This makes them easy to test, move, and deploy.
- **Dynamic management:** Using cloud-based servers that can be flexibly provisioned on demand; if on a public cloud, which is typical, companies pay only for resources when they are actually used.
- **Microservices:** Designing applications as a collection of small, decoupled component services. Each microservice can be deployed, upgraded, scaled, and restarted independent of other services in the application, and with no impact on the end user. Microservices increase velocity by allowing teams to develop in parallel, working on their components simultaneously yet independently, thanks to the elimination of dependencies and the coordination efforts that come with them.
- **Automation:** Replacing manual tasks, like maintenance and updating, with scripts or code so they happen seamlessly and reliably.
- **Orchestration:** Tying it all together by automating the deployment, scaling, and management of containerized applications. Specifically, using Kubernetes (or another orchestration tool) to control and automate tasks such as the availability, provisioning, and deployment of containers, load balancing of containers across infrastructure, and scaling up/down by adding/removing containers as needed.

The two cultural principles are:

- **Delegation:** Offering individuals the tools, training, and discretion they need to safely make changes, then deploying and monitoring them as autonomously as possible (i.e., without needing to hand off to other teams or seek permission through a slow management approval process).
- **Dynamic strategy:** Communicating strategy to teams, but allowing them to modify that strategy in response to their results. That is the ultimate purpose of

the fast, experimental deployment that cloud native provides: there's no point running experiments if you don't make use of what you learn.

Ultimately, **cloud native** *is about how we create and deliver, not where.* So, when you see an application built and deployed in rapid iterations by a squad of independent, compact feature development teams—and those teams are collaborating via an integrated platform that decouples infrastructure while providing automated monitoring and testing—that is when you know you are looking at the cloud native approach in action.

We are not considering the cloud native approach because it's the current hot tech (though this is undeniably true). Our motivation is pragmatic: cloud native works well with fast, modern software delivery methods like continuous delivery to provide faster time to value; it scales horizontally and effortlessly; and it can be very efficient to operate. Cloud native architecture also allows us to create complex systems by dividing them into smaller components built by independent teams. This differs from traditional monolithic application complexity, which is limited by the ability of the developers and architects to fully understand it even as it chains them together to deliver in unison.

Most importantly, cloud native can help reduce risk in a new way: going fast but small, limiting the blast radius in case changes ever go wrong, and rolling them back instantly if they do. So how and where do we start building?

It's All About Services

The heart of cloud native is cloud-based services. This is the platform upon which we build, launch, and operate our distributed, containerized, and automated modular application empire. There are different types of services available from public cloud providers:

- **Infrastructure-as-a-Service:** This is the obvious one, and it includes off-premises hardware, data storage, and networking. Hiring infrastructure rather than owning it allows you to maximize the creativity of each team instead of limiting it to the capabilities of a central architecture team.

- **Platform-as-a-Service:** This can be used to manage and maintain all that virtualized infrastructure, greatly reducing the load on your Ops (or Platform) team.

- **Software-as-a-Service:** This allows you to pick and choose component applications, everything from traditional business software (think MS Office 365 or Adobe Creative Cloud) to virtual infrastructure management tools, all delivered via—and operated over—the web. The provider ensures security, availability, and performance.

- **Container-as-a-Service:** This lets you hand over container engines, orchestration, and all underlying compute resources for delivery to users as a service from your cloud provider.
- ***-as-a-Service:** If you can dream it, if your business requires it, there is probably a service for it. If it doesn't exist right now, just wait a month or two. Backend-as-a-Service, Functions-as-a-Service—these once pie-in-the-sky services are now crossing the chasm into full enterprise introduction even as we write this book.

All cloud services arrive pre-built and ready to wire up with any other services, so you can get right to work more or less instantly. However, in order to use them effectively, you must use the right architecture.

Understanding the Principles

Cloud native is a lot to wrap your head around: it's an architecture, a tech stack, an approach to software development and delivery, and a complete paradigm shift all rolled into one! To confuse things even more, cloud native implementations vary widely between enterprises thanks to the sheer number of tools available as well as the complexity they offer. However, simply understanding these five fundamental principles of cloud native architecture—and, even more importantly, how they interrelate and support each other—gives you the keys to the cloud native kingdom, no matter how complicated it gets.

To reiterate, the five principles consist of:

- Containerization
- Dynamic management
- Microservices
- Automation
- Orchestration

Containerization

Once you've defined your service-based architecture, it only makes sense (for just about everybody, everywhere) to containerize things. Containers are lightweight, standalone executable software packages that include everything required to run an application: code, runtime, system tools, libraries, and settings. They are a sort of "standard unit" of software that packages up the code with all of its dependencies so it can run anywhere, in any computing environment. You can link containers together, set security policies, limit resource usage, and more.

Think of them as scalable and isolated virtual machines in which you run your applications. (We know this statement has historically launched a thousand flame wars, so let's at least agree that containers are simply much faster, OK?). Containers isolate an application and its dependencies, even its own operating system, into a self-contained unit that can run on any platform, anywhere. This means you can host and deploy duplicate containers worldwide (thanks to your Infrastructure-as-a-Service!) so your operations are flexible, reliable, and fast.

Dynamic management

This is where your new system absolutely shines. In short, dynamic management means making optimum use of the benefits conferred by your new cloud platform. Compute, network, and storage resources are provisioned on-demand, using standardized APIs, without up-front costs—and in real-time response to real business needs.

Dynamic management takes away the costs typically involved in capacity planning and provisioning of hardware resources. Instead, a team of engineers can start deploying value to production in a matter of hours. Resources can also be de-allocated just as quickly, closely mirroring changes in customer demand.

Operating compute, network, and storage resources is traditionally a difficult task that requires specialized skills. Obtaining these skills is often time-consuming and expensive. Even more important, though, is speed: humans are never going to be able to respond as quickly to cycle up and down as demand surges and sinks. Letting your chosen cloud platform run things dynamically means resource life cycles get managed automatically and according to unwaveringly high availability, reliability, and security standards.

Microservices

Microservices (microservice architecture) are an approach to application development in which a large application is built as a suite of modular components or services. Each service runs a unique process and often manages its own database. A service can generate alerts, log data, support UIs and authentication, and perform various other tasks. Microservices communicate via APIs and enable each service to be isolated, rebuilt, redeployed, and managed independently.

They also enable development teams to take a more decentralized (non-hierarchical) and cross-functional approach to building software. By using microservices to break up a monolithic entity into smaller distinct pieces, each team can own one piece of the process and deliver it independently. Ideally, some of these parts can even be acquired as an on-demand *-as-a-Service from the cloud.

Think about the companies setting the bar for everyone else in terms of performance, availability, and user experience: Netflix, Amazon, the instant messaging platform WhatsApp, the customer-relationship management application Salesforce, even Google's core search application. Each of these systems requires everything from login functionality, user profiles, recommendation engines, personalization, relational databases, object databases, content delivery networks, and numerous other components all served up cohesively to the user. By breaking all this functionality into modular pieces and delivering each service separately and independently, you increase agility. Each microservice can be written in the most appropriate language for its particular purpose, managed by its own dedicated team, and scaled up or down independently as needed. And, unlike in a tightly coupled monolithic application, the blast radius from any change is contained within that microservice's footprint.

Automation

Manual tasks are replaced with automated steps in scripts or code. Examples are automated test frameworks, configuration management, continuous integration, and continuous deployment tools. Automation improves the reliability of the system by limiting human errors in repetitive tasks and operationally intensive procedures. In turn, this frees up people and resources to focus on the core business instead of endless maintenance tasks.

Simply put, if you are trying to go cloud native but don't have automation, then you are rapidly going to get yourself in a mess. Enterprises come to the cloud to deploy more quickly and frequently. If you haven't fully automated your deployment processes, then suddenly your Ops staffers are spending all that time they save by no longer managing those on-premises servers to instead manually deploy your new, expedited production cycle. More frequent deployments also mean more opportunities to screw up every week; putting things into production faster and scaling them faster also means generating bugs faster. Automated deployment takes the grunt work out of constant implementation, while automated testing finds problems before they become crises.

Orchestration

Once a microservices architecture is in place and containerized, it is time to orchestrate the pieces. A true enterprise-level application will span multiple containers, which must be deployed across multiple server hosts that form a comprehensive container infrastructure, including security, networking, storage, and other services. An orchestration engine deploys the containers, at scale, for required workloads while scheduling them across a cluster while scaling and maintaining them—all the while integrating everything with the container infrastructure.

Orchestration encourages the use of common patterns when planning the architecture of services and applications, which both improves reliability and reduces engineering efforts. Developers are freed from solving lower-level abstractions and get to focus on the application's overall architecture.

This is where Kubernetes comes in, and it is one of the very last things to be done in a cloud native migration. If you implement an orchestrator first, you are fighting a battle on simultaneous fronts. Using an orchestrator effectively is a highly complex endeavor; getting that right often depends on the flexibility, speed, and ability to iterate you have put in place first. Other cloud native principles—cloud infrastructure/dynamic management and automation—must be in place first. Quite often, when experts are called in to work with a company whose cloud migration has gone wrong, what we find is that they have put in an orchestrator before things were otherwise in place.

Use your platform to build your platform—before you start worrying about orchestrating all the pieces!

Fitting Everything Together

The five (technical) principles, constructed in the proper order, are all essential supports in a cloud native architecture. One, however, may be even more important than all the others: microservices.

Microservices occupy a central role among the five principles. In order to get microservices right, you must have a mature approach to all four of the other principles. At the same time, containers, dynamic management, automation, and orchestration are truly powerful only when combined with microservices architecture. Figure 1-1 shows how everything fits together.

For example, one of the main advantages of containerization is that it enables heterogeneous applications to be packaged in a standardized way. This is not very compelling if your entire business logic is built inside a monolith. Similarly, you could apply dynamic management to such a classic homogeneous enterprise application on public infrastructure or a Platform-as-a-Service cloud provider. Doing so, though, means wasting the capability of scaling up and down in response to your business needs.

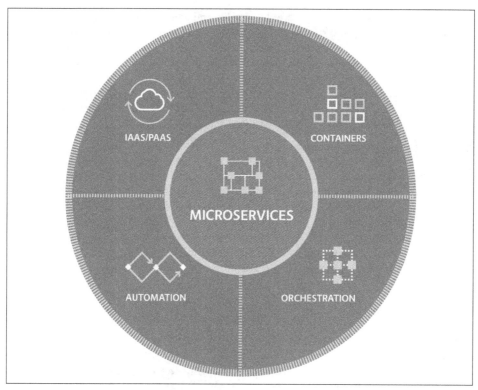

IAAS/PAAS

CONTAINERS

MICROSERVICES

AUTOMATION

ORCHESTRATION

Figure 1-1. The relationship diagram between the five principles of cloud native architecture

And, yes, while it is true that automation can still be applied to monolithic architecture, at least to a certain degree, the level of automation achievable with microservices is vastly higher given their self-contained, independent nature. Finally, modern orchestration platforms assume that applications will be composed of smaller, containerized services. A "lift and shift" cloud migration of a traditional application to run in containers on top of modern orchestrators is possible. However, it requires a great deal of adaptation and investment—all while failing to capture the significant benefits of microservices architecture.

There are cases where doing a lift and shift of an existing mono-lithic app to run on a cloud native platform is a reasonable choice. Companies with existing cloud native expertise can find advantages in moving an application to the cloud first, before re-architecting to optimize it to run there. This doesn't get you to full cloud native, but instead jump-starts your journey in two out of five areas as a starting point for further transformation. So, in the right circum-stances, there can be some value in this approach.

Experience is essential, however: if you're going to use an experi-enced partner to guide your cloud native transformation, you may get it right. But the risk of doing it on your own is way too high for the value. We too often see companies with limited cloud knowl-edge trying to simply shift their existing monolith onto the cloud as an end goal rather than a starting point. This requires a lot of time and resource investment with only limited benefits—at which point many companies will get discouraged and delay, or even cancel, further transformation efforts.

The most compelling argument for placing microservices at the center of cloud native principles is the fact that they encapsulate business logic, the differentiating factor for any enterprise. Microservices are capable of representing the processes by which a business delivers value to its customers. Ultimately, this shortens the distance between strategy definition and execution—serving the need for speed that brings most enterprises to cloud native in the first place.

However they are deployed, these five principles now have techniques and tools behind them that are approaching full maturity and commoditization. The ease of use and robust tooling offered by current containers and orchestration platforms is truly impressive. Once upon a time (four years ago) the world's most advanced technolo-gies were attainable at true production scale only by large companies who could maintain in-house IT teams dedicated to the development, care, and feeding of pow-erful but still immature innovations like containers and microservices. The competi-tive advantages these technologies confer are now publicly available, commoditized, and available to anyone with an internet connection and a credit card.

What Could Possibly Go Wrong?

So, yes, it is truly amazing that anybody with an idea can go to Amazon, Microsoft, or Google, sign up for a fully provisioned Platform-as-a-Service, and be up and running in minutes. Competition is fierce, and prices are falling, while features are expanding exponentially. The cloud now seems to be disrupting every industry it touches, and companies are understandably eager to migrate operations and embrace cloud native as fast as they can.

What can possibly go wrong? Well, rather a lot of things, actually. But the reasons behind cloud native transformations that go wrong tend to fall into one of three main categories:

- Difficulties due to the complexity of distributed systems

- The relative immaturity of the cloud native ecosystem with its Wild West landscape of tools and platforms

- The failure to adapt and evolve organizational culture to keep pace with changing technologies and delivery expectations

(Distributed) Systems Shock

We now live in a highly mobile world where apps get accessed and used across a plethora of platforms and devices. Users expect a fast, seamless, and always-on experience. To fulfill these expectations and keep the users happy, we have evolved distributed systems to manage the inevitable fluctuations and failures of the complex, behind-the-scenes services required to run it all. Many of cloud native's superpowers are granted by the sheer merit of its distributed-systems architecture.

A simple way to think about distributed systems is as multiple independent functions all harnessed together to present to the end user as a single, unified experience. Even a monolithic application talking to a database is a distributed system—albeit a very simple one. The primary benefit of a distributed system is reliability; when computing processes are spread across an entire network of machines, they happen independently from each other. If one fails, the process still keeps going.

Likewise, distribution makes it easy to add nodes and functionality as needed—the much vaunted scalability of cloud native systems. Distributed systems are also able to deliver the performance users now expect from every interaction, thanks to companies like Google and Amazon raising the bar for online user experience. Requests and workloads get split into pieces and spread over multiple computers, so the work gets completed in parallel and returned very quickly.

All these benefits, though, come with a significant side effect: complexity. When distributed systems become complex, then design, construction, and debugging all get much, much harder. Failure is pretty much inevitable, and engineering teams need to accept that and build in contingency plans for failure so that the end users hardly notice when it does happen. Peering inside a distributed systems technology stack to understand those failures is an enormous challenge, though, and so sophisticated observability is essential. The tools and knowledge necessary for detecting those failure points—such as distributed tracing, chaos engineering, incident reviews, and understanding the complexities of upstream and downstream dependencies—are extremely advanced. Few companies have the ability to do this for themselves.

Shocking Immaturity

That brings us to the second place things go wrong during cloud migrations: the relative immaturity of the cloud native ecosystem. Public cloud platforms like Amazon Web Services and Azure are presented as full end-to-end solutions, but they are far from plug and play. Companies used to the full functionality of virtual machines, or any other fully mature tech solution, are unpleasantly surprised to find that configuration is manual, and not all the necessary pieces are even present.

Imagine buying a TV, bringing it home, and opening the box to find there are no cables, no power cord, no remote. None of the peripherals we expect to find and that are essential for operating the TV. It's literally just a screen. The manufacturer tells you, "Now go buy this piece here, that piece there, and assemble your TV—eventually it will be fine!" So it is with cloud providers: they claim to be full solutions, but half of the necessary stuff is missing. Because you believed your vendor that their platform was a full solution, you haven't allocated people or budget or time to build or buy the missing or incomplete pieces. And it is highly unlikely that you have people inside your company who can handle assembling all of it anyway.

Because cloud native is still so new, the current landscape of cloud technologies and vendor offerings is constantly evolving. The CNCF maintains a roster of the ever-proliferating technologies in the cloud native landscape. Trying them all is probably out of the question: as we write this book, the CNCF counts more than 1,200 technologies, vendors, and projects to choose from when mapping a cloud migration.

Many of the patterns we introduce later in this book are directly concerned with managing the complexities of distributed systems. There are also patterns for narrowing down the intimidating array of choices of cloud native tools and platforms, no matter how often they change, in order to choose the most effective for your specific context.

The Executive Summary

In short, to get the best from the cloud, use cloud native architecture: microservices, containers, orchestration, automation. Since the first three may introduce new problems, automation should be among the very first things put in place—you want the sanitation system laid down before you build your city in the clouds.

Microservices and cloud services are key to truly harnessing the power of cloud operations. On the surface, the win might look like getting rid of physical machines. *The true win, though, is accessing all the extraordinarily sophisticated services—every kind of specialized software as a service, turnkey and ready to hook into your application.* With cloud and microservices in place, you'll be ready to iterate and deploy quickly and more often, which is where automation and orchestration come in. It can be complex, yes, but orchestrators exist to optimize all this—and these days, you can simply hire those as a service as well!

The online European fashion retailer ASOS provides a very good example of how to curate the perfect set of services. Their big win in the cloud was the ability to choose a different database for every piece of data they had, from stock to shipping to customer information—all without the need to manage the complexities of different databases. With microservices, ASOS could make their apps smaller and specifically tied to a particular database optimized for that exact use case. A relational database for some, key/value store for something very fast, but in every case it was State-as-a-Service. Even better, they could buy off the shelf from the provider—without needing specialists to run it all. Not one giant monolith that talks to one giant relational database, but many smaller microservices, each talking to their appropriate database counterparts. This example shows how far and how fast we have come: in the "old" days five years ago if you wanted, say, a Cassandra database, you also needed a really expensive database expert to run it. Now you can get both on demand from your public cloud provider.

Cloud native is a powerful, promising (and, yes, much-hyped) technology. Enterprises are understandably eager to get there as fast as they can. But reaping the full benefit of the cloud means first looking past the hype to build a solid foundation—one based upon the principles of cloud native architecture. And, meanwhile, evolving your organization's culture, its structure and processes, to an equally new way of working. We will explore how to achieve these human-centered changes next, in Chapter 2.

CHAPTER 2

The Human Challenge of Cloud Native

Cloud native is more than just a technology or tool set. It is a philosophical approach for building applications that take full advantage of cloud computing. This new paradigm requires not only embracing new technology but also a new way of working.

As this book is being written, we have already helped several dozen companies integrate their cloud native systems. These enterprises have widely varied in size, sector, and background, but all had one thing in common: when they first began migrating their operations to the cloud, they firmly believed that a cloud native transformation meant simply a change in technology.

The thinking seems to go like this: *just start using containers and Kubernetes/microservices/cloud infrastructure, and whatever problems our organization is currently experiencing will suddenly be better.* While this is certainly a possible outcome for most companies moving to cloud native technology, it is also a very unlikely one—unless the organization also addresses the human challenge of cloud native.

We call it a cloud native *transformation* because, in order to make a successful, effective, and above all worthwhile migration to the cloud, the entire organization—not just the tech stack—must change. This means evolving nontechnical aspects such as management practices, organizational structure, and team responsibilities—even your fundamental delivery processes—to work in your new cloud native context. Otherwise, if you simply layer the latest tech on top of the same old way you have always done things, you will create a whole new slew of problems, including but not restricted to, slow delivery, reduced quality, and difficulties in both project and team management.

Quite simply, your organization's culture needs to change along with the technology. If it doesn't, you are very likely about to waste a lot of time and money on an ultimately unproductive transformation.

Talking about tech is easy because it's concrete. We can see it and interact with it and observe direct effects and clear causality: when we change X, then Y happens. Culture, even though we all act and interact within it constantly, is much more abstract and indirect. Invisible, even. Nevertheless, organizational culture plays a crucial role when a company undertakes a cloud native transformation.

This chapter takes a look at the people-centric parts of a cloud native transformation. From an architectural standpoint, all the human aspects of a cloud native transformation fall into the overall category of "culture." But what does "culture" really mean in this context, and why is it so important?

Culture Vulture

> "Culture is not something vague and undefined, but a set of living relationships working together toward a shared goal. Culture is not something you are—it's something you *do*."
>
> —Daniel Coyle, *Culture Code*

In a business context, the "do" is how the people within your organization interact, communicate, and work with each other. In short, culture is the way your enterprise goes about creating and delivering your service or product. If you have the perfect set of cloud platform, tools, and techniques yet go about using them in the wrong way—if you apply the right tools in an improper way because that is how your culture has always dictated you use any and every kind of tool—it's simply not going to work. At best, you'll be functional but far from capturing the value that the system you've just built can deliver. At worst, your system simply won't work at all.

How do we know what we are talking about when we talk about a company's culture? What does the word even mean inside an enterprise? The answer is surprisingly concrete for such an abstract concept.

Culture is the sum of the daily actions that you take. At the most fundamental level, your regular routines are your culture. For example, if you talk to people, listen to what everyone is saying, and incorporate that into decision making, you have collaborative culture. Needing to seek permission from higher up before trying something new means you have hierarchical culture.

Add up all the things you do in the course of a normal workday and then step back to look at them from the perspective of the collective, yet generally unexamined, assumptions that shape and drive these actions. These assumptions, about how work gets done and how people interact in your company, will reveal your culture. And this is not fixed or immutable—culture is slow to shift, but it can be done.

If you change your actions, you change your culture.

A (Brief) Field Guide to Organizational Culture

The three major types of culture within enterprises track closely with the type of product/service delivery process the organization follows: Waterfall, Agile, and cloud native. At least, these are the ones that we've identified; there must be more, but those three cover the absolute majority of the companies we see in our work. So we will be framing our discussion in terms of Waterfall, Agile, and cloud native organizations, and we further realize that in the real world there are as many different ways to characterize—and implement—these different approaches as there are companies. Bear in mind that when we say "Waterfall organization" we are talking about a company that mostly, if not entirely, uses the corresponding process.

First, a quick guide to the terms as we will be using them.

Waterfall organizations are all about long-term planning. They deliver a single large, solidly built, and thoroughly tested deployment every six months to one year (perhaps even longer). They are risk-averse, with a long decision-making chain and rigid hierarchy. There are a lot of managers, including project managers.

Waterfall organizations tend to have specialist teams handling very specific skills—security, testing, database administration, and so on. Although market estimations (from vendors of Agile tools and solutions) suggest most companies have adopted at least some Agile practices, our estimation (based on our own observations—remember, this is book is drawn from our direct experiences and not intended as any kind of definitive Ten Commandments of cloud native) is that about 80% of software today is still produced using a development approach that is still primarily Waterfall in style.

Agile organizations recognize the limitations imposed by monolithic long-term releases and have adapted to deliver faster by using a more iterative, feature-driven approach to releasing in one- to four-week "sprints." Agile development breaks applications into their functional components, each of which is worked on start to finish by a single team. Instead of handoffs between specialist teams, Agile has cross-functional teams whose members hold all the skills necessary to design, build, and test the service they are responsible for developing. The result: there are wide responsibilities *in* a team, but a very narrow responsibility *for* the team. Scrum is one functional implementation of Agile process. Roles in this system include the teams themselves; Scrum Masters, who facilitate between the different process-owner teams; and Product Owners, who have full ownership of the delivered functionality and the deadlines.

Agile-ish organizations are a hybrid breed. Typically they are Waterfall organizations that have made some moves toward Agile, such as adopting Scrum (a common term in the industry is to say they follow a "Scrum-fall" process). For example, teams may work in sprints, but they are still building tightly coupled services on a longer term (six plus months) release schedule. Truly Agile companies are actually pretty rare, because fully implementing Agile across an entire organization is a serious challenge. Agile-ish is a much more commonly found culture type.

WealthGrid, our example enterprise, is an Agile-ish organization. Although they use Scrum and their teams have become somewhat cross-functional, WealthGrid's culture is still the kind typically found in organizations using the Waterfall software development approach: hierarchical, permission-seeking, focused on proficiency over innovation, and driven by tight, rigid deadlines.

Cloud native organizations are built to take optimum advantage of functioning in cloud technologies; the cloud of course will continue to evolve and will look quite different in the future, but we also build to anticipate this. Applications are built and deployed in a rapid cadence by small, dedicated feature teams made up of developers who also know how to build in networking, security, and all other necessities so all parts of the distributed system become part of the application. Meanwhile a platform team sits off to one side, designing and assembling the platform the devs will deploy to. This highly automated platform uses an orchestrator like Kubernetes to manage the complexity.

This organization could also work in an Infrastructure-as-a-Service or a traditional virtualized VMware environment. However, taking maximum advantage of cloud technology means moving to approaches like minimum viable product (MVP) development, multivariate testing, abandoning specialist teams for DevOps, and embracing not just rapid iteration but rapid delivery/deployment (i.e., continuous integration and continuous delivery, even continuous deployment). Some of these are part of Agile, at least when fully practiced, but they are all necessary for cloud native.

Cloud native architecture centers on microservices architecture (i.e., de-composing applications into small, loosely coupled services that operate completely independently from one another). Architecture then influences process: each of these services maps to smaller, independent development teams that release iterative software updates as soon as they are ready. Rapid release of software creates a tighter feedback loop, allowing enterprises to easily adapt and respond to customer demands and desires.

Although cloud native is powerful and can provide a serious competitive edge in many cases, it is not automatically the "right" solution in every case. By the same token, Waterfall is not inevitably wrong or bad. There are times when Waterfall is absolutely the best process for the situation at hand—when, for example, there is a strong product that is stable and will require few future changes. In that case, riding along on Waterfall is effective and efficient. Agile, too, has circumstances where it is the optimal choice. "Good" versus "bad" has little meaning when applied to culture, because culture itself simply *is*.

"Right" Solutions, "Wrong" Culture

So, then, what matters is not culture itself, but the *type* of culture. Our daily actions inside an organization are dictated by our collective culture. So when a "right" solution (or, sometimes, a mishmash combination of solutions) gets applied in the "wrong" culture, the solution and the culture conflict, undermine, and ultimately gridlock each other.

It is a little like sitting down behind the wheel of a car when you have spent all your life riding horseback. Fundamentally, both are means of transport. You can be an expert equestrian, but that skill set is of little use in your new automobile. And, actually, driving the machine is not the problem; it's not hard to figure out that the steering wheel makes the car turn, one pedal makes it go, and the other makes it stop. The truly difficult—not to mention most dangerous—part is figuring out how to take it out on the road, or how to jointly navigate with all the other cars also driving the same route, so nobody collides. The rules and assumptions of good horsemanship simply don't apply when suddenly you can go 100 mph on a superhighway.

Either mode transports you from point A to point B. But the rules of the road—the collective understanding you share with all the other drivers out there—is suddenly vastly different. When we went from horses to automobiles, our daily actions changed. And this eventually changed the way we worked, where we lived (suddenly, suburbs became possible), how we communicated, and even how we interacted. Everything around us was affected, and our culture shifted in response. Anyone who tried to keep riding horses as their main form of transportation found themselves left behind, no matter how swift their steed.

Today there are laws in most parts of the world against taking a horse-drawn vehicle onto a highway because doing so is perilous for all involved. Conflict arises when new technology gets applied through the old way of doing things. Trying to do cloud native by using methods from your previous paradigm will wreck your initiative. This is in fact the root cause of most of the problems we find when we get called into a company to rescue a stalled cloud native transformation.

The Culture Clash Conundrum

In software development, as in real-world geopolitics, the worst problems happen when cultures clash.

The issue is not so dramatic in companies that merge Waterfall and Agile practices. Despite some surface differences, there are many functional similarities that enable such a hybrid approach to function. Both share the very strong presence of Product Owners who decide what should be built. In Waterfall, architects and managers are expected to understand the entire product with all its complexity, while the teams themselves need to understand only the part they are specifically responsible for. Similarly, in Agile, each team only needs to understand the components of the product they're charged with delivering (which will create strong separation for that part from all other parts, due to Conway's law wherein software will resemble the communication and organizational structure of the company producing it). But in both cases teams are still not really in charge of *what* they are building; their authority is limited to *how* to build whatever they are assigned.

 It is worth noting that companies following truly Agile practices, or especially Agile combined with Lean, display culture very similar to what we are identifying as cloud native here. True Agile is very, very different from Waterfall. However, in our experience very few companies are able to reach completely Agile status, thanks in part to deeply ingrained Waterfall culture (or perhaps it's because truly Agile companies are able to make the move to cloud native fairly easily, without help from consultants, so we rarely encounter them). The ones that call us for help, however, most often are working with significant baggage in terms of Waterfall culture: risk-averse, predictive, and, above all, slow.

Technology itself doesn't deliver velocity, though it can certainly help. Changing your culture—the way you work every day—is how an organization gains true velocity.

Furthermore, both Agile and Waterfall require coordination across teams to deliver the separate parts together. The only difference is frequency, with Agile delivering much more frequently than in Waterfall. And while Waterfall teams are building a single monolith, Agile teams are effectively building a number of monoliths. In a typical Agile organization, the number of independent components is usually three to ten, with one team (sometimes two) working on each. This does mean that Agile teams can take on three to ten times more complexity compared to Waterfall teams, but they are all still building monoliths. By the same token, in Agile many teams can work on the same, single monolithic component, effectively splitting it up into a smaller waterfall. The result is still central planning and a lot of coordination, including joint delivery of all components every one or few sprints.

So you can see how in some ways the cultural differences between Waterfall and Agile are actually compatibilities, rather than true differences! Working in cloud native, however, requires a completely new and different culture.

The most common culture problem we find when we are called in to help save an attempted cloud native migration gone wrong is where a company has tried to add a single element of cloud native while not changing anything else. "We will keep delivering software the same way we always have, except now we will have DevOps!" So we have a clash between the new cloud native technique, DevOps—where a single team, working independently, first develops and then deploys and maintains an application—and the "old" approach of building a tightly coupled system of apps and delivering everything all at once, every year or so.

Can you do DevOps in a Waterfall organization? Well, sort of. On the Dev side you can apply cloud native practices like continuous delivery to optimize and accelerate your development process. Meanwhile on the Ops side you can automate deployment to make your provisioning and infrastructure faster and more efficient than ever before. This is all great…except for the fact that your beautiful, containerized microservices and their state-of-the-art platform won't actually get in front of users until the next release cycle is completed, many months from now, because you never changed your delivery process to match. Yes, you are doing cloud native—from inside the linear, sequential, and tightly coupled Waterfall approach. All that speed and efficiency? Simply wasted.

The culture-clash conundrum works backwards, too: you can't have otherwise full-on cloud native culture but not have microservices. If it takes you six months to deliver, you can't be truly distributed. There is nothing to be gained in simply re-creating a monolith on the cloud—yet companies try do it all the time.

Which Brings Us Back to…Culture

This is why understanding your organizational culture is critical for functioning well in the world—i.e., succeeding as a business. Knowing your culture means being able to choose the path that best fits your organization…or not choosing some hot new tech that, however promising, conflicts with your organization's fundamental nature.

Cultural awareness also grants the ability to start changing your organization from within, by a myriad of steps all leading in the same direction. This lets you evolve gradually and naturally alongside a rapidly changing world. "Long-term direction" is basically the definition of strategy. It's a myth that strategy has to be "big." Egos are big. Taking small steps toward your direction is a solid strategic move. Strategy is incremental: setting a direction and then moving in that direction through intentional, iterative, intelligent moves, each one small, each building upon the last.

So: Your culture is the sum of the practices that add up to and define how you function. You can identify these forces that shape your organization so fundamentally by examining the actions that define your day-to-day operation. Then you can decide the best next steps. This is far from new advice. Long, long before cloud native, Confucian philosophy advised us that, in order to slowly change one action over time, you must first change yourself. Really it all comes down to two simple words from Socrates: know thyself.

A practical tool for creating this organizational self-awareness can be found in Chapter 5.

Meet Our WealthGrid Team

Now it's time to meet the protagonists of the WealthGrid story. Jenny, the program manager, is the character we will be following most closely through WealthGrid's journey to cloud native. Jenny is first to realize that her company is facing pressure—that the stranger is coming to WealthGrid's town—and needs to evolve. Even if others have perhaps also recognized this, she is the first to take real action. Either way, Jenny is the catalyst for WealthGrid's cloud native initiative. In later chapters we will also meet Steve, WealthGrid's CEO, who plays an equally important role in the company's cloud native transformation efforts.

So where were we? Oh, yes: a stranger has come to town. WealthGrid is facing pressure, perhaps even genuine existential threat, to adapt to this change in their market/environment.

Jenny has been a program manager at WealthGrid for several years, and she is good at her job. At WealthGrid, as in any mid-size or larger Waterfall or Agile-ish company, program managers are quite literally middle management. They sit squarely between upper-level executive leadership, which is responsible for defining strategy and project initiatives, and the engineers responsible for delivering the actual product. Program managers act as project facilitators and keep communication flowing smoothly between these two groups. Working with the engineers, project managers have detailed boots-on-the-ground insight into a project's progress. In turn they keep upper management informed, only without bogging them down with unnecessary details. Project managers also spend a lot of time interfacing with other middle managers, facilitating project handoffs between WealthGrid's specialized teams, and trying to keep production schedules on track.

Jenny likes her work and finds her position an interesting challenge. Being a good program (or project) manager means having enough technical knowledge to understand the engineers and their work, balanced with enough business knowledge to explain things to the executives. In short, Jenny acts as a translator between the otherwise fairly separate enterprise and technical cohorts within the same organization. She can explain the business case of a proposed feature in terms that rally the engineers to get behind a new project. She can also respectfully communicate upward, in proper C-suite speak, when a suggested new feature might be impractical, maybe even infeasible, from a technical standpoint.

Thus Jenny's job as program manager requires high exposure to the business side: customer conversations, understanding the market forces that shape the company's path, and involvement with planning and improving internal processes. It also involves daily immersion with the teams themselves, closely tracking the decisions they make and the outcomes they produce. She enjoys this because, like most good engineering managers, Jenny herself is a former engineer. Even though she has moved into a management role, she tries to stay up to date and knowledgeable in the latest trends. No matter which hat she's wearing, though, Jenny's natural ability as an organizer and her solid people skills serve her well.

Jenny's job requires her to manage both downward and upward at the same time—to make things happen, but still make everyone reasonably happy on both sides. But being in the middle also means that she gets pressure from both above and below.

Pressure from Both Sides

One particular pressure that has been subtly building for a while now has to do with WealthGrid's response to the cloud computing revolution. Cloud-based services have been radically altering both how enterprises can deliver products and services and how customers can consume them. Jenny herself is aware of the rapid evolution of cloud native tools and techniques—of course she has heard about containers and microservices. But she doesn't have deep knowledge in this cutting-edge tech. Hardly anyone at the company does since it's so very new.

That doesn't stop her engineering team from badgering her about Kubernetes and how cool it is—most tech folks love exploring the latest and greatest innovations in their field, and her team is no exception. For Jenny, this means every time someone comes back from a conference, they are excited about the possibilities of putting together their next project using microservices architecture, orchestrated by Kubernetes. Heck, she's excited too—she goes to a few conferences herself and has heard first-hand about the power of cloud native to revolutionize a company's delivery model to make it responsive, iterative, and, above all, fast. She has been doing some research, and it seems like cloud native is real and here to stay.

But where could this fit within WealthGrid's well-defined, proficient, and long-standing (i.e., legacy) systems and processes?

Interestingly, this pressure from her engineering team dovetails with pressure that Jenny has recently experienced from above, regarding hiring. Recently, hiring for technical positions at WealthGrid has become surprisingly challenging—surprising because WealthGrid's compensation is at the top of industry pay scales. However, openings simply aren't drawing many good candidates. Concerned, Steve, the company's CEO, ordered some internal surveys to identify how the hiring process might be improved.

The answer was plain: WealthGrid's systems are legacy tech. Nobody just emerging from university with a computer science degree wants to work on boring old stuff. They want new and cutting edge! Worse, while high pay may entice some into applying anyway, these hires don't tend to stay long once they realize that there is little opportunity for professional growth. Pretty much the only way to advance professionally if you are an engineer is to move into management. And forget about developing new skills: WealthGrid is really good at what WealthGrid does, but that is all they do.

Some of the company's executive managers have started mentioning cloud native architecture in other contexts beyond the hiring issue. They have read Gartner and similar publications talking about how the cloud is how modern companies now need to operate their business—so they think, of course, that WealthGrid should do this too. This gets considerable pushback from other managers, though, who say that business is good and there is no need to rock the boat.

So, from her position at the nexus of enterprise and technology, Jenny hears a thousand different voices, each one telling her different things. But it is just this simultaneous, often conflicting view into both worlds that gives Jenny a unique perspective. The business-savvy side of her recognizes the stranger danger that threatens to disrupt WealthGrid's comfortable world. Her technical knowledge and experience give her the confidence to do something about it.

In the end, those thousand voices all seem to add up to the same message: it's time for WealthGrid to make a move to the cloud.

CHAPTER 3

What's the Pattern? Architecture, Pattern Languages, and Design

This chapter is split into two sections. The first introduces Christopher Alexander's groundbreaking work on evolutionary growth versus big-bang projects. We also look at software design patterns, discuss the need for a pattern language specific to cloud native, and explain why having a pattern language increases the chance of a quick and successful transformation. In the second part, we discuss patterns themselves, how they are made, how they work—and our process for creating cloud native patterns for this book.

Architecture: "The complex or carefully designed structure of something."

There is a reason that we apply the term "architecture" to both buildings and computer systems. The term describes a non-trivial system whose shape has come about through careful thought, imagination, and planning—also known as design.

In his book *A Pattern Language*, first published in 1977, Christopher Alexander consolidated decades of intelligent observation of architecture. He thoughtfully analyzed what works—and what does not—when we undertake to design and build human systems. Alexander points out that "right" architecture has nothing to do with classical beauty. Rather, it creates a structure that is comfortable and easy to use and maintain. It's one that feels like a responsive, even living, place that supports and extends those who use it rather than constraining or frustrating them.

Alexander's quality of "rightness" is difficult to quantify or describe yet innately recognized when we experience it. We have all seen houses or cities that feel right, that we'd like to live in, just as we've been in ones that simply feel wrong. A gorgeous city square lacking shade from the sun and offering awkward seating, or none at all, does not encourage visitors to linger. A courtyard with a mixture of sunshine and shade, offering trees and fountains and comfortable places to sit, is a far more human venue —a "right" place people will be happy to spend their time in and work to maintain.

As software engineers we have all experienced, in the same way, computer systems and teams that are not "right"—brittle systems that constrain and frustrate us, that fail to support us as users or maintainers. Hopefully we've also worked on systems that made us proud and that were a genuine pleasure to develop and grow, and collaborated with teams that feel like a circle of friends who happen to share high productivity and a passion for clean code.

But how do we make the good stuff happen? How do we move from instinct to actuality?

Patterns

Alexander's key to building "right" architecture was the creation of context-specific patterns that were easy to explain and teach and were above all deliverable. He developed these patterns over a long career spent observing what did and did not work on the ground.

The pattern languages Alexander developed cover all levels of design, from micro to macro. At the micro end of the spectrum he describes individual spaces and how to make them comfortably habitable and instinctively "right" using templates such as "Pattern 128: Indoor Sunlight" and "Pattern 236: Windows Which Open Wide." Alexander slowly widens his lens from single rooms to whole buildings and the relationship between them, then outward further to towns, cities, and entire geographic regions. These macro patterns include planning for both urban and rural settings since different contexts produce different needs. Examples like "Pattern 11: Local Transport Areas" and "Pattern 52: Network of Paths and Cars" show how broadly scoped patterns can be applied to benefit large populations, not just single dwellings.

> The fact is that very few things have so much effect on the feeling inside a room as the sun shining into it.
>
> —Pattern 128: Indoor Sunlight

Collectively the patterns serve as universal guiding principles for design. "Each pattern describes a problem which occurs over and over again in our environment, and then describes the core of the solution to that problem, in such a way that you can use this solution a million times over, without ever doing it the same way twice." (Christopher Alexander, *A Pattern Language*, 1977).

So when does an actual pattern language emerge from all these building blocks? Individual patterns themselves are not a language, but more like vocabulary terms. A group of individual patterns can be put together to describe a vocabulary (still not a language). A pattern language, though, presents the patterns along with guidance on how to construct solutions (e.g., A follows B, or C may follow from B in certain cases). Once you have these "grammar" rules in addition to the vocabulary, then you have a language.

The notion of patterns for constructing buildings and even towns was instantly embraced by architects, and more than 40 years later *A Pattern Language* remains in print. The concept also piqued the interest of computer scientists, who recognized the value of applying similarly concise, specific, and reusable solutions within the field of software development.

In 1987 two software engineers, Ward Cunningham and Kent Beck, inspired by Alexander's work, presented a paper on applying the idea of design patterns to computer programs. This was the catalyst for a whole new pattern-based philosophy of software design, and the new school of thought attracted many converts. The software design patterns movement crossed over to the mainstream in 1994 when the Gang of Four—software engineers and researchers Erich Gamma, Richard Helm, Ralph Johnson, and John Vlissides—published *Design Patterns: Elements of Reusable Object-Oriented Software*. A quarter of a century later, this hugely influential book can still be found in the personal reference libraries of many a software developer.

The appeal is obvious: a software design pattern, just like an architectural pattern, is a reusable solution to a commonly recurring predicament. A software design pattern is *not* a finished design directly translatable into code, but a platform-agnostic description of how to solve a specific problem. It also functions as a language, one that helps developers to communicate better since they can now name the important things and agree on basic principles. Having this common language grants a shared understanding that allows devs to save time while elevating discussions to a higher level, because the basics have been agreed upon and settled.

Cloud native itself is a particular approach to software design, a paradigm shift to a new way of designing, building, and running computer applications. It is based on cloud Infrastructure-as-a-Service combined with new operational tools and techniques like continuous integration, container engines, and orchestrators.

The objective is, almost always, to improve speed. Companies can no longer simply deliver a product or service. To survive and prosper in the new age of instant information in the palms of our hands, they must also help customers seamlessly use, consume, or purchase their wares. You can no longer be "just" a healthcare or financial services or retail enterprise: like it or not, realize it or not, all companies are now software companies.

Existing software design patterns may still be useful to cloud native systems so long as the different context is carefully considered, though architectural patterns certainly do not apply. Thanks to the aforementioned paradigm shift, new patterns have been emerging to address the new cloud native architecture.

When Container Solutions was founded in 2014, we didn't even have a name for this new approach to developing software applications, much less a shared understanding of common scenarios and effective methods. Cloud native, as we now call it, has reached the point where we can create a new pattern language allowing us to name—and, of course, implement—optimal context-specific practices in this rapidly evolving technology.

A Time for Design

Having established the benefits of cloud native architecture, you might now reasonably expect the assertion that cloud native systems are intrinsically "right." We would love to say this, but unfortunately it isn't true. Cloud native systems, no matter how robustly containerized, microserviced, and orchestrated they might be, are no more likely to exhibit rightness than any other computing architecture. In fact, in some cases, they can be worse.

This is because there are times where cloud native complexity is simply not called for. Highly stable and proficient systems that require little change or updating, for example, make for ideal monoliths and should be run as such. Attempting to split such a system into containerized microservices would be an interesting thought experiment, costing time and resources to do while ultimately producing little functional improvement. "Monolith" is not a dirty word. It is simply another kind of architecture, and there are some contexts where it is absolutely the right approach.

Most of the time, though, given the complexity of modern software and the sky-high expectations of users, cloud native is likely the right approach. Unfortunately this is a highly complex process; while almost all transformation initiatives start off well, many quickly go wrong. Why does this happen?

Cloud native can be deceptively easy to implement at first. Anyone with a credit card can log onto a public cloud provider and have an initial instance up and running in a matter of hours. And it is indeed true that the first few experiments with cloud native technology, typically in a careful testing-the-waters context, are almost always easy and successful. This unfortunately creates the hopeful illusion that full migration to cloud native will be equally easy: just install a few tools and go live! However, implementing full-scale enterprise cloud native is in fact very difficult due to the complexity of distributed systems, which increases exponentially with scale.

This next step, after the easy first experiment, is in fact where cloud native migrations usually go wrong. This is a very new technology, and there simply is not enough knowledge within most organizations to successfully navigate cloud native's complexities. And currently, given the immature state of the ecosystem, it is not yet possible to go forth and purchase one full-service solution that can simply "make you" cloud native.

This is also, however, the right time to begin constructing a set of sound strategies and design practices in order to facilitate cloud native migrations. We are far enough along in the evolution to understand at least the basics of what works, what does not, and why.

Even once you have successfully transitioned to cloud native and are enjoying all the benefits of this latest and greatest technology, you don't get to simply stop. There will eventually come a day, probably sooner rather than later given the accelerating pace of technological advancement, when a new technology or paradigm emerges to change the rules yet again. So, ultimately, what we need is not best practices for adopting cloud native or Kubernetes. The most enduring and valuable thing we can take from a transformation is the ability to change and adapt to new circumstances, whatever they are. The foundation of cloud native philosophy is evolving right along with your environment through constant small innovations and experiments. This is how we de-risk change: by building continual evolution and learning into the architecture itself. If you do it all the time, suddenly change is no longer scary.

What we now require is a way to identify, describe, and name these evolution-friendly strategies and practices—all the better to share our hard-earned knowledge and help organizations create "right" cloud native systems. A cloud native pattern language does exactly that.

A Cloud Native Pattern Language

Alexander wrote that "each pattern can exist in the world only to the extent that it is supported by other patterns." A design is incomplete if it doesn't contain mutually supportive patterns to address the entirety of the system, from the largest problem to the most detailed. In addition, he concluded the overall vision cannot be delivered in one big bang, but must grow toward the envisioned ideal.

Sound familiar? Alexander's pattern parameters correlate quite well with the cloud native principles of interrelated microservices, collaboratively developed and delivered in small, iterative steps toward the overall goal.

Just as Alexander's building patterns must interrelate and support each other, so must the patterns of cloud native architecture. For example, a "Distributed System" may depend upon "Microservices Architecture," "Containerized Applications," and "Dynamic Scheduling" while existing within a larger context/goal, such as a "Highly Secure System."

The point of a pattern language is to make it easier for developers to discuss, learn, and apply the best practices in cloud native. In this book we will share some of the patterns that we've learned from over five years of helping enterprises move to cloud native.

The patterns themselves come from experience working with our clients and with cloud native itself, but they also pull in years of reading books and articles in every conceivable related area. Other patterns publications, management and strategy books, and seminal papers like *Manifesto for Agile Software Development* and Mintzberg's *Of Strategies, Deliberate and Emergent* all fed our understanding and helped form the thoughts in the book.

Patterns inherently build upon other patterns; that is how patterns and pattern languages work. Similarly, we the authors are indebted to the work of many who came before us. Since it is impossible for us to acknowledge every one of the countless influences and sources of inspiration that fed into our own work, however, we elected to cite sources only when directly referenced or quoted.

Patterns in Context

Cloud native systems are innately complex. This means having a high likelihood of failing to deliver even the table stakes of good system design: being stable, efficient, and fit for their purpose. Sometimes one cloud native approach might be better than another—or perhaps a different architecture entirely could be the superior choice. There is no one design that will work well in every circumstance, and so design patterns must be context-specific. A design that ignores context will almost certainly be a painful one to deliver and difficult to live with—if it works at all.

What kind of contexts should we consider when making software design choices? There are a lot! For example:

- The existing skills of your teams
- The time frame and goals of your project
- The internal political situation (how much buy-in exists for the project)
- Budgets
- Legacy products and tools
- Existing infrastructure
- Emotional or commercial tie-in to vendors or products
- Ongoing maintenance preference

The right choice almost always depends on where you are now and where you want to be. This is as true in designing, say, distributed system architecture as it is in designing a townhouse.

As an example, one effective and popular cloud native pattern is Dynamic Scheduling —that is, the use of a container orchestrator like Kubernetes to handle the deployment and live management of applications on your physical infrastructure. Though dynamic scheduling is great in most contexts, there are some where it can be disastrous. Nothing is perfect in every environment, Kubernetes included. Let's say you decide, as part of your transformation, to apply the Lift & Shift at the End pattern to move one or more of your existing VMs straight onto the cloud, without refactoring. VMs are designed to run in highly stable environments, though, and so require either re-architecting or some kind of wrapper to shield them from the highly animated environment of a cloud native platform where they could be switched on and off randomly as load demand requires. Your team doesn't really know how to handle orchestration yet, though, so if you encase your VMs inside Kubernetes without teaching the engineers how to maintain them, what you have is a pure (and totally unnecessary) disaster in the making. And it happens not due to the Dynamic Scheduling pattern itself, but the context where it gets applied.

This is why it is vitally important that, before selecting which cloud native patterns to implement, enterprises first understand the current context for their organizational needs and aspirations as well as identifying the proper target context. But how to pragmatically assess these contexts?

A tool was required and, in the course of guiding companies of all sizes over a wide spectrum of sectors (from financial services to manufacturing to healthcare, to name but a few), our cloud native engineers developed one. The Container Solutions cloud native Maturity Matrix is an assessment tool for helping enterprises understand where they are now as well as identifying where they want to go: their existing versus desired contexts. The Maturity Matrix is discussed in depth in Chapter 6.

It is important to note that not all cloud native contexts are concerned with technology. Migrations are not just about software; psychological and social forces within the organization heavily influence success or failure as well. The context of an organization's management process, team structure, and internal culture must be assessed before assigning patterns. These human-centered context areas are as important as tech-centered ones like provisioning and maintenance/automation (see Chapter 2).

Cloud Native Context in the Real World

Continuous integration (CI) is an example of a high-level pattern that seems to nearly always apply in the cloud native context. Within any developer's codebase, the more it diverges from the main code branch, the harder it becomes to merge working changes back into the mainline—eventually, the merge may even become impossible. This seriously reduces a system's stability and availability. CI calls for putting in place tooling that makes it very easy for devs to merge their changes back into the main codebase, on a daily or even more frequent basis, while simultaneously checking that no bugs have been introduced.

There are contexts, though, where CI would be less useful. When there is a single developer and a single codebase, for example, an automatic merging tool provides less value. A context where CI would be not just useless but actively bad as a pattern is in a situation where there is no automated testing. If everyone is merging insufficiently tested changes into the main codebase, you soon end up with a malfunctioning mess.

Continuous integration and continuous delivery (CD) use automation to ensure that new application code is always tested, secure, and ready for deployment. The automation and stability provided by CI/CD are so essential to cloud native architecture that few, if any, enterprise cloud migrations would choose to *not* adopt this pattern—as long as their existing technological context includes thorough automated tests.

There is, however, another nontechnological prerequisite context for CI/CD to be adopted successfully, and that is executive commitment: the culture context. These projects are difficult and expensive. They require Executive Commitment, one of the core organizational patterns we will discuss later. If you tried to implement CI/CD in an enterprise without the cultural context of senior-level support, you would quickly run out of corporate patience and budget.

So CI and CD are both key cloud native patterns that vitally depend on context. No matter how fundamental to the architecture, if they are executed in the wrong circumstances, they will fail. This shows us why "the right pattern" can only be the right pattern *in the right context*.

Common Contexts

Many companies looking to commence a migration to cloud native share a consistent and typical setup. Often, they are organized in traditional Waterfall style, with perhaps some transition to Agile (typically, in their use of Scrum), and have:

- Traditional Waterfall process with deliveries every few months
- Monolithic applications
- Older languages (typically Java/C#, but sometimes even Cobol)
- Strong, inflexible hierarchy
- Little or no automation of infrastructure and development processes

WealthGrid, our example enterprise, is an extremely typical example. For a long time WealthGrid found success in its traditional financial services market by delivering reasonable updates, fairly often. However, it can take up to six months for a new feature to reach customers. This makes it pretty much impossible to incorporate user feedback and requests in a useful time frame, meaning that WealthGrid instead has to more or less guess in advance what customers want—and hope that they guess right.

Now organizations like WealthGrid have realized they need to compete with new, web-based companies such as contender banks—mobile-only banks providing full-service accounts solely accessed from Android and iOS devices. It's not only financial companies finding themselves under pressure to keep up with tech-savvy competitors. Perhaps they are online retailers led by customer expectations of near-instant feature updates and a highly personalized user experience. No matter the business model, fast innovation has become essential for survival in a marketplace that is becoming increasingly global yet customized. These days, thanks to technology, any company can compete in any market—Amazon can become your hometown brick and mortar grocery store—and do so while providing each customer with personally tailored services.

Simply put, a high level of customized services, delivered with little or no downtime, is what customers now expect. This means that, for a business, velocity, time to market, and ease of innovation are more important than cost saving.

Staying abreast with the newest technology in order to provide the same cutting-edge user experience as the competition requires attracting developers who want (and are able) to work with the very newest tech. Since modern applications tend to be distributed, this is a competitive hiring arena.

Given that these enterprises, no matter what their core business, all originate from similar circumstances and are driven by similar needs, it is not surprising that they face similar difficulties:

- Decisions are typically made according to existing practices. This is appropriate for stable tech ecosystems like virtual machines. In cloud native, though, currently there are few established practices.

- In a traditional hierarchy, the top managers decide, but they don't fully understand the complexity of building and maintaining distributed systems—and therefore allocate insufficient resources.

- For the next three to five years, cloud native will still require a lot of investment due to the technology's relative immaturity.

- Dealing with immature tech requires more experimentation and research than straightforward project management typically allows. Processes such as Scrum create problems in particular by placing massive pressure on delivery, which reduces resources for research and innovation.

- Large enterprises are optimized to preserve the status quo and embrace change slowly and reluctantly, while cloud native requires quick changes and the ability to work in an ambiguous environment. Such organizations must undergo a fundamental culture shift.

- There is not enough cloud native knowledge in enterprises, or indeed in the current tech sector overall, to support effective widespread migration. Companies don't even know how much they do not know.

Successful cloud native transformation requires most enterprises to make changes in both technology and internal processes and culture in order to prepare the path. As a straight-up technology, due to the complexity of distributed systems, full-scale cloud native is very difficult to implement. When coupled with organizational and cultural challenges, the way forward can seem formidable indeed.

When the right patterns are applied in the proper context, the results can be powerful. Time is saved. Money is saved. People get to work in cloud implementations that feel "right"—for both the enterprise's business mission and the humans who work to execute it.

Patterns, Pattern Languages, and Designs

Here we get deeper into pattern languages and explain the details of good patterns: how they work, how to create them, and what is the best way to use them.

Originally, Alexander developed pattern languages to bridge the gap between professional architects and citizens in the community so that ordinary people could design their own dwellings. Software design patterns subsequently arose for constructing non-concrete objects: computer programs. In both cases these patterns allow us to fill technical gaps between expert practitioners and those with less experience. When junior developers can read, understand, and apply patterns created by experienced engineers, this greatly accelerates the production of new software/systems. Software-design patterns can speed up the development process by providing tested, proven development paradigms.

Even more importantly, though, effective software design requires awareness of conflicts and issues that may not become apparent until much later in the implementation. With patterns, the juniors benefit from the design knowledge that the more advanced practitioners worked hard to gain—without needing to spend years building the deep understanding of the subtleties of contextual relativity that makes this kind of foresight possible.

When it comes to cloud native, most of us are junior. The technology is so new, and our understanding of the architecture so nascent, that sharing our rapidly evolving knowledge is especially valuable. Creating cloud native–specific patterns is a way to name the things we are learning so developers and engineers can communicate using common names for software interactions. As we learn and continue, the design patterns will evolve and improve alongside our understanding.

How Patterns Work

Patterns are not a hack. That is, they are not a quick and easy way to solve difficult problems without careful thought. (In fact, that's where the application of patterns often fails: because people try to treat patterns, particularly the Gang of Four patterns, in just this way.)

Instead, patterns are a language for sharing context-specific working solutions. Context comes in when we select and fit together patterns to form a design—which brings us to the three core concepts at hand: patterns, pattern languages, and design.

- **Pattern:** A contained and specific approach to addressing one particular, commonly occurring need. A pattern is designed to be re-usable and applicable whenever the appropriate context occurs. There are many ways to implement each pattern, depending on different circumstances.

- **Pattern language:** The method of describing patterns, their useful organization, and good design practices within a particular field of expertise. Alexander had architecture, which begat software design patterns, which in turn spawned pattern languages in hundreds of abstract areas, including disaster prevention, innovation, cooking, and even a pattern language for writing patterns.

- **Design:** Patterns fitted together to define a full system, or perhaps one part of a larger system, with some guidance for selecting and applying them in a particular order. Designs provide general solutions, a sort of road map even, documented in a format that doesn't require specifics tied to a particular problem.

These terms vary based on which patterns are being applied and how. In the context of Alexander's building patterns we use "patterns," "pattern languages," and "designs" to construct, from micro to macro scope, individual rooms, buildings, neighborhoods, cities, regions, and so on. Gang of Four and other software-related patterns, on the other hand, pretty much only discuss "design patterns" with no concept of "language" or "design" as a system for putting them together. For the purpose of this book, we are taking the Alexandrian approach; we have "patterns" to form a "cloud native pattern language" and "designs" of typical cloud native transformations.

For example, the cloud native pattern "Distributed System" may depend upon "Microservices Architecture," "Containerized Applications," and "Dynamic Scheduling". Together they can also form part of an overarching design, such as a "Highly Secure System." We'll describe these specific cloud native patterns and present sample designs in future chapters. For now, let's talk about what goes into creating a good pattern of any kind.

What Makes a Pattern?

Taken together, patterns, pattern languages, and design form the way to simply but fully describe a complex system. However, there is no one right—or, for that matter, wrong—way of creating and presenting patterns.

Fundamentally, however, all patterns convey the same areas of information:

- A *title* that immediately and concisely conveys the problem being addressed
- A *context* statement describing the problem at hand
- *Forces* that influence the problem and make it difficult to solve
- A *solution* (or solutions) presented in detail
- The *consequences* of applying the solution

A good pattern is precise and concise. It concerns itself with a very specific and limited problem, isolates and identifies the forces that shape that problem, and tells us what to do about it. It ends by describing the new context that will be created once the problem is addressed. And it does all this in simple language accessible to almost any reader—you do not need deep expert knowledge to understand a pattern. The whole idea is to make deep understanding beside the point; we are trusting in the experience and knowledge of the pattern writers to create a guided and reliable path for us to follow.

How do patterns get made? Quite honestly, just as there is no "official" template for presenting a pattern, there is no authority in charge of creating—or overseeing the creation of—pattern languages.

The closest thing the patterns world has to a governing body is the Hillside Group, an educational nonprofit organization based in the United States. It was founded in 1993 to organize the efforts of various thought leaders in the then-emerging software design patterns movement to converge their separate efforts toward defining and documenting common development and design problems into a pattern language.

The Hillside Group functions as the de facto hub of the global patterns community, which gathers at annual Pattern Languages of Programs (PLoP) conferences that Hillside sponsors. The conferences focus on pattern writing workshops and invited talks related to pattern development. One frequent PLoP conference presenter is Takashi Iba, a prominent patterns researcher at Keio University in Japan. Iba is also a prolific patterns author who, working with his students over the past decade, has created more than 20 pattern languages containing more than 600 patterns covering many different topics. As a part of this process Iba has developed his own process for creating patterns and a protocol for presenting them.

How (Iba) Patterns Are Made

When developing a new pattern language, Iba discovered that it is important to "mine the seeds" of the patterns from real-world examples of optimal experiences or best practices. He named this approach "pattern mining."

> In the pattern mining, first, miners explore their experiences, observations, episodes, or documented past work related to the subject at hand. Through this exploration, they look for and identify hidden knowledge used for the target. This knowledge may include associated rules, methods, tips, or customs. Next, the miner finds critical connections among these related items so that prospective pattern begins to form a meaningful whole.
>
> —Takashi Iba, "Pattern Language 3.0 and Fundamental Behavioral Properties," keynote address, PURPLSOC Conference 2015

In Iba's pattern mining process, group members start by identifying a subject and then brainstorming any and every rule, custom, insight, or method they deem to be important about the subject. These are all written down on sticky notes. They briefly describe each insight to the group and then add its sticky note onto a large sheet of paper. Everyone in the group brainstorms ideas and takes turns talking about them until no one has any more thoughts to share. At that point, they examine the mosaic of sticky notes and collaborate to organize similar ideas into groups. The groupings that emerge from this process are the "seeds" of potential patterns.

The group approach is important for creating the most accurate and incisive definition of a problem. As humans, we are all subject to cognitive biases and wrong assumptions (see Chapter 4 for more about behavior and biases); eliciting multiple points of view helps authors to avoid patterns becoming skewed by individual prejudices or cognitive blind spots.

Presentation

The next step is to write up the pattern seeds into a formal pattern format. An Iba-style pattern states the essential elements of title, context, forces, and solution very simply, and preferably in no more than one page of text. In addition, an Iba-style pattern will also contain a simple diagram.

The format is presented in three sections. The first consists of the pattern name, introduction, and illustration; these three elements serve to provide a summary of the pattern.

- The *Pattern Name* is a short, memorable name that concisely and accurately describes the pattern.
- It is followed by the *Introduction*, a one-sentence executive summary of the problem that the pattern addresses.

- The *Illustration* comes next to provides a visual representation of the pattern's core concept.

The second section provides more details about the problem being addressed and presents the pattern's context, problem, and forces:

- *Context* describes when and under which circumstances the pattern should be used.
- *Problem* is the undesired but common consequence that typically arises in this context.
- *Forces* are unavoidable factors that influence the problem and make it difficult to overcome.

The final section presents the solution, related actions, and consequences of applying them.

- The *Solution* is one way to resolve the problem.
- *Actions* provide some concrete, practical steps to address the situation.
- *Consequences* describe the outcome when this pattern is applied to the problem.

As an aid to envisioning and articulating patterns, Iba also created a Pattern Writing Sheet, which he has made freely available under Creative Commons licensing. Figure 3-1 shows the template, which contains instructions for identifying elements of a pattern and spaces for defining the Context, Forces, Solution, and so on.

Our Approach

The authors of this book followed largely in Iba's footsteps. Some patterns were mined during whiteboard sessions with Container Solutions engineers, others during collaborative brainstorming and epic patterns-writing sessions in London, Amsterdam, and Baltimore. Early versions of six patterns were produced as part of a paper presented at the 2018 PLoP conference. That paper, titled "A Cloud Native Transformation Pattern Language," inspired the creation of many more patterns and eventually grew into this book.

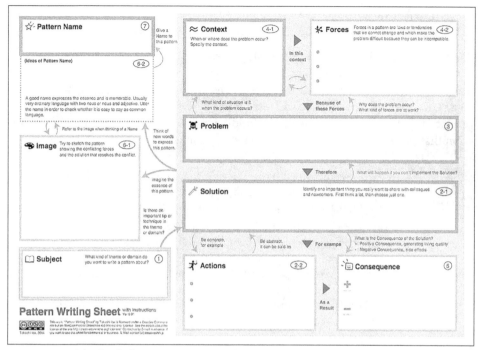

Figure 3-1. Takashi Iba's Pattern Writing Sheet

We have, however, expanded upon Iba's minimalist format. The fundamental components of Context, Problem, and Solution are all there, but explained in greater depth than true Iba style would dictate. We have also listed related patterns and added common pitfalls related to the pattern that we have observed occurring during actual cloud migrations. We are also going to include any cognitive biases that contribute to the problems described in the patterns or that are a basis for solution nudges. All of this is an effort to help the reader contemplating their own cloud native transformation project.

As is typical, the patterns are presented as a library for readers to draw from. However, we also wanted to present them in the vibrant, living context of a typical migration initiative. So we came up with the story of WealthGrid as a way to bring them to life. We hope you will find yourself in this story, imagine yourself a bank, a travel agency, whatever your business, suddenly finding yourself under pressure from a radical new competitor. You need to evolve by building a new way to deliver your services or products, or else this new paradigm or company entering your sector is going to drive you out of business. The effective way to adapt quickly is to use a pattern design as the roadmap to your new system.

Patterns are the foundation layer of this solution, but they are not the story itself. Think of them more like Legos, interchangeable building blocks that can fit together in any number of ways. We are giving you the pieces you need to put together for designing, creating, and envisioning your own custom solution.

You don't need to know much, if anything, about the cloud to use cloud native patterns. Patterns give you the ability to describe your own ideas and solutions for your new home to your architect, but that doesn't mean you have to build the house yourself. Patterns are just a means to express yourself. They don't tell you exactly how it's going to be done—they describe the scaffolding you will work inside to build the solution that exactly fits you, in whatever context you inhabit.

 New cloud native patterns are emerging constantly. To continue sharing them and extending the cloud native pattern language we have established here, please visit www.CNpatterns.org.

This is where to find the latest pattern developments, but also an online community for discussing and creating new patterns. We are inviting people from across the industry, thought leaders and influencers but most importantly everyday engineers and managers—those out there working elbows-deep in cloud native code and architecture—to contribute and participate. Hope to see you there!

CHAPTER 4

Beyond Patterns: Behavior, Biases, and Managing Evolution

We humans, sitting as we do atop the evolutionary apex, like to think we are logical and rational—not animals driven by impulse and instinct. In fact, though, we are prone to all kinds of proven biases, cognitive quirks, and mental shortcuts. These cognitive biases presumably served our hunter-gatherer ancestors well by allowing fast decision making: when facing down a predator, speed was more valuable than accuracy.

Many of these biases continue to serve us well. If followed by a stranger when we walk alone at night, our fight-or-flight instinct is more valuable than engaging that stranger in a discussion about the unequal distribution of wealth in our society. Other times, however, these very same biases can cause us to think and act quite irrationally, to our own detriment.

In cloud native, cognitive biases can lead us to try to build a cutting-edge, distributed microservice system by following traditional (comfortable) approaches we've used to build software for the past two decades. In this chapter we take a look at cognitive biases and discuss the ones most likely to impact a cloud transformation—and how some biases can be harnessed to work for, instead of against, success.

Imagine a commercial construction company in your town, one that is well established and successful, and known for producing solid, high-quality apartment buildings. Now imagine that the company's leaders decide to broaden the business mission: they start building bridges. Halfway through the very first bridge project, however, it becomes obvious that something is not right. This bridge has doors, chimneys, and even decorative bay windows—all things that the company has always included, to great acclaim, in previous projects. Of course, chimneys and windows have zero utility in a bridgespan. These features may even render the new construction less stable and secure. But this is how the company has always built things, so it continued doing just that in their newest project.

Sounds ridiculous, right? A mistake that no one would ever make. A thing that could never happen in the real world.

Unfortunately, it *does* happen. The cloud native equivalent occurs distressingly often when companies attempt to transition to the cloud. We have observed over and over that, ironically, these migrations can contain a great deal of internal resistance to the very changes being sought. As a result, companies rebuild their operations and infrastructure in the cloud but then start trying to build cloud native applications exactly the same way they've built software for the past 10 or even 20 years. It's the cloud native equivalent of building a nice fieldstone fireplace right in the center lane of that new highway bridge.

Implementing the complex technology portion of a cloud native transformation can actually be the easiest part of the overall project. A successful migration depends on more than simply embracing, say, microservices and Kubernetes. As we talked about in Chapter 2, the organization itself must also change significantly in terms of culture and psychology in order to make effective use of its shiny new cloud native tech. These human-centered changes are the areas we most often see causing the greatest problems for a company undertaking a cloud native migration. But why is this?

Conway's Law

The answer is simple but also difficult: human-centered changes are hard because, well, we are human. We like doing the things we are good at, in the familiar ways we are comfortable doing them. These biases toward sticking with the easy and familiar are not inherently bad. In fact, they exist for a reason: most of the time they work pretty well to save effort and energy. We just need to be careful to catch those times when they don't.

In the same way, pre-cloud techniques and technologies once served us well too, and for a long time. The tricky part in any of these instances is to recognize the point when change becomes required—such as when the decision is made to transform an organization into a cloud native entity.

Going cloud native requires giving up those old familiar ways no matter how successful they have been for us previously. For many organizations, this means no longer operating as a hierarchy while they construct monolithic applications. These design patterns are useful, valuable even, in their original context. In a cloud setting, however, they conflict with cloud native principles and can even cause the best-supported migration to fail.

Why do the old ways conflict with cloud native? The reason is Conway's law.[1]

Conway's law essentially states that system architecture will come to resemble the structure of the organization that contains it. Cloud native architecture requires distributed systems, period. This means succeeding as a cloud native entity requires enterprises to transform themselves from traditional hierarchical processes—or even relatively modern Agile practices—to a decentralized organizational structure. Cloud native systems architecture literally dictates this reality; Conway's law merely describes it.

This is a transformational change due to the distributed nature of cloud native, which is based on an architecture of small, loosely coupled modular components, and it leads directly to more decentralized organizations. In order to successfully transform themselves into cloud native entities, organizations must evolve a collaborative, experimental culture to truly take advantage of innovations offered by the cloud. This is harder than it sounds! Traditionally, organizations needed to be massively risk averse, to minimize uncertainty at all costs. Wholesale risk-aversion becomes embedded in the company psychology to the point where the idea of experimentation, of exploring and testing many different answers, can feel genuinely terrifying.

Cognitive Biases

We can explain all day long to these clients how and why cloud native's experimental culture and other organizational changes are the path to success, but we can't carry them to the destination. They have to walk there for themselves. No matter how many cloud native transformation patterns we map for an enterprise, they simply will not be effective until its people are ready to apply them to their work.

Understanding the underlying causes—and that they exist in the first place—is the way to move beyond these self-inflicted limitations. We are finding that an effective form for both understanding and explaining this comes in the form of cognitive biases.

A cognitive bias is a kind of systematic error in thinking that affects the decisions and judgments that people make. They are basically hardwired into the human brain. We all have such biases in one way or another, even if we think that we're personally immune to them (there is even a specific bias named for this: "bias blind spot"). This is understandable—when making judgments and decisions about the world around us, we of course like to think of ourselves as objective, logical, and capable of evaluating all relevant available information. Cognitive biases, though, are an unavoidable

---

1 The original paper (*http://bit.ly/2L1fi65*) introducing Melvin Conway's theory.

part of being human. They are baked into our thought processes and decision making.

Such biases are not always bad, though. In fact, they evolved for a reason.

Why Biases Are Useful

Biases can sometimes trip us up, leading to poor decisions and bad judgments. But they also serve us.

The human brain is a powerful processor that is constantly taking in and making decisions/acting on innumerable inputs. But, just like any computer processor, it also has limits. If we had to think about every possible option when making even the simplest of decisions, it would take a ridiculously long time. Due to the sheer complexity of our surrounding environment and the staggering amount of information it contains, our brains developed adaptive methods for simplifying the information processing load. Cognitive biases, in effect, are mental shortcuts—known as *heuristics*—designed to help us to selectively attend to input, make decisions, and then act on them quickly.

Such shortcuts served us well as early humans, back when our greatest existential threat involved becoming dinner for a saber-toothed tiger. Cognitive biases serve us in dangerous or threatening situations.

For example, imagine walking alone on a city street late at night and spotting sudden movement in the nearby shadows. Cognitive bias has us wired to assume this likely to be some sort of predator—muggers being the modern equivalent of saber-toothed tigers—and that we need to get to safety as fast as possible. Even though the perceived threat could actually be an alley cat or stray plastic grocery sack blowing in the breeze, we are unlikely to stick around to find out. Our "mysterious movement in nearby darkness" mental shortcut leads directly to worst-case scenario (*Predator! Run!*) to get us out of the way of potential danger.

That is an example of attribution bias—attributing a cause to an event without knowing what was actually happening and then responding to that limited interpretation regardless of reality. This and similar automatic responses are rooted in human evolution and are pretty easy to recognize. Though they can be surprisingly accurate, they still represent an error in thinking.

Things get even more complicated, though, when emotions, personal motivation, and social or cultural pressures inevitably get mixed in. When we use these pre-programmed shortcuts to assess situations and then make decisions, it all happens unconsciously–and beneath an overlay of those emotional factors. This is how subtle biases can creep in without us ever noticing to influence and distort the way we see, understand, and respond to the world.

Fortunately, simply being aware that this happens at all, that biases exist and influence everyone, is a powerful first step toward combating such distortion and influence. The second step is recognizing what biases might be at play in our own processes, whether personal or organizational.

Biases, Patterns, and Behavior

The idea that cognitive biases exist and influence us has become widely accepted over the past few decades and has even inspired various fields of academic research and study.

The concept of cognitive bias was first established in the 1970s by Amos Tversky and Daniel Kahneman. Both were Israeli social scientists who eventually relocated to the United States, Tversky teaching at Stanford and Kahneman at Princeton. They continued working closely, however, and together they pretty much invented the field of behavioral economics while racking up both a MacArthur Foundation "Genius Grant" and the 2002 Nobel Prize in Economic Sciences. Kahneman summarized several decades of their joint discoveries in his 2011 best seller, *Thinking, Fast and Slow*.

In his book, Kahneman identified two "systems" of thinking in the human brain: one conscious and deliberate, the other impulsive and automatic. System 1, our instinctive "fight or flight" wiring, resides in our lower brain and is a legacy of our saber-toothed tiger days. System 2 represents our rational and, above all, aware mental processes required to apply logic to decisions, exert self-control, and deliberately focus attention on non-life-threatening things like office work.

At only a few thousand years old, System 2 is a relatively new feature in the human brain. It evolved to help us function in a more complex world as our primary functioning became less about hunting for dinner (while avoiding becoming anyone else's dinner) and more about engaging in more abstract survival activities like earning money and posting on social media.

Unfortunately, these two systems don't play nicely together, or even take turns. Instead, they often fight over which system gets to be in charge in any given situation you face. Whichever one wins determines how you respond.

The way things are supposed to work when we encounter a problem is for System 1 to activate first. If the problem turns out to be too complex or difficult for System 1 to solve quickly, it hands off to analytical and slow-thinking System 2 to figure things out. The reason is because, again, we are wired to cut corners and save energy whenever possible: the law of least effort states that, given any task, the human brain will apply the minimum amount of energy it can get away with. This is why System 1, our impulsive snap-decision brain, gets first crack at most situations.

Trouble arises when the brain perceives problems to be simpler than they actually are. System 1 thinks, "I can handle this!"—even though it actually can't—and we end up making a bad decision or reaching an erroneous conclusion. To illustrate this in action, Kahneman uses a simple math logic challenge called the "bat and ball problem":

> A baseball bat and a ball have a total price of $1.10. The bat costs $1 more than the ball. How much does the ball cost?

Take your time. Think it over. Got it?

If your instant answer is $0.10, we regret to inform you that System 1 just led you astray. If the ball costs 10 cents and the bat costs $1 more than the ball, you ended up with $0.10 plus $1.10, which equals $1.20. Try working the problem again.

After actively pondering things for a minute or two—i.e., activating System 2—you'll see that the ball must cost $0.05. At $1 more than the ball, that means the bat costs $1.05. Combine the two and you reach the correct $1.10 total.

What just happened here? Well, if the brain gauges that System 1 can just handle things, it won't bother to activate System 2. We make a snap judgment and then happily move forward in the wrong direction. The process is so automatic and deeply rooted as to be completely unnoticeable when it's happening. At least, when it gets pointed out to us that our solution to the bat and ball problem is wrong, our System 2 brain can get called into action to overrule System 1's unmediated impulse answer. But that's not so easy in the real world, when we're dealing with unpredictable people and unexpected situations rather than a straightforward arithmetic problem.

Failing to realize that System 1 does not suffice and therefore it's time to activate System 2 is a universal human problem, according to Kahneman. "Unfortunately, this sensible procedure is least likely to be applied when it is needed most," he wrote in *Thinking, Fast and Slow.* "We would all like to have a warning bell that rings loudly whenever we are about to make a serious error, but no such bell is available, and cognitive illusions are generally more difficult to recognize than perceptual illusions. The voice of reason may be much fainter than the loud and clear voice of an erroneous intuition, and questioning your intuitions is unpleasant when you face the stress of a big decision."

This is the process that happens when we apply cognitive biases in a decision-making situation: we too often take the mental shortcut. Unfortunately, according to Kahneman and others who have studied bias, it is basically impossible to alter the leap-before-you-look System 1 part of our brain. We simply can't control the human hardwiring that served us so well for so long, though we can strive to be aware that it does exist and is always trying to jump into the driver's seat.

The most effective check against letting System 1 auto-drive our responses ultimately lies not within ourselves but in the people around us: others can perceive our biases and errors more readily than we ourselves are able to. Ultimately, the good news is that we can use external observation to create strategies and policies to help us monitor our individual decisions and predictions. With this approach we can weed out cognitive biases and faulty heuristics in order to make decisions more slowly but correctly, instead of fast but wrong.

This is where patterns come in. (This is, after all, a book about patterns.) Patterns, pattern languages, and transformation designs are all highly intentional and carefully crafted. As such, they function as System 2 tools that can be applied in complex scenarios of many kinds to help keep us on a rational and reasonable path. Patterns themselves can also function as a kind of external observer: later, when we get to our actual cloud native patterns, you will find that they each include a list of the biases that are likely to emerge in that situation.

Linking each pattern to potential biases is our effort to help with your situational awareness—to show the reason that you may be doing (or not doing) certain things is because of a particular bias or to overcome another specific bias. Let's start by taking a look at the common biases that we have seen influence people and organizations when they undertake a cloud native transformation.

Nudges

Over the decades, the idea of cognitive biases has become widely accepted as one of those things that simply make us humans. Research has made it clear, furthermore, that they are hardwired and inalterable.

The only possible thing we can change is our behavior—the actions we take while under the influence of a bias. The best way to change bias-driven behavior takes the form of incentives or "nudges." A nudge is a subtle cue or context change that prods you toward making a certain decision, while leaving all options open. Nudges don't force us toward any one action; our actions are entirely voluntary. However, nudges do subtly guide us in a particular direction.

The notion was introduced by Richard Thaler, a University of Chicago behavioral economist, and Cass Sunstein, a Harvard legal scholar, in their book *Nudge: Improving Decisions about Health, Wealth, and Happiness*, first published in 2008. They draw directly on Kahneman's work, particularly the concept that there are fast and slow systems of human thinking. (Thaler and Sunstein call System 1 "the automatic system" and System 2 "the reflective system" but the upshot is the same.) The book demonstrates quite powerfully that we all are being nudged all day, every day—sometimes toward good decisions, sometimes toward bad ones.

For example, if your company's cafeteria places fresh fruit by the cash register instead of pastries, you are more likely to take the nudge to choose a healthier snack or dessert. Conversely, when a server asks "Would you like fries with that?" you are being nudged toward a choice that benefits the restaurant's profit margin (though not your own healthy best interest). The good news is that we can design systems and environments to counter—or even harness—biases so that we will be nudged toward making a beneficial choice.

The most powerful form of nudge is known as the default. Default nudges are choices set up so that if you do nothing, you will be choosing the desired thing by simply going with the option presented. This has been used to raise the number of people who become organ donors in the United States. Many states have tried to boost organ donor rates by implementing a default nudge. They have shifted from an explicit opt-in question when people apply for a driver's license or renewal ("Would you like to be an organ donor?") to making all applicants organ donors by default, with the chance to explicitly opt out. The default doesn't force anything—applicants may still freely choose whether they'd like to be a donor. But the change leads to many more organ donors, and more lives saved, because social and behavioral sciences research shows most people accept whatever is listed as the default option.

So, ultimately nudges are a way to manage bias—maybe even the only way.

Take, for example, the cognitive bias known as *present bias*—the tendency to favor immediate rewards at the expense of our long-term goals. This is well demonstrated by how a large majority of people will say that putting money into a retirement savings account is important and how few people will actually follow through and do so. They mean to take some money out of their next paycheck and start an account eventually…just, not right now.

In this case, present bias has contributed to a severe shortfall in retirement savings in the United States, where millions of Americans face the very real likelihood of getting too old to continue working—but without the means to stop. According to a 2018 study by Northwestern Mutual, a financial services company, 21% of Americans have no retirement savings at all, while an additional 10% have less than $5,000 in savings. A third of the population currently at, or about to reach, retirement age has less than $25,000 set aside for financial support for their golden years. How did this happen? Historically, participation in retirement savings programs has been voluntary. Present bias led most people to keep that money in their current paychecks, rather than opting in to set money aside for their golden years.

While present bias has so far proved intractable, employers have been able to nudge employees into contributing to retirement plans by making saving the default option: now you have to take active steps in order to not participate. Yes, laziness or inertia can be even more powerful than bias!

This is a classic example of "choice architecture"—the way in which our decisions are influenced by how the choices are presented. People can be nudged by arranging their choice architecture in a certain way, like by placing healthy foods in a school cafeteria direct at eye level while putting less healthy choices like chips and cookies in harder-to-reach places. Individuals are not actually prevented from eating whatever they want, but arranging the food choices that way causes people to eat less junk food and more healthy food.

"How does this apply in cloud native software development?" you may well ask. Well, biases permeate all human undertakings, and cloud native's decentralized hierarchy means that teams, as well as individuals, are no longer tightly overseen and directly managed—and so sometimes biases climb into the driver's seat. Even more importantly, however, is that transforming into a cloud native organization requires getting comfortable with uncertainty and change (more about this in later chapters).

Both of these cloud native realities, thus, make it important to understand that biases are operating in the first place and must be taken into consideration and countered—often, interestingly, with more bias. For example, ambiguity provokes anxiety, which in turn leads us down a well-worn path to many different biases. Knowing this, in the cloud native context we can counteract with an abundance of information and small, manageable experiments to build certainty and familiarity while reducing anxiety. You fight phobias with exposure to the thing that is feared, right? Well, the very common bias known as "status quo effect" is essentially change phobia…but when change becomes a way of life, you aren't afraid anymore. When experimentation becomes routine, the new is no longer to be feared. Innovation as a routine process is, after all, a core cloud native principle.

Common Biases and Nudges

Cognitive bias has become a popular mainstream topic, and many, many examples have been defined. Wikipedia's "List of Cognitive Biases" contains, as of this writing, 193 entries. The list of the many different flavors of flawed thinking, all apparently hardwired into the human brain, literally ranges from A (the ambiguity effect, or "The tendency to avoid options for which the probability of a favorable outcome is unknown") to Z (the Zeigarnik effect, where "uncompleted or interrupted tasks are remembered better than completed ones").

The list is broken down into three types of bias:

- *Decision-making, belief, and behavioral biases* that affect belief formation, business and economic decisions, and human behavior in general
- *Social biases*, a form of *attribution bias* that describes the faulty assumptions that affect our thinking when we try to explain the cause of our own behavior or that of other people ("Rather than operating as objective perceivers, people are prone to perceptual errors that lead to biased interpretations of their social world," Wikipedia helpfully explains.)

- *Memory biases* that either enhance or impair the recall of a memory or that alter or shift its details

All of these are things that can hold a project back, slow it down, or even cause it to fail.

We have identified the 24 cognitive biases that, in our experience, most commonly show up during cloud migration projects. Most of these biases fall into the category of decision-making, belief, and behavioral biases, with a couple of social biases thrown in. We have also included any related nudges that can flip a bias from being a problem to being a force for positive change.

These commonly occurring biases are presented in the following list, starting with each one's Wikipedia[5] definition followed by a description of how it tends to present itself in the course of a cloud native transformation.

Ambiguity effect
> The tendency to avoid options for which missing information makes the probability of the outcome seem "unknown." An example of ambiguity effect is that most people would choose a regular paycheck over the unknown payoff of a business venture.
>
> *Cloud native relationship*: This bias is the main reason to run experiments early in a transformation, to understand the project's scope and fill in the missing information gaps. Otherwise, people tend to do what they have always done, because they know exactly how that worked, even when it no longer applies to the new context.

Authority bias
> The tendency to attribute greater accuracy to the opinion of an authority figure (unrelated to its content) and be more influenced by that opinion.
>
> *Cloud native relationship*: In traditional hierarchical (Waterfall) organizations, authority figures have to know more than others below them in the hierarchy. In cloud native, this bias is even more dangerous, as the managers have less understanding of what's going on in a highly complex distributed architecture based on new technologies. They need to be careful to avoid giving orders or even providing opinions as they will be automatically received as "correct."

Availability heuristic
> The tendency to overestimate the likelihood of events with greater "availability" in memory, which can be influenced by how recent the memories are or how unusual or emotionally charged they may be.
>
> *Cloud native relationship*: "Everyone is talking about Kubernetes so suddenly it must be the right thing to do!"

Bandwagon effect

The tendency to do (or believe) things because many other people do (or believe) the same thing. Related to groupthink and herd behavior.

Cloud native relationship: When Gartner puts certain tech on their chart, everyone decides to adopt it even without understanding how it relates to their use case.

Bystander effect

The tendency to think that others will act in an emergency situation.

Cloud native relationship: This is very relevant for overlapping responsibilities. In a Waterfall organization with its many specialized teams, for example, when a task doesn't officially belong to anyone, no one will volunteer to pick it up. In cloud native, where teams are responsible for independent execution, there needs to be clear communication so all necessary tasks get covered.

Confirmation bias

The tendency to search for, interpret, focus on, and remember information in a way that confirms one's preconceptions.

Cloud native relationship: Ignore all those inconvenient facts and embrace the information that supports your opinion. There is always plenty of data to choose from, so it's easy to cherry-pick. If you have a system administrator with 20 years of traditional IT experience, he'll be very creative in finding lots of very important reasons not to move to the cloud. If an engineer is dead set on using some cool tool he heard about at a conference, he will ignore all information showing that another tool might actually be a better fit.

Congruence bias

The tendency to test hypotheses exclusively through direct single testing, instead of testing multiple hypotheses for possible alternatives.

Cloud native relationship: When you run an experiment to prove your point rather than to find new information. So, you would run only one proof of concept (PoC), and if it works, you'll automatically dismiss all other alternatives even without evaluating them. This is why we have a PoC pattern and a separate Exploratory Experiments pattern.

Curse of knowledge

When better informed people find it extremely difficult to think about problems from the perspective of less well-informed people.

Cloud native relationship: Our clients' engineers frequently struggle to sell cloud native ideas to their managers due to this bias: they see so clearly why this is the right thing to do that they forget the managers have no background knowledge that enables them to understand it with equal clarity. Even our own engineers and consultants, so immersed in cloud native, need to stay mindful of seeing things from the perspective of clients who are new to cloud native.

Default effect

When given a choice between several options, the tendency is to favor the default one.

Cloud native relationship: Solutions to any problem have to consider the correct defaults, as those defaults will be adopted more frequently compared to any customized option. In other words, if you set up a cloud native platform, most people are probably going to use it exactly as you gave it to them. This is true both for the tools built into cloud platforms like Amazon Web Services or Azure as well as internal tools provided to employees. It's why we have the Starter Pack pattern.

Dunning-Kruger effect

The tendency for unskilled individuals to overestimate their own knowledge/ability, and for experts to underestimate their own knowledge/ability.

Cloud native relationship: This bias leads to overestimating your competency at things you're not intimately familiar with. We see this with managers who try to dictate which tools or methods will be used as part of a transformation. They have no actual cloud native experience or knowledge, but they are accustomed to calling all the shots.

Hostile attribution bias

The "hostile attribution bias" is the tendency to interpret others' behaviors as having hostile intent, even when the behavior is ambiguous or benign.

Cloud native relationship: We need to consider this bias whenever we go into a new client's organization and when working with internal transformation leaders who can run into this same form of resistance. In both scenarios we meet people who think that we're there to destroy their work and wreck their company. We shouldn't think that this is their real opinion, as it is a normal human bias arising from the fact that change frequently creates anxiety in those poised to undergo it.

IKEA effect

The tendency for people to place a disproportionately high value on objects that they partially assembled themselves, such as furniture from IKEA, regardless of the quality of the end result.

Cloud native relationship: This one can be used positively, as a nudge, and explains why we have to involve everyone in the client's organization in every stage of planning and executing a transformation. Whoever is involved is biased to like and support the solution.

Illusion of control

The tendency to overestimate one's degree of influence over other external events.

Cloud native relationship: This is especially common in the uncertain circumstances of a cloud native transformation. Engineers think that they know how to build microservices, and managers think that they know what it takes to do DevOps. But in reality, it is only an illusion of control. Many complex and emergent processes are very difficult to even steer, much less control. Sometimes we need to embrace some uncertainty to ultimately get results.

Information bias

The tendency to seek information even when it cannot affect action.

Cloud native relationship: Analysis paralysis. Very common in a Waterfall organization's efforts to try to find more and more answers for more and more questions, regardless of the fact that there are only two or three possible actions to take and the benefits of one of them are very clear.

Irrational escalation (also known as sunk-cost fallacy)

The phenomenon where people justify increased investment in a decision, based on the cumulative prior investment, despite new evidence suggesting that the decision was probably wrong.

Cloud native relationship: If you've spent six months working on setting up an OpenShift cluster and bought all the licenses, it is very unlikely that you're going to switch to another tool even if it's proven to be superior. People routinely push forward with projects that are obviously not going to bring any value.

Law of the instrument

An over-reliance on a familiar tool or methods, ignoring or under-valuing alternative approaches. "If all you have is a hammer, everything looks like a nail."

Cloud native relationship: Moving to cloud native while using old techniques/processes. Examples of this include using Scrum for innovation; deploying many microservices coupled tightly together; telling people what to do in a highly distributed team building microservices; or acting in other ways that avoid change in favor of what is already familiar.

Ostrich effect

Ignoring an obvious (negative) situation.

Cloud native relationship: Hardly requires explaining. We know that when we move to cloud native we need to make significant cultural shifts, not just change the tech. However, many companies choose to either ignore this altogether or make only small cosmetic changes meant to signal they've transformed their culture—and, either way, try to work in the new paradigm using old processes that no longer apply.

Parkinson's law of triviality ("bikeshedding")
The tendency to give disproportionate weight to trivial issues. Also known as bikeshedding, this bias explains why an organization may avoid specialized or complex subjects, such as the design of a nuclear reactor, and instead focus on something easy to grasp or rewarding to the average participant, such as the design of a bike shed next to the reactor.

Cloud native relationship: When people get together for three days of discussion and planning their cloud native migration—and then talk about tiny trivial things like which machine will Kubernetes run on or how to schedule a specific microservice. All this while avoiding large challenges, like changing organizational culture or overall architecture.

Planning fallacy
The tendency to underestimate task completion times. Closely related to the well-traveled road effect, or underestimation of the duration taken to traverse oft-traveled routes and overestimation of the duration taken to traverse less familiar routes.

Cloud native relationship: Especially operative in uncertain situations like moving to cloud native for the first time. We are eager to estimate the time and resources required but have no idea what it actually takes to move to cloud native. So, some people estimate it as a few weeks of work, maybe a couple months at most. Reality: often a year or longer. Basically if you don't have baselines from previous experience, any estimation is totally worthless.

Pro innovation bias
The tendency to have an excessive optimism toward an invention or innovation's usefulness throughout society, while failing to recognize its limitations and weaknesses.

Cloud native relationship: "Let's do Kubernetes, regardless if it's a good fit or even necessary. Because it is new and cool."

Pseudocertainty effect
The tendency to make risk-averse choices if the expected outcome is positive, but make risk-seeking choices to avoid negative outcomes.

Cloud native relationship: Successful teams will avoid investing in improvements while everything is going OK. But once a crisis erupts they will jump on any crazy new tool or process to save themselves. This is also a challenge for us: how do we help successful teams and companies overcome this and invest in continual improvement? The best motivator is recognizing the existential risk of standing still.

Shared information bias
> The tendency for group members to spend more time and energy discussing information that all members are already familiar with (i.e., shared information), and less time and energy discussing information that only some members are aware of.

> *Cloud native relationship*: The whole team went to a Docker training, so they spend a lot of time talking about Docker—and no time at all about Kubernetes, which is equally necessary but they don't know much about it. To reduce this one, especially in new and complex environments, teams have to learn new things all the time.

Status quo bias
> The tendency to like things to stay relatively the same.

> *Cloud native relationship*: Entire companies, and/or people within the organization, will resist moving to cloud native due to this bias: everyone wants to remain comfortably right where they are right now, which is known and understood.

Zero-risk bias
> Preference for reducing a small risk to zero over a greater reduction in a larger risk.

> *Cloud native relationship*: This is the opposite of low-hanging fruit. For example, companies want to reach 99.9999% availability, which is very difficult, yet they have no CI/CD to deliver the changes in the first place.

What to Watch For, and How to Overcome

A few of these biases are particularly hazardous to cloud native transformations. In particular we see the status quo bias operating in many client migration initiatives, especially in long-established companies. In this scenario, people have been doing the same set things in the same set way for 20 years and they simply don't want to change. They may not actively protest the move to cloud native, but neither do they actively help make it happen. Such inertia, repeated in person after person across an entire organization, can seriously hinder a transformation initiative.

There are several others. Law of the instrument bias—where people tend to rely on old skills and methods for doing new things, often unconsciously—leads to more individualized problems. One example happens when a project leader within a digitally transformed company still reflexively insists on approving each small change or experiment their team may want to try. This was the policy in the previous Waterfall hierarchy, but applying it now effectively blocks their team's autonomy—when it is just this independence and ability to iterate and experiment that drives the velocity and responsiveness of a cloud native system. Planning fallacy is another extremely common hazard; most companies enter into a transformation thinking it will be relatively quick and simple. They budget time and resources for only a few weeks or months, only to find that a proper transformation can require a year or more to successfully complete. And, finally, the ostrich effect explains the common scenario that arises when a company tries to transform its tech while ignoring the need to also transform its organizational culture and processes.

Fortunately, we can apply patterns to overcome these and other globally dysfunctional behaviors caused by bias. Committing to full change is difficult, and also anxiety-provoking, which can trigger our reflexive System 1 thinking. Patterns lift us into our rational and intentional System 2 brains by giving us a series of small steps to follow, so as to slowly and gradually shift in the right direction.

Cognitive biases evolved for a reason, and as we have seen there are ways they serve us still. But we need to recognize them and move beyond them. By consistently engaging our highest and most-evolved thought processes—by applying patterns, for example—we can easily evolve along with the completely new—and ever-changing—environment that cloud technologies have created.

First Attempt at Transformation–Cloud Native "Side Project"

This interlude includes a description of Jenny's first attempt to lead WealthGrid through a cloud native transformation. One of the most frequent mistakes we see is a company trying to treat a cloud native transformation as just another simple technology shift. Instead of allocating the resources necessary to implement a major organization-wide evolution of both tech and culture, the initiative gets treated as just another minor upgrade. It's assigned as a side project, or as just another system upgrade added to the backlog of standard tasks. Since getting started with cloud native can be deceptively easy, this may even seem to work well at first. But the reasons why this is a poor way to approach a transformation begin to reveal themselves as the project progresses. Things rapidly grow more complex, however, and more and more problems arise; meanwhile, the transformation team still has to keep working on existing system, too. Eventually the initiative will grind to a halt, though no one is quite sure why or what happened.

When last we saw Jenny, our technical program manager, she had come to the realization that now is the time for WealthGrid to make the move to the cloud.

She had been experiencing pressure for just such a move from both above and below. The engineering team she oversees really wants to try out new tools and technology. Some of WealthGrid's executive leadership, meanwhile, has been reading about how all modern businesses must go cloud native. Recently, upper management also realized that having cutting-edge cloud tech would help them attract and retain engineering talent.

Jenny agrees with the engineers *and* the C-suite. Furthermore, she had identified a third clear driving force that unites both sides: keeping the company's bottom line strong and healthy. WealthGrid needs to move to the cloud, for sure, and doing this now is key to keeping the company competitive.

She is astute enough to recognize that not only is the imminent arrival of a disruptive new cloud-powered competitor a very real possibility, but that if you wait until they show up in your market and begin showing significant strength, it could very well be too late for you to catch up. Remember our exponential versus traditional growth graph? Take a look at Figure II-1 as a reminder.

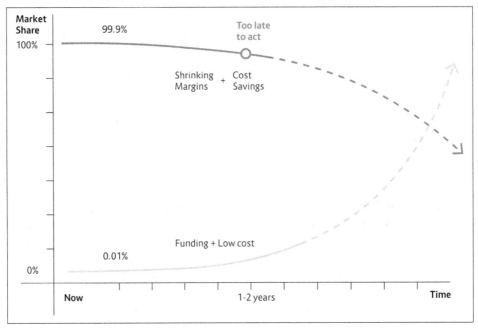

Figure II-1. When a disruptive new competitor comes to your market, they may seem small and nonthreatening at first—but their progress will be fast and relentless

Even if at first the stranger is just a small startup taking only a tiny bite of your market, pretty soon they are going to be eating your whole lunch! WealthGrid must take action before they even appear on the scene. And Jenny thinks she knows what to do.

Jenny has been to conferences, listened to talks, and read a lot of tech-industry articles. She understands that technology is the main factor in winning this competition. And that, furthermore, all of these technologies—public cloud, microservices, Kubernetes—are widely available to everyone. Many are even open source technologies, so they are available for free!

Really, this will just be a technical shift, she thinks. No need to put together a formal proposal and take it up the chain of command, because this falls into the category of pragmatic operations details that the C-suite avoids getting involved with. She can easily spare money out of her budget—have you seen how cheap it is to get started on the public cloud providers?!—and ask the engineers to work on implementing it alongside their usual tasks on the existing system.

This is how, without even going to her managers for approval, Jenny—together with the technical team she oversees—decides that they must go ahead and implement those things. Then they can show the entire company, once they have it ready. This should take a few months, no problem.

How Hard Can This Be?

The engineers are thrilled. Finally, a chance to roll up their sleeves and play with something really cool. They are eager to get started right away with their plan to put together a new platform for WealthGrid's software development system using Kubernetes, Docker containers, and microservices. Although they are accustomed to working with older technologies, the engineering team is confident they can figure things out as they go along. Jenny is confident, too—she knows her team is smart and capable. How hard can this be?

Their enthusiasm is only slightly dimmed when they realize that of course their first priority is the existing system—keeping it up and running well while still delivering new functionality. This, after all, is WealthGrid's core business, and where the company's profits come from. There are projects underway for building out new features, and those also need to keep moving forward. Even so, building a new cloud system shouldn't take too long, everyone agrees. They can work on it as a side project, when there is time, and still turn it around in a few months.

At first, things go pretty well. The team kicks off its cloud native transformation by setting up an account on a public cloud provider like Amazon Web Services or Google Cloud—all you need is a credit card, and you can be up and working almost instantly. If you want to run a single container, you can go online, click, and in 10 seconds you have a fully provisioned container running. It's practically magic!

Or perhaps they decide to go with a private cloud on their own infrastructure, à la VMware, and set up a Kubernetes cluster on a couple of spare servers ... or get a free version of one of the commercial cloud native integration platforms like RedHat's OpenShift or Mesosphere DC/OS.

After that, setting up a small project is also pretty easy. The engineers play around with a single container, begin learning the ropes, and it goes really well. So then they try adding a small experimental app they whip together, or perhaps place an existing Java app exactly as is into a container and get that running on the cloud. Either way, at the beginning this initial trial project seems very easy—but quickly gets harder. A *lot* harder.

Dividing everything into related, containerized microservices makes intuitive sense, but no one at WealthGrid has ever worked with a distributed system before. The complexities inherent in even a single small and isolated project present a major learning curve, and there seem to be more and more things going wrong that they just don't understand. Still, they are confident they can figure it all out, if they just find some time to focus.

Unfortunately, this dedicated time to focus on the new cloud platform simply never happens. Every time the engineering team starts to work on building out the new system, the work gets interrupted by a higher-priority feature request that comes from the market—from the customers out there using the existing WealthGrid products. The problem is, there is always pressure from customers. New or improved features are always winning the battle for assigning time to projects, and the new system always loses.

A Year Later, with Little to Show for It

So time passes, and after 12 months only a tiny portion of the new technologies is implemented. Even these are still strictly experimental. The engineers maybe have a few microservices running nicely on some Kubernetes clusters off on the side, but there is no significant impact on the current production environment. The results are intriguing—and also completely stalled. The team is constantly pulled away from any work on constructing the new platform by the need to continue rolling out features and support for the existing one.

This is not true failure, but there is no real success either. A year ago Jenny decided, along with her team, to go get for WealthGrid the same kind of responsive development and speed that their cloud native competitors enjoy. Their expectation was this would take maybe three to four months. Suddenly it's a year later, and there is little to show.

Jenny's first wakeup call was that WealthGrid needed to evolve into a cloud native company, and she responded using the resources at hand to start the transformation. Now she has a second wakeup call: what they're doing isn't working. It's not leading them fast enough to the goal of successfully competing with the disruptive newcomers crowding into WealthGrid's market.

Jenny needs to try a different approach. But what should she do?

CHAPTER 5

Knowing Thyself: The Cloud Native Maturity Matrix Tool

Cloud native is no longer the exclusive domain of massive tech-forward pioneers like Google, Uber, and Netflix. Cloud native tools and tech have matured to the point where the vast benefits of going cloud native have become available to companies of any size, from every sector. You are likely reading this book because you realize that cloud native's very tangible benefits—the ability to iterate and produce results quickly without getting bogged down in infrastructure setup and maintenance—are now realistically within your grasp.

Having read this far, however, means you've also gotten the news that achieving a cloud native transformation is not as simple or as easy to do as those peppy conference presenters like to make it sound. Transformation patterns certainly help facilitate the process, but that requires awareness and understanding of your current organizational context in order to know which patterns apply, and in what order.

So how *do* you go about launching a successful migration, patterns and all?

The first crucial step, as we saw in Chapter 2, is Know Thyself. This means truly understanding your company's existing architecture, processes, and organizational culture. You must evaluate these crucial but often overlooked realities before you can tackle the technical aspects of a migration—that is, if you want a successful outcome. Enterprises that just grab for the new tech without first understanding how it will fit into and function within their existing organizational culture (spoiler alert: it won't) are setting themselves up for wasting time and resources on an ultimately ineffective effort. Or, worse, complete failure.

Mirror, Mirror, on the Wall...

Realistically, this is easier said than done. It's hard to objectively observe and evaluate your own systems and culture from the inside as an active participant. Honestly it's not the easiest thing to do from the outside, either. Take the many interwoven forces and factors at play and then combine those with the unique circumstances any enterprise brings to a migration: it's a complex tangle.

Cloud service providers are no help in this area. Amazon Web Services, Google Cloud Services, Azure, et al., are doing their level best to anticipate and solve every onboarding problem a business may encounter, but thus far none of them offers any help with the crucial first step (i.e., that "Know Thyself" task). They don't even acknowledge its existence. Why would they? Their business model centers upon getting you to sign up and use their systems, not analyzing your own existing one.

Thus, the temptation to just pick a provider and get on with the show is utterly understandable. In the early stages it will also likely feel like a successful move. However, the complexity inherent within cloud native's distributed systems architecture is relentlessly exponential. An "unexamined" organization will inevitably reach a point where its existing systems and culture will clash with—and, ultimately, short-circuit —its transition attempt.

Though still new and evolving, cloud native has been around long enough for those of us in the sector to observe and identify common elements appearing in successfully completed migrations, as well as frequent points when attempts stall or even fail outright. Having cataloged some things that help drive a successful migration, and some that definitely do not, the next logical step was to create an assessment tool.

For Mature Audiences Only: The Maturity Matrix

Maturity models can be a useful and effective mechanism for evaluating status in all kinds of systems. When it comes to software development, unfortunately, traditional maturity models often lack context and/or fail to provide pragmatic guidance for undertaking their recommended steps. Even when they do try to help with actual implementation, maturity models too often either (a) oversimplify reality or (b) prescribe a one-size-fits-all progression path.

Since every organization has unique circumstances, challenges, and needs, we developed a detailed and accurate yet flexible and, above all, pragmatic version for organizations seeking a cloud native transformation.

We distilled four years' worth of observation and experience gained from helping clients onto the cloud and used it to build this assessment tool. We call it the Cloud Native Maturity Matrix, a unique framework for evaluating and understanding your company where it is right now. The matrix is a pragmatic process you can apply to map your current maturity, identify gap analysis, and discern where they should focus their efforts in order to reap the most benefits. This is a model which has proved very useful for our clients.

Organizations tend to call upon cloud consultancy services in one of two ways. Helping a company commence a brand-new cloud migration and getting it right from the start is our preferred mode. But, as is happening more and more frequently, we are also called in to rescue stalled implementations. Either way, our approach starts the same with each and every client.

We spend two days on site evaluating their unique circumstances and specific needs by taking them through the Cloud Native Maturity Matrix. Together, we create an accurate snapshot of the enterprise along nine different axes. We then use this to define, analyze, and describe organizational status and begin to map the migration process. This data—constantly re-assessed as the process moves forward—allows us to customize transformation goals and monitor progress while working to keep all the different aspects involved in a migration moving forward smoothly and in alignment.

In other words, the Maturity Matrix is how we create the custom map for each company's unique migratory path to the cloud. And it's also how we monitor the process to remain on track.

The concepts that form the Maturity Matrix framework are essential background knowledge for talking about cloud native transformation patterns. Understanding what we assess, and why, is key to understanding your own global organizational context—so you can identify the applicable patterns and use them properly for your own transformation design.

Staying in Sync

In this chapter we are going to walk you through the nine different areas on the Maturity Matrix and how to identify your organization's status in each one. These areas are:

- **Culture:** The way individuals in your organization interact with one another
- **Product/Service Design:** How decisions are made within your organization about what work to do next (e.g., which new products to build or what new features to add or improvements to make to existing ones)
- **Team:** How responsibilities, communication, and collaboration works across and between teams in your organization
- **Process:** How your organization handles the execution of work and assigned projects

- **Architecture:** Describes the overall structure of your technology system
- **Maintenance and Operations:** How software is deployed and then run in a production environment in your organization
- **Delivery:** How and when software from your development teams gets to run in your live (production) environment
- **Provisioning:** The processes by which you create or update your systems in your live production environment
- **Infrastructure:** The physical servers or instances that your production environment consists of—what they are, where they are, and how they are managed

Once assessed, each area's status is mapped on the corresponding Maturity Matrix axis. We then literally "connect the dots" by drawing a line through each area's current status point, from Culture all the way to Infrastructure.

Graphing status in this way provides an instant, powerful, and above all easy to grasp visual representation of your company's state. It also clearly demonstrates the distance that we will need to close in each area in order to achieve full cloud native functioning.

Figure 5-1 shows Maturity Matrix results from a real-world client assessment.

In the sample Maturity Matrix in Figure 5-1, we see both the current situation for an actual company, as well as the progression points necessary for a cloud native transformation. For example, Culture has progressed somewhat beyond Waterfall, while Process has nearly reached Agile.

This allows us to identify the worst bottleneck (i.e., the least developed areas) and focus our initial migration efforts there, so as to immediately begin to increase the flow. In this example matrix, we would be looking at Infrastructure, Product/Service Design, and Teams as first priorities.

Stage	NO PROCESS	WATERFALL	AGILE	CLOUD NATIVE	NEXT
CULTURE	Individualist	Predictive	Iterative	Collaborative	Experimental
	O	O	O	O	O
PROD/SERVICE DESIGN	Arbitrary	Long-term plan	Feature driven	Data driven	All driven
	O	O	O	O	O
TEAM	No organization, single contributor	Hierarchy	Cross-functional teams	DevOps / SRE	Internal supply chains
	O	O	O	O	O
PROCESS	Random	Waterfall	Agile (Scrum/Kanban)	Design Thinking + Agile + Lean	Distributed, self-organized
	O	O	O	O	O
ARCHITECTURE	Emerging from trial and error	Tightly coupled monolith	Client server	Microservices	Functions
	O	O	O	O	O
MAINTENANCE	Respond to users complaints	Ad-hoc monitoring	Alerting	Full observability & self-healing	Preventive ML, AI
	O	O	O	O	O
DELIVERY	Irregular releases	Periodic releases	Continuous Integration	Continuous Delivery	Continuous Deployment
	O	O	O	O	O
PROVISIONING	Manual	Scripted	Config. management (Puppet/Chef/Ansible)	Orchestration (Kubernetes)	Serverless
	O	O	O	O	O
INFRASTRUCTURE	Single server	Multiple servers	VMs (pets)	Containers/ hybrid cloud (cattle)	Edge computing
	O	O	O	O	O

CURRENT SITUATION   GOAL

Figure 5-1. Cloud Native Maturity Matrix results from an enterprise assessment/discovery, with the cloud native "goal line" defined

This, however, does not mean that other areas stay on hold while one or more bottlenecks are addressed. It's OK for different teams to progress at different rates—especially if some of these teams are preparing the ground for an easier overall transition.

 It is important to note that a company doesn't need to go through intermediate stages in order to reach cloud native—that is, if they are in Waterfall, they can jump directly to cloud native without going through Agile first.

Transitions progress gradually, and different teams move forward at different rates. Aligning the Maturity Matrix does not mean moving in lockstep to maintain some inflexible, perfectly even line during transition. It's more about staying in sync: making sure that each of the axes is adequately and appropriately addressed, working together holistically and in context with the entire complex system.

Applying the Matrix

The Cloud Native Maturity Matrix is typically administered by trained facilitators over the course of a few days spent on-site with an enterprise and its employees. However, it is still an extremely useful thought experiment to work through it on your own to try to identify where your organization currently falls.

As we have seen, the Maturity Matrix is divided into nine separate areas (or axes), each one an individual and essential member of an integrated, interdependent system. Each axis is further divided into four specific stages of organizational development a company may currently occupy: no process, Waterfall, Agile, and cloud native. (An additional "Next" category is also included to show possible directions that could happen in the future, given current trends and tech developments.) Over our next few sections we will examine what exactly organizational status typically looks like in each of these same query stages, compared across each of the nine axes. We move across them from left to right, from older/less agile states in a progression toward resilient and responsive cloud native. But the Cloud Native Maturity Matrix does not end with a successful migration onto the cloud! As we've discussed, cloud native is not only focused on what to do now—it is just as much about building in the ability to easily adapt to whatever comes *next*.

Culture

The Maturity Matrix begins with Culture because it is the toughest transition axis to progress—no matter the organization. Culture is abstract, hard to transform, and evolving it is a slow process. The other axes are faster and easier to achieve because, ultimately, they are mainly code and planning. Changing culture also requires a lot of buy-in across the entire organization, while the other axes can generally function in a more independent way.

We discussed culture in depth in Chapter 2, but here is a quick overview. Figure 5-2 shows the range of Culture indicators we investigate in a Maturity Matrix assessment.

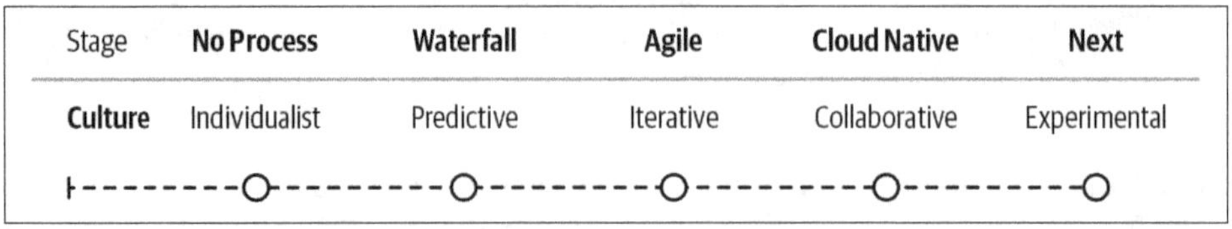

Stage	No Process	Waterfall	Agile	Cloud Native	Next
Culture	Individualist	Predictive	Iterative	Collaborative	Experimental

├ - - - - - - -O - - - - - - - - O - - - - - - - - O - - - - - - - - O - - - - - - - -O

Figure 5-2. Culture axis of the Cloud Native Maturity Matrix

No process: Individualistic

There is no set or specified way to interact with peers, superiors, or subordinates. Instead, communications are rooted in personal preferences. This is a common culture for startups but is unsustainable as you scale up.

Waterfall: Predictive

A Predictive organization has a strong preference for long-term planning and firm deadlines. The goal is to deliver a complex system exactly as specified; delivering it fast is not a priority. These organizations tend to suppress experimentation or introducing new ideas because these are inherently unpredictable. Typically there are large amounts of documentation; procedures for changes, improvements, and daily tasks; segregation of teams by specialization; tools for every situation; and regular (e.g., weekly), lengthy planning meetings. Delivering a complex system exactly as specified and on time is a complex and difficult endeavor.

This culture is common in medium-to-large enterprises.

Agile: Iterative

An Agile organization chooses smaller and simpler goals, which it aims to deliver as fast as possible. Agile organizations tend to focus on the short term rather than following a long-term plan. Communication is often by short, daily meetings. Emphasis is on fast responses and quick fixes, which can lead to a "hero culture" where individuals regularly display superhuman efforts to keep everything on track. They commonly use the Scrum project management methodology, with inter-team communication by Scrum Masters and other coordinators. Agile organizations normally have wide responsibilities *within* cross-functional teams but narrow responsibilities *for* each team.

This culture is common throughout startups and enterprises of all sizes.

Cloud native: Collaborative

A **Collaborative** organization tends to have big but not deeply specific goals (i.e., there may be a wide vision but without a detailed specification or a fixed delivery date). This culture embraces learning and consistent, continuous improvement over predictability. Emphasis is on self-education, experimentation, and research. Results are coldly assessed based on field data.

A collaborative culture is crucial for companies operating in areas of high uncertainty or fast change.

Next: Generative

We predict the next type of organization will be a **Generative** one. An extension of a collaborative organization, in a generative organization IT will co-create solutions as equal partners with the business.

Product/Service Design

This is the place where we assess just what it is you do and how you go about doing it. We evaluate whether you are organized around long-term planning, delivering a tightly coupled product on a slow and deliberate schedule—or whether you iterate rapidly in shorter sprints, ideally using customer feedback to drive the changes. Figure 5-3 shows the range of Product/Service Design situations we look for in a Maturity Matrix assessment.

Stage	No Process	Waterfall	Agile	Cloud Native	Next
Prod/ Service Design	Arbitrary	Long-term plan	Feature driven	Data driven	All driven

├ ─ ─ ─ ─ ─ ─ ─O ─ ─ ─ ─ ─ ─ ─ ─O ─ ─ ─ ─ ─ ─ ─ ─O ─ ─ ─ ─ ─ ─ ─ ─O ─ ─ ─ ─ ─ ─ ─ ─O

Figure 5-3. Product/Service Design axis of the Cloud Native Maturity Matrix

No process: Arbitrary

An arbitrary design process is fad/wild-idea driven, somewhat random, and not deeply discussed. It is a common way to operate in startups where ideas usually come from the founders. On the upside, it can be highly creative. On the downside, it may result in partial features or an incoherent product.

Waterfall: Long-term plan

This design process focuses on collating and assessing product feature requests by customers, potential customers (via sales), users, or product managers. Individual features are then turned into team projects and multiple features are combined into large releases that happen every six to twelve months. This process is a very common model for larger enterprises.

Agile: Feature Driven

A feature-driven design process speeds things up by allowing small new features to be selected with less planning. The aim is that these more modest features will be delivered to clients every few weeks or months in small batches. A feature-driven organization focuses on fast change often without an overarching long-term plan.

Cloud native: Data Driven

The final say on which features stay in a product is based on data collected from real users. Potential new features are chosen based on client requests or designs by product owners without a long selection process. They are rapidly prototyped and then developed and delivered to users with copious monitoring and instrumentation. They are assessed against the previous features (better or worse?) based on A/B or multivariate testing. If the new feature performs better, it stays; if worse, it is switched off or improved.

Next: AI Driven

In the future, humans will be cut out of this process entirely! AI-driven systems will make evolutionary tweaks and test themselves with little developer interaction.

Team

Does your enterprise take a top-down, "Do what the boss says" approach, likely with highly specialized teams? Or one that is more cross-functional, composed of teams where each member has specific skills? Possibly you have progressed all the way to DevOps—an effective approach that takes advantage of cloud native architecture. Figure 5-4 shows the range of Team structures we look for in a Maturity Matrix assessment.

Stage	No Process	Waterfall	Agile	Cloud Native	Next
Team	No organization, single contributor	Hierarchy	Cross-functional teams	DevOps/SRE	Internal supply chains

Figure 5-4. Team axis of the Cloud Native Maturity Matrix

No process: No organization, single contributor

In this type of organization we find little structure, typically one or possibly a few independent contributors with no consistent management. This is most commonly found in small startups.

Waterfall: Hierarchy

Organized via considerable top-down order, both within and between the teams. Decisions are made by upper managers, and implementation is done by specialized teams (making it difficult to move individuals between teams). There will be separate teams of architects, designers, developers, testers, and operations. Inter-team communication is generally through tools like JIRA or via managers. Historically, this has been the most common structure of large organizations.

Agile: Cross-functional teams

A cross-functional organization has less specialization across teams and more cross-capability *within* teams. For example, development teams will often include testing and planning capabilities. Scrum Masters, Product Owners, etc., facilitate communication between teams. However, a hierarchical organizational structure remains outside the teams themselves.

Cloud native: DevOps/SRE

Traditionally, developers/engineers have been responsible for building software and then handing it off to the operations team for deployment. A DevOps team joins the two in a single team capable of designing and building applications as part of a distributed system, and also operating the production platform/tools. Across the organization, each team has full responsibility for delivering an individual set of microservices and supporting them. DevOps teams typically include planning, architecture, testing, dev, and operational capabilities.

There will still often remain a separation of tasks. For example, it is common to see a platform DevOps team in charge of building the cloud native platform, while site reliability engineering (SRE) or first-level support teams respond to incidents (and spend the rest of their time working on automation to prevent them from happening in the first place). However, there is considerable collaboration between those teams and individuals can easily move between them.

Next: Internal supply chains

In an Internal Supply Chain organization, each service is a separate product with full tech and business generation responsibilities in the teams—much as many ecommerce teams have been managed for a decade.

Process

Does your enterprise do long-term planning up front and then follow with execution? Or do you change things responsively and on the fly? Currently, Scrum/Kanban is what we find most enterprises using. Cloud native and CI/CD require the next jump in speed: now developers need to be able to deliver every day—and do so independently from other developers. Figure 5-5 shows the range of process approaches we look for in a Maturity Matrix assessment.

Stage	No Process	Waterfall	Agile	Cloud Native	Next
Process	Random	Waterfall	Agile (Scrum/Kanban)	Design Thinking + Agile + Lean	Distributed, self-organized

├--------O---------O---------O---------O---------O

Figure 5-5. Process axis of the Cloud Native Maturity Matrix

No process: Random

In a random organization there is no change-management process, just random changes made at will. There is often no consistent versioning. This is common in many small companies with only a couple of engineers.

Waterfall: Waterfall

In a Waterfall organization, the product development process is tightly controlled through up-front planning and change management processes. A sequential process is followed of planning, execution, testing, and (finally) delivery. There is usually an Integration stage before delivery where work from different streams is combined.

The process is run by managers; every handover is well documented and requires forms and procedures.

Agile: Agile (Scrum/Kanban)

Product development is run in sprints using an Agile technique such as Scrum or Kanban. Documentation is limited (the product is the documentation), and teams are heavily involved in their own management through daily consultation. There is usually considerable pressure to deliver fast and no defined provision for experiments or research. Limited or no changes are allowed during sprints to protect the delivery deadlines.

Cloud native: Design Thinking + Agile + Lean

Design Thinking and other research and experimentation techniques are used for de-risking large and complex projects. Many proofs of concept (PoCs) are developed to compare options. Kanban is often then used to clarify the project further, and finally Agile methods like Scrum can be applied once the project is well understood by the entire team. Highly proficient organizations might choose to follow the Lean model.

This relatively new approach is very effective in situations of high uncertainty or where the technology is changing rapidly.

Next: Distributed, self-organized

In the future, self-organized systems will be highly experimental. There will be less up-front design. Individuals or small teams will generate ideas, which will then form the seeds of a new product or feature. Once implemented, these will be iterated and improved on automatically by the platform.

Architecture

Is your enterprise trying "batteries included" to provide everything needed for most use cases—the Tightly Coupled Monolith? Or perhaps you have reached the next step in the evolutionary architecture chain, Client–Server. The cloud native goal is to use microservices architecture where a large application is built as a suite of modular components or services. Microservices enable development teams to take a more decentralized (non-hierarchical) approach to building software. Microservices enable each service to be isolated, rebuilt, redeployed and managed independently. Figure 5-6 shows the range of Architecture approaches we look for in a Maturity Matrix assessment.

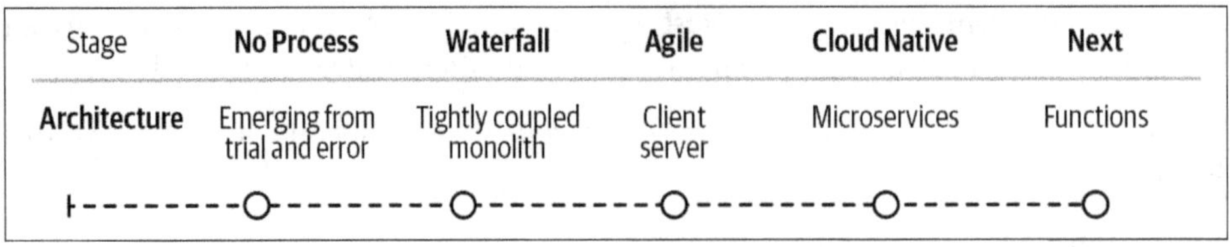

Stage	No Process	Waterfall	Agile	Cloud Native	Next
Architecture	Emerging from trial and error	Tightly coupled monolith	Client server	Microservices	Functions

├ - - - - - - - -O- - - - - - - - -O- - - - - - - - -O- - - - - - - - -O- - - - - - - -O

Figure 5-6. Architecture axis of the Cloud Native Maturity Matrix

No process: Emerging from trial and error

In an architecture described as emerging from trial and error, there are no clear architectural principles or practices. Developers just write code independently, and all system-level communication is ad-hoc. Integrations between components tend to be poorly documented, unclear, and hard to extend and maintain.

Waterfall: Tightly coupled monolith

A tightly coupled monolith is an architectural model where the entire codebase is built as one to five modules, with many developers working on the same components. A layered architecture (database, business logic, presentation layer, etc.) is common. Although interfaces have been defined, changes in one part often require changes in other parts because, typically, the code is divided into components with very strong coupling.

Delivery is done in a coordinated way, all together, and typically the monolith is written in a single programming language with strong standardization on tooling. The application is usually vertically scalable (you can support more users by adding more resources on single server). The design and maintenance of the monolith is usually led by a system architect or her team, many of whom are not hands-on developers.

Agile: Client–server

This architecture is the most basic form of distributed system. The client–server model partitions tasks or workloads between service providers—the servers—which deliver requested resources to the service-seeking clients.

Like a monolith, in a client–server architecture multiple teams work on services at once, and all services need to be deployed together. However, because the network-induced separation provides a degree of decoupling, it is usually possible to at least some degree to develop on the system in parallel (one group handles the client part, one the server).

Cloud native: Microservices

Microservices architecture is highly distributed. It comprises a large number (usually more than 10) of independent services that communicate only via well-defined, versioned APIs. Often, each microservice is developed and maintained by one team.

Each microservice can be deployed independently, and each has a separate code repository. Hence, each microservice team can work and deploy in a highly parallel fashion, using their own preferred languages and operational tools and datastores (such as databases or queues).

Because the system is distributed and components are decoupled, not only from each other but from other copies of themselves, is it easy to scale the system up by deploying more copies of each service. Operationally, microservice deployment must be managed in a fully automated way.

Next: Functions-as-a-Service/Serverless

A Functions-as-a-Service (FaaS, also known as Serverless) architecture is one where no infrastructure needs to be provisioned. Each piece of business logic is in separate function, which is operated by a fully managed Function-as-a-Service such as AWS' Lambda, Azure Functions, or Google's Cloud Functions. No operations tasks such as up-front provisioning, scaling, or patching are required. There is a pay-as-you-go/pay-per-invocation model.

Maintenance

On this axis we assess how you monitor your systems and keep them running. It's a broad spectrum, from having no process whatsoever to full automation with little or no human intervention. No Process/Ad Hoc means every now and then going in to see if the server is up and what the response time is. (And the somewhat embarrassing fact is, a lot of folks still do just that.) Alerting means having some form of automation to warn when problems arrive, but it is nowhere near fast enough for this new world because once a problem is alerted, a human being still needs to intervene. Comprehensive monitoring and full observability, where system behavior is observed and analyzed so problems can be predicted (and prevented) in advance, rather than responded to when they do happen, are an absolute necessity for cloud native. Figure 5-7 shows the range of Maintenance approaches we look for in a Maturity Matrix assessment.

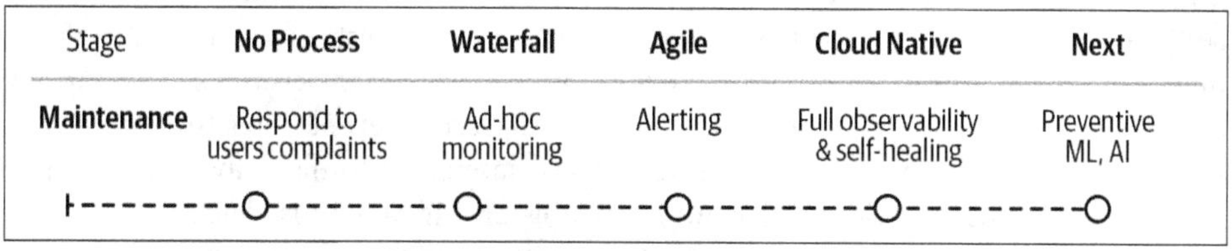

Stage	No Process	Waterfall	Agile	Cloud Native	Next
Maintenance	Respond to users complaints	Ad-hoc monitoring	Alerting	Full observability & self-healing	Preventive ML, AI

Figure 5-7. Maintenance axis of the Cloud Native Maturity Matrix

No process: Respond to users' complaints

The development and operations teams are alerted to most problems only when users encounter them. There is insufficient monitoring to flag issues in advance and allow engineers to fix them before the majority of users will hit them. System downtime may only be discovered by clients, or randomly. There is no alerting.

For diagnosing issues, administrators usually need to log in to servers and view each tool/app log separately. As a result, multiple individuals need security access to production. When fixes to systems are applied, there is a manual upgrade procedure.

This is a common situation in startups or small enterprises, but it has significant security, reliability, and resilience issues, as well as single points of failure (often individual engineers).

Waterfall: Ad-hoc monitoring

This consists of partial, and mostly manual, monitoring of system infrastructure and apps. This includes constant monitoring and alerting on basic, fundamental downtime events such as the main server becoming unresponsive.

Live problems are generally handled by the operations team and only they have access to production. Usually, there's no central access to logs, and engineers must log in to individual servers for diagnosis, maintenance operations, and troubleshooting. Formal runbooks (documentation) and checklists exist for performing manual update procedures; this is very common in larger enterprises but still does not completely mitigate security, reliability, and resilience issues.

Agile: Alerting

Alerts are preconfigured on a variety of live system events. There is typically some log collection in a central location, but most of the logs are still in separate places.

Operations teams normally respond to these alerts and will escalate to developers if they can't resolve the issue. Operations engineers still need to be able to log in to individual servers. Update processes, however, may be partially or fully scripted.

Cloud native: Full observability and self-healing

In full observability and self-healing scenarios, the system relies upon logging, tracing, alerting, and metrics to continually collect information about all the running services in a system. In cloud native you must observe the system to see what is going on. Monitoring is how we see this information; observability describes the property we architect into a system so that we are able to discern internal states through monitoring external outputs. Many issue responses happen automatically; for example, system health checks may trigger automatic restarts if failure is detected. Alternatively, the system may gradually degrade its own service to keep itself alive if, for example, resource shortages such as low disk space are detected (Netflix is famous for this). Status dashboards are often accessible to everyone in the business so that they can check the availability of the services.

Operations (sometimes now referred to as "platform") engineers respond to infrastructure and platform issues that are not handled automatically. Live application issues are handled by development teams or system reliability engineers (SREs). The SRE role may be filled by individuals embedded in a DevOps team or separated into a dedicated SRE team.

Logs are all collected into a single place. This often includes distributed tracing output. Operations, developers, and SREs all have access to the logging location. They no longer have (or need) security access to production servers.

All update processes are fully automated and do not require access by individual engineers to individual servers.

Next: Machine learning (ML) and artificial intelligence (AI)

In the next generation of systems, ML and AI will handle operational and maintenance processes. Systems learn on their own how to prevent failures by, for instance, automatically scaling up capacity. Self-healing is the optimal way for systems to be operated and maintained. It is faster, more secure, and more reliable.

Delivery

Delivery is really all about how quickly you can get things out and in how automated a fashion. The Maturity Matrix moves from traditional major version releases every six to 12 months to Agile's more rapid iterations of weekly to monthly releases. Reaching cloud native grants the ability to release daily, or even multiple times per day. Figure 5-8 shows the range of delivery approaches we look for in a Maturity Matrix assessment.

Stage	No Process	Waterfall	Agile	Cloud Native	Next
Delivery	Irregular releases	Periodic releases	Continuous Integration	Continuous Delivery	Continuous Deployment

Figure 5-8. Delivery axis of the Cloud Native Maturity Matrix

No process: Irregular releases

In many small organizations, irregular software releases (new function or fixes) are delivered into production at random times based on IT or management decisions about the urgency of the change. For highly urgent issues, like fixes for production problems, changes are delivered by developers directly to production ASAP.

This is a common situation for startups and small enterprises.

Waterfall: Periodic scheduled releases

Many organizations have periodic scheduled releases, for example every six months. The contents of these (usually infrequent) releases becomes extremely important and is the result of long planning sessions. Extensive architectural documents for each release are produced by enterprise architects; no coding is done before the full architecture is ready. Once the release contents are agreed on, any change is subject to a change approval board (CAB). A key driver behind infrequent releases is the need to perform expensive manual testing of each release prior to deployment.

Highly sequential processes are followed for each release:

1. System and software requirements are captured in a product requirements document.

2. Analysis is performed, resulting in documented models, schema, and business rules.

3. Design of the software architecture is completed and documented.

4. Coding is done: the development, proving, and integration of software (i.e., merging the work done by different teams).

5. Testing of that integrated new code is performed, including manual tests.

6. The installation and migration of the software is completed by the operations team.

After the release, the Operations teams support and maintain the completed system.

Agile: Continuous Integration (CI)

Continuous integration describes an organization that ensures new functionality is ready to be released at will—without needing to follow a strict release schedule (although a formal release schedule may still be followed). It often results in more frequent releases of new code to production.

A tech organization using CI typically has:

- A single codebase (aka source repository) that all developers add their code to. This ensures that merging and integration happen constantly rather than occasionally. That tends to make merging much easier.

- A fully automated build process that turns new code into runnable applications.

- Automated testing of all code as part of the build. This forces developers to fix bugs as they go along (which, again, is easier).

- A requirement for developers to add their new code to the single repository every day, which forces them to merge and fix bugs incrementally as they go along.

- A way to deploy code to test or production hardware in an automated fashion.

Cloud native: Continuous Delivery (CD)

Continuous delivery describes an organization that ensures new functionality is released to production at high frequency, often several times per day. That does not mean the new functionality is exposed to all users immediately. It might be temporarily hidden or reserved for a subset of experimental or preview users.

With CD we typically see:

- A so-called "deployment pipeline" where new code from developers is automatically moved through build and test phases.
- Automatic acceptance (or rejection) of new code for deployment.
- Thorough testing of functionality, integration, load, and performance happens automatically.
- Once a developer has put their code into the pipeline, they cannot manually change it.
- Individual engineers do not have permission to change the production (live) servers.

Cloud native organizations typically combine integration and deployment processes, known as "CI/CD," to drive continuous improvements to their systems. They also run tests on their production systems using methods such as "chaos engineering" (a way of forcing outages to occur on production systems to ensure those systems recover automatically) or live testing for subsets of users (e.g. "A/B testing").

Next: Continuous Deployment

The next evolution of delivery is continuous deployment, where we see fully automatic deployment to production with no approval process—just a continuous flow of changes to customers. The system will automatically roll back (uninstall) new changes if certain key metrics are negatively impacted, such as user conversion.

Provisioning

How do you create new infrastructure and new machines? How quickly can you deploy everything, and how automated is this process? Provisioning is the Maturity Matrix axis where we are happiest to see a company leading the other eight areas! Figure 5-9 shows the range of delivery approaches we look for in a Maturity Matrix assessment.

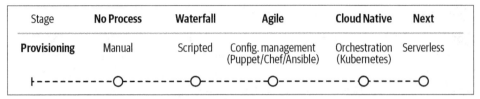

Stage	No Process	Waterfall	Agile	Cloud Native	Next
Provisioning	Manual	Scripted	Config. management (Puppet/Chef/Ansible)	Orchestration (Kubernetes)	Serverless

Figure 5-9. Provisioning axis of the Cloud Native Maturity Matrix

No process: Manual

In a manual system, a developer (who is also your operations person) logs in to a server and starts apps manually or with rudimentary scripting. Servers are accessed using primitive file transfer mechanisms like FTP.

This is a common situation in startups. It is slow, labor-intensive, insecure, and doesn't scale.

Waterfall: Scripted

Developers build an app and hand it over to the operations team to deploy it. The ops team will have a scripted mechanism for copying the application and all its dependencies onto a machine to run. They will also have a scripted mechanism for configuring that machine, or they may have pre-configured virtual machines (VMs).

In this case, because the development team "throws their app over the wall" to operations, there is a risk that the development team built and tested their app using different tools, versions, or environments to those available to or used by the ops team. This can cause an application that worked fine for the dev team to fail to work when operations puts it on their test or live servers. This introduces confusion when issues are subsequently seen: is there a bug in the app delivered by dev, or is it an issue in the production environment?

Agile: Configuration Management (Puppet/Chef/Ansible)

In a system with configuration management, applications are developed to run on specific hardware or virtual machines. Tools like Puppet, Chef, or Ansible allow operations engineers to create standardized scripts, which are run to ensure a production system is configured exactly as required for the application provided by development. This can be done at will (i.e., fast) but there is limited automation (mostly a human still needs to press a button to run the scripts).

Developers often deploy on their local test environments with different, simpler tooling. Therefore, mismatches can still occur between developer environments and production ones, which may cause issues with the live system. However, this is less common and faster to resolve than with more ad-hoc scripting.

Cloud native: Dynamic Scheduling/Orchestration (Kubernetes)

Applications in production are managed by a combination of containerization (a type of packaging that guarantees applications are delivered from development with all their local operational dependencies included) and a commercially available or open source orchestrator such as Kubernetes.

The risk of a mismatch between development and live environments is reduced or eliminated by delivering applications from Dev to Ops in containers along with all of the app's dependencies. The Ops team then configures Kubernetes to support the new application by describing the final system they want to produce in production. This is called declarative configuration.

The resulting system is highly resilient, automated, and abstracted. Neither engineers nor the apps themselves need to be aware of hardware specifics. Everything is automatic. Detailed decision making about where and when applications will be deployed is made by the orchestrator itself, not a human.

Next: Serverless

All hardware maintenance and configuration is done in a fully automated way by your cloud provider's platform. Code is packaged by developers, submitted to the serverless service(s), and can potentially be distributed and executed on many different platforms. The same function can run for testing or live. Inputs, outputs, and dependencies are tightly specified and standardized. Serverless is rapidly being adopted across the cloud native ecosystem and is well on its way to becoming standard cloud native best practice.

Infrastructure

Everyone knows this one: single server to multiple servers to VMs running in your own data center. Then shifting to Hybrid cloud for a computing environment that mixes on-premises infrastructure with private and/or public cloud services best tailored to your company's specific needs and use case. Figure 5-10 shows the different Infrastructure options we look for in a Maturity Matrix assessment.

Stage	No Process	Waterfall	Agile	Cloud Native	Next
Infrastructure	Single server	Multiple servers	VMs (pets)	Containers/ hybrid cloud (cattle)	Edge computing

Figure 5-10. Infrastructure axis of the Cloud Native Maturity Matrix

No process: Single server

In a single server environment you run all of production on a single physical machine. This may be an old desktop sitting under a desk in the office. You have no failover servers (resilience), and you deploy to your server using copy-and-paste file transfers. You probably have some rudimentary documents to describe the setup.

Waterfall: Multiple servers

A multiple servers (physical) infrastructure will handle a moderately complex application. You can have a sophisticated system of multiple interacting applications, for example front ends and a clustered database. Redundancy ensures that if one machine fails, another will take over. This is probably all sitting in a simple co-located data center.

Your operations team may use manual problem solving, and it might take days or weeks to provision new infrastructure because it's hard to get more rackspace! Compute, storage, networking, and security are usually managed separately and require separate requests to ops. New infrastructure is ordered through a ticketing system and provisioned by ops.

Agile: VMs ("pets")

A VM-based environment is similar to a multiple-servers environment in that you have a set of machines and manual server setup. (VMs are sometimes referred to as "pets," due to the small number of machines and the personal relationship that arises from needing to interact with each of them regularly.) However, this is made easier by using standardized virtual machine images. You use virtualization software such as VMware to help manage your virtual machine instances. You get better resource utilization (and therefore an effectively larger system for your money) by running multiple VM instances on each physical server.

Your operations team uses manual or semi-automated provisioning of new infrastructure resources. Your VMs are "mutable"—engineers can log on to them and change them by, for example, installing new software or fixes. Each machine is maintained separately, and it would be painful if one died (hence, "pets"). It will generally take hours or days to provision new infrastructure, mainly due to handovers between Dev and Ops teams.

Cloud native: Containers/hybrid cloud (cattle)

Here, individual machines don't matter: they are called "cattle" because there is a big herd and they are interchangeable. There is usually full automation of environment creation and maintenance. If any piece of infrastructure fails, you don't care—it can be easily and almost instantly recreated.

Unlike VMs, these are never directly provisioned; they are accessed only through automated processes exposed through APIs. This automation means new infrastructure takes minutes, even seconds, to provision. Containers are used for application packaging, which makes it easier to run those applications anywhere, including different "hybrid" cloud environments, whether public or on-premises.

Next: Edge computing

The next evolution for infrastructure is edge computing. Decentralized computer processing as the edge of your network. Edge computing takes applications, data, and computing power (services) out of a centralized location and distributes them to locations closer to the user. (Kind of like microservices for compute loads, really.) Edge computing returns results fast and works well in applications where, for example, adequate data is available locally.

Connecting the Dots

OK! Now you have read through the nine Maturity Matrix axes and identified, at least roughly, your company's current practices, from Culture to Process to Infrastructure. Now it is time to copy your answers from each individual axis onto the full blank matrix in order to graph your own real-time status. Figure 5-11 provides a blank version of the matrix, or you can visit *https://container-solutions.com* (*http://bit.ly/ 37L69Ij*) to find a full-size downloadable version.

Stage	NO PROCESS	WATERFALL	AGILE	CLOUD NATIVE	NEXT
CULTURE	Individualist	Predictive	Iterative	Collaborative	Experimental
PROD/SERVICE DESIGN	Arbitrary	Long-term plan	Feature driven	Data driven	All driven
TEAM	No organization, single contributor	Hierarchy	Cross-functional teams	DevOps / SRE	Internal supply chains
PROCESS	Random	Waterfall	Agile (Scrum/Kanban)	Design Thinking + Agile + Lean	Distributed, self-organized
ARCHITECTURE	Emerging from trial and error	Tightly coupled monolith	Client server	Microservices	Functions
MAINTENANCE	Respond to users complaints	Ad-hoc monitoring	Alerting	Full observability & self-healing	Preventive ML, AI
DELIVERY	Irregular releases	Periodic releases	Continuous Integration	Continuous Delivery	Continuous Deployment
PROVISIONING	Manual	Scripted	Config. management (Puppet/Chef/Ansible)	Orchestration (Kubernetes)	Serverless
INFRASTRUCTURE	Single server	Multiple servers	VMs (pets)	Containers/ hybrid cloud (cattle)	Edge computing

Figure 5-11. The blank Cloud Native Maturity Matrix template, ready for you to fill in and then connect your very own dots

It's very simple: match your answer from the section above, where we explained each individual axis, to draw a point on the corresponding place on the full blank matrix. Then literally connect the dots by drawing a line through each status point. Graphing status in this way gives instant valuable feedback and provides a powerful visual of your company's current state.

At this point we are using the Maturity Matrix specifically in a "know thyself" capacity. You have mapped where you are right now and where you want to go—a crucial first step in preparing for a migration.

However, there is much more we can do with this useful data! See Chapter 9, Antipatterns and Common Challenges, for problems that commonly arise during transformation initiatives and what the Maturity Matrix looks like in each scenario. (It's kind of like a field guide for what not to do.) It is very useful to match your results against typical scenarios that we have observed at other enterprises seeking to migrate their legacy systems and transform into a true cloud native entity. If they are strikingly similar, well, then we have patterns for fixing exactly that problem!

The Axes, United

The cloud native approach empowers enterprises to design their product exclusively around the user, with no concern for the needs of the underlying system. This lets them deliver better products with less risk, which is the true heart of cloud native. That they also can now deliver them faster and cheaper is a pleasant corollary outcome.

By undergoing the Cloud Native Maturity Matrix assessment, a company generates an intelligent, flexible, and constantly updatable status check. Granted this understanding and perspective, companies can begin to plan their cloud native transition with knowledge—and confidence that they will be able to avoid common pitfalls along the way.

We will revisit the Maturity Matrix again in Chapter 13, when we use it to identify common problems arising during the cloud native transformation process. These typical scenarios occur often enough that they are a valuable source of useful patterns (and even antipatterns) for constructing a proper migration path. It is wise to examine them first as a valuable lesson of what *not* to do in a cloud transformation and then as an aid in custom-mapping the right path.

Second Attempt at Cloud Native

Jenny's second wake-up call and WealthGrid's attempts to reapproach their cloud migration from a more creative direction.

Jenny's first wake-up call was that WealthGrid needed to take action now on making the move to the cloud. Her second is that, unfortunately, her effort to lead a cloud native transformation using a small internal team (working entirely on their own, and only part-time) simply isn't working. It's not getting them ready fast enough to handle the arrival of a disruptive new cloud-powered competitor.

The trouble, she realizes now, comes from treating their cloud migration as just another tech changeover. They ran this project the same way they always handled, say, moving to a new database. This was an approach, it now becomes apparent, that was destined to fail. Going cloud native, she understands at last, requires so much more than simply lifting and shifting WealthGrid's existing systems to run on the cloud.

It's fine, though. They may have lost some time, but Jenny has learned a few things from this first go-round. Her team has gained experience as well. She is confident that a second effort—one that has more resources, more people helping out, even a dedicated budget allotment—will go right and go quickly this time. Based on the chatter she has heard from upper management, she is further confident that WealthGrid's executives will support it.

Jenny gets to work preparing a very significant plan, complete with technology goals, documentation, cost projections, and all the many, many predictive details that WealthGrid execs like to see. The document takes her weeks to pull together. She must involve enterprise architects to create complex diagrams and meet with other program managers and department heads to get them on board too. Finally, however,

Jenny creates a comprehensive vision for building a new platform and adopting new technologies—in other words, building cloud native like it's meant to be.

She takes this plan, complete with deadlines and deliverables, to Steve, WealthGrid's CEO. Steve is happy to see Jenny taking the initiative on a migration, because he also understands that to survive in this market, the company needs to evolve. In fact, the board has even had some preliminary discussions about whether it's time for the company to move to the cloud, so this is good timing. Jenny seems knowledgeable, and certainly well prepared. She is given permission to launch her project, with a budget and a mandate for all of WealthGrid to support the initiative.

Embracing Innovation

Having learned that cloud native can't simply be installed like some new software suite, or even a whole new operating system, Jenny has come up with a much more ambitious plan.

The original migration effort had a major block to progress: the team kept getting pulled away from building the new cloud platform in order to work on the current system. In response, Jenny has devised a "divide and conquer" strategy.

The plan is to divide their efforts. There is a legacy platform team, staffed with just a few people, to keep things going while everyone else works on getting the new system put into place. The legacy team will be delivering slowly, if at all, when it comes to any new features or functionality, because this is just a placeholder until the brand-new cloud native platform gets built. Any new upgrades to current functionality and all new features will be part of that. After all, it makes no sense to keep building things for the previous platform when it's going away very soon. The general idea is that, once up and running on the new platform, teams will be able to produce so much and so fast that they will very quickly pay back any delay in deliverables.

Meanwhile the newly created cloud native team is of course responsible for building this new platform. It's an all-hands-on-deck effort: WealthGrid is going all in on cloud native. There is a generous budget. A large crew of engineers—comprised, in fact, of most of the company's developers and IT people, except for the skeleton crew keeping the current system going—has been mobilized to work on the initiative full time. This time, they have no constraints.

Jenny's promise to WealthGrid's board is that all of this will take six months.

Experimentation Time

The first three months go by quickly, with a lot of exploration. In typical Waterfall predictive style, the teams start by doing a lot of theoretical research and comparing features. They are trying to think ahead about all possible system architecture outcomes while simultaneously trying to guess all future situations that could arise. Their efforts are thoroughly documented, as is standard WealthGrid procedure.

No one really anticipated the sheer number of possible implementation combinations available, though! There are literally hundreds of projects and products available—more than 1,200 as of this writing, both open source and commercial vendor offerings—with more added all the time. The ecosystem is evolving so rapidly that the Cloud Native Computing Foundation offers a cloud native "landscape" that is updated daily to keep track of it all.

The result: 10 different teams have gone out to do research on the various choices available for public and/or private cloud implementations, and they are all doing it in different ways. No one is worried, though, because the idea right now is just to explore the best options for WealthGrid's new platform.

It seems like things are going pretty well, actually—by now some of the teams even have a small application actually running in production on the cloud. Each team's app experiment, however, is dramatically different: different clouds, different tools, different technologies—and there are seven of them. It doesn't help that, because WealthGrid's technical teams are organized by functionality, each team has built something that works really well for their highly specialized area of responsibility…if maybe not so well for the other teams. They are all working hard on the thing they think is right, even if it looks nothing like what the next group is doing. Of course they are each really proud of their version and believe it to be the right one for WealthGrid to adopt (remember the IKEA effect bias, where people value something much more highly if they assemble it themselves).

Once they realize the level of extreme divergence between efforts—and opinions—on the best platform, Jenny and the other project managers (there is one at the head of each team) try their best to work out a compromise.

Unfortunately, there is no way to standardize the various versions, even a few of them, onto one unified platform. They simply don't share enough commonalities to be compatible. By the time all of this has been figured out, argued about, and argued about some more, two more months have gone by. They are nearing the project deadline, and the company's executives are expecting to see some results.

A new argument arises: Why not just let each of the specialist teams use their own cloud implementation, then? They've always been able to choose their own tools before, at least within reason. We don't want to waste all of this effort, after all (remember the sunk cost bias?). Ultimately, however, the Operations team makes it clear that there is no way they could ever possibly run seven different platforms, much less support seven different teams in production. That would result in complete chaos!

All of this takes yet more time to analyze, discuss, and debate. Eventually, Jenny and some other managers go back to the board and the CEO to explain why six months have passed but the promised cloud native platform has not been built. WealthGrid's execs are supportive: this is a comprehensive initiative affecting the entire company. We can see that six months might not be enough time to get it all done. Take another six months and finish it up, we can wait a little while longer for you guys to do this right—but not *much* longer.

Back to the Drawing Board

So, back to the drawing board. This time, the decision is made to try a unified approach. The teams work with one of WealthGrid's systems architects to make a plan and make sure that everyone is on the same page before anything else gets built. Microservices and Kubernetes are definitely going to be part of the implementation— this is one area where everyone is in firm agreement.

So the architect sits down to design a consistent plan for all the engineers on all the teams to implement Kubernetes running microservices. It's a big diagram, with a very (very) detailed description of how it will be installed—writing the document alone takes four months before the tool itself can ever be installed. The senior managers are happy; they see a very good document, which to them represents very good progress.

Great, right? Well…Now the next step is for everyone to attempt putting into place a plan for Kubernetes that was written by someone who has never actually used Kubernetes. He doesn't even understand that he doesn't understand—though this does not stop him from creating and presenting a complex diagram with the very strong conviction that this is how it should work (this is a classic illustration of the cognitive bias known as the Dunning-Kruger effect, or the tendency for unskilled individuals to overestimate their own ability).

Except that it doesn't work. Everyone is astonished: here are microservices, there is Kubernetes, those are the core cloud native pieces. So what is wrong?

Yes, you have an impressive document, a tool installed, and maybe even a nice demo for upper management. But what exactly are you showing them? Kubernetes is included, but the one application the cloud native team (which at this point, remember, consists of most of WealthGrid's engineers) was finally able to get running on it is simply terrible: full of holes, no security, no automation. It's in a container but still falls apart every two weeks.

Everything is configured wrong. It turns out that even these so-called "full solution" platforms still require a great deal of complex initial configuration, so even this small platform they have built is very difficult to maintain. There is no preparation for production, no monitoring, and no attempt to create the continuous integration and continuous development processes and practices necessary to effectively develop a cloud native app in the first place. The developers don't know how to use it. The ops team is frankly afraid of it. And everyone is complaining because instead of fewer tasks, there are now so very many more (because the new system is much more complex, but zero automation has been put in place to handle that complexity).

At this point maybe 2% of the implementation is complete. The cloud native team can claim that they do have something running on K8s, but realistically nothing is actually delivered. They tried building a microservice architecture, yet there is not a single microservice in production even though six months have, once again, gone by.

Managerial trust in the engineering team is at an all-time low. The engineers feel this is extremely unfair because they have been working very hard to build the thing they were told to build. They've always succeeded before in delivering technical projects, and they are truly surprised that they can't seem to finish this one.

The problem is, after a six-month extension on the project, it is now one year since the full-company cloud native initiative launched—and two years since Jenny first began trying to shift WealthGrid to the cloud in the first place. The full-company cloud native team is nowhere close to being finished. Maybe 30% of the platform is delivered, and it's not even close to production ready.

Meanwhile, the skeleton team left in charge of WealthGrid's original platform has just been maintaining the status quo. They have been holding off on delivering features—features that customers are demanding—because they were waiting for the new system to come online. They wouldn't have been able to deliver a meaningful amount of new work, anyway, because so much of the team was moved over to building the new system.

Third Time's the Charm?

WealthGrid can't wait any longer: they *have* to deliver these delayed features to the market as soon as possible or they risk losing customers. Customers expect new functionality and constantly increasing quality of experience; if they don't get them, they will simply move over to one of WealthGrid's competitors.

At this point the executive team and the sales team have so much pent-up pressure coming from the market that they finally lose patience. They summon Jenny to a meeting and deliver the following message:

"You know what? We've had enough. You promised certain deliverables in six months and this hasn't happened. We gave you six more months and you still couldn't deliver. You can't even tell us what will happen in the *next* six months.

"We know this is complex stuff and we still trust you to deliver this platform, but we really, really need to get these backlogged features out to the customer. We don't care where they run, but we *must* have these five features out in the next three months. What are you going to do about it?"

Jenny's third and final wake-up call has arrived.

The message from WealthGrid's leadership is crystal clear: show us value in 90 days. If she can't deliver, Jenny could very well lose her job. Her engineers are going to be extremely unhappy as well, since they would have to stop working with this cool new tech and go back to churning out features on the boring old legacy system.

But what to do? There is no practical way to get these five do-or-die features out on the new cloud native platform, because the new platform is not production ready and no one really knows when it will be ready. So they have to do something else. The problem is, *what*? First they tried doing the new system off to the side while continuing to roll out the current system features. That didn't work. Next they tried going all in, sidelining the current system to focus on building a brand new one as fast as possible. That didn't work either.

What else is there?!

This is the point where cloud native consultants often get called in to rescue a stalled or failing transformation. But even summoning external experts won't always help much if a client organization doesn't take the necessary global approach. That is, consultants who primarily offer Kubernetes knowledge will indeed get a platform up and running pretty quickly—but the company will still struggle with the other essential pieces of the cloud native puzzle: microservices architecture, team structure, DevOps, hierarchy, culture, and so on. So, WealthGrid needs to be careful not to call a consultant that will only address the tech aspect of its situation. However, also calling a management consultancy to help with the organizational and process side of things would probably not help the company much, either, as that scenario will almost certainly involve a massive transformation plan that will cost millions and take years.

We don't want to leave you hanging too much (and also this is a book about patterns). So suffice it to say there is a path to success, and we plan to tell you all about it. Coming up next in Chapter 6 we will present some tools that will help Jenny solve the problems keeping her team from delivering a functional cloud native platform in a timely fashion. The chapters after that introduce the patterns themselves. Then, in Chapter 11 and Chapter 12, we will demonstrate a successful pattern design for actually delivering the system in 90 days—while also delivering the five do-or-die features WealthGrid needs now.

CHAPTER 6

Tools for Understanding and Using Cloud Native Patterns

OK, so what just happened during WealthGrid's second attempt at a cloud native transformation? Why is WealthGrid having such a difficult time building a new cloud native system, even when they are putting tons of money and people into the project?

The short answer: cloud native is new, complex, and requires a very different way of thinking. Alas, this is apparent only once you have already moved a significant distance down the migration.

These eventual but inevitable difficulties take everyone by surprise because the first stages of a cloud native transformation are genuinely (and deceptively) easy. Engineers go to the conferences and they see Google Cloud Platform guru Kelsey Hightower or someone like that doing magic on the stage and producing results very quickly and efficiently. Then they go try it themselves by setting up one container, or maybe a simple application with a few containers running Java, and it goes great. It's actually pretty simple and can be done in just a few hours and they feel like they've got this, no problem-o. This is the point where most engineers go to management and say, "We have to adopt this technology! We love it—it's excellent and so easy we can do it without any big investment." So they get the approval, and move happily forward, expecting things to continue on being just that easy and successful—while they continue working the same way they've always done.

This kind of bottom-up push to go cloud native, originating from the engineers, is one of the two ways most enterprises enter into a migration.

The other type of push is top-down, where an enterprise's executives are hearing how hot cloud native tech is and decide that their company must do it too, even if they have no idea what it is all about. They are reading articles in professional publications about how amazing cloud native is and hearing from vendors how easy it will be if they just spend money on the right products. Due to this lack of understanding, the tendency in the top-down scenario is to grab onto one concept—DevOps, Kubernetes, etc.—and order the tech staff to adopt it.

In both scenarios there is no actual adoption strategy, and the decision to move ahead is made based on lack of understanding coupled with the misbelief that the process will be fairly simple and straightforward. The problem is that the complexity of this is dramatically different as you start moving to a large-scale production environment. At some point you realize, *Uh oh, this is not going at all like we thought it would.* Figure 6-1 shows the cloud native adoption curve and how it moves from simplicity to complexity—and where the "Uh oh" moment inevitably occurs.

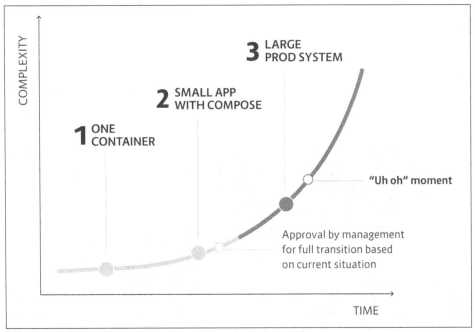

Figure 6-1. The cloud native adoption curve starts out fairly flat as transformation initiative starts out with early experiments with single containers and small test applications (using an external cloud database platform like Compose, to keep things simple). The curve gets steep fast, though, when it's time to turn these small experiments into an actual production system

This is exactly what happened at WealthGrid.

WealthGrid's first attempt to adopt cloud native was a classic bottom-up approach. Due to lack of resources, though, the initiative didn't get far enough for the team to reach the point where difficulties would begin to reveal themselves. Jenny's engineers had had some success with building small pieces of the system, even if they had to start and stop a lot. Jenny's natural assumption, and theirs too, is that this seems actually pretty easy; the only thing holding us back is lack of time to focus on it. Based on their experience they fully believe that, if they just have more help and no distractions, they could crank out a new cloud native platform in just a few months.

So when Jenny first approached the CEO and board asking for support to go all in, company-wide, on a cloud migration initiative, this is what she told them. Naturally they approved her request and allotted significant resources. After all, top-down pressure had also been building at WealthGrid. The engineers just acted first.

For the second attempt the whole company tried going all in, sidelining the current system to focus on building a brand-new one as fast as possible. That didn't work either. In fact it went quite terribly wrong. What happened? And what else is there for them to do?!

So Many (Deceptively Simple) Tools

What happens? Why do things fall apart? The reason for this is best explained by the Cloud Native Computing Foundation's landscape—there are more than 1,200 projects currently monitored by the CNCF representing the cloud native ecosystem and its landscape. And there are new projects added every week!

Figure 6-2 shows the landscape at the time this book is being written, with its plethora of options. You don't have to become intimately familiar with all of them, but you do need to understand the basics of what they do, how they work, and how they fit together.

Gaining even the most basic grasp of this insanely large landscape means first understanding what the different tools do. Next, how all those tools fit together. Then, both how they integrate between themselves and how they integrate with older systems. Finally, you have to establish what kind of development and delivery processes you need to use in order to be successful using them all.

This requires a lot of new knowledge. It's not simply installing some new tech, "lifting and shifting" to the cloud. Not just updating the tools you use, but revolutionizing *how* you go about using them.

Let's introduce some tools. A few things that will help Jenny solve WealthGrid's problem.

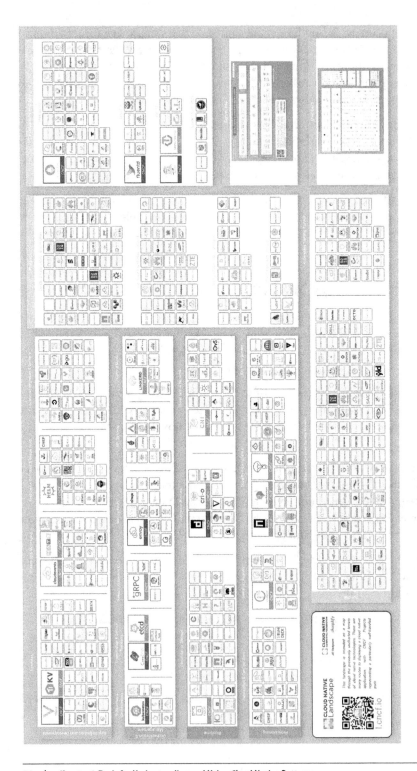

Figure 6-2. The Cloud Native Computing Foundation's cloud native Interactive Landscape (November 2019)

Tools to Take You the Rest of the Way

Before we can dive completely into the patterns, we first need to establish some of this new knowledge. The two concepts introduced in this chapter will provide crucial background understanding for applying the pattern design that follows. We are going to examine the important difference between proficiency and creativity and why managing them correctly is key to succeeding in any kind of digital transformation... like the one WealthGrid is attempting. Next, we work with McKinsey's Three Horizons model for visualizing how and when to apply creativity versus proficiency and, most important of all, how to balance them properly,

Proficiency Versus Creativity

WealthGrid is a highly proficient company. Things are optimized for delivering its core business mission consistently and well. This is a good thing, right? Stability, reliability, and quality drive profits and thus are valuable assets in any system.

Most traditional companies prize proficiency, the ability to complete well-defined and predictable tasks with maximum efficiency. This is how you deliver maximum value in a relatively stable context with few, if any, unknowns or surprises. In this context, creativity and innovation are viewed with skepticism. Innovation introduces unknowns into a highly regimented system—and with unknowns come risk.

However, as we have seen, companies in nearly every imaginable sector no longer have the luxury of a stable, predictable environment. Things are changing fast in every way, from new tech to new competitors. This calls for being able to respond— being able to change—to meet these new challenges whenever they arise. It means switching out of highly efficient, algorithmic delivery (proficiency) temporarily in order to change what needs changing—your product, your way of working, your company itself—through innovation and creativity. Once you've made the changes, then focus returns to proficient delivery of your improved products/service...until the next time a new challenge calls for a creative response.

So, yes, proficiency is a good thing...up until the moment that it isn't and you need to adapt to new circumstances. Most struggle to adjust, however, because they are trapped in proficiency mode. Again, many successful companies got that way through focusing on the bottom line: proficient delivery of their core product/service. They are really good at what they do, but in the process of becoming exactly that good at exactly that thing, they forgot how to work any other way.

Fortunately, once a company recognizes this reality it's possible to take corrective moves toward creativity. But which moves, and how?

Want Fries with That?

A useful tool for conceptualizing the flow between creativity and proficiency, which are essentially two sides of the same coin, is called the Knowledge Funnel, shown in Figure 6-3.

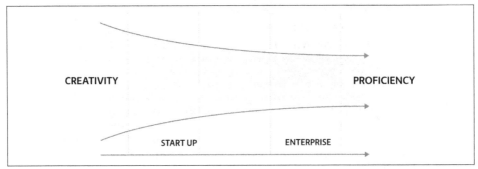

Figure 6-3. Roger Martin's Knowledge Funnel concept as applied to the process of moving from a highly creative startup to highly proficient enterprise delivery of products/services

The Knowledge Funnel was introduced by Roger Martin in his book *The Design of Business: Why Design Thinking is the Next Competitive Advantage.* According to Martin, every new idea goes through three major stages as it progresses to full adoption: Mystery, Heuristics, and Algorithmic. We are going to look at these stages in terms of McDonald's fast-food restaurants, because it is such an excellent example of pure proficiency at work.

Mystery comes first: you have a new idea and you think it's good, but you have no real understanding of how (or even if) it will work or how to implement it.

Imagine the very first McDonald's hamburger restaurant, founded in 1948 in San Bernardino, California, by brothers Richard and Maurice McDonald. It was a business serving food, but with one brilliant twist: you could walk up to the counter and get food right away instead of needing to sit down at a table and wait for service. No one knew at that point if this was a good idea or a bad idea; it was simply a new idea.

Heuristic follows the mystery stage. A heuristic is any approach to discovering something new or solving a problem that applies a practical method to reach the immediate next goals. A heuristic is not guaranteed to be optimal or perfect, only sufficient for getting things working well enough for the time being.

This new idea was apparently one whose time had come, because the first McDonald's restaurant was instantly successful. The McDonald brothers naturally thought to expand, opening new locations until they had four total. Things were still going very very well—Americans were eagerly embracing the concept of fast food—and they wanted to keep expanding. Starting with restaurant number five, however, they ran into a problem. The quality of their hamburgers was not scaling along with the growth; it was going down, actually, because they couldn't keep things consistent. The McDonald brothers realized they had to keep production fast and quality high, but they didn't know how to scale.

The *Algorithmic* stage is the next stop on the Knowledge Funnel, representing fully optimized and streamlined proficiency.

Ray Kroc was a restaurant-supply salesman who was intrigued by the fact that the first McDonald's restaurant had ordered eight milkshake mixers. Most restaurants had one, at most two, and Kroc was curious to see what this new place was doing with so many more than the usual hamburger joint required. When he visited the place, he was instantly intrigued by their innovative approach. He was so impressed, in fact, that he persuaded the founders to let him try turning their concept into a nationwide chain of restaurants all based on a single, easily replicable model.

Kroc eventually bought the brand from the McDonald brothers and made McDonald's what it is today: essentially, a fully algorithmic operation. When a new franchise opens, it is done literally by the book: each franchisee is given a guide in which every step in running a McDonald's restaurant is well defined, extremely specific, and very clear. Every decision has already been made in order to optimize quality, consistency (a Big Mac in Birmingham, Alabama, tastes exactly like a Big Mac in Buenos Aires, Barcelona, or Beijing), and, above all, speed.

In short, the McDonald brothers came up with a truly innovative idea, but Kroc was the one who recognized what it could become—if proficiency were applied.

Creativity, Proficiency, and Enterprise

Unfortunately, when businesses evolve from a scrappy new startup to become a proficient and as-algorithmic-as-possible operation, they often forget how to be a startup —that is, how to re-enter the mystery state over and over in order to research and introduce new ideas to their business. This would be like McDonald's sticking to their original menu of regular burgers, fries, and shakes, never to invent their famous triple-patty Big Mac, much less Chicken McNuggets. McDonald's again is an excellent metaphor for our exploration of proficiency versus creativity, because the company has historically continued to introduce innovative new menu items (produced in, of course, a fully proficient fashion).

How do these concepts apply beyond fast food to the world of businesses and software, though? Figure 6-4 helps us visualize this.

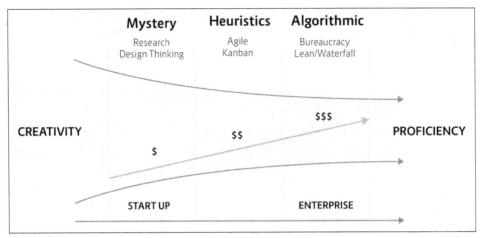

Figure 6-4. The flow between creativity and proficiency through the different stages of a company's journey from startup to enterprise, and from mystery to algorithmic delivery

In Figure 6-4 we still see the Mystery, Heuristics, and Algorithmic stages. Let's look at how they apply to typical enterprises.

Mystery: Startups by nature inhabit the creative phase—when building a new thing, by definition you don't know if it is going to succeed or not. The beginning phase, for a startup, is almost purely creative: the time when you have an idea and need to develop it. There are many, many ideas in the world, which is why there are so many startups. Most of these ideas are probably not very good, which is why so many startups fail.

Heuristics: Once your brilliant new idea has found success in your market, it's time to move to this next phase. In order to begin building up the company, to grow and find success in your market, you must become more proficient. This means turning focus from figuring out how to get your idea working at all (an inherently creative process) to how to get it working efficiently.

Algorithmic: You improve the idea until it becomes a viable business, and you can deliver reliably and steadily. Congrats, you have now reached full enterprise status!

Just as each of the three stages of business development has specific characteristics, how an organization functions internally while moving through each of them is also very different. There are whole books dedicated to exploring the mysteries of group behavior at different points along the path from crazy idea to fully established and delivered business value. Two of these in particular helped us crystallize our thinking around creativity, proficiency, and how to address and balance both through cloud native transformation patterns.

Loonshots: How to Nurture the Crazy Ideas That Win Wars, Cure Diseases, and Transform Industries, by Sahfi Bahcall, is a compelling look at how companies, individual teams, or really any group having a common mission will suddenly change from a culture of embracing wild new ideas (while in Mystery mode) to rigidly rejecting them (once Algorithmic stage is reached), just as flowing water can transform into inflexible ice. Bahcall draws upon the scientific field of phase transition to illustrate how group behavior is influenced by the structure of its containing organization.

Likewise, Daniel Coyle's *The Culture Code: The Secrets of Highly Successful Groups* examines how diverse groups end up internalizing the same homogenous mindset and how this can lead to the stifling of innovation within an organization.

What do these look like over the life cycle of a typical enterprise? In the beginning you want to use research, design thinking, all kinds of creative ways of doing things, because this time is all about exploration. As a successful direction emerges, you begin to define your product or service and your process for delivering it. However, you are still able to pivot quickly and change direction because there is still some flexibility and creativity in your processes. If things turn out not to be working, it's still possible to change course.

At some point, though, when you have honed things down to delivering a core value proposition, you reach the algorithmic stage. The inevitable outcome of this is building in bureaucracy to keep things running smoothly and consistently. This happens because it is only by reaching the algorithmic stage and full proficiency that you can generate significant revenue. Simply by being successful, you undergo a process of organizational evolution. Early on, you are a handful of crazy people trying all kinds of wild things, and the point is not to make money (well, not yet, anyway) but grow your idea. Once you prove your idea works, though, you want to grow the business.

In such cases, companies tend to become Waterfall organizations with a strong hierarchy, or perhaps a Lean one like the Toyota Production System. The Lean production model focuses only on that which adds value, mainly through reducing everything else (because it is not adding value). Unfortunately, this almost always means jettisoning creativity, which has no functionality in a proficient system because you no longer have an idea you need to explore. Now you have a successful product and the sole need becomes only to keep delivering that product as cheaply as possible. Perhaps that product improves over time, but the focus is now all on proficiency and no longer on evolution.

This does not mean proficiency is inherently bad or creativity is automatically good. An enterprise needs both, in proper balance—a balance that can shift according to need. There always needs to be at least a small portion of effort going to improving and trying new things. Because if you are only proficient and some kind of disruption or other significant change happens unexpectedly—one that requires you to shift to a new or different way of doing business—you have no way to respond.

When an existing business gets challenged by the stranger in their town, they swing from proficiency to overvaluing creativity, because they suddenly realize they don't have enough of it. Startups, meanwhile, tend to overvalue proficiency, which is what *they* don't have since they are often seat-of-the-pants organizations with few resources. They aspire to the stability that proficiency represents, but this leads to a different problem. Many startups jump too soon in trying to introduce quality and so try to establish an algorithmic delivery model too early, locking themselves in and diverting resources when they still need to be focused on fully developing their idea. Thus, they are trying to leave creativity prematurely in favor of proficient delivery of a product that is not yet fully baked.

So, yes, you need both proficiency *and* creativity. One is not better than the other, or more important than the other—it's the balance that is important. You need both, but not at the same time. This is because they both need to be managed differently. You cannot have teams that are working both proficiently and creatively at the same time, since these are conflicting mandates:

- Proficient teams require high repetition to deliver the same thing, over and over, very efficiently and reliably, and at the highest quality possible. High repetition, high feedback, small set of very specific rules. The emphasis is on skills and repetition.

- Creative teams, on the other hand, have no specific list of tasks. Their work requires open-ended thinking that is more like puzzle solving. This doesn't mean that creativity equals chaos: there is still a guiding purpose behind it, and tools to use. To effectively nurture innovation there must be a goal and the strong support and safety of a space that allows open-ended experimentation. Autonomy is crucial: once the goal is established, let the team find solutions in whatever way they can discover.

- Both types of teams are just teams, composed however your organization's team structure works. It's their jobs that are different: the proficient teams are your bottom-line delivery workers, the creative teams are focused on research and next steps. Typically you're going to have more teams tasked with delivery than innovation/creativity.

Trying to have one team work using both proficient and creative approaches at the same time is simply futile. They are two different mandates, and they conflict with each other. You are asking a single team to focus on optimizing repetitive ongoing delivery processes while simultaneously innovating on them, which means neither area is going to get full attention or best effort, and both are going to suffer.

Thus an organization needs both kinds of teams, and they need to be distinct and separate.

They also, of course, need to work together. The proficient teams focused on bottom-line delivery of product need to tell the creative teams—who are in charge of keeping the company looking forward and engaged with innovation—what the actual problems are in the market that the company needs to solve. The creative teams, meanwhile, need to return something from their development pipelines that the proficient teams can use in real life that is useful to customers.

Ideally this is a dynamic relationship—a well-adapted organization can move as needed between times of greater proficiency versus times of increased creativity.

It is difficult to achieve this, but possible. Striking the balance requires maintaining the separation of proficient and creative teams while closely coordinating between them. Different styles of management are required for each, and a designated champion (or two, or even more) is needed to act as a kind of translator to manage whenever there are handoffs between their respective efforts.

The way to integrate proficiency and creativity, organizationally speaking, uses our next tool: McKinsey's Three Horizons model.

Three Horizons

Once you understand the differences between creativity and proficiency, and the relationship between them, we use the Three Horizons model to understand how to blend and balance investment in developing new products within a company, while still delivering efficiently and reliably (and, of course, profitably).

The Three Horizons is an incredibly useful tool for identifying your business's current state and then strategizing adaptive actions—either to take now or to hold for when they might be needed in the future. In order to use it most accurately, we break creativity into two different categories: innovation and research (more about those below). Let's jump right in: Figure 6-5 shows the three stages.

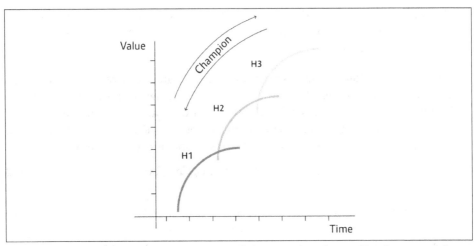

Figure 6-5. McKinsey's Three Horizons Model showing the relationships between delivery, innovation, and research

- **H1:** Horizon 1 represents your current core business—presumably, the things that provide your cash flow and main profits. This also includes logical next-step development of/iteration upon any product or service you are making right now.

- **H2:** Horizon 2 is investment in innovation: taking ideas that have been shown to work in the H3 incubator and productizing them for real customer use. This means both introducing new technologies and new ideas into existing products or changing your existing products themselves to something entirely new. At this point you are working with a promising idea that looks like it is going to grow to become a successful part of your bottom-line business. (Interestingly, cloud native itself is now still mostly at H2: it's working at many organizations but is far from easy or even completely stable and requires special knowledge to implement.)

- **H3:** Horizon 3 is research. Pure exploration of new ideas, research projects, pilot programs. Nothing that you can really use right now—here is where you are looking at the long term, things you may need to know or use a few years down the line. H3 is about awareness: staying abreast of what is coming next so you at least have some understanding when it does get here. Some of what you discover in H3 will get moved to H2 for further investment and development. Not everything you investigate in H3 will pan out or end up being useful, but that's OK. Sometimes experiments just don't work.

- **Time:** The x-axis does not represent a linear progression of time; it is not telling you when to apply each stage—now, later, or far in the future. *Companies must work within all three horizons at the same time.* In this model, "time" demonstrates how an enterprise moves, throughout the course of a normal venture's life cycle, between the three interrelated cycles.

- **Value:** The y-axis represents the growth in value that organically occurs when an organization addresses all three horizons simultaneously and, as we shall see, in proper balance.

Companies start with some crazy big idea and founders who create a company around it. If you find success, you have to hire more people, which means starting to create specific heuristics so everyone can work together. If you are really successful, at some inevitable point you form a hierarchy, with set positions, routines, processes— it's a one-way ratchet. Nobody wants to go back to the zero-process chaos of an early startup, no matter how creative a time it was.

What this means, though, is that most enterprises in the world use economy of scale to optimize both operations and profits; naturally, then, it becomes where all their efforts focus. Only a very few companies keep creativity on the side and keep it feeding in.

An adaptive business constantly evaluates and recalibrates the relationship between its three horizons, pursuing the optimal balance between proficiency and creativity. To manage this across an organization, it's important to have people called "champions," who understand those different horizons and move the technology across those three horizons.

We Are the Champions?

The champion is the person who keeps a firm fix on the bottom line while also pushing the likely next step—and keeping an eye on whatever crazy future thing could be coming next. It's a lot to track, and so it's good to have someone officially in charge of doing just that.

Champions are well aware that for a good company in a stable market, a good general ratio between the three horizons means putting most of the company's efforts into delivering the core business. A small, but still significant, portion gets directed into practical innovation: basically, building the logical, market-demanded next step in terms of feature or functionality. Finally, a little bit gets left open for research.

Of course, this ratio represents a "business as usual" situation. It should change whenever the business environment shifts, in direct response to the type of change— like when a disruptive stranger suddenly shows up in your market.

Companies who lack a champion (or, more to the point, aren't even aware of what a champion does and why they should have one) often skew the balance. This happens unintentionally, because they are fully focused on the business at hand and forgetting to build in some innovation to keep their creative juices flowing.

Figure 6-6 puts some numbers behind these varying scenarios and the proper ratio for each of the horizons, in different circumstances. Note that these are approximate numbers to demonstrate the relationship between proficiency, innovation, and research, not hard-and-fast definitions that you must hit exactly (or else). They are based on our own experience with what we have observed works well in companies that achieved not just a successful cloud native transformation but also a new ability to respond to changing circumstances as they arrive.

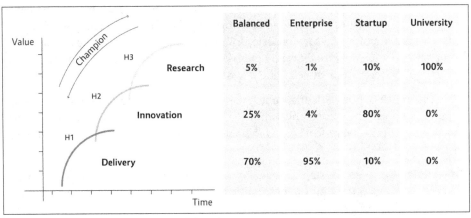

	Balanced	Enterprise	Startup	University
Research	5%	1%	10%	100%
Innovation	25%	4%	80%	0%
Delivery	70%	95%	10%	0%

Figure 6-6. Recommended ratios of the Three Horizons in different business environments

- **Balanced:** Normally you would want to invest 70%–80% of effort into delivery, invest 15%–25% into innovation, and maintain a small budget for research (5%).

- **Enterprise/Full Proficiency Focus:** Many enterprises, though—the ones we mentioned earlier, who forget how to be creative in the pursuit of pure proficiency—look more like 95/4/1. To be honest, this is even more realistically 95/5/0 at most traditional Waterfall companies. Too many focus solely on delivery, caring only about the products they are selling right now.

- **Startups/Mostly Innovation Focus:** By nature, startups are an innovative type of company. They are in the process of building a proper product, so they mostly live in the middle. They may dabble a bit in H3 (10%), and of course they are working their way as fast as they can to inhabit H1, so there is some groundwork already laid there (10%). But H2 is their home turf (80%).

- **Research:** Universities are pretty much the only entities you will find spending 100% of their time and effort on research. These are the only places that can do pure exploration without needing to worry about monetization in the near future.

Dedicating 5% of a company's resources to research may not sound like a lot, but it's crucial. That 5% is where you are gaining knowledge and retaining your ability to be creative when necessary. Where this goes wrong, where companies end up in trouble, is when they are not thinking—there is no strategy—and they try to move straight from research to delivery.

For example, in a cloud native transition, a company's engineers might try to adopt a microservices architecture when they know nothing about it, have no background, and so end up approaching it all wrong. They researched enough about microservices to recognize that this is the right thing to do, but they are rushing to get things working, which means they skip the middle stage and try to squeeze it directly into delivery. Skipping H2, which is the pragmatic development phase for creating heuristics around delivering new ideas, might sound like a way to speed things up. But instead it's a recipe for failure, since they haven't taken time to understand how it works and fits together. An innovation champion's job is to prevent just this sort of short-sighted corner cutting.

Now let's look at the flip side. Sometimes, proficiency is, for the most part, what a company needs, with side initiatives into innovation and pure research. And these can even go to zero, temporarily, if needed. An example would be when quality is suffering in an enterprise's main offering, and focus needs to be fully on delivery for a while. But this is a temporary pause, and in a healthy company (especially one with a champion on the job) once the crisis passes, the ratio gets rebalanced.

There is another scenario, however, where many companies do exactly this—pull all resources out of innovation and research in order to focus on the bottom line—and it is absolutely the wrong move. This would be when a company is under serious pressure from a new competitor, or a previous competitor that has introduced something new that is disrupting the whole market. Suddenly the established company is rapidly losing market share, and its leaders panic. The most likely path for a traditional company in this case would be to start cutting costs, especially in development. In times of distress, the R&D department is the first to suffer. But by doing this, the company is basically guaranteeing that it will not ever be able to adapt to the new market conditions and emerge as an equally strong contender.

So What the Heck Happened at WealthGrid?

How do we use these tools to understand what went wrong—and make it go right?

When we first met WealthGrid, it was a classic Waterfall-process company focused on the bottom line: delivering its core business value as efficiently and profitably as possible. If WealthGrid had an innovation champion, which they most assuredly did not, this person would have analyzed the Three Horizon ratio as 95% of efforts invested in proficiency, 5% in innovation, and 0% in research.

It was in this 95/5/0 context that Jenny and her team first attempted to move Wealth-Grid onto the cloud. As we have seen, this did not work. At the time, they chalked it up to not having enough time to focus on the migration because the existing system always took priority. We now have new tools to gain a deeper understanding into the broader forces that caused this to happen.

Essentially, WealthGrid's first attempt failed because they tried to implement cloud native—which requires a creative and innovative approach—from a proficiency mindset.

Jenny and the engineers put cloud native technologies and tools into the Scrum backlog along with all their other tasks for running the existing proficient system. Then they tried to execute it using the same type of processes they've always used, using the same sort of management by deadlines, sprints, and stress. Many companies use sprints as a development framework; Scrum usually sets a goal with two weeks to deliver it. The problem is that when you are running as fast as you can to deliver, it's hard to look around you with a mind open to innovation: it is impossible to be predictively creative.

So this initial attempt did not work. The dirty secret here is that, even had Jenny's team been able to work 100% only on building the new system, they still would have failed. And for the same reasons, though perhaps from a different direction, that attempt number two also then proceeded to fail.

WealthGrid's second attempt to go cloud native was basically the full reverse: *Now we will go into complete creativity!* The company moved a majority of resources—in this case, people—to the transformation project. That is, they redeployed most of their engineers from working on the original proficient system to building the new one. Dedicating resources to a transformation is a great first step. Unfortunately Wealth-Grid then took multiple wrong steps, all of which added up to the same thing: still attempting to deliver this brand-new technology and way of working by using proficiency-centered processes and culture.

There was no adoption of new ways of thinking or doing things, no application of a design thinking process to identify new ways to do creative problem solving, no purpose setting. The second attempt to build a cloud native system still used a Scrum and/or Waterfall approach to building. Just about every engineer in the company may have been playing around with different tools and cloud providers, but they were all using the same old knowledge and the same old way they have been doing successfully (and proficiently) for so long. This is why things went wrong for WealthGrid— *both* times.

Cloud native is a new way of doing things. It is not predictable, at least not to people who lack a good understanding of how it works. Most of the people at WealthGrid did not have this knowledge. Probably no one, not even Jenny, truly understood the full intricacies of cloud native architecture; certainly, no one at WealthGrid had any experience actually building a cloud native system. Lacking this understanding and experience, they of course used what they knew, the tools and techniques at hand. They didn't know what they didn't know.

The initiative may have moved forward pretty well at first, but inevitably the complexities multiplied as the system grew in size. Things slowed down more and more until the entire project simply could no longer progress at all. Meanwhile, the old system—the one WealthGrid is still running on!—had been languishing, with no new features or functionalities being delivered to the customer for over a year.

This was the third crisis point. WealthGrid was still committed to becoming a fully cloud native company. But it also needed a way to continue delivering value to customers while it worked to find the right path—the middle path between proficiency and creativity—to finally deliver the long-delayed new platform.

Summary

Digital transformation, ultimately, requires a balance between innovation and pragmatism, between creativity and proficiency. Some companies attempt to innovate but do so by trying to deliver creativity using proficient processes—that is, long-held practices and beliefs that worked well for them historically but don't work with cloud native architecture. This leads to failure, or at best a low-functioning, improperly implemented attempt. There may be a few microservices running on a few Kubernetes clusters, but no real value is being delivered—especially in comparison with how much time and money has just been invested.

Others go all in on innovation, attempt to abandon the old system completely to build a new one from scratch, and still get lost. Many times these companies are trying to be like Google, one of the most creative (not to mention fully cloud native) organizations around. The common misbelief is that being like Google means being all in on creativity—let's say something like 98% creative. Google's real focus, however, is very much on proficiently delivering their existing products and services while investing very intentionally in small but targeted and highly impactful creative initiatives. Putting in the terms we have been using in this chapter, Google's balance would actually be closer to 2% creativity and 98% delivery. The point is, they do have a balance, and it is what works for them. The real problem for most established and successful companies is that they have no idea how to be creative at all, in an effective way, at any number.

Proficiency is important. Creativity is important. Neither is better, and both are necessary. Proficient teams need to be managed in a way that supports their focused, stable and efficient delivery of bottom-line core business value for the company. Creative teams are managed for open-ended exploration of next steps, so the company stays innovative and ready to take responsive and adaptive next steps whenever needed.

It's not surprising at all that WealthGrid attempted to transform itself into a creative cloud native company using proficiency-focused Waterfall/Agile processes. This is an extremely common thing, and we have seen it many times, in enterprises of all sizes and from all sectors. Certainly, if they knew better, they would do things a different way. The right way.

Now let's see what the right way looks like.

CHAPTER 7

Patterns for Strategy and Risk Reduction

What is a chapter about strategy and business risk reduction doing in a book about cloud native patterns?

The biggest risk factor enterprises now face is not being able to respond fast enough to a changing environment. No matter what your sector, disruptor companies can show up at any time, and your existing competitors are also seeking the ability to shift direction and choose new markets very, very quickly. If you have a competitor that can shift in 6 months and you can only manage to shift in 12 months, then you are in trouble. Risk reduction today is the ability to respond to sudden or unexpected changes in market conditions when you don't have much notice, in time to meet or beat the competition. And you achieve this ability through strategy.

How does this all play out in the real world? Well, we just witnessed WealthGrid making a smart move: realizing that the company's long-term viability depends on adapting to changing environmental (market) conditions, the pragmatic implementation of which is to transform itself into a cloud native company.

In the effort to do just that, however, we also saw WealthGrid do some not so smart things during its two separate attempts at a cloud migration. So maybe now is actually a great time for a little strategy, with a nice side of risk reduction.

In this chapter we will introduce patterns that specifically shape and drive overall strategy in a cloud native organization. And, better yet, how to use them to reduce risk and build for long-term success, both during a transformation and then on into the future. We will examine patterns for:

- Dynamic Strategy
- Value Hierarchy
- Business Case

- Executive Commitment
- Transformation Champion
- Vision First
- Objective Setting
- Involve the Business
- Periodic Checkups
- Data-Driven Decision Making
- Learning Loop
- Learning Organization
- Measure What Matters
- Research Through Action
- Gradually Raising the Stakes
- No Regret Moves
- Options and Hedges
- Big Bet
- Reduce Cost of Experimentation
- Exit Strategy Over Vendor Lock-in
- Three Horizons
- Reflective Breaks
- Designated Strategist

But first, let's set the scene for how and when these patterns come into play. We will do this by getting acquainted with the leader of strategy and decision making at WealthGrid and taking a quick look at the challenges he faces in leading the company through an uncertain environment.

Meet Steve

Steve is WealthGrid's CEO. He has always been a numbers/business kind of guy, never an engineer. Nonetheless, he recognizes the importance of investing in new technology to keep WealthGrid relevant in the market and healthy as a company overall.

Steve has spent his entire career in traditional companies with hierarchical structures that followed the Waterfall delivery approach. Working this way is now second nature to him. He has deep-rooted assumptions about how an organization works: there is of course a hierarchy. Certain people handle certain jobs, and everyone stays in their lane unless explicitly reassigned. Experimentation is bad, because novelty means risk.

This kind of company is all about doing one thing, and doing that one thing predictably, reliably, and well.

So Steve's one thing is running a bank: he is a banker, with deep expertise in how banks work. But banks are not just banks anymore; they are tech companies—or at least they need to act like one, if they want to stay in business. This puts a lot of pressure on Steve, and also WealthGrid's other uppermost managers. They are all intelligent, well-educated executives who see the trend of IT becoming of central importance to any company like theirs. All the publications for senior execs are advising investment in machine learning, in automation, in cloud everything. But what the heck does all of that even mean? Steve has always had an IT department to handle the technical side of things; he has never needed to understand anything about it (in fact, Steve personally is so tech-shy that he just had his kids set up his new iPhone for him).

The good news for Steve is that what the company needs from him now is not deep tech knowledge. Or any technical knowledge at all, for that matter. What WealthGrid needs from Steve at this point is strategy.

Strategize, Then Delegate

Steve doesn't know it yet, but being a banker actually gives him all the strategic skills needed to help WealthGrid navigate its way onto the cloud. The core business of a bank, after all, is to buy and sell money while taking a percentage in the middle, in the form of loan rates. What is really at work? Simple risk management: knowing the right time to borrow money and choosing the right customers to lend it to. It turns out Steve knows all about analyzing current state, establishing a desired goal, and identifying and evaluating procedures to avoid or minimize getting lost along the way.

There is one thing, however, that will get in Steve's way: Steve.

Steve brings a strong risk management skill set to any cloud native initiative WealthGrid might undertake. But he is also a product of the environment where he built that experience: the traditional hierarchy using Waterfall delivery methods. In that environment, the executives make all the decisions—not just strategy, but many execution details as well. They bring in both inside and outside experts and architects, create many reports and documentation, and in general take a long time to think things through. Once the plan is set, it is handed off to middle managers to oversee the plan's execution, exactly as created with no diverging allowed, at the team level.

Waterfall and predictability and planning and documentation: we don't mean to make it sound like these are bad things. Far from it. They are tools for creating a consistent, stable, and efficient delivery environment and, used at the right time and in the right way, are good and important things. The right time for them, however, is not during the creative and innovative process that a company must undergo to transform itself into a cloud native entity. But it doesn't stay in creative mode forever. Once the new system is in place and cloud native knowledge has been infused into the company, things will rebalance to focus mainly once again on proficient delivery of core business value.

Companies like WealthGrid, with their highly proficient and historically profitable way of working, are accustomed to operating in a stable environment. Their market had long been steady and reasonably predictable, their competition known and manageable. They were good at deciding a smart course of action, doing a lot of research to create the best implementation, and then producing a detailed plan of action to make it happen on time—usually, a two-year span—and on budget. During that time span the focus was on execution, not re-evaluating the original goals, so the plan never changed.

We call this type of long-term, predictive, and above all fixed way of working *static strategy*. This was how business worked, and worked very well, for a very long time… until the steady and predictable world became today's reality of constant rapid change.

Now a strategic leader's job is to create dynamic strategy. This means watching the company's market, competitors, and other environmental factors both current and emergent in order to make comparatively quick and short-term decisions about how to respond and which direction to go next. Quick and short-term moves that are frequently re-evaluated, and adjusted if necessary, are what's needed now in order to respond to ever-faster change conditions. The Dynamic Strategy pattern, inspired by Henry Mintzberg's theories on emergent strategy,[1] describes the practical application of these concepts.

---

1 Henry Mintzberg's original whitepaper, "On Strategy, Deliberate and Emergent." (*http://bit.ly/2OkMSpJ*)

Pattern: Dynamic Strategy

Today's tech-driven marketplace is a constantly shifting environment, no matter what business you are in—so your game plan needs to shift right along with it (Figure 7-1).

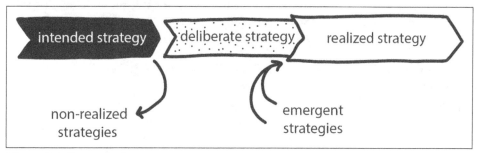

Figure 7-1. Dynamic Strategy

A company is commencing a cloud native transformation, has completely and successfully migrated its platform, or is at any point along the way. Traditionally, companies could set strategy, translate to objectives, and then move comfortably into long-term execution without ever looking back to re-evaluate. Today's environment is uncertain and constantly changing. Cloud native evolved in response to this reality as a nimble, scalable, and fast framework for handling constant variability.

In This Context

Not responding quickly enough to market changes or new information may lead the company to continue building products according to an old strategy that is no longer fully relevant. The original strategy could be realized in its totality, but in the meanwhile competitors could come up with better products, technology could change, and much better opportunities could be missed.

Ultimately, the company may end up with exactly what was planned in the beginning of the project—only to find that this is not what they actually need when they finally go to market.

- New technologies are constantly introduced, bringing unexpected new competitors to every sector.

- Low-certainty projects carry extremely high risk. Any decision made early in the project is highly likely to be uncovered as a wrong decision later.

Continually re-evaluate circumstances as the initiative moves forward.

Check if the relevant products are still in demand and if the chosen technologies, organizational structure, and development processes are still the best for the most successful delivery. Always monitor the competition to adjust delivery planning and releasing optimal functionality to maximize market impact.

- If adjustment is required, use the Gradually Raising the Stakes pattern to reduce risk and make better decisions.
- Dynamic Strategy is essential for doing cloud native right, from inception to completion. This pattern is so essential that it is built into our transformation design from the beginning.
- Use Reflective Breaks for the executive team to review and reassess strategy.

The executive leaders are aware when the environment changes and adjust strategic goals to keep the company heading in the right direction.

+ Digital transformation is a constant balancing act between innovation and pragmatism—delivering what earns the company's money right now.

+ If a disruptive new competitor enters the market unexpectedly, the CEO and board can shift the company toward increased creativity to keep up.

+ If quality is suffering, the leaders can redirect strategy to refocus on delivery until the situation improves.

Common Pitfalls

Being overly reactive and changing direction *too* often, which is distracting, wastes time, causes instability, and can siphon resources away from delivery. The company's Designated Strategist can provide helpful perspective when leaders are contemplating a potential strategy adjustment.

Related Biases

Irrational escalation/sunk-cost fallacy
The urge to keep investing in a project, despite new evidence that the decision was probably wrong, because you've already sunk so much into it.

Illusion of control

The tendency to overestimate one's degree of influence over external events. Many complex and emergent processes are difficult to steer, much less control. Sometimes we need to embrace some uncertainty to ultimately get results.

Related Patterns

- Designated Strategist
- Reflective Breaks
- Three Horizons
- Executive Commitment
- Value Hierarchy

Today's tech-driven marketplace, no matter what business you are in, is the ultimate uncertain environment. If you have a strategy, it needs to change all the time. Dynamic Strategy is the transformation pattern that teaches us to observe how the world is changing and to continually evolve and adjust strategy to match. And this responsibility sits squarely with the company's executive leadership.

WealthGrid's first transformation attempt doesn't really count, since it was Jenny and her team trying to do it as a side project. There was not any strategy at all and upper management, other than perhaps granting permission, was barely involved. But they should have been. Ideally, Jenny would present a problem to the board, demonstrate the need for a strategic decision, ask for the decision, and then get authorization to execute on that strategic decision. Obviously this didn't happen, so instead Jenny and her team did their best but ultimately stumbled around for six months.

For the second attempt, though, everyone got on board and things still went sideways. The problem? WealthGrid's leadership was involved, true, but they fell victim to the very common pitfall of static strategy: give scope, allocate budget, set deadline, trust team to deliver...and never look back to reassess the original goals and plans to see if they are still needed and still working.

Once a working strategy is defined, the middle managers take over to translate the strategy into specific objectives and deliverable goals. Their job is to explain these to their teams and then step back and let the teams decide exactly how to execute them. The delivery schedule emerges bottom up: the teams report the timeline of when they can achieve what. The teams have the freedom to choose their own tools and approach (within a set of company standards, since too much freedom leads to chaos and conflicting technologies) so long as they deliver functional results. This is all a single chain that has to function in coordination. If any of the links in the chains go too fast or too slow, the overall throughput suffers. (This is described more deeply in the Decide Closest to the Action pattern, which is described in Chapter 8.)

Since decisions regarding strategy now need to be made quickly and since the power —and responsibility for making all other kinds of decisions—is being distributed to middle management and execution teams, it's essential to share a consistent set of values and priorities that guide decision making across the organization.

Pattern: Value Hierarchy

When an organization's values are clearly stated and prioritized, as well as fully internalized across the company, people have the basis for making day-to-day decisions without needing to seek consent or permission/approval (Figure 7-2).

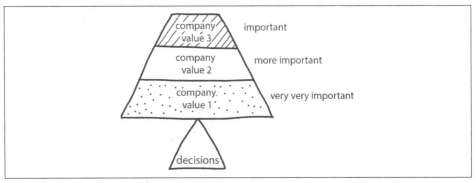

Figure 7-2. Value Hierarchy

The company's cloud native transformation has just begun, and there is a lot of uncertainty. People are still learning about the tech, and the organizational structure is evolving. Teams are becoming independent, and there are many moving pieces.

In This Context

Without a clear understanding of the company values and the priorities, people have no easy way to connect their daily work to the company strategy. In such a situation, different teams may make conflicting decisions or waste a lot of effort on low-priority tasks.

- Gaining consensus from all stakeholders is time-consuming.
- In traditional organizations managers make all the decisions.
- The market is changing frequently, with new competitors appearing unexpectedly.
- Cloud native technology is constantly and rapidly evolving.

Create an ordered list of clearly stated values to simplify decision making and guide behavior in an uncertain environment.

- Identify the company's values: what is important to us?
- Formulate these simply and clearly.
- Rank these values in order of importance.
- Incorporate this value hierarchy into the company's culture and identity by broadcasting it across the organization.

Consequently

Teams and individuals in an organization are able to make decisions with confidence.

+ Organizational principles and priorities are clear and commonly understood by all.

+ People can easily make informed choices that reflect both the company's values and best interest.

+ In a constantly changing environment, there is a stable and constant point of orientation.

– Too-frequent changes to the value hierarchy can cause confusion and chaos.

Related Patterns

- Decide Closest to the Action
- Objective Setting
- Dynamic Strategy
- Vision First

Once a Value Hierarchy is in place, the next step is to make sure the company will truly benefit from investing in a cloud native transformation.

Pattern: Business Case

Before launching a cloud native transformation, an enterprise's leadership must make sure the initiative is needed and that the benefits will justify the investment (Figure 7-3).

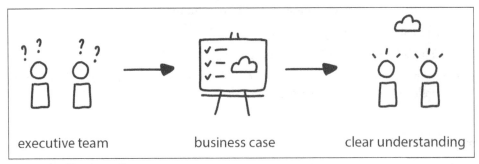

Figure 7-3. *Business Case*

A company is experiencing pressure, whether from the market or internally, to move to cloud native. The executive team is contemplating making the move to cloud native, but there is little internal knowledge of cloud native tech and culture or understanding of its benefits.

In This Context

Cloud native transformations are a big commitment, requiring significant investment of budget, time, and team talent. Too many organizations, though, get caught up in the hype of the cloud conversation and make decisions without understanding how exactly a transformation fits their business needs and goals. The risk is especially high for organizations that have already established rapid and significant internal momentum toward making this move.

- The traditional model is for organizations to be massively risk-averse to minimize uncertainty at all costs.
- Change-averse culture avoids new technologies or experimental approaches. Cloud native architectures are conceptually different from traditional approaches, merging careful upfront planning with flexible and mutable, experimentation-based implementation.
- Tech teams are eager to get started with the transformation, even before a business case is established.
- Cloud native is complex, and the benefits are not easily visible.

- Companies often don't have good baselines for how much it actually costs them to do development in their current approach, so trying to evaluate cost savings or time savings in a new approach is difficult.

Create a formal business case to help educate the organization's executive team, to evaluate how the transformation will serve the company's goals, and to create a clear vision for where the organization is headed.

- Discussion should involve business stakeholders, as well as information-gathering interviews with internal and external resources.
- Explain key cloud native advantages, including acceleration of business velocity, resilience, scalability, potential cost savings, and the ability to quickly act on feedback from customers to improve products.
- Evaluate the realistic scope and cost of the transformation, including technical and organizational changes.

The business case for a cloud native transformation is clear. The company's decision makers have a clear understanding of the initiative and the advantages it will confer when complete. They are ready to move forward.

+ They are prepared to allocate the necessary budget and resources that such a large project will require.

+ Enhanced recruitment and retention of tech staff eager to work with modern systems.

Common Pitfalls

If the company has recently invested in new (non-cloud-native) infrastructure or other modernization efforts, there can be significant resistance to now investing in cloud native.

Executive team underestimates the cost, time, and resource demands of the transformation as they perceive it a purely technological change with a reasonably predictable scope. They may have a long history of collaboration and trust in their IT team, but in the case of the cloud native transformation, the IT team is typically not in a position to evaluate the full impact that an initiative will have upon the entire business.

Related Biases

Bandwagon bias
> Everyone is talking about doing Kubernetes, so we better do it too!

Status quo bias
> Everything is fine right now, there is no need to rock the boat by introducing new tech or changing how we do things. That is risky!

Ostrich effect
> Competition is stable in our sector; we don't need to worry about disruption.

Ambiguity effect
> Cloud native is complex and the benefits are not easily visible, so better just to keep things the way they are.

Sunk-cost effect
> If a company has invested significant budgets into existing infra or other modernization projects, the tendency will be to continue investing there instead of switching to a new architecture—even if it is demonstrably superior.

Pro-innovation bias
> The belief that technology can fix all problems can be used as a nudge toward positive action: increase the chance of approval by showing innovation as an explicit benefit

Related Patterns

- Executive Commitment

Once a genuine business case has been established, it's a quick next step to our next pattern: Executive Commitment.

Pattern: Executive Commitment

To ensure allocation of sufficient resources and reasonable delivery time frames, large-scale projects such as cloud native transformation require strong commitment from the top executive team (Figure 7-4).

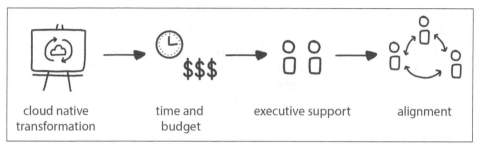

cloud native   time and   executive support   alignment
transformation   budget

Figure 7-4. Executive Commitment

An enterprise that is using Waterfall or Agile software development practices has made a clear decision to adopt cloud native, with a business case supporting the transformation.

In This Context

Cloud native transformations require significant changes in all areas of an organization, from infrastructure to processes to culture. These changes place large demands on the organization's budget and time.

- Clients continue demanding fast delivery of new functionality, leaving no slack for structural changes.

- Executive performance is measured by P&L (profit and loss statement), reducing incentives to invest in long-term structural improvement such as cloud native transformation.

- Executives likely don't understand the full scope of the cloud native transformation.

- Successful adoption of cloud native may significantly speed up feature development and increase tech teams' job satisfaction.

Announce the cloud native transformation as a high-priority strategic initiative that is important to the company and that has explicit support from the executive management.

+ Prepare a transformation strategy and the allocation of adequate resources and budget.

+ Publicly announce the cloud native transformation as a strategic initiative. This creates company-wide alignment and awareness, while setting the expectation of collaboration from all departments.

Consequently

The company is aligned around common goals and everyone understands priorities for the transformation.

+ All departments follow a unified vision, thus avoiding independent silos that lead to inconsistent, or even conflicting, implementation.

− Personal public commitment by execs makes it difficult for them to reverse the decision later, due to public embarrassment related to changing their minds.

Common Pitfalls

The focus is on technical changes only, without including the organizational changes that are also essential for a cloud native transformation to succeed. Or the initiative gets treated like just another tech/infrastructure upgrade, instead of a true paradigm shift. In such cases Executive Commitment exists, only for a wrong scope of the initiative.

Related Biases

Authority bias
   The tendency to attribute greater accuracy to the opinion of an authority figure and be more influenced by that opinion can be used as a nudge for the team to act. Even if those leading the decision to go cloud native are not deeply technical, their status in the company grants them authority to drive the change.

Bandwagon effect

The tendency to do (or believe) things because many other people do (or believe) the same thing, related to groupthink and herd behavior, can be used in this case as a nudge to enlist wide support for the initiative.

Related Patterns

- Business Case
- Vision First
- Core Team
- Objective Setting
- Transformation Champion
- Internal Evangelism

Establishing executive commitment to the initiative is essential, but you're still going to need a designated hands-on person to lead it. That person is the transformation champion.

From Theory to Execution

Choosing a transformation champion is an important early milestone in the transformation's forward progress. We talk much more about this role later in Chapter 11, but for now the short version is: this is where things start getting real! Now come the first functional steps for getting the transformation underway.

Pattern: Transformation Champion

When a person is promoting a good new idea that can take the company's goals and values into the future, recognize and empower them to lead the action (Figure 7-5).

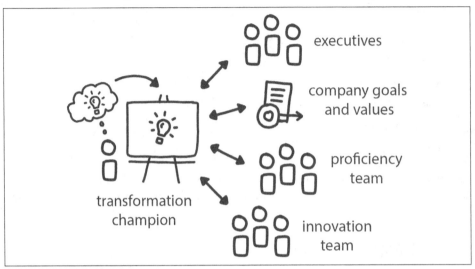

Figure 7-5. Transformation Champion

Market conditions are changing fast, and the company needs to evolve to keep up.

In This Context

Successful established enterprises focus on proficient delivery of their core products or services and often forget how to be innovative. When a disruptive competitor appears, it is difficult for them to respond quickly and effectively. There are always a few people within the organization who see the future better than others. An even smaller subset of these are willing and able to take organized action, but many organizations ignore them and waste the opportunity to encourage healthy leadership.

Without such motivational leaders, the initiative often falls flat and keeps going only after management exerts some bureaucratic pressure to push it forward.

- Change creates anxiety, so people tend to avoid it.
- There is little knowledge or experience within the organization around cloud native architecture/tech.

- An established enterprise accustomed to delivering a highly proficient product/service will likely struggle to innovate.

Therefore

Recognize the person (or group) who has triggered the movement and name them transformation champion. Authorize them as designated advocate for the initiative. Name a different person to this role only if there is a very compelling reason to do so.

There are conditions under which the person who started things is not the right transformation champion. It could be that they are not able to see the wider business perspective, as sometimes happens with technical people, or it may be that they are abrasive (as sometimes also happens with technical people). In that case, you want to let them lead the technical portion of the transformation and then find a partner for them who can share the lead on the cultural and organizational aspects of the transformation.

The transformation champion is a person or a small team who understands both the transformation and the company objectives, is well-connected within the organization, and is highly motivated to promote the transformation. Unless they are given authority, however, they will be unable to stimulate effective change across the organization.

- Don't create a champion: discover the one who is already there.
- Empower this person/group to lead the initiative.
- Publicize their role as authorized champion.

Consequently

The transition has a focal point for organizing the transformation initiative and a champion in charge of driving it forward. The transformation champion is connected with both the proficient and innovative branches of the transformation and can act as a bridge between them.

+ The transformation champion evangelizes the initiative across the organization.

+ The organization's leaders publicly empower the champion with the authority to lead.

+ The company now has a channel for reintroducing innovation while maintaining proficiency.

Common Pitfalls

The transformation champion can come from anywhere within a company, but in an organization with a strong internal hierarchy there is always pressure to name higher-up managers to leadership positions. The wrong person in this role—and they can be wrong for a variety of reasons—can seriously hinder the migration.

Related Biases

Status quo bias
> Overcome the natural resistance/anxiety around organizational change with internal marketing about the cloud native initiative and how it will help everyone.

Hostile attribution bias
> Internal transformation leaders run into this form of resistance where people fear that a new cloud native will take their jobs away or threaten their position in the company. We shouldn't think that this is their real opinion, as it is a normal human bias, but those acting under this bias can do real damage by passively resisting, or even actively thwarting, a transformation.

Related Patterns

- Business Case
- Executive Commitment
- Core Team
- Vision First
- Objective Setting
- Internal Evangelism
- Gradually Raising the Stakes

The transformation champion's very first task is to create a big-picture vision for the transformation, defining its initial shape and direction. This doesn't have to be exact or detailed, and it's important to not let this vision become set in stone. Dynamic Strategy means we will refine and adjust as necessary as we go along.

Pattern: Vision First

Defining a high-level transformation path as the very first step helps set the right course through an uncertain environment (Figure 7-6).

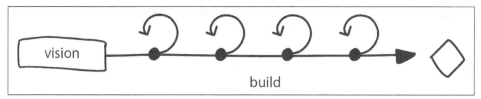

Figure 7-6. Vision First

The company has established a Business Case for going cloud native, achieved Executive Commitment, and is ready to move forward with a transformation initiative.

The company needs to define a clear and achievable vision that can be translated into specific executable steps.

- Without an overall consistent vision, different teams will make independent and, frequently, conflicting architectural decisions.
- The combination of limited experience and lack of extra time and flexibility for research leads to pursuing cloud native implementation using "well-known ways."
- In many companies, enterprise architects are responsible for creating a detailed architecture. Many enterprise architects lack sufficient theoretical or practical experience in the cloud native approach.
- Agile methodologies, widely adopted in the contemporary business world, create pressure to produce results early and onboard teams to new systems very quickly.

Therefore

Define and visualize the organizational structure and architecture of the whole system upfront.

- This can be either requested from external sources or uncovered by a series of small research and prototyping projects ranging from a few hours to a few days each.

- Keep the vision high-level to allow freedom of choice during implementation (not dictating specific tools or approaches) yet also specific enough to provide clear goals and desired outcomes.

- Revisit the vision regularly to evaluate status and adjust the plan if necessary.

- Executive Commitment paired with leadership by the Transformation Champion are essential for successful vision creation—this indicates the path for the teams to follow.

Consequently

All teams have a clear guiding principle for the implementation phase.

+ The teams can start producing the lower-level architecture and translate it to the backlog of tasks.

Common Pitfalls

Attempting to move to cloud native by using old techniques/processes, because that is what you know how to do.

Related Biases

Law of the instrument
An overreliance on a familiar tool or methods, ignoring or undervaluing alternative approaches. "If all you have is a hammer, everything looks like a nail."

Related Patterns

- Executive Commitment
- Transformation Champion
- Core Team
- Objective Setting

From Vision First we move directly into Objective Setting. This is the stage where responsibility begins to shift from the organization's executive leadership into the hands of middle managers/project leaders. Now it is their turn to begin converting high-level vision into explicit and visible goals and actions.

Pattern: Objective Setting

After establishing a transformation vision, the next step is to translate it into pragmatic goals and actions for moving the initiative ahead (Figure 7-7).

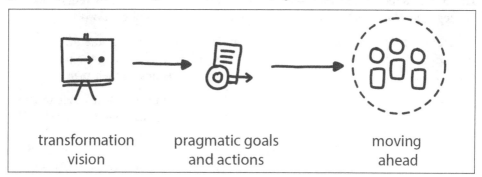

transformation vision   pragmatic goals and actions   moving ahead

Figure 7-7. Objective Setting

A company is committed to adopting cloud native technology and transforming its culture to suit. The Business Case is established; the executive team is fully committed and has devised the initial Dynamic Strategy. Middle management and the rest of the company are ready to take the next steps.

There is still an overall low level of cloud native knowledge on all levels of the company, and the transformation plan is still very high-level.

In This Context

There is commitment to and a vision for transformation, but concrete steps for getting there still need to be defined.

- There is little knowledge or understanding of cloud native tech and culture within the organization.
- Change creates anxiety and uncertainty.
- Change also creates opportunities: if you keep doing the same thing, what is the chance that you are going to get new results?
- When scope changes significantly, new executive commitment must be made to the altered project.

Executives need to hand over the high-level strategy to middle managers to translate it into specific and tangible objectives for their teams. Keep redefining the strategy and the objectives based on known information, not guesswork.

Objective-setting is done by mid-level managers. It is essentially the art of taking high-level vision, making it explicit and visible, and then explaining the priorities to those involved in execution so they can make better decisions on their own.

For example, a company may establish the high-level strategy of being able to run a full experimental cycle within days (define, build, deliver, and collect feedback). The specific and tangible objectives for this strategy would be: use cloud native tech (containers, microservices, dynamic scheduling, etc.) and a Continuous Integration/ Continuous Delivery build approach. These objectives in turn can be divided into even more specific sub-areas, with more detailed objectives created for each one.

- Keep learning about the market.
- Keep adjusting the strategy in response to new conditions in order to uncover new information.
- Make the strategy explicit and visible, and explain the priorities to all involved so they can make better decisions on their own.

The initial strategy is continually improved, adjusted, and translated into clear and tangible objectives. The relevant teams in the company know what they need to achieve and are constantly providing new information to upper management.

+ The team is aware of the latest direction and priorities.

− There is cost to monitoring the market and current conditions; requires time and effort.

− Continuous changes in the strategy lead to confusion and possibly frustration in the teams.

− Difficult to change direction, especially once you have momentum in a certain direction.

Common Pitfalls

- The executive team itself does continuous, detailed planning and objective-setting for the rest of the company without significant input from the teams, or alternatively seeks input from an enterprise architect with almost no knowledge or experience in cloud native. Objectives defined this way and with no experimentation will have no chance of being correct and will provide little motivation for the rest of the company.

- The executives will just give an order to middle management to execute the cloud native transformation without closely observing the progress and providing executive support. In such cases, the commitment is less than complete, as the full responsibility gets rolled onto middle managers, who will have limited time, budget, and other resources to allocate to a full-scale transformation.

- Adjusting strategy only every two to three years is the most common mistake. It is a relic of the long-range predictive Waterfall planning process, and executives will stick to a strategy for a very long time—regardless of the actual state of the market and the company—because they are accustomed to following a "set it and forget it" static strategy.

Related Biases

(Most of them, really—the majority of biases are against making any changes, and here we are saying "Make all the changes!")

Related Patterns

- Dynamic Strategy
- Executive Commitment
- Vision First
- Gradually Raising the Stakes
- No Regret Moves
- Big Bet
- Options and Hedges
- Value Hierarchy

How do we know what the most valuable, and useful, goals for this transformation might be? As the engineering teams start to get hands on with executing the technical objectives, business teams need to be involved as well to help target the right enterprise outcomes.

Pattern: Involve the Business

The business teams and the tech teams need to collaborate to create an effective customer-feedback loop that drives product improvement (see Figure 7-8).

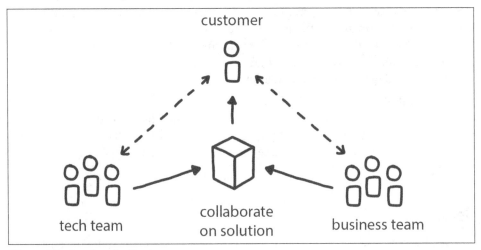

Figure 7-8. Involve the Business

The company is aiming to deliver value to customers as fast as possible while learning from customer feedback and steadily improving the product.

In This Context

When developers are running quick iterations without involving customer-facing people, the value could be limited to tech solutions only. Businesspeople, however, can't run full-tech experiments.

- Departments in large enterprises tend to focus on their own tasks.
- Long development cycles can make it difficult to incorporate customer feedback in a meaningful way.

Therefore

Create close collaboration between dev teams and the business to define experiments for testing new customer value and quickly executing them.

To close the learning loop, experiments and changes should include everyone from developers to the business teams to the customer and back, and the results should then be used to define and drive the next change.

- Customer feedback drives new ideas, and fast turnaround on a smaller scale (shorter delivery cycle) helps both dev and business teams learn more quickly.

- Development teams need to embed measurement of customer feedback into products.

- The business teams need to work with developers to define what is valuable for customers.

Consequently

Your products (or services) can change quickly in response to actual customer needs and desires.

+ Teams are learning from each other.

− Effort is required to build this communication and collaboration into the delivery cycle as a regular event, and it creates one more step in the process.

Related Biases

Curse of knowledge
When better-informed people find it extremely difficult to think about problems from the perspective of less-informed people—in this case, tech teams needing to explain technical things to the businesspeople, and the businesspeople needing to explain customer-facing needs/issues as executable deliverables.

Dunning-Kruger effect
The technical people make decisions because they think they know what the business needs. Not only is this not their area of expertise, but tech teams are generally inward-facing. They are not engaged in the kinds of customer-facing roles that would grant them the perspective to also deeply understand business needs.

Related Patterns

- Data-Driven Decision Making
- Personalized Relationships for Co-Creation
- Learning Loop
- Measure What Matters

As the transformation moves ahead, it's important to continue re-assessing the objectives—the business environment can change without warning, and the transformation goals need to change to match it.

Pattern: Periodic Checkups

Frequently reassess vision and objectives to ensure these remain the correct direction to proceed as the business environment shifts (Figure 7-9).

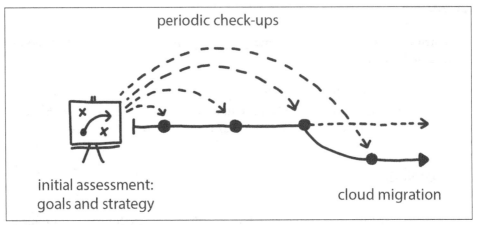

Figure 7-9. Periodic Checkups

The company is immersed in the new and changing environment of cloud native. Goals and strategy are set, the Core Team is underway, and the transformation is going full speed ahead. But the business goals might be changing as the environment changes.

In This Context

Teams focused solely on execution without pausing to assess and reappraise the direction they're going in might achieve what they originally planned—but not what they ultimately needed, because circumstances changed along the way.

- Teams tend to work by creating strategy, choosing a direction, and then continuing on without reviewing changes in environment or goals.

- Visions and plans require adjustment to meet real-world conditions. In the words of German military strategist Helmuth von Moltke, "No battle plan survives contact with the enemy."

- Cloud native ecosystem changes quickly, with new tech emerging all the time.

- It is impossible to predict what the cloud native world will look like in a year.

- Under delivery pressure, teams don't have a chance to look around them, only straight ahead.
- The process itself may require adjustments as the team matures.

Make sure that you and your team are still on the right path. Assess the current situation with regard to initial strategic decisions.

- Run a gap analysis assessment every month during the transformation.
- Have a standard assessment template.
- Invite independent experts to provide a second opinion.

The Core Team meets regularly to assess current conditions and can adjust direction as circumstances require.

+ Time to reflect and celebrate progress.

− Frequent adjustments may distract from overall delivery.

Related Biases

Ostrich effect
> The tendency to ignore an obvious problem because you don't have time to investigate it, or perhaps simply don't understand it well enough to see any solution.

Pro-innovation bias
> The tendency to be excessively optimistic about a new technology, assuming it will solve all your problems while failing to recognize its limitations and weaknesses.

Related Patterns

- Dynamic Strategy
- Reflective Breaks
- Designated Strategist
- Three Horizons

The best decision is an informed decision. In cloud native, we collect information and draw insights to guide strategy and next steps. The Data-Driven Decision Making and Learning Loop patterns describe how to incorporate this into your company in a practical way.

Pattern: Data-Driven Decision Making

Collect data, extract patterns and facts, and use them to make inferences to drive objective decision making (Figure 7-10).

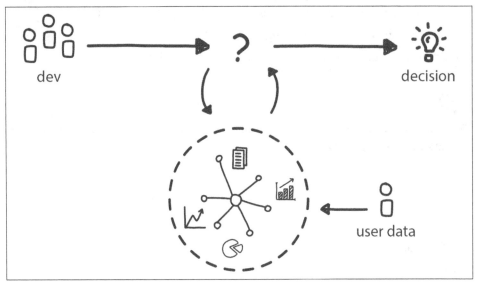

Figure 7-10. Data-Driven Decision Making

A company is moving to cloud native and sees the complexity and number of components growing exponentially. Each component is built separately. Competitors are changing products on a daily basis.

Managers make decisions based on their expectations from previous experience, which might not apply in the new and unknown environment of a cloud native system.

- Long development and release cycles (six months to a year, or even longer) that are typical in the Waterfall development approach result in products that are no longer relevant by the time they reach the customer.

- Software systems and users are complex systems. It's impossible to predict behavior.
- In hierarchical organizations managers protect their status by knowing everything and deciding everything.
- Technically it is easy to collect data.
- Measuring the wrong things may lead to bad results.

Therefore

Make product decisions based on data collected from actual users (observability, measure what matters).

Data can be collected automatically by embedding the data collection tools into the platform and all applications before they are released to customers. However, developers need to be careful not to be overly reliant on, or trusting of, user feedback/data. Users often don't know what they want, especially in regards to radical innovation.

- Apply the A/B Testing pattern to evaluate different options by exposing them to the real customers.
- Similarly, the Learning Loop pattern builds on Data-Driven Decision Making.
- Collect feedback and clicks/business measurements following the release of changes.

Consequently

The team can quickly make decisions based on objective measurements.

+ Instead of arguing on direction, team can set up experiments and measure.

− It is easier to follow the herd.

− It is not always easy to measure and interpret the right things.

− Sometimes data and users are wrong, and the team needs to trust their instinct and pivot to a radical change.

Common Pitfalls

The first pitfall is collecting insufficient data to make real decisions. The team has a feeling that they have everything they need while really they have plenty of blind spots and the full picture is different.

On the other side, teams become overly reliant on the data collected from users and forget that *users themselves don't always know what they really want*. Human intuition is a valuable resource based on thousands of years of evolution and is especially valuable to the process of radical innovation. If back in 2012, a year before Twitter was founded, you had asked people how much they would want or need an SMS service over the internet, the answer would probably have led Twitter's founders to drop their idea to create such a service.

Related Biases

Law of the instrument
> Overreliance on a familiar tool or methods, ignoring or undervaluing new or alternative approaches. In this context we would see managers attempting to lead a move to cloud native using old techniques/processes and cultural assumptions. For example, micromanaging work done in a highly distributed team building microservices or insisting that component services all release together instead of independently.

Status quo bias
> Why change things if they have always worked before?

Hostile attribution bias
> Assuming that others who are driving a change are doing so from hostile intent, trying to make the manager's position ineffective or irrelevant.

Related Patterns

- A/B Testing
- Learning Loop
- Measure What Matters

Pattern: Learning Loop

Building feedback collection into the delivery process closes the loop between engineers and the people who use their products, putting the customer at the center of the product development cycle (Figure 7-11).

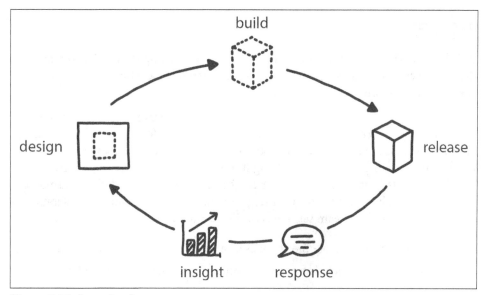

Figure 7-11. Learning Loop

A company is working to transform its culture to align with the delivery approach required by cloud native's distributed architecture of containerized microservices delivered via the cloud.

Learning happens in a three-part cycle: goal-setting, execution, and reflection. The first stage is identifying a challenge or problem and devising a likely solution. The second stage is carrying out the plan until it succeeds or fails. The third is studying the result—thinking back over what happened and how it worked out. In a very long delivery process this cycle is of limited use when lessons learned can be applied only months later, when the information is not fresh in the developer's minds or perhaps no longer relevant.

The learning loop is useful in an organizational context only when it is closed (one stage leads directly to the next and the next, then the cycle repeats).

Most companies adopting cloud native cite increasing product velocity as their main motive.

Tightly coupled Waterfall-approach release cycles may be as long as six months to one year, or even two.

Build mechanisms for collecting user feedback and feeding it rapidly back into the delivery cycle, enabling responses to flow back from the customer so the business can make better-informed decisions.

In cloud native, organizations can make extremely effective use of this three-part learning cycle as a feedback loop to developers that allows for fast iteration and adaptation to changing market conditions and customer needs. When a team is building its piece of an application and deploying it quickly and frequently to production, the team's work gets in to users right away. If client feedback is collected at that point, it can be fed directly into the reflection stage for the team to take into consideration as the loop repeats and the team sets goals for its next work cycle.

- Use the feedback to create the changes customers are telling you they want.
- Not collecting feedback decreases the value of cloud native's shorter time to market.

Apply Data-Driven Decision Making to cloud native's rapid delivery cycle so that the output of the system continually goes back in to improve the system (you *can* go fast without breaking things).

+ Developers capture the momentum of improvements, leading to more improvements.

− Observability is complicated and needs to be carefully engineered to provide the right insights.

− What customers want is not always feasible or cost-effective.

Common Pitfalls

Collecting feedback but not making it available or using it to gain meaningful insight. Engineers need to have observability into the outcome of their work so they can feed that knowledge into future work.

Related Biases

Planning fallacy
Make sure that the scope of the changes/improvements indicated by feedback actually fits into the delivery cycle.

Related Patterns

- Observability
- Measure What Matters
- Reflective Breaks
- Continuous Delivery
- Continuous Deployment
- Data-Driven Decision Making

Events don't occur in a vacuum. Effective decisions require not just situational awareness of events but also comprehending their context in order to interpret them and
define the best response. Applying the Learning Organization pattern approach in
your culture helps create and maintain a high level of understanding throughout the
organization.

Pattern: Learning Organization

*An organization skilled at acquiring information, creating insight, and transferring
knowledge can tolerate risk with confidence and solve difficult problems through experimentation and innovation (Figure 7-12).*

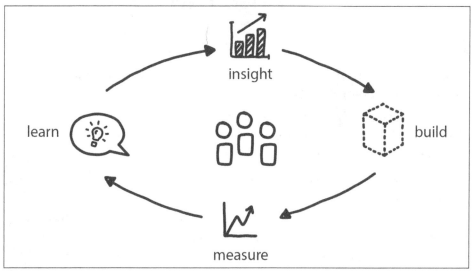

Figure 7-12. Learning Organization

A company is launching a cloud native transformation and needs to create a new culture in the organization that supports innovation and accepts uncertainty. In the new

and complex world of cloud native technology, there is no "right" way to go about a cloud native transformation.

Organizations migrating from Waterfall or Agile paradigms to cloud native don't typically have the skill set for working in a highly uncertain and ambiguous environment: open-mindedness, a willingness to experiment and tolerate risk, and above all the ability to enter into the transformation process without a detailed map.

Traditionally, before starting large projects managers would require all the answers and full work estimations. Then once the project was approved there would be no real possibility to adjust course. Such bureaucratic habits reinforce stability and reduce risks by eliminating change, but they conflict with the need to innovate and lead to re-creating the same old monolithic systems and organization, only now with newer tools.

- Teams are coming in with proficient, rather than creative, skills.
- Innovation requires the ability to tolerate risk and ambiguity.
- The process of innovation depends on failures and improvements over time.
- Few people are trained to think or work in a creative, open-ended way.

Therefore

Take an honest look at your current culture. Build in the willingness to accept ambiguity and risk as part of your daily organizational process.

Rather than demanding a full detailed plan with clear estimation upfront, embrace Dynamic Strategy and help teams to structure effective experiments. Make sure there is enough Psychological Safety to allow people to take risks.

- Leaders need to lead by example and show everyone that it's safe to try new things even if they fail.
- Consider your company's current relationship to risk and change. Does experimentation require permission? Is failure considered automatically "bad"?
- Treat change as an opportunity rather than a cause for anxiety.

Teams are co-creating solutions and challenging each other with Productive Feedback as they experiment their way toward the right answers.

+ People learn how to act autonomously while being willing to fail—and then mine what went wrong so they can learn from it.

− Training for cognitive resilience and creativity is possible, but it requires investment and work.

Common Pitfalls

Expecting teams to learn to work innovatively, experiment, and fail willingly, etc., while trying to use a proficient management approach that demands steady results.

Long-term precise and predictive planning is the norm in most enterprises, and it is also the biggest obstacle to meaningful change.

Related Biases

Law of the instrument
> An overreliance on a familiar tool or methods, ignoring or undervaluing alternative approaches. "If all you have is a hammer, everything looks like a nail."

Shared information bias
> Group members are likely to spend more time and energy discussing information that all members are already familiar with (i.e., shared information). For example, the whole team did Docker training, so they spend a lot of time talking about Docker—and no time at all about Kubernetes, which is equally necessary but they don't know much about it. To counter this bias, especially in new and complex environments, teams should learn new things all the time.

Related Patterns

- Psychological Safety
- Personal Relationships for Co-Creation
- Manage for Creativity
- Manage for Proficiency
- Blameless Inquiry

- Learning Loop
- Productive Feedback

Of course, in order to understand what's really happening and the best way to respond, you need to be looking at the right things.

Pattern: Measure What Matters

People optimize their actions based on how their work is measured. Assessing the wrong things leads people to optimize for the wrong goals (Figure 7-13).

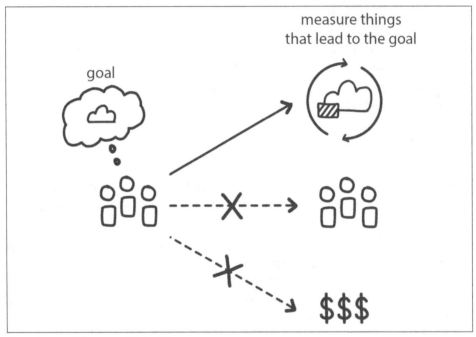

Figure 7-13. Measure What Matters

The company has strategic and tactical goals, and the management team wants to establish company performance metrics to measure and monitor progress.

In This Context

People tend to optimize their work output based on what is measured. Incorrect measurements will result in flawed deliveries (delivering the wrong things) and suboptimal performance.

For example, measuring velocity in Scrum will lead to inflation of story points. If the key performance indicator (KPI) doesn't reflect the company's actual needs, the result will be poor. This is an example of Goodhart's law, which states "When a measure becomes a target, it ceases to be a good measure." What happens is that which this can occur is individuals trying to anticipate the effect of a policy and then taking actions that alter its outcome.

- People tend to optimize for best measurements.
- Most methodologies bring their own metrics.
- Different teams may have different goals.

Therefore

Always adjust performance measurements to fit the organization's strategic and tactical needs. Keep measuring the most important KPI and stop when specific behavior becomes routine. Only measure a few KPIs at a time, choosing ones related to the current worst bottlenecks. Prioritizing customer value as the main metric helps to focus on customer needs.

- Keep KPIs measurable and achievable but also stretched for delivery progress.
- Measure differently for creativity versus proficiency.
- Avoid getting stuck in vanity metrics like number of site visitors and focus on measuring customer value.

Consequently

Managers set up KPIs in conjunction with goals and adjust them as the goals are changing.

+ Higher awareness from all involved.

+ All stakeholders have more clarity about priorities and goals.

− It is difficult—and confusing to the teams—if metrics change frequently.

Common Pitfalls

Having too many measurements is a common pitfall. People can't be effective when they try to achieve too many simultaneous goals. Although a company may have a variety of strategic and tactical goals, it must choose only the most critical ones—or risk achieving none at all.

Related Biases

Information bias
> The tendency to seek information even when it cannot affect the outcome; in A/B testing this would lead to choosing meaningless variables to test.

Confirmation bias
> Picking test variables that will "prove" your existing opinion, rather than genuinely exploring alternatives.

Congruence bias
> If you have a preconceived outcome in mind and test results that confirm this, you stop testing instead of seeking further information.

Parkinson's law of triviality/"Bikeshedding."
> Choosing something easy but unimportant to test and evaluate instead of something that is complex and difficult but meaningful.

Related Patterns

- Dynamic Strategy
- Involve the Business
- A/B Testing
- Manage for Creativity
- Manage for Proficiency
- Learning Loop

It's a mistake to think of measurement as merely the passive collection of data. It's the same with research. Figuring things out through trial and error keeps teams engaged and builds skills by doing.

Pattern: Research Through Action

People can sometimes use research as a way to avoid making decisions, so hands-on learning through small experiments builds confidence and jumpstarts progress (Figure 7-14).

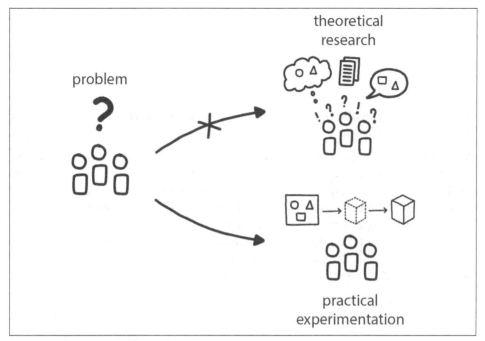

Figure 7-14. Research Through Action

The challenges are new and complex, information is scarce, and the company is pushing to go fast.

In a new or unfamiliar environment, people can analyze things too much and fail to make progress: analysis paralysis.

The tendency is to spend a lot of time on research, because making an actual decision is daunting—particularly in an environment where failure historically resulted in punishment. The effort to take in so much new information can also be overwhelming. As a result, people will often skip from one idea to the next before getting enough understanding to guide informed decision making. All of this adds up to procrastination because it is not effective data gathering related to actually moving ahead with a plan—it is research for research's sake.

- When people are not allowed to fail, they avoid taking risks.
- Quick actions carry a lot of risk.

- If the cost of action is high, people tend to delay and wait for more info.
- In a world with many dependencies, taking action requires involving others.

Run small experiments instead of full analysis and research; choose action over extensive contemplation and exhaustive research.

We all find ourselves from time to time in front of a massive pile of work without the faintest idea where to start. Doing nothing is the easiest choice, of course, but this won't lead very far. So then we try some thorough planning to "make sense" of all these tasks, doing lots of reading and Googling. In an uncertain environment, however, we won't be much smarter after all that work—the best course of action is to simply pick the first task from the pile and do it! Then another one and another one. Keep doing this until you gather enough information about what's going on, and at that point a bit of planning could be appropriate.

- Experiments and PoCs instead of in-depth architectural documents.
- Limit the risk of action with short deadlines and low cost.

You are making minor yet tangible progress through taking small, iterative steps.

+ Uncover unknown-unknowns through experimentation.

+ Increase team motivation and joint learning.

+ Many experiments fail—this is OK.

+ A solution that is not fully baked can still be a valid choice.

Related Biases

Ambiguity effect
   The tendency to avoid options where information is missing or difficult to gather.

Information bias
   The tendency to seek information even when it cannot affect action. "Analysis paralysis" is very common—continuing to find more answers for more questions, even though there are only two or three possible actions to take and the benefits of one of them are very clear.

Parkinson's law of triviality/"Bikeshedding."
Choosing something easy but unimportant to test and evaluate instead of something that is complex and difficult but meaningful.

Related Patterns

- Exploratory Experiments
- PoCs
- Avoid Reinventing the Wheel
- Reduce Cost of Experimentation
- Gradually Raising the Stakes

Practical Patterns for Managing Any Kind of Risk

Whenever you need to create strategy around any big change for your organization because there is no clear next step, much less an obvious path to success, Gradually Raising the Stakes is the pattern that will take you there. It gives us the tools to address uncertainty and gradually reduce risk by moving step by logical next step. The way it works is through three graduated levels of risk taking: little risk, moderate risk, high risk. In terms of pure strategy formation we are guided through the process by unpacking Gradually Raising the Stakes' related next-steps patterns: No Regret Moves, Options and Hedges, and Big Bet.[2]

When it comes to setting the right technical path in a transformation design, however, there is a different set of sub-patterns correlating with this three incremental stages de-risking approach: Exploratory Experiments, PoCs (Proof of Concepts), and MVP Platform. You can find these in Chapter 9.

Low-certainty projects carry extremely high risk. Any decision you make early in the project is highly likely to be uncovered later as wrong. In a predictable environment like Waterfall, you can start a big project without doing experiments/PoCs because, although the project itself is new, it is still very similar to previous projects. In an uncertain environment where the next move is not clear (and the one after that a complete mystery) this strategy may lead you to make major technical and organizational decisions too early—with little chance of reversing them later, due to the sunk-cost fallacy. This often leads to a wrong solution remaining in place—sticking with

---

2 Gradually Raising the Stakes and its Related Patterns are drawn from multiple significant sources, including the book *Exploring Strategy: Text and Cases* by Duncan Angwin et al. (Pearson) and the Harvard Business Review article "Strategy Under Uncertainty," by Hugh Courtney et al.

the original choice because so much is already invested—and possibly the punishment of key people involved in choosing the solution.

So how *do* you undertake a major new initiative—and avoid making major and costly mistakes—when you have no previous knowledge or experience in this area? Patterns help us move through uncertain situations, and Gradually Raising the Stakes opens the door to this process.

Pattern: Gradually Raising the Stakes

In an uncertain environment, slowly increase investment in learning and information-gathering; eventually you uncover enough information to reduce risk and make better-informed decisions (Figure 7-15).

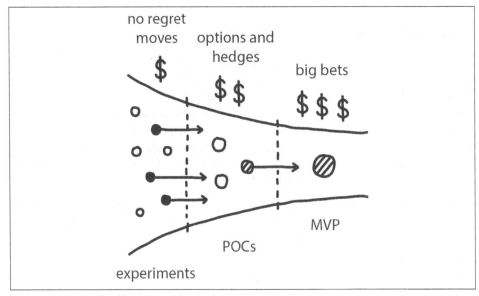

Figure 7-15. Gradually Raising the Stakes

You are in the beginning of a transformation, and the executive team is committed to moving forward but needs to map how it will proceed. The company is new to cloud native, and the team has little knowledge or experience in the field.

In This Context

Making major decisions before having enough information to understand the parameters carries a great deal of risk. However, in the uncertain environment of an early cloud native transformation when there is not much knowledge or a clear path, grabbing right away for a "big bang" solution is very tempting.

- In traditional environments budgets are allocated based on full estimation of scope and a clear execution plan.
- In the cloud native environment high uncertainty makes estimation difficult; next steps are not predefined but uncovered one at a time.
- Executives still expect problems to have a well-defined and reasonably predictable solution, because that is how they have always worked before.

Avoid making big decisions early; do a series of small projects, always growing slowly in size, until you have enough information to make a big bet.

Begin the initiative with small no-risk actions that benefit the organization in any circumstances (see: *No Regret Moves*). Once a baseline understanding is in place, move to actions that help deepen understanding in areas that seem especially relevant to the organization's transformation goals, and begin narrowing down the field of options (see: Options and Hedges). Eventually a reasonably clear best path will emerge, and the company can then make a reasonably confident Big Bet commitment. This, in the cloud native context, means building an MVP version of the most likely large-scale solution.

- Move incrementally through three stages: first, learn the basics. Then deepen knowledge through more detailed investigation and experimentation, which helps eliminate wrong choices. Finally, gather the information revealed and use it to decide the best likely path.
- Once the big bet is taken, stay on the path until the circumstances are stable.
- If circumstances change due to new information uncovered by experiments, or if the market changes, then remember to refactor the strategy using Dynamic Strategy.

The project has been gradually refined/decided without taking disproportionately high risks, and appropriate budget and resources have been allocated to each stage based on its level of uncertainty.

+ You know how much resource each project will require as you uncover next steps; you are allocating just that, no more, no less.

+ The level of detail of the project, and the understanding of the scope and the context, gradually increases with each step—which proportionally lowers the embedded risk.

– There is great ambiguity in the project, which prevents thorough financial and resource planning. Ambiguity typically feeds anxiety.

Common Pitfalls

Making big decisions before having all the information—committing to a solution without doing enough experimenting to uncover risks (or simply not experimenting at all); conversely, endlessly experimenting with everything to minimize risk never quite reaching a decision or committing to a plan.

Related Biases

Irrational escalation/Sunk-cost fallacy
  The urge to keep investing in a project, despite new evidence that the decision was probably wrong, because you've already sunk so much into it.

Confirmation bias
  Picking test variables that will "prove" your existing opinion, rather than genuinely exploring alternatives.

Ambiguity effect
  Cloud native is complex and the benefits are not easily visible, so better just to keep things the way they are.

Zero-risk bias
  Preference for reducing a small risk to zero over a greater reduction in a larger risk. People keep experimenting thinking they can eventually get something perfect, and so never stop doing research and experimentation because there is always a better solution if you wait long enough and keep looking.

Related Patterns

- No Regret Moves
- Options and Hedges
- Big Bet
- Dynamic Strategy

Cloud native transformation is a massive project with a variety of risky moves embedded in it. Making a totally wrong technical or organizational turn early on might be much worse than just a small loss of time and money. In the past five years observing cloud native transformations, we've seen companies struggling in a transformation for two to three years without ever reaching satisfactory results. Instead, they stay stuck fighting with the wrong tools and an organization that doesn't allow innovation.

In a situation with high embedded risk and little knowledge, how do you identify, classify, and investigate possible solutions in such an unknown environment? The No Regret Moves pattern show us the place to begin.

Pattern: No Regret Moves

Small, quick actions that require little investment of time and money but increase knowledge, reduce risk, and benefit the entire organization—inside or outside of a transformation scenario (Figure 7-16).

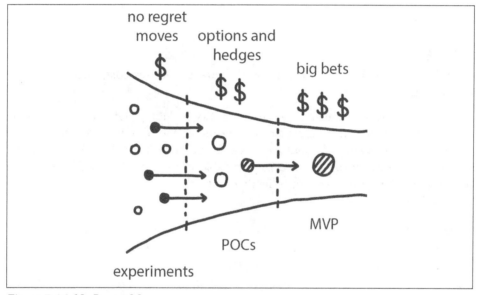

Figure 7-16. No Regret Moves

A company is in the beginning of a cloud native transformation initiative or facing any other difficult technical or organizational question with no obvious or readily available answer.

Lacking adequate information, the team has no practical way to make an educated decision—and essentially will have to gamble on a semi-random solution and hope for the best.

Unfortunately for traditional Waterfall organizations, managers are measured based on their success in leading large initiatives. Thus, many ignore initial small exploratory steps in favor of jumping into a game-changing project that will earn them a fat bonus and a nice promotion. In Waterfall organizations, which typically operate with known technologies in reasonably stable markets, that strategy often works. But in a highly volatile cloud native environment, it can easily lead to disaster or, worse, wasted years without either clear success or failure.

- Change creates anxiety, so people tend to avoid it.
- In the early stages of a cloud native transformation there is little knowledge or experience within the organization around cloud native architecture/tech/culture.
- The situation is highly uncertain, and making big commitments early carries a lot of risk.

Therefore

Take first-stage risk-reduction actions that are quick, low-cost, and benefit the company no matter what.

Some improvements to operational effectiveness—including training and coaching, and, in a project context, running small experiments and technical exercises—would benefit any business in just about any circumstance. These small but beneficial and practically no-risk moves are especially valuable during the first, highly uncertain days of a cloud migration and form the first of the three stages of graduated transformation risk-management strategy.

- An in-depth quality assessment like the cloud native Maturity Matrix creates situational awareness that is universally valuable to the organization now, but also serves as a gap analysis for future moves.
- Trainings and educational offerings keep employees engaged and constantly refresh their knowledge.
- Hackathons and small experiments uncover technical answers via hands-on actions.

Consequently

The organization has gained self-awareness and knowledge without investing huge amounts of time or money. Risk has been incrementally lowered, and the company's leaders are ready to take the next step in setting the transformation path.

+ When people know more, they feel more confident, which increases their ability to meet challenges creatively and proactively.

– Since No Risk Moves are so affordable and beneficial, the company could stay stuck in this stage for too long and delay getting the transformation underway.

Common Pitfalls

Doing things like training and education for only some, but not all, teams. Likewise, having an assessment done but not sharing the results across the organization. The more people know, the more risk is reduced—so don't limit information sharing to only certain groups

Related Patterns

- Gradually Raising the Stakes
- Options and Hedges
- Big Bet
- Learning Organization
- Research Through Action
- Exploratory Experiments
- Reduce Cost of Experiments

At the beginning of a transformation risk is high and knowledge is low, so it's easy to just keep running experiments (especially when they are quick, low-cost, and generally beneficial No Regret Moves). Your research has given you a better understanding of what is going on, but there is still fairly high risk involved. Making a big decision at this point can still lead to unnecessarily high expense, while running additional tiny experiments that uncover no new information is just a waste of time.

Once some promising potential solutions have been identified, how do you further test their durability and fitness? The Options and Hedges pattern shows us the next logical step to follow No Regret Moves.

Pattern: Options and Hedges

Research has created deeper understanding, and a few potentially promising transformation paths have begun to emerge. Continue reducing the risk by focusing on the most promising options and developing them further (Figure 7-17).

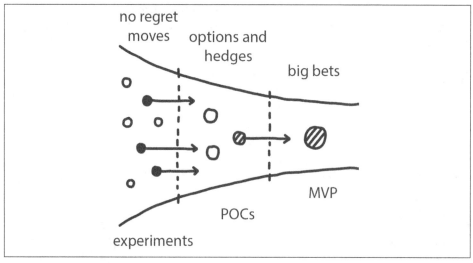

Figure 7-17. Options and Hedges

You have achieved moderate certainty by running a series of small experiments, research projects, and trainings, but the team is not yet confident enough to make major decisions about the transformation.

In This Context

Your research has given you a better understanding of what is going on, but major decisions are still not obvious. Commitment to a large solution at this point still carries serious high risk of choosing the wrong solution, while running additional tiny experiments that uncover no new information is just a waste of time.

- Pressure is rising to make commitments.
- Too easy to keep running experiments forever.
- There will always be some uncertainty, no matter how much research you do.

Make small tactical decisions aimed at creating and understanding a new path forward. They can be rolled back or forward, ramped up or down, and will at least eliminate some options while you create new plans.

The goal is to validate the results of any successful experiments performed so far.

- Do mid-size proof-of-concept projects that take a few weeks to a couple of months.
- Stay aware of biases like the IKEA effect and sunk-cost fallacy that could lead to sticking with a solution even when it's not really working.
- No commitments yet! Maintaining the ability to change direction reasonably easily is still important here.
- Take a vendor-neutral approach: companies need the best tools and techniques for their cloud native platform, and these are not necessarily the ones offered in bundled solutions.

Consequently

You have uncovered the majority of the important information required and are reasonably certain where you are going next.

+ Risk declines because, as you experiment, you eliminate things that don't work and reveal the ones that do.

+ Next steps come into stark relief. The results of all these little experiments actually shape the architecture of the new system.

+ You are ready to take the next big steps (Big Bet) because you have gained knowledge and experience.

Common Pitfalls

Jumping too soon by committing to a Big Bet move prematurely. Or the opposite, never jumping because you are doing endless research in the form of No Regret Moves.

Related Biases

Information bias
> The tendency to seek information even when it cannot affect action. "Analysis paralysis" is common—continuing to find more answers for more questions,

even though there are only two or three possible actions to take and the benefits of one of them are clear.

Confirmation bias
Picking test variables that will "prove" your existing opinion, rather than genuinely exploring alternatives.

Congruence bias
The tendency to test hypotheses exclusively through direct single testing, instead of testing possible alternative hypotheses.

Ambiguity effect
The tendency to avoid options for which missing information makes the probability of the outcome seem "unknown."

Related Patterns

- Gradually Raising the Stakes
- PoCs
- MVP
- Big Bet
- No Regret Moves

When decisions are made too early, before enough information was uncovered by experiments and research, it's easy to commit to a solution that turns out to be less than ideal. This means risking reversal at high cost in order to change to a better one —or sticking with a wrong solution anyway due to sunk costs.

Conversely, sometimes the team is hesitant to make a big decision. This often leads to wasting time and resources on research that adds only marginally useful information or, worse, on parallel investment into multiple solutions for the same problem. The answer to both these conundrums is to make the Big Bet, but at the right time. But how do you know when it's the right time to finally choose a single solution, even if there is still some uncertainty—when is the right time to finally end the research? How do you convince the organization that the approach you are outlining can solve real problems at real scale? The next step after Options and Hedges, the Big Bet pattern, shows us how.

Pattern: Big Bet

When enough information is available, commit to a significant solution for moving the cloud migration forward. Focus on execution rather than research (Figure 7-18).

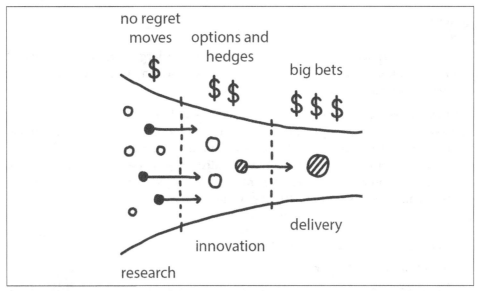

Figure 7-18. Big Bet

A company is facing a big technical or organizational decision. Experiments were performed, research done, major points validated, and the team has a good understanding of the company's needs and the problem domain. Multiple major directions are still open.

Continuing research and experimentation without ever making any big decision leads to significant waste of resources as the teams are not focused on solving the problem and the direction is not chosen yet. It means that there is no clear alignment across teams regarding a solution, and no stable and focused delivery process has been established.

- In Waterfall, teams tend to do too much research and try to find all the answers for all questions.
- Many times any decision is better than none.
- Large corporations hate risk and therefore push for more research.
- In Waterfall organizations, managers' success is measured by their ability to decide on and execute major changes.

Make a commitment to a large-scale solution, like a large rebuild, architectural change, migration, purchase of new products, etc., bearing in mind that it might require organizational change.

After exploring the options with No Regret Moves and increasing the chance of success even more with Options and Hedges, we now can make a big commitment toward the right longer-term solution. Once the commitment is made, the teams switch from research to execution mode, provided there are no significant changes in the market or other game-changing information. This creates alignment among teams and allows quick product delivery, without endless discussions about the direction.

- Make the commitment clear to the team.
- Stop doing competing projects.
- Consider an exit strategy (evaluate related costs should it be necessary to reverse the decision).

There is full commitment to the chosen direction. It is clear to everyone that this is a commitment moment: at this time we stop experimenting and move forward. Unless there is a significant change in market or strategy conditions, teams stay committed to the chosen path.

+ A single solution is chosen, and the team is focused on making it work.

+ No effort is wasted on work that doesn't improve the decision process.

− There is always a chance that the decision can turn out to not be the right one.

Common Pitfalls

Almost always: people make the Big Bet too early. In some cases the decision proves to be successful, which reinforces the confidence of the managers even if that success was a result of pure luck. Other decisions are not so good, and in those cases, managers will work hard to either hide the failure or present it as a success. Sunk-cost fallacy is a very strong factor in such situations.

Forgetting to get back to experimenting/No Regret Moves when conditions shift and change is in order.

Related Biases

Irrational escalation/Sunk-cost fallacy
> The urge to keep investing in a project, despite new evidence that the decision was probably wrong, because you've already sunk so much into it.

Zero-risk bias
> Preference for reducing a small risk to zero over a greater reduction in a larger risk.

Status quo
> Once you commit to something, you stop looking around—but you still need to keep situational awareness to be able to adjust to market/environment changes with Dynamic Strategy.

Related Patterns

- Gradually Raising the Stakes
- No Regret Moves
- Options and Hedges
- Dynamic Strategy
- Three Horizons
- Exit Strategy Over Vendor Lock-in

Cloud native processes are iterative; they incorporate rapid feedback and data from a change to then make more changes. Thus these patterns operate as loops, and the essential process can be summed up as "investigate, iterate, incorporate, repeat." That methodology is at the heart of the Gradually Raising the Stakes pattern: No Regret Moves is about investigating many possible solutions/paths to narrow down to the most promising ones. Options and Hedges then takes a deeper look at the best options, iterating them forward to see how they hold up. This provides more data to make a best-fit Big Bet decision. This set of patterns is shown here as a way to de-risk major situations like a transformation initiative, but the loop is equally applicable to smaller scale and more minor decisions as well.

Since experimentation is the main tool for working our way through the incremental stages of curating solutions through investigation and elimination—no matter how large or small the problem at hand—it is imperative that your company removes any barriers that prevent or bottlenecks that slow these small but impactful investigations.

Running an experiment in a traditional organization is difficult. Trying something new in a complex monolithic software system requires extensive planning and complex setup to order and install servers running the experiment: it may be months before you get results. If each experiment costs $100,000 and takes several months, not to mention a lot of meetings and paperwork to get permission in the first place, then you won't run many. In most cases the team will simply skip experimentation altogether and move directly to full execution, ignoring the massive risks that this approach entails.

Pattern: Reduce Cost of Experimentation

When someone has an idea that requires validation, the cost of doing experiments around it needs to be as low as possible (Figure 7-19).

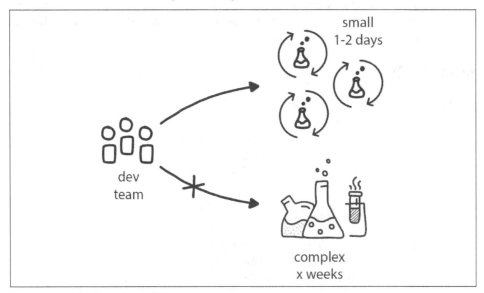

Figure 7-19. Reduce Cost of Experimentation

A company is moving into cloud native with little understanding of tooling and technologies. Uncertainty is very high. New ideas and solutions come up all the time, and the team has to run a variety of validation experiments to select the best ones.

In This Context

There are significant barriers to experimentation in the organization: permission is required, and the related planning, documentation, and coordination meetings take a lot of time. Then actually getting the results afterward typically requires a significant wait. As a result, engineers will often skip experimentation and move directly to execution.

- Very little chance that any experiment will lead to canceling a project because there is already high commitment to that path.
- Higher cost means an experiment is less likely to be done.
- If cost is low enough, people can experiment even with things that lead to failure.
- The higher the cost, the lower the willingness to abandon the experiment (sunk-cost effect).
- Traditional organizations require extensive documentation with any experimentation, which by definition makes costs high.

Put in place a simple, straightforward, and seamless process for doing experiments. When experimentation is central to an organization's process and progress, it needs to be an inexpensive and easily accessible action.

Outline and publicize a process, or provide periodic training. for how to create appropriate hypotheses with measures and then design small experiments to test them. Aim to remove bureaucratic roadblocks such as managerial approvals and extensive documentation for every action, while providing technical infrastructure that is light, fully automated, and requires only a tiny budget.

- Create a framework around experimentation: the tools, facilitation techniques, project-management structure, and guidelines for allocation.
- Such facilitation makes it faster to obtain and understand the results of an experiment.

More experiments take place. Instead of extensive research and guessing when a complex problem arises, a rapid process of hypothesis/results/analysis provides the solution.

+ Teams can be more innovative when they know they can easily try out ideas.
− There is cost to experiments, even if it is low.

Common Pitfalls

Potential for over-experimentation—people love experiments. If they are too cheap and easy, people will do nothing but experiment, and nothing ever moves forward (analysis paralysis).

Trying for a "sure thing"—If experiments require a long process of approval and documentation, then they typically become less like true explorations to test hypotheses and gather conclusions and more like PoCs to reassure that the proposed plan is working as described or intended.

Related Biases

Irrational escalation/Sunk-cost fallacy
> The urge to keep investing in a project despite new evidence that the decision was probably wrong, because you've already sunk so much into it.

Information bias
> The tendency to seek information even when it cannot affect action. Also known as "analysis paralysis," this is very common—continuing to find more answers to more questions, even though there are only two or three possible actions to take and the benefits of one of them are clear.

Parkinson's law of triviality
> Choosing something easy but unimportant to test and evaluate, instead of something that is complex and difficult but meaningful.

Related Patterns

- Exploratory Experiments
- PoCs
- Measure What Matters
- Psychological Safety
- Productive Feedback
- Manage for Creativity
- Blameless Inquiry

Even as the company is working to identify the best transformation path, it's important to keep an eye out for second-best options too. This information comes in handy when evaluating backup plans, and even more so for deciding whether to commit to a particularly global set of solutions.

Pattern: Exit Strategy Over Vendor Lock-in

Public cloud or other major product vendors can handle all aspects of building and oper-ating a cloud native platform, and their tools are often excellent—but when committing to a vendor/technology/platform, it's important to identify an alternate solution and any costs associated with switching over (Figure 7-20).

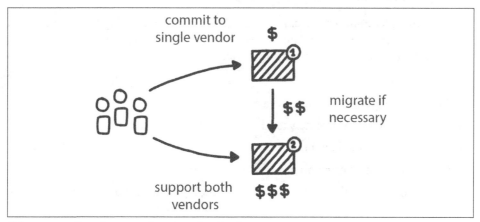

Figure 7-20. Exit Strategy Over Vendor Lock-in

Companies need to use tools/products provided by vendors (commercial or open source communities) but are afraid to get locked into a single vendor. Some indus-tries require supporting multiple choices for some key platforms, tools, or technolo-gies used to develop company products. Being fully committed to a single tool or technology can drive costs up or hinder tech progress down the line.

In This Context

Committing to a single vendor (or simply a single large solution) creates reliance upon their ongoing stability and availability and pricing, but the cost of maintain-ing active alternative/backup options is prohibitive.

This leads to full dependency on the vendor. If the vendor is in trouble or when a better option becomes available on the market, the company cannot afford to switch —which leads to using unmaintained or inferior technology.

- There is risk in any choice.
- Every decision can be reversed; it's just a matter of cost.
- Some industries require multiple vendors for each solution.

Instead of blindly refusing to commit to a single vendor, explore the options for a second migration, if necessary, and what they would cost. Then make an educated decision based on the tradeoff between short-term gains from a vendor with the best tool and the long-term risk of migrating out of it if needed. Often lower costs and higher productivity outweigh the risk.

Consider implementing architectural changes that will reduce the cost of migration in case it will be required. Such changes can be inexpensive if done in the earliest stages of the project, and they can significantly reduce the risk of the future migration.

- Prepare a migration plan just in case.
- Consider reducing dependencies that significantly increase risk.
- AWS could be a big help now.
- Closed ecosystems often offer an excellent set of tools/options.
- Invest in commonly used tools and technologies that may become industry standards.

The team can focus on getting the maximum performance out of and benefit from each tool, and they are aware of what it would cost to migrate to alternative solutions should the need arise.

+ There is a good understanding of the different backup options.

+ High-level plan is in place for a major migration scenario.

− There is always risk when only one tool is used.

Common Pitfalls

Sub-prime solutions: A team may waste effort seeking, evaluating, or implementing solutions that will work with many different tools in order to optimize portability in the event of emergency. In many cases the resulting solution is far from optimal for the company's actual needs, due to the need to get down to the lowest common denominator across chosen tools.

Related Biases

Zero-risk bias
> Preference for reducing a small risk to zero over a greater reduction in a larger risk; in this case, building/buying an expensive backup solution in case of the unlikely need to suddenly and completely migrate between options.

Related Patterns

- Public Cloud
- Private Cloud
- Avoid Reinventing the Wheel
- Open Source Internal Projects

Maintaining Strategic Momentum

One of the reasons that WealthGrid found it so very hard to find a successful path to cloud native was pretty ironic: they were so good at doing what they did that they forgot how to do anything else. In other words, they were beautifully effective at the proficient delivery process. In the process of perfecting this near-algorithmic state, however, the company moved away from exploration and experimentation, and so stopped investing in creativity and innovation. Three Horizons[3] is the pattern that makes sure this never happens again and that any company is able to adapt to change when it comes even while operating at maximum proficiency for the situation.

---

3 This pattern is drawn from the concepts in the McKinsey Quarterly article "Enduring Ideas: The Three Horizons of Growth," (*https://mck.co/35wZFLj*).

Pattern: Three Horizons

Proportional allocation of resources among delivery, innovation, and research makes an organization responsive to change while reliably delivering core business value (Figure 7-21).

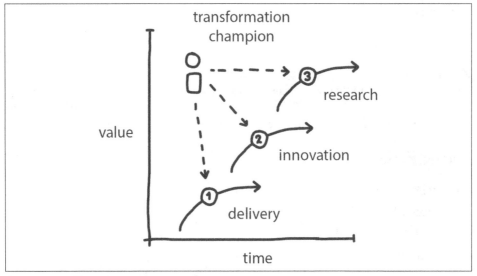

Figure 7-21. Three Horizons

An established enterprise is aiming to run a large innovation initiative while all current teams are dedicated to incremental (proficient) work on existing products. Or, a startup is building a new product and devotes all resources to research and innovation.

In This Context

In general, companies seldom keep the right balance between delivery and innovation. Enterprises tend to allocate almost all resources to Horizon 1, proficient delivery of core business product/service, which eventually leads to stagnation. Startups tend to overcommit to innovation, Horizon 2, which leads to poor product quality and lack of focus on delivery value to customers. At the very far end lies Horizon 3, researching ideas that are promising but will not lead to any practical solutions in the foreseeable future.

- Creative and proficient teams need to be managed differently.
- Startups tend to focus on innovation, enterprises on incremental improvements.

- Complex innovation many times looks like just another technology project.

Always allocate resources to delivery (current products or services), innovation (refining new products/services or significantly improving existing ones, relevant within 12–24 months), and research (long-term ideas and technologies). Champions are responsible for moving technology and knowledge across the teams.

An adaptive business constantly evaluates and recalibrates the relationship among its three horizons, pursuing the optimal balance between proficiency and creativity. To manage the Three Horizons in the context of a cloud native transformation across an organization, it's important to have a Transformation Champion who understands the different stages and helps the company's teams and leaders distribute the focus, technology, and strategy as needed. Once the transformation is complete, a Designated Strategist can serve in the same role to keep the company in balance going forward. (For a deeper explanation of McKinsey's Three Horizons model, see Chapter 6.)

- Give 70%–80% of resources to Horizon 1, proficiency; 15%–25% to Horizon 2, innovation; and 3%–5% to Horizon 3, research.
- Adjust investment in horizons when circumstances change (to improve quality or prod innovation).
- After significant investment in innovation, move people back to improve quality on H1 projects.

The company is always prepared for whatever the future brings while still delivering existing products frequently and at high quality.

+ Continuous innovation.

+ Continuous improvement.

+ Stable delivery of core business value.

– Some resources are not allocated to products that immediately generate revenue.

Common Pitfalls

Enterprises begin as startups but over time lose the capability to work on Horizons 2 and 3. This happens because they are fully optimized for delivery of their current products, which is a totally proficient task. When the market changes or a new big opportunity arises, they approach the challenge as any other proficient project to be delivered under constant pressure of frequent deadlines and with long and detailed documentation. Even if the company sets very innovative goals, such initiatives will fall short, since the teams are given no space for free thinking and no psychological safety to experiment and make mistakes.

Related Patterns

- Manage for Creativity
- Manage for Proficiency
- Dynamic Strategy
- Transformation Champion
- Designated Strategist

Our last two patterns are essential for working in the Three Horizons model. Reflective Breaks make sure that everyone in the organization has a regular opportunity to take a step back and contemplate their current path and process. Naming a Designated Strategist means the company has someone specifically in charge of keeping an eye on the future.

Pattern: Reflective Breaks

Build periodic times into the business delivery cycle dedicated to reviewing current strategy in light of shifting market conditions or other new information (Figure 7-22).

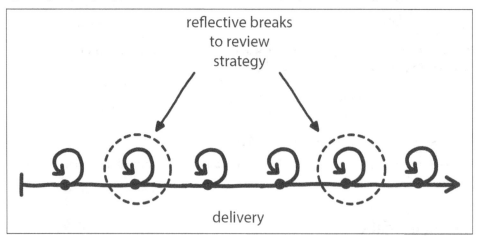

Figure 7-22. Reflective Breaks

Strategy is in place, and the execution roadmap is clear. People are working under pressure to deliver according to the plan. The environment is still changing frequently and drastically.

When you run as fast as you can, you stop looking around to evaluate the situation and focus on only a single point—the finish line. Most modern delivery processes are designed to create stable pressure to help people focus on delivery. There is no planned and structured time set aside for periodic strategy reviews and for creative thinking.

This is a good way to manage for proficiency and fast delivery of incremental, well-understood changes, but it leaves out the opportunity for radical change of direction that requires unstructured, open-ended time to think.

- People under pressure don't reflect: to run fast, you look straight ahead—not side to side.

- It's difficult to generate new ideas when focused on delivery. Innovation requires free time for thinking.

- The typical Agile environment creates continuous pressure to deliver new features in an unbroken cadence.

Build periodic planned "time-outs" into the business cycle across the entire organization.

People think "taking a break" means that they get to stop working, but that is not the case in cloud native, or in any other big innovation initiative. The cloud native delivery cadence should include time for everyone in the organization to occasionally step back from their everyday responsibilities in order to do a different kind of work. Temporarily reducing the pressure to deliver your usual responsibilities makes room for thoughtful consideration of current conditions, both inside and outside the organization.

This periodic planned time-out applies across the entire organization. The cycle must reflect the enterprise's specific circumstances, of course, but quarterly break periods across the calendar year are a logical approach that can be effective in many organizations. Other break examples could be an Agile org making every fourth (or fifth, sixth, or eighth) sprint a "rest" period before stepping back into focused delivery mode. Again, timing depends on factors specific to each company, such as development cycles and delivery schedule.

For the company's leaders, Reflective Breaks are a pause from concentrating on forward-focused actions in order to review the existing environment—an opportunity to reflect on the strategy, review the architecture, inventory the backlogs, and basically re-evaluate the plan for the entire company.

For the development and business teams, it means taking time out from regular responsibilities like building new features and iterating improvements (or pursuing sales and marketing efforts, or administering internal company functions, etc.) in order to refocus on the strategic aspects of their work. The chance to step back and examine how everything you do every day as part of your job, from process to product, might be improved.

People don't change strategy unless they have time to look at it. This is the chance to review architecture, adjust it if needed, and invest in nonfunctional improvements that will make everyone's life better when the next sprint puts everybody back to busily executing their tasks.

- Make breaks on all levels.
- Use reflective breaks for executive team to review strategy, middle managers to review objectives, and execution teams to review backlogs and make nonfunctional improvements.

Consequently

Teams are focused on execution but also have the regular opportunity to review and adjust on all levels of the company.

+ Company spends the majority of time on focused delivery of profitable products/services but is still able to adjust direction.

+ Cyclical breaks are a crucible for innovation, which requires free time and bandwidth to think and create.

– People tend to schedule their vacation time for these breaks and may not take full advantage of the opportunity to reflect on their day-to-day work.

Common Pitfalls

Trying to remain always 100% focused, which means people are overworked and don't see anything around them. Sometimes a company claims to value reflective breaks but then embeds them as just another part of the delivery process. This means you are relying on individuals to take this time for reflection; some will do it and some will not. If there is a lot of time pressure, people will almost always choose what is urgent over what is merely important. This is why you need to build it in as a company-wide cycle.

Related Patterns

- Dynamic Strategy
- Learning Organization
- Decide Closest to the Action
- Manage for Proficiency
- Manage for Creativity

Pattern: Designated Strategist

When you're running forward as fast as you can, it's difficult to look around you—so make one person within the organization in charge of situational awareness (Figure 7-23).

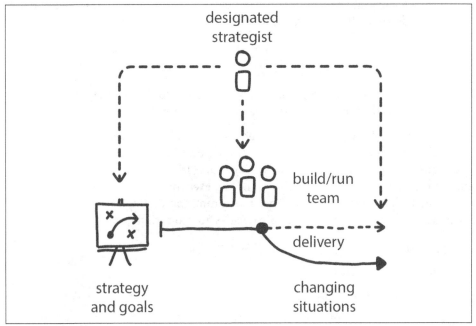

Figure 7-23. Designated Strategist

The company has a strategy and a clear execution backlog. The entire team is focused on proficiently delivering the best products. The market and the company situation are changing as the project progresses.

Once your transformation strategy has been defined, the team will tend to enter full execution mode—and stop refactoring the goals. This leads to the achievement of the original goals, but with no ongoing evaluation as circumstances evolve/ change. People under stress of delivery can't look around and re-evaluate the situation since they are pressured to focus solely on the set goals. The problem is that you might arrive at the finish line only to find that the problem has changed completely while you weren't paying attention and your original solution no longer applies.

- It's difficult for people to do broad strategic and deep tactical tasks at the same time.
- Scrum, the most widely used software delivery methodology, is heavily focused on proficiency and creates pressure to deliver as much as possible as fast as possible. By default, it leaves no space for reflection.

Therefore

Free one of the experienced architects or managers to focus solely on the future and evaluate all the scheduled tasks based on long-term goals.

The Designated Strategist should have no short-term commitments in order to prevent them from getting drawn into "all hands on deck" delivery deadlines or firefighting mode. This person functions as the "lookout" (as in, the person with the spyglass on the crow's nest of a sailing ship) while the executive team is at the wheel of the ship. The lookout warns of rocks ahead, or promising destinations to explore—and then the company's strategic leadership decides how to turn the ship.

- Make sure strategist is not working on daily tasks.
- Strategist has no executive power.
- Can also do evangelizing.
- Connected well to both customer desires and business goals.
- Balance is important.

Teams can focus mainly on delivery while the company still maintains a strategic perspective.

+ Teams are in charge of their work.

+ Strategist acts as advisor for adjusting goals and direction.

− Strategist may create distractions and constant instability by suggesting too many direction changes.

Common Pitfalls

Making this only a part-time responsibility and giving the Designated Strategist other, unrelated tasks that distract from their focus on strategic analysis and planning. Urgent tasks almost always get prioritized higher than important tasks.

Related Biases

Authority bias
The tendency to attribute greater accuracy to the opinion of an authority figure (unrelated to its content) and to be more influenced by that opinion.

Related Patterns

- Dynamic Strategy
- Three Horizons
- Periodic Checkups

Ready for Next

Our next three chapters introduce many more patterns for optimizing your organization and culture for cloud native, evolving your development processes, and building your new infrastructure. These are all things that you will do, actions you will take in the process of transforming your company.

These upcoming chapters deal with technologies and how to use them, and will need to be updated eventually. And sooner rather than later: technology changes fast, and how we use it also changes. The patterns and material in this chapter, by contrast, won't really change. They exist to teach you *how* to do these things. Together, they form a roadmap and a cognitive tool set for managing change no matter where, and no matter when—whether in the middle of your transformation, when a sudden new competitor appears, or a few years from now when the next paradigm shift arrives to replace cloud native. These patterns for strategy and risk management aren't simply tools to make you ready for cloud native: they help make you ready for *next*.

 New cloud native patterns are emerging constantly. To continue sharing them and extending the cloud native pattern language we have established here, please visit www.CNpatterns.org.

This is where to find the latest pattern developments, but also an online community for discussing and creating new patterns. We are inviting people from across the industry, thought leaders and influencers but most importantly everyday engineers and managers—those out there working elbows-deep in cloud native code and architecture—to contribute and participate. Hope to see you there!

CHAPTER 8

Patterns for Organization and Culture

Traditional organizations are structured to protect and reinforce the existing order: static strategy, top-down decision making, and little freedom for teams to deviate from the dictated path. This is in no way a bad thing! It is in fact an efficient structure for executing on a well-honed plan in a predictable and stable environment, but top-down flow takes a long time. This is fine if everything else is slow too, and releases happen only once every year or so.

Attempting to deliver on a new cloud native system by following the old ways is, however, a disaster in the making: things will break down very quickly because a hierarchical organizational structure simply can't keep up with a cloud native delivery approach.

To succeed as a cloud native entity an organization must embrace freedom of choice, delegation, and individual independence and responsibility. Not because this is an inherently superior way to do things, but because it is the better way to support a dynamic strategy. The main power of cloud native is the ability to adjust whatever you are doing (or the way you are doing it) to adapt in response to market or other environmental changes. If change happens every few months—which it will—but requires coordinating a massive rollout through many layers of bureaucracy each time, this basically derails any strategic shift. By the time you finally get it out there the market (and, likely, some of your customers) will have moved on.

Becoming a cloud native organization requires more than just opening an Amazon Web Services account and installing Kubernetes. Your culture needs to evolve along with your tech (something we discussed in depth in Chapter 2). Culture is a consistent set of basic actions that add up to how people are encouraged to do their daily work. Having a cloud native culture means moving to be more proactive and more experimental, allowing your teams to be independent and to make their own decisions—and take their own risks. It means, essentially, deconstructing the waterfall.

This chapter collects a series of patterns to guide your evolution toward cloud native culture, to help you cut down dependencies and move toward decentralization. You are stepping out into an uncertain world and, yes, it's a little scary. The old world was a well-charted, comfortable place. You knew how to get around, and also there were plenty of maps. This new landscape, though, changes all the time. Worse, there are few fixed landmarks—and no map at all. But you don't need one. After all, the only way to find your way in this new territory is to explore it until you get your bearings and can navigate instinctively. Or, to frame it in terms of Simon Wardley's seminal essays on optimizing organizational structure for continuous innovation, be a Pioneer rather than a Town Planner:[1]

> *Pioneers are brilliant people. They are able to explore never before discovered concepts, the uncharted land. They show you wonder, but they fail a lot. Half the time the thing doesn't work properly. You wouldn't trust what they build. They create 'crazy' ideas. Their type of innovation is what we call core research. They make future success possible…*
>
> *…Town Planners are also brilliant people. They are able to take something and industrialise it taking advantage of economies of scale. This requires immense skill. You trust what they build. They find ways to make things faster, better, smaller, more efficient, more economic, and good enough. They build the services that Pioneers build upon.*

These patterns are the survival kit of tools and techniques that will help you forge your own particular trail as a true pioneer in this new world among the clouds.

The following patterns describe and address cloud native culture and organizational structure. They are presented in an order that we believe will be useful or helpful for the reader, but there is no right (or wrong) order for approaching them: Patterns are building blocks for a design and can be combined in different ways according to context.

This chapter is intended as an introduction to the patterns themselves, and there is intentionally little explanation relating them to each other at this point. When considering an individual pattern, the decision is not just where and when to apply it, but whether to apply it at all—not every pattern is going to apply in every transformation or organization. Once the concepts are introduced we will fit them together, in progressive order and in context, in Chapter 11 and Chapter 12, as a design that demonstrates how patterns are applied in a typical cloud native transformation.

- Core Team
- Build-Run Teams ("Cloud Native DevOps")
- Platform Team
- SRE Team
- Remote Teams

---

1 Simon Wardley's original essay "On Pioneers, Settlers, Town Planners and Theft." (*http://bit.ly/2KUPZm1*).

- Co-Located Teams
- Communicate Through Tribes
- Manage for Creativity
- Manage for Proficiency
- Strangle Monolithic Organization
- Gradual Onboarding
- Design Thinking for Radical Innovation
- Agile for New Development
- Lean for Optimization
- Internal Evangelism
- Ongoing Education
- Exploratory Experiments
- Proof of Concept (PoC)
- MVP Platform
- Decide Closest to the Action
- Productive Feedback
- Psychological Safety
- Personalized Relationships for Co-Creation
- Blameless Inquiry

Pattern: Core Team

Dedicate a team of engineers and architects to the task of uncovering the best transformation path and implementing it along the way. This reduces risk embedded in the transformation while the team gains experience helpful for onboarding the remaining teams later (Figure 8-1).

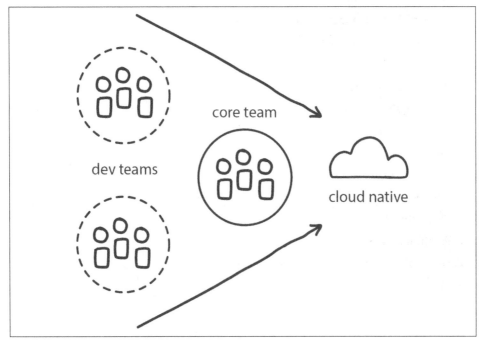

Figure 8-1. Core Team

With Vision First in place, the company is now allocating resources to the cloud native transformation and choosing the best teams for leading the initial stages.

In This Context

Making an existing team or teams responsible for delivering the new cloud native system while still requiring them to work on their regular duties means they will have conflicting priorities—and struggle to deliver either of them at all, much less do it well.

This happens very commonly when companies fail to recognize the size and scope of a cloud native transformation—both the time and resources it will require and the many ways it will impact the organization. Instead, they treat it like another system upgrade added to the backlog of standard tasks. This leads to insufficient resource allocation to the cloud native transformation project and conflicting priorities for the engineers working on it and will almost certainly cause the initiative to stall or simply fail.

- Teams working on both urgent and important tasks will tend to prioritize urgent tasks first, leading to deprioritization of important tasks such as cloud native transformation.
- Cloud native technologies are new and complex. They require intense time investment for learning and experimentation.
- Some of the cloud native challenges are too difficult for one person to handle.
- A team responsible (and trusted) for delivering a new solution will have full commitment to the solution and later evangelize about it across the organization.

Therefore

Create a single Core Team of five to eight engineers and architects to lead the transformation.

- Team responsibilities will include ownership of the technical vision and architecture and derisking the transformation by running a series of experiments to uncover the best transformation path.
- Later, the Core Team can use its experience to onboard other teams to the new way of working and to create the Dev Starter Pack materials.
- The team may continue improving the platform after the major parts of the transformation are done.

Consequently

The Core Team rapidly works through the most challenging parts of the transformation (identifying the best migration path, tools and technologies, and then implementing a minimum viable product version of a platform) and paves the way for the rest of the teams in the company toward successful cloud native adoption.

+ The team is building knowledge and experience in the cloud native area.

+ It can use this growing knowledge to adjust the vision and the architecture of the applications as it goes.

+ Progress is visible and measurable.

Common Pitfalls

Underestimating the complexity of cloud native work and treating it as just another technical upgrade. See Chapter 9.

Related Biases

Planning fallacy
    The tendency to underestimate task-completion times.

Related Patterns

- Vision First
- Gradually Raising the Stakes
- Reference Architecture
- Demo Apps
- Build-Run Teams
- Avoid Reinventing the Wheel
- Gradual Onboarding
- Developer Starter Pack

Pattern: Build-Run Teams ("Cloud Native DevOps")

Dev teams have full authority over the services they build, not only creating but also deploying and supporting them (Figure 8-2).

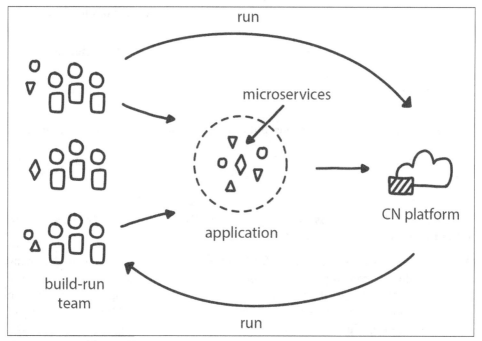

Figure 8-2. Build-Run Teams

The company has cross-functional teams (Agile) or teams siloed by technical specialty (Waterfall) and needs to move to a structure compatible with cloud native. Development teams rely on the Ops team to deploy artifacts to production. The company is looking for the right balance between independence and standardization for their dev teams.

In This Context

When development teams are responsible for building an application and supporting it in production, if they also try to build the build the platform to run it, the organization can end up with multiple irreconcilable platforms. This is unnecessary, expensive to operate (if even possible), and takes time away from teams that should be focusing on delivering features, not the platform they run on.

- Handover between development and operations teams kills production speed and agility.

- Adding an Ops person on each developer team is how you end up with 10 irreconcilable platforms.

- Conway's law says that software architecture will come to resemble the organization's structure, so if we want the platform to be independent, then the teams developing an application need to be separate from the team running the production platform.

- There is a limit to the capabilities a team can have. Devs are devs; they can extend their knowledge to a certain level, but they are not Ops.

- Maintaining Ops and Development as separate disciplines/teams is not sustainable in cloud native.

- Too much freedom brings chaos, but too much standardization strangles innovation.

Therefore

Create teams that each have their own capability to build a distributed system with microservices managed by dynamic scheduling.

Build-Run teams will be responsible for building distributed applications, deploying them, and then supporting the applications once running. Build-Run teams all use the same standardized set of platform services and deploy to a single unified platform that runs all applications for the entire company. This platform is the responsibility of the Platform Team, which implements and supports it.

- Build-Run teams are not DevOps teams in the traditional sense that devs and operations people sit together.

- In Agile, the development team also includes software testing capabilities, but the products are handed over to a separate Ops team to be delivered to production.

- In cloud native a true cross-functional team must be able to build distributed systems.

- The Platform Team is a specific kind of Build-Run team in that it builds, deploys, provisions, and supports the cloud native platform and infrastructure, but it works separately from the application development teams.

There is strong separation of defined responsibilities: Build-Run teams handle the applications. The Platform Team is responsible for building and maintaining the operating platform.

The Platform Team doesn't have to be part of the company—public clouds like Google/AWS/Azure, etc., with their automated platforms, could make an internal Platform Team unnecessary. If a Platform Team is designated, they are typically global, supporting all services/applications; Build-Run teams are separate and rely on standardized platform delivered by the Platform Team.

+ Teams have a bounded level of autonomy and ability to focus on their true tasks.

+ Developers still have freedom to choose components to run on top of the standardized platform so long as they are compatible.

Common Pitfalls

Giving Build-Run teams the responsibility for creating their own platforms. They deploy Kubernetes for their service, in their own way; but then there are 10 other teams creating their own platforms for their own services in *their* own way.

Adding Ops engineers to development teams (basic DevOps principle) instead of having a designated Platform Team (see pattern). This leads to each team having its own platform, producing a multitude of competing cloud native platforms that are difficult to develop and coordinate, and expensive to maintain.

Related Patterns

- Platform Team
- SRE Team
- Avoid Reinventing the Wheel
- Public Cloud

Pattern: Platform Team

Create a team to be in charge of architecting, building, and running a single, consistent, and stable cloud native platform for use by the entire organization so that developers can focus on building applications instead of configuring infrastructure (Figure 8-3).

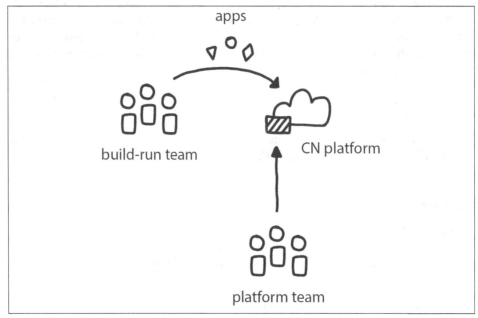

Figure 8-3. Platform Team

An enterprise is moving to the cloud and adopting microservices architecture. Many teams are building many different services, and they need extra tools to create the infrastructure to run their pieces of the application.

In This Context

If there is no single team in charge of creating an official cloud native production platform for the transformation, each team responsible for different microservices will have to build its own platform.

This duplicates effort, wastes time, and—most critically—sows conflict when it comes time to deploy. Because each service was built using a different approach on a bespoke platform, they will have conflicting needs and be difficult, if not impossible, to run all on one unified platform. Ops is stuck trying to come up with some kind of Frankenstein solution, but it's unlikely they will be able to make it work.

- Different teams will build different solutions if not coordinated.
- Basic cloud is not enough; complex and custom configuration is required.
- Standardization maximizes the possibility of reuse.
- Freedom of choice is needed for finding the best solutions.
- People are creative in finding ways to circumvent the roadblock set by lack of platform, leading to a "shadow IT" effect.

Therefore

The Platform Team will handle the platform itself—everything between the cloud and the apps (or, to put this in terms of the current technological landscape, Kubernetes and below)—while developers are responsible only for building the applications themselves (again, in the current tech landscape, Kubernetes and above).

- Set up a separate team responsible for choosing, building, and configuring a basic set of tools and practices to be used by all of the development teams.
- Build one platform to be used by the entire organization.
- Create a standard and reusable set of tools to simplify work for the devs.

Consequently

Developers are able to focus on building individual application services, features, and functionality while the Platform Team takes care of running the platform itself. Developers are allowed to introduce custom tools but they will have to support them as part of their own application unless the tools are proven stable and/or requested by other development teams.

+ There is a consistent, reusable, and, above all, stable platform that ensures all services work together seamlessly.

+ There is less work for developers: they can just focus on building apps and not worry about the platform they will run on.

− There is also less freedom for developers to choose their tools, although choice is still possible.

Common Pitfalls

The Platform Team forgets about its main goal of building a good and useful platform for the development teams and instead sets off to build the best ever, most scalable, and most technically amazing platform with availability of 99.999999%. Why? Because they can.

Imagine your company wants to build a nice three-story office building, but the architect comes back with a plan for a 100-story skyscraper. Constructing such a massive edifice would obviously be a crazy waste of time and money, right? Well, the same is happening with cloud native platforms.

Such projects get approved because managers don't fully understand the technology and fear confronting the head architect head-on. In most cases, early versions of the platform can be quite basic because the applications that are initially going to run on it are themselves quite basic. The quality and scalability of the platform should be built gradually as both the development teams and their applications mature and grow, and their actual platform requirements emerge more clearly.

Related Patterns

- Core Team
- Build-Run Teams
- Reference Architecture

Pattern: SRE Team

The SRE (Site Reliability Engineering) team helps the development teams to maintain and improve the application (not the platform or infrastructure) (Figure 8-4).

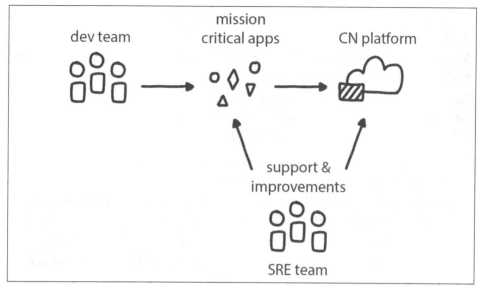

Figure 8-4. SRE Team

A big company has a large, mission-critical application with very high demands for quality and availability, and significant resources for creating dedicated improvement teams.

Once a platform is built and in production, attention is often directed away from improving internal processes and runtime performance. This can cause degradation over time, reducing quality and performance.

- Dev teams are measured on functionality, Ops on stability, SRE on improvements.

- SRE is a very expensive team to operate because it requires the most experienced and knowledgeable engineers.

- Opportunity cost arises when you pull your best engineers from development teams to SRE.

- If improvements are the priority for this team, then this is somewhat removed as a responsibility/priority for the Build-Run teams.

- SRE is more relevant when an application enters maintenance mode, rather than during the initial build.

Create a team that is focused 50% on reliability and 50% on continuous improvement of internal processes and development practices.

This SRE team worries about overall site (platform) availability. However, each individual service has its own operational needs as well. It can be helpful to add SREs into each individual build squad (or at least tribe) to focus on service availability.

- SRE engineers are in charge of improving whatever it takes to create better infrastructure, better runtime, and better user support.
- The SRE team makes the error budgets and helps the dev team define its operational model and the Platform Team to improve the platform.
- Most tasks are automation rather than manual support.
- Every 18 months the SRE team needs to automate everything it is doing manually (so it can move to the Platform Team's responsibility).
- You have a highly knowledgeable and experienced team, with good knowledge of operations but also devs who can write code.

Consequently

The runtime stability and quality is continuously increasing, and automation is also increasing.

+ Developers are aware of operational concerns and incorporate that knowledge into their development cycle.

+ The SRE team works closely with the Build-Run teams and the Platform Team.

− SRE teams are expensive and take top engineering talent away from other projects.

Common Pitfalls

Taking your best five engineers away from other work to try to capture the last 1% of performance gain.

Having an SRE team when the application has no actual need for this kind of improvement, instead of using that brainpower to build products. It's expensive in both money and opportunity cost, but people will do it anyway because they think they need an SRE team because other companies have them (Bandwagon effect). In such companies, SRE will typically not live up to the expectations and will forever remain a normal Ops team, only with a fancier title.

Related Biases

Bystander bias
> If no one is in charge of improving internal processes, improvement is not likely to happen. Conversely, if the SRE team is in charge of improvements, that takes some responsibility off Build-Run teams to optimize their contributions.

Bandwagon effect
> Everyone is talking about doing Kubernetes, so we'd better do it too!

Status quo bias
> It's working just fine, so let's just leave it alone (and changing something that works feels risky).

Related Patterns

- Build-Run Teams
- Platform Team
- Delayed Automation

Pattern: Remote Teams

If teams must be distributed, whether across a city or a continent, build in regular in-person retreats/work sessions as well as robust channels for close and free-flowing communication (Figure 8-5).

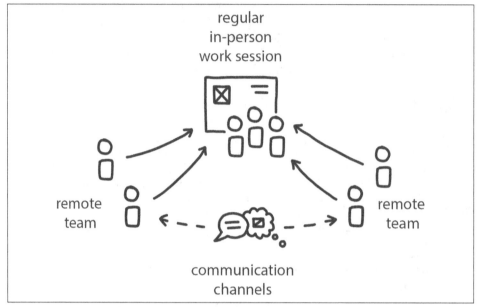

Figure 8-5. Remote Teams

A company is solving complex and relatively difficult business problems, and many team members are working remotely from one another.

In This Context

In many organizations remote team members may rarely, or even never, meet face to face. That works as long as the problems being solved by those teams are reasonably well-defined and not very complex. In the complex world of cloud native, however, problems are often messy and difficult, and require a more open-ended and collaborative approach.

Without a strong aim for collaborative co-creation, the team's ability to generate innovative solutions is typically limited to the creative abilities of individual team members working separately.

- Distributed workforces are increasingly common, and a team can have members scattered across a country, a continent, or the entire globe.
- The cloud native approach rests upon teams being given goals to achieve along with the freedom to decide how to execute them.
- In a predictable environment, little communication is required for executing stable workloads.
- Problem-solving without talking to anyone else means you are solving the problem separately, not collaboratively.

Therefore

Put programs in place to connect remote teams and bring them together in every way possible, both physically and virtually.

In the complex world of cloud native, problems are often messy and difficult, and require a more open-ended and collaborative approach. Working well this way requires in-person relationships, honest feedback, and close communication. If teams must be scattered, then regular face-to-face meeting times and other ways to connect the individual members need to be prioritized in order for them to be an effective cloud native workforce.

- Hold regularly scheduled in-person team retreats/gatherings/offsite work sessions.
- Open multiple channels of communication using tools like Slack to keep teams in constant and fluent contact.
- Make use of other tools like video conferencing, remote whiteboarding, and virtual *fika* sessions (see below) to keep members connected and working closely.
- In the end, there is no real substitute for personal interaction, sharing a meal, etc.
- If possible, don't distribute a team until it is already mature and has created strong internal connections.

Consequently

Teams see each other regularly in person and in between stay engaged via multiple channels and practices that promote fluent communication. Ideas are created, validated, and implemented in groups instead of coming from individuals.

+ Increased productivity and innovation are a natural outcome of closer ties with co-collaborators.

+ Regularly scheduled events—both daily hangout sessions and quarterly meet-ups—are easy to plan around so work is not disrupted.

– Offsite retreats, though important, are an additional operating expense.

Common Pitfalls

Confusing time spent sitting at one's desk with productivity. Swedish culture has a tradition known as *fika*. While it roughly translates to drinking coffee, in the workplace *fika* is a scheduled opportunity to connect and bond with others. To some work-obsessed cultures, stepping away from your desk to mingle with coworkers may sound like a waste of billable workday time units. However, recent data from the Organization for Economic Cooperation and Development suggests that Sweden's higher productivity rates per hours worked, compared with countries known for their long work hours such as the United States, Japan, and Korea, are at least in part due to *fika*.

Related Patterns

- Co-Located Teams
- Personalized Relationships for Co-Creation
- Communicate Through Tribes

Pattern: Co-Located Teams

Teams that work together in person develop naturally closer relationships and better collaborative problem-solving abilities, which in turn nurtures greater innovation (Figure 8-6).

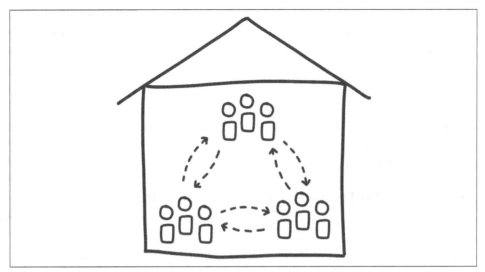

Figure 8-6. Co-located Teams

An organization that is moving to cloud native has multiple offices and office buildings. Teams that are targeted to move to cloud native have individual members located in multiple physical locations.

When team members are located in different places, they tend to communicate less and focus on their jobs rather than personal relationships. This hobbles team problem-solving, because individuals will attempt to solve problems separately and then contribute that solution back to the team—rather than solving them collaboratively with teammates.

- Creative teams especially are more effective when personal relationships are on a higher level.
- Complex communication is better in person.
- Cloud native is a paradigm shift that requires new ways of working and creative problem-solving.

All members of a given dev team will work in the same physical location and meet daily.

All meetings and collaboration will be first done using whiteboards, pen and paper, etc. Teams will be chosen based on location. If the team is in the same office, then move the members to sit at adjacent desks.

- Periodic team-building events to strengthen personal relationships.
- Encourage the team to talk to one another in person.
- Consider pair programming.

High level of trust and proximity naturally increases collaboration.

+ Quick and effective communication.

– Not always possible due to distribution of teams.

– Possibility of personal conflict exists.

Common Pitfalls

Assuming that just because people sit together, they are a team and will be effective working together. Team-building efforts are still required—see *Personalized Relationships for Co-Creation* for specific ways to create a bonded team.

Related Biases

Bandwagon effect
> The tendency to do (or believe) things because many other people do (or believe) the same thing can be a hazard in groups.

Bystander effect
> The tendency to think that others will act in an emergency situation translates, in the team context, to no one volunteering to take responsibility for a task unless it officially "belongs" to them.

Curse of knowledge
> A group of people sharing the same knowledge and experience tends to forget that others outside the group don't have access to that same knowledge base.

Shared information bias
> Group members are likely to spend more time and energy discussing information that all members are already familiar with (i.e., shared information). For example, the whole team did Docker training, so they spend a lot of time talking about Docker—and no time at all about Kubernetes, which is equally necessary

but they don't know much about it. To counter this, especially in new and complex environments, teams should learn new things all the time.

Related Patterns

- Personalized Relationships for Co-Creation
- Remote Teams
- Manage for Creativity
- Ongoing Education
- Communicate Through Tribes

Pattern: Communicate Through Tribes

Create groups of people who have similar skills but are on different teams to cross-pollinate ideas across the company and provide valuable whole-organization perspective (Figure 8-7).

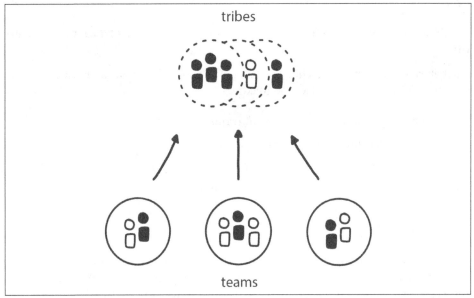

Figure 8-7. Communicate Through Tribes

A company is moving from a hierarchical Waterfall approach to the quickly evolving and complex world of cloud native. In traditional organizations, decision making and knowledge sharing are done according to hierarchy, and managers or lead architects are responsible for knowing everything about their assigned projects. In cloud native, however, engineers are given ownership over microservices and need to make decisions quickly and independently. Delivery processes are being fully automated.

In This Context

In a changing cloud native world, with ownership for application services divided across teams, managers don't know enough to provide effective advice, much less make good decisions. At the same time, managers have the illusion of knowledge and control—they don't know what they don't know—so the team's abilities and effectiveness are only as great as its manager's capability.

- Cloud native tech is complex and takes time to learn.
- Most delivery decisions in cloud native happen during automated delivery process or very close to it.
- Dependencies between teams and a need to get permission for any change slow down delivery.

Therefore

Create domain-specific tribes that operate outside of normal management hierarchy.

Use tribes to share specific technical and organizational info and to provide perspective and advice for complex decision making.

- Members of tribes belong to different teams.
- Meetings are regular and open-ended.
- Tribes play advisory and coordination roles but have no decision-making power.
- All the tribe members are knowledgeable in the tribe's domain.

Consequently

The company has groups that cross-cut traditional organizational units. This helps those people who are closest to and most knowledgeable in a particular domain subject identify areas for running experiments and making changes.

+ Tribe members share ideas and advise one another on issues and problems.

+ Managers have limited ability to intervene.

Common Pitfalls

Tribe meetings need to be interactive and discussion-oriented, but too many turn into "Here's some lunch while you watch this slide talk" sessions. This type of passive format stifles communication and the free exchange of ideas, which is the entire point of these meetings.

Related Biases

Curse of knowledge
> A group of people sharing the same knowledge and experience tends to forget that others outside the group don't have access to that same knowledge base.

Shared information bias
> Group members are likely to spend more time and energy discussing information that all members are already familiar with (i.e., shared information). For example, the whole team did Docker training, so they spend a lot of time talking about Docker—and no time at all about Kubernetes, which is equally necessary but they don't know much about it. To counter this, especially in new and complex environments, teams should learn new things all the time.

Related Patterns

- Co-Located Teams
- Remote Teams
- Personalized Relationships for Co-Creation

Pattern: Manage for Creativity

Teams charged with innovation need the open-ended freedom to experiment their way to solutions without pressure for delivering specific results on a set schedule—and the freedom to sometimes fail along the way (Figure 8-8).

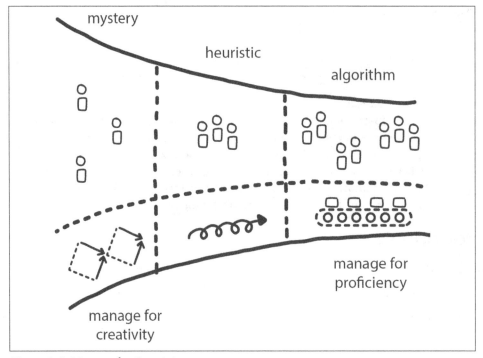

Figure 8-8. Manage for Creativity

The company is investing in all Three Horizons—H1, proficiency; H2, innovation; and H3, research. Some teams are working to deliver H1 core value and improve proficiency. Other teams are dedicated to innovation projects, which require a creative approach.

In This Context

Teams charged with identifying and building promising future products are often managed using the same known methodologies that are popular in the enterprises. One of the most common, Scrum, helps clarify what's going to be built and creates pressure to build it as fast as possible. Running endless numbers of strings without much reflection on the way drives most of the creativity out of the development project.

No inventor can tell when and what exactly she is going to invent.

- Creative thinking requires time and freedom to explore, and safety to fail.
- Startups tend to manage for creativity.
- Enterprises tend to strongly promote proficiency, speed, and quality of delivery.
- Scrum and similar methodologies create pressure to deliver and reduce free thinking.

Therefore

Manage the teams responsible for innovation by stating a purpose or desired outcome, which gives the team a direction toward which they will be creating new ideas. The team will require time, funding, and other resources to support its work, safety to fail, and autonomy to explore. Team dynamics will be more important than deadlines and delivery management.

Cloud native companies need creative thinkers. This new tech-driven environment requires companies to be innovative, flexible, and responsive. While many teams within the organization can be focused on delivering the core business product, at least one should be in charge of innovation. Because its job is to investigate likely next steps for the company's near future, it needs to work differently than the teams executing processes in the existing system.

- Psychological safety is essential for creativity to flourish.
- Purpose needs to be practical and achievable.
- Creative teams should be dedicated to innovation and have no regular delivery tasks.
- Innovation Champions are responsible for ushering projects that prove to be of value toward production, moving them along among the H1/H2/H3 teams. This role can be covered by the Designated Strategist or another person who can be officially responsible.

Innovation thrives in the company, and the innovative teams are separated from the proficient teams.

+ Creative teams have the opportunity to invent and the safety to fail.

– No certainty in delivery, but the projects are always time-bound.

– Difficult to predict results looking forward, but easy to measure success looking back.

Common Pitfalls

Taking creativity too far: digital transformation is the balance between innovation and pragmatism. When faced with the pressure to evolve due to some new disruptive competitor, some companies go all in on innovation and get lost. They miss the point of balance: you need to be *more* creative, not *all* creative. For example, Google is one of the most innovative companies in the world, but it has 2% creativity and 98% delivery. Companies that want to be like Google almost always get this backward, thinking Google is 98% creative, when in fact it is laser-focused on optimum delivery of its services.

Trying to manage creative teams to deliver in a proficient way, i.e., specific deliverables on a set schedule. This creates pressure to deliver and reduces the ability to think creatively. Creative teams under proficient management work hard to produce the illusion of innovation by performing many different tasks, but they rarely create any meaningful breakthroughs.

Related Biases

Shared information bias
If an innovation team is functioning under delivery pressure (that is, being managed for proficiency instead of creativity), it risks trying to speed things up by focusing on things it already knows about. In this context it can feel like there is no time for branching outward into new or untried possibilities.

Related Patterns

- Three Horizons
- Manage for Proficiency

- Learning Organization
- Reduce Cost of Experimentation

Pattern: Manage for Proficiency

Teams delivering stable and highly repetitive or algorithmic work should be managed for high quality and optimal efficiency (Figure 8-9).

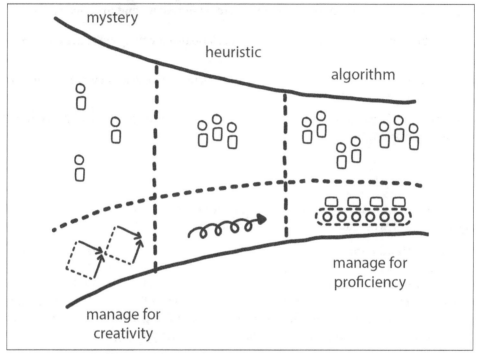

Figure 8-9. Manage for Proficiency

A transformation is underway. Some teams are working creatively to build the new system while other teams remain focused on keeping the existing system delivering the company's core products/services.

Alternatively, a cloud native transformation is at its end, and all the teams onboarded to the platform know very well what they are doing. They are ready to deliver excellent products to customers as fast as needed.

When the teams responsible for delivering stable and scalable products are given too much freedom to innovate and explore, they introduce new risks that harm product quality and increase the cost of development.

In many cases the new cloud native platform is not yet ready or stable enough to accommodate all the new teams, while most of the teams have to maintain old systems and release new incremental updates. Allowing those teams to start innovating too early may come at a significant cost to productivity and product quality.

- Established companies desire creativity because usually they don't have enough of it.
- Startups are highly creative yet desire proficiency because they are striving to build a consistent, deliverable product.
- The typical enterprise culture strongly supports a proficient, even algorithmic, way of working.

Therefore

Run the execution teams the way they have always been run. Focus on repeatability and optimize on quality and speed of delivery.

As an organization transforms itself into a cloud native entity, most teams will eventually need to evolve to cloud native's more flexible, intuitive, and problem-solving way of working. During the transition, however, there will be teams still tasked with delivery of the core business on the existing system while the new platform is built. It's important to keep the proficient teams proficient and run them as they have always been run, not changing to cloud native techniques yet.

Once a system (or new product) has left the innovation phase and is in steady production, most resources can typically be moved away from research and experimentation, and back to a mostly proficient approach.

- Let them know that they are valued: keeping existing product lines going at high quality is important to the business.
- Promise them that they will be onboarded to the new system when the time is right.
- Aim to create team pride around the best possible results and highest-quality products.
- Management of proficient teams requires high repetition, high feedback, and a strong sense of belonging.

- Emphasize that both types of teams are needed and important to the organization; avoid the perception or reality that creative work is rewarded more.

Teams in charge of delivering the company's profit-generating products/services in a proficient way are being managed to optimize this. Proficient and creative teams are loved and appreciated equally.

+ If the market changes in a large and/or frequent way, the company can shift resources into creativity and innovation when necessary. But creative is expensive, so drop back to proficient when things are stable/predictable.

– Some teams may need to work in the legacy codebase permanently (see "Lift and Shift at the End").

Common Pitfalls

Trying to train all the teams at the same time in the new cloud native tools and methods. Delays before a team is onboarded to the new system because it is still running the old one can sow frustration or, worse, fear among its members that they could be made redundant, or resentment that they are being left out. Also, training well before team members have a chance to practice new skills typically is a waste, and the training will need to be repeated later anyway. Keep managing these teams for the old proficient system until the time is right for them to move over.

Related Patterns

- Manage for Creativity
- Lift and Shift at the End
- Strangle Monolithic Organization

Pattern: Strangle Monolithic Organizations

Just as the new tools, technologies, and infrastructure gradually roll out over the course of a transformation initiative, the organization and its teams must also evolve to work with them properly (Figure 8-10).

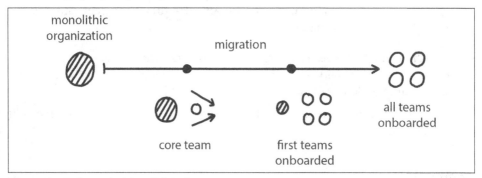

Figure 8-10. Strangle Monolithic Organizations

A cloud native transformation is in progress and some teams are moving to cloud native, while others may not move to cloud native for a long time.

In This Context

Migrating an existing company to the cloud can take years, and it happens very gradually.

There are two types of moves that rarely work. First, trying to move everyone over at once does not lend itself to good training. Without a solid background in the new tech, teams will be less effective and get frustrated over time or fall back on old habits that don't work well in cloud native. If the cultural and organizational change is not supported to evolve equally along with the cloud native technology, this also creates frustration.

Second, simply leaving one part of the organization in legacy while everyone else moves to cloud native stratifies the company so that the teams that never get moved to cloud native are stalled professionally. They'll never get to play with the cool new tech and build modern developer skills if they are left behind to babysit the legacy system. This, naturally, leads to frustration, resentment, and reduced motivation, not to mention difficulty hiring and retaining engineers.

- Cloud native transformation takes a long time.
- When people learn something, they need to apply it very soon.

- Tech and org/culture misalignment leads to frustration.
- People are motivated by hope of future improvements or frustrated by lack of hope.

Therefore

Move the teams from the legacy organizational structure to the new one gradually (Gradual Onboarding pattern). Restructure teams and change from hierarchy shortly before the new onboarding to the cloud native platform when it is fully ready.

This is an organizational version of Martin Fowler's architectural strangler pattern: Slowly strangle the process, and Waterfall cultural relics like specialized teams, along with the monolith itself. The two systems, old and new, can coexist well during the migration process. Once complete, the remaining pieces of the legacy system can be ported over to the new cloud native platform (Lift and Shift at the End) and gradually refactored into microservices until the old monolith is no more, and the maintainers are now experienced with cloud native.

- Educate constantly.
- Promote experimentation.
- Shift from hierarchy to tribes and delegation.
- Avoid training and restructuring if the team is not planning to move to cloud native soon.
- Create a plan for all legacy teams but execute only when the move is close.

Consequently

The old system keeps working as always while the new one is built, and teams are gradually moved over. Teams get restructured and retrained only when it is time for them to actually move. While you are on the old platform you keep delivering with excellence; then you move to the new one and deliver equally well there.

+ There is a clear plan for all the teams.

+ Organizational/cultural changes are aligned with tech changes.

+ Original and new cultures are coexisting but only temporarily until the full cloud native transfer is complete.

– Potential clashes between teams.

– Legacy teams could be disappointed by lack of change.

Related Patterns

- Decide Closest to the Action
- Communicate Through Tribes
- Lift and Shift at the End
- Gradual Onboarding
- Manage for Proficiency
- Ongoing Education
- Internal Evangelism

Pattern: Gradual Onboarding

One to three months before the new platform goes live, begin training a couple of teams at a time with a pause between each cohort to incorporate feedback and improve the process/materials (Figure 8-11).

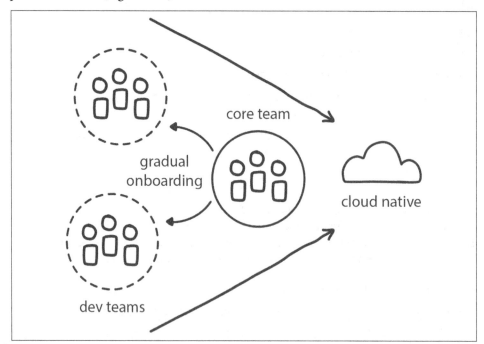

Figure 8-11. Gradual Onboarding

There is pressure from the top, the executives and board, to start using the cloud native platform as soon as possible and pressure from below, from the development teams, to move to cool technology. The company spent a lot of time and money building the new system, and everyone is eager to reap the rewards. Developers want to learn and use new technology.

Onboarding too many teams at once will stress the Core Team and reduce its ability to continue improving the platform. Educating people too early, however, will create anxiety in the teams and desire to start as soon as possible (and frustration if there is a long wait before the new system is available).

- A team that releases a tool on a large scale with low quality will struggle to improve it.
- People have little patience and are eager to apply recent learning.
- If you learn something new, you need to start using that knowledge soon or risk losing it.
- Good people may go to other companies to have a chance to work with the new and exciting technologies.

Therefore

Start small organizational changes early in the cloud native transformation. Prepare materials to onboard other teams and execute it slowly when teams are ready.

Continue onboarding the rest of the organization gradually over a period of 3 to 12 months.

- Start educating teams one to three months before onboarding.
- Prepare Developer Starter Packs and all relevant educational materials to simplify the onboarding.
- Onboard two to five teams at a time. Take breaks in between to use their feedback to improve the platform.
- Continuously improve the platform and the onboarding materials based on the feedback from the recently onboarded teams.

Consequently

The Core Team can support teams as they onboard and improve the process as they go. The first few teams onboarded to the platform can help educate and support the teams onboarded later.

– Some teams may not join for one to three years.

– Slower perception of scale.

Related Patterns

- Core Team
- Developer Starter Pack
- Ongoing Education
- Reference Architecture

Pattern: Design Thinking for Radical Innovation

Whether faced with a radical new idea or a big problem, Design Thinking can be used as a process for first brainstorming a robust list of solutions and then narrowing it down to the best possibilities for actual exploration (Figure 8-12).

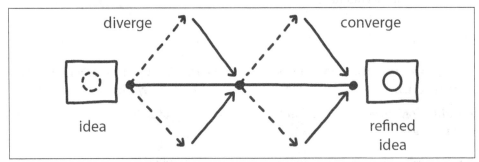

Figure 8-12. Design Thinking for Radical Innovation

We have a big idea or a difficult problem that may change the business. There are possible solutions, but also many uncertainties.

In This Context

When faced with a problem, people typically spend only the minimum time required to find the first satisfactory solution, even if it's not the best one or doesn't involve all stakeholders. This leads to reasonable solutions, but misses the opportunity to find excellent ones.

- Law of preservation of cognitive energy leads people to choose the first good solution.

- Developers typically are decision makers on tech solutions.
- Devs aren't trained in business or market forces.
- Elegance and beauty are also relevant for internal systems.

Take the basic first idea and run it through a series of divergent and convergent thinking exercises to rethink the idea's boundaries and explore alternatives.

Ideation/brainstorming is followed by application experiments. In-depth explanation of Design Thinking is beyond the scope of this pattern, but guidelines for running Design Thinking workshops can be found online[2]

- Create 10 to 20 new solutions/problems/ideas based on the first idea, narrow that list to the two to three best ones. Then expand and iterate these two to three best ones into 10 to 20 new possible variations, and then again choose two to three of the most promising to run longer experiments and choose to implement.
- Hold regular Design Thinking workshops.
- Use the workshops to refine big ideas/problems.
- Invite major stakeholders.
- Facilitate collaboration to help excellent solutions emerge.

Ideas are thoroughly explored. Cost of initial exploration is still low, as it requires little to no actual development (No Regret Moves).

- Too many people involved slows down the decision-making process.

Common Pitfalls

People without experience in running Design Thinking workshops may end up running them more like Scrum planning exercises. Instead of helping with a wider exploration and evaluation of new and often radical ideas, it reaffirms the existing leading solution and effectively becomes an execution-planning session. A correctly led Design Thinking workshop does not have to lead to a new solution, but its main pur-

---

2 Introductory article on Design Thinking (*http://bit.ly/2sgeK5B*), with links to resources and many expert facilitators are available to run high-quality workshops.

pose is to question the assumption of the problem and brainstorm a variety of possible solutions.

Related Biases

Ambiguity effect
> The tendency to avoid options for which missing information makes the probability of the outcome seem "unknown."

Confirmation bias.
> Picking test variables that will "prove" your existing opinion, rather than genuinely exploring alternatives.

Related Patterns

- Involve the Business
- Vision First
- Exploratory Experiments
- PoCs
- Reduce Costs of Experimentation

Pattern: Agile for New Development (Innovation Breaks)

Balance proficiency and innovation by building a separate time for each into your development cycle (Figure 8-13).

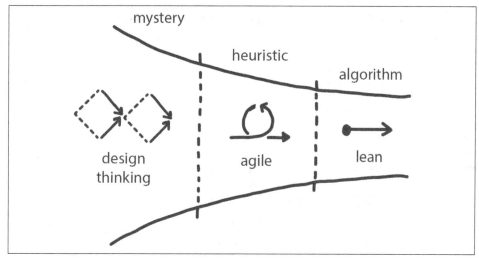

Figure 8-13. Agile for New Development

Strategy is defined and solution direction is chosen after experimentation. There are still many uncertainties and not all knowledge is available within the team.

Teams are either endlessly researching and collecting information or, conversely, starting to deliver and optimize very early. In the first case, value is delivered to customers late, ends up being of poor quality, or never gets delivered at all. In the second case, the solutions are too simple and underdeveloped and miss the opportunity to solve customer problems.

- Many processes aiming to increase productivity attempt to do so by pushing out innovation.
- Radical innovation and proficient delivery can't be done in the same way.
- Innovation without delivery is academic research.
- Delivery without innovation is blind to market changes.

Run alternating iterations of research and development.

Spend about 20%–30% of the time running proof-of-concept experiments and other research activities. Use the rest of the time to implement the discovered solutions and increase the quality.

- Every third or fourth sprint in Scrum should be used for research.
- 20%–30% of Kanban backlog should be dedicated to innovation and improvement tasks.
- When a solution is not clear, use experiments or PoCs to discover and eliminate options.

Consequently

Delivery and innovation are separate and in balance.

+ Team can still change product direction relatively easily.

+ Quality of the products constantly increases.

− One-third of the time is not immediately monetized.

Common Pitfalls

Using Scrum by the book without leaving any space for PoCs and innovation. This leads to team exhaustion and to overly high focus on delivery too early in product development.

Related Biases

Status quo bias
It's always worked to do it this way before, so let's just keep doing that. It might not be optimal, but we know it works (and changing something that works feels risky).

Related Patterns

- Three Horizons
- PoCs
- Exploratory Experiments
- Dynamic Strategy
- Manage for Creativity
- Reflective Breaks
- Gradually Raising the Stakes

Pattern: Lean for Optimization

When a stable system delivers the value that's intended and is not a target for technical innovation, focus on improving the system by continuously and incrementally improving delivery and maintenance processes with emphasis on repeatability (Figure 8-14).

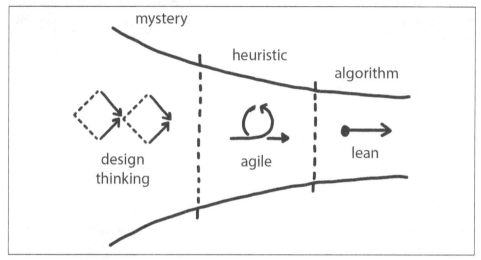

Figure 8-14. Lean for Optimization

Your product is stable and in demand (a "Cash Cow" on the BCG growth-share matrix), and it is in a state of incremental improvement and support. Tech used in the product is known and well-understood. All capabilities are present in the team.

In This Context

Innovation and evolution are inevitable in technology. However, there is little need to innovate when a proficient system is delivering stable value and maintenance cost is low. And we often see that, in an otherwise proficient system, the team continues to introduce new tools and solutions that constantly destabilize the product while needlessly consuming time and budget.

- Repeatability leads to boredom.
- Quality demands investment.
- Creativity and proficiency require different management frameworks.
- Proficiency and mastery require repeatability and standards.
- Creativity requires freedom and psychological safety for generating experimentation.

Reduce work in progress, focus on optimizing delivery process, measure quality and speed of delivery, and aim to improve both.

Lean management optimizes proficiency and value to customers while eliminating anything that does not bring value to the end product/service and ensuring continuous incremental improvement.

- Use Kanban with optimization and new features backlog.
- Measure everything that matters.
- Optimize price versus performance ratio.
- Optimize proficient processes.
- Automate repeatable tasks.

Consequently

Delivery is fast and proficient. System is stable, and quality is consistently going up.

+ No destruction of an efficient system.

+ Gradually increasing quality.

− Very limited innovation.

− Some people are bored.

Related Biases

Pro-innovation bias

"This brand new tool/technique must be better than these boring old ones we have been using!"

Related Patterns

- Manage for Proficiency
- Measure What Matters
- Three Horizons

Pattern: Internal Evangelism

Provide plenty of information about the transformation across the entire company right from the start to create understanding, acceptance of, and support for the initiative (Figure 8-15).

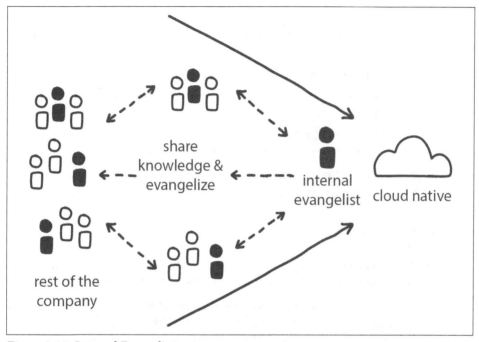

Figure 8-15. Internal Evangelism

Cloud native transformation is underway, and the Core Team is working hard to understand the challenge and build a high-quality platform with a clear way to onboard old and new applications to it. The rest of the teams are not yet involved in the transformation, and it may take a few months, even a year, before they are all onboarded to the cloud native new platform.

In This Context

When there is little information about an ongoing cloud native transformation, people don't automatically assume it's a good idea. People don't resist the transformation because they think it is the wrong thing to do—they resist because it is new and scary. Change creates anxiety, and most people just don't know much about cloud native in general. Without clarity, people tend to fill in the gaps with imaginary negative information (negative attribution bias), and they may fear their jobs will be dramatically different—or even eliminated.

Most people enter the transformation process from a traditional Waterfall hierarchy. In such organizations, managers have always just told them what to do. Cloud native teams, however, are highly independent and so require full participation and active involvement from all members. Without motivation to learn and do it right, the result could be disastrous for the company, as only a few teams will fully embrace the cloud native way of working.

- People have a lot of ways to resist by dragging their feet or even actively sabotaging an initiative.
- People need to be encouraged to behave differently.
- Punishment works to stop behaviors, but it will not work to inspire and engage people with new behaviors.
- People do not automatically receive a new message. They need many touch points to hear the new story until they accept and internalize it.
- Negative attribution bias: if you aren't telling them about the change, they assume no progress is being made/nothing is happening.

Therefore

Share positive, clear, and abundant information about the transformation to create acceptance, support, and even excitement across the company.

Metamorphosing an organization's tech and especially culture is a tribal movement. If people are not sure whether it's a good idea, then you need to help them understand. Negative attribution bias can be powerful here: without enough info, you fill in the gaps with negativity. The solution is to fill in the gaps with a lot of information all the time—not just about what is happening, but why, how these changes will benefit the entire organization.

- Organize events, send newsletters, show demos. Essentially, do internal marketing.
- Tell the story over and over in a positive and inspirational way, rather than a "do this or else" way.
- Internal Evangelism should be led by someone who is committed and knowledgeable and involved. This person makes it public, involves people, and creates the movement.
- It's imperative the evangelist demonstrates good knowledge of the business itself and what it does now, so their opinion is trusted as being informed and based on thoughtful judgment.

- The Transformation Champion is a possible candidate for this role, but only if it does not distract from their duties leading the transformation itself.

The transformation is understood across the organization, and people feel motivated to join and support it. There is plenty of time and opportunity to mitigate any resistance originating through fear of uncertainty.

+ People have had time to get comfortable with the idea.

+ The message starts out very simple and gradually grows more detailed as both the project and the acceptance progress.

+ Small projects and experiments are opportunities for evangelism.

Common Pitfalls

No one actually promotes the initiative across the whole organization. Engineers may be hacking around building amazing systems but then they never talk about it. They don't think it's their job to tell others, but it is—part of the job of building anything is to make it successful. Not just rolling it out one day, but telling people what you are doing and why. The best way to see cloud native transformation is to consider it an internal startup that not only needs to build the platform but also to sell to internal customers.

The management version of this is to buy a very expensive, comprehensive tool and just force it on everyone, including the team that just built a very nice, small-scale custom solution that is perfect for the company's needs. This is actually one of the biggest problems in transformations and easily avoidable with Internal Evangelism— yet very few companies do it.

Related Biases

Curse of knowledge
Transformation information has to be understandable to the people you are seeking to sway. You already know you need to simplify the message when broadcasting cloud native transformation info across the organization. But because you are deeply involved in the initiative, with expert knowledge level of 9 on a scale of 10, you boil the message down to 5 or 6 when talking to others, even if they only understand it to maybe 2.

Negative attribution bias. People assume that if they are hearing nothing about the transformation, then no progress is being made/nothing is happening.

Related Patterns

- Transformation Champion
- Executive Commitment

Pattern: Ongoing Education

Continuously introduce new ways and improve existing ones to help teams continually develop their cloud native knowledge and skills (Figure 8-16).

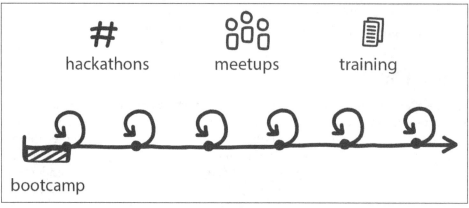

Figure 8-16. Ongoing Education

The company is moving to cloud native, and some teams have never worked with cloud native technology or processes. In their previous environment, knowledge and learning were reasonably stable and linear (learn a bit and exploit the knowledge a lot).

Other teams are already deep into building the cloud native platform or microservices and so have gained basic cloud native knowledge, but still are not advanced enough to support the entire transformation.

People are joining the organization's cloud native initiative without fully understanding the possibilities it offers or the wide variety of solutions available. New technology is introduced all the time that renders current tools and techniques out of date. When this happens, productivity suffers, and change slows down.

- Only some people are motivated to learn on their own.

- People learn better in groups.
- Formal education is more effective after some initial exposure to/experience with new information.
- Most people need to learn something a few times before they fully understand it.
- The cloud native ecosystem is changing fast.

Therefore

Build and continuously run an education program about cloud native for everyone in the company, from basic education for newly onboarded or new joiners to continuous and more advanced trainings for more experienced engineers.

- Onboarding bootcamps
- Hackathons
- Periodic knowledge updates
- Management trainings
- Online self-learning opportunities
- Books, blog posts, and other reading
- On-the-job learning by pair programming, whiteboarding, etc.

Consequently

Team knowledge is constantly refreshed and updated.

+ Easy ways to roll out new information.

+ A lot of inspiration arises for trying out changes.

+ Developers are better able to adapt to technology shifts.

+ Technology changes, which are inevitable, will be minimally disruptive since developers are better able to adapt to shifts in tech.

+ By disseminating best practices and successful ways of using technology, you can replicate success and avoid missteps.

− There is cost related to frequent education.

Common Pitfalls

In most companies, teams onboarded to the cloud native platform would typically get at least some training, even if it is very simple and incomplete. The more common problem is with the engineers who are perceived to be cloud native experts after spending 6 to 12 months building the initial cloud native platform. While they would know significantly more about the cloud native field than their peers, they still need to learn much more before they become real experts. Engineers working in the cloud native field, and any other innovative areas, should continue their education indefinitely.

Related Biases

Authority bias
> The tendency to attribute greater accuracy to the opinion of a perceived authority figure, whether or not they are truly expert, and thus be more influenced by that opinion. In this situation, the company may overly rely on the perceived expertise of the Core Team in making key decisions, when they might not yet have sufficient knowledge and experience to make informed choices.

Related Patterns

- Learning Organization
- Internal Evangelism
- Demo Apps
- Gradual Onboarding

Pattern: Exploratory Experiments

When dealing with a complex problem with no obvious available solution, run a series of small experiments to evaluate the possible alternatives and learn by doing (Figure 8-17).

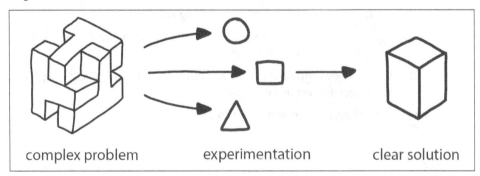

complex problem   experimentation   clear solution

Figure 8-17. Exploratory Experiments

The challenge is new and complex, and the team can't solve it by using its existing knowledge or through simple research (i.e., you can't Google it). There is not enough information to make the next step, much less a proper decision.

In This Context

Committing too early to a solution you don't yet fully understand. Teams are likely to do one of three things: Choose a known solution that is not a good fit for the problem, because they are familiar with this solution; undertake a lengthy analysis of the solution that leads nowhere (analysis paralysis); or else jump on the first available solution (availability bias).

- In Waterfall all questions need to be answered before actions are taken.
- People learn best by doing.
- Difficult problems are better solved by a team.

Therefore

Explore the problem space. Mitigate the risk by delaying critical decisions long enough to run a series of small scientific-style experiments to uncover missing information and evaluate alternatives.

Each experiment should have a hypothesis that can be proved or disproved by the experiment. When a hypothesis is disproved, the experiment itself can still be called a success. It is critical to avoid assigning blame or punishing those involved in the experiment in cases where the results are not satisfactory.

- Identify one problem/idea and choose two to five small—taking a few hours to a few days—experiments to test it.
- Form a hypothesis to query: *What is my problem in the first place, does this solve it, what is the cost, and can we afford it?*
- Identify and compare possible alternative solutions.
- Establish clear and measurable criteria for success or failure. Collect data and evaluate it.

Consequently

The team is granted time and given a process for experimenting with solutions when it encounters a complex problem.

+ Teams learn by doing this, which helps them in future decisions and work.

+ By showing a small, quick success with an experiment, you are able to make a first small and easy step in a new direction.

− When experiments are cheap and easy enough to run, it can be hard to determine when it is time to stop experimenting and make a decision/move forward.

Common Pitfalls

If the problem is known or the solution is simple, running experiments is a waste of time and a diversion from actual work. Avoid experimentation simply for the sake of experimenting.

Can lead to endless experimentation and analysis paralysis when no decisions are made, as there are always plenty of assumptions to test and tools to evaluate.

Focusing on tactical experiments (which server to provision, which tool to choose) instead of tackling the big, difficult problem.

When there are multiple options but only one is realistic or available, experimentation is a waste of time if the path is already determined.

Introducing experimentation in teams that will not be moving to the new system soon can create unrest.

Related Biases

Confirmation bias
> The risk of running experiments to prove a point instead of checking alternatives. If you are testing only one hypothesis, you're not experimenting. You are jumping to a solution because it's easier, which is S1 thinking. This book's entire purpose is to point you to S2 (see Chapter 4: Behavior and Biases).

Shared information bias
> Everyone talks only about the things that are already commonly known and then chooses a solution without considering and experimenting with lesser-known alternatives.

Information bias
> The tendency to seek information even when it cannot affect action. You need to limit the experiments and make decisions at the end of the experiment to avoid analysis paralysis.

IKEA effect
> If you get teams involved in building an experiment, there will be a bigger commitment to the idea, for two reasons. First, they may be reluctant to abandon an experimental version even when it is complete, because they built it themselves.

Second, involvement in building the early portions of a new cloud native system can generate greater ownership of and support for the entire transition initiative.

Irrational escalation/Sunk-cost effect
Keeping experiments small before making a decision makes it easier to drop the results of any given experiment because there has only been a small investment.

Status quo.
Can use this as a nudge: by showing a small, quick success you can take a first small and easy step away from the status quo.

Parkinson's law of triviality, a.k.a. "Bikeshedding"
Choosing something easy but unimportant to test and evaluate, over something else that is complex and difficult but meaningful.

Related Patterns

- Proof of Concept (PoC)
- Reduce Cost of Experimentation
- Design Thinking for Radical Innovation
- Learning Organization
- Blameless Inquiry
- Manage for Creativity

Pattern: Proof of Concept (PoC)

Before fully committing to a solution that can significantly affect the future, build a small prototype to demonstrate viability and gain a better understanding (Figure 8-18).

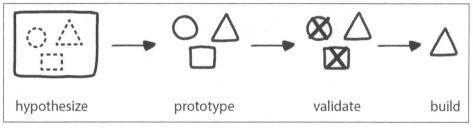

Figure 8-18. Proof of Concept

You have run experiments and identified a solution path that you think could be the right one, but there are still some big unknowns. You are at a decision point: adopt this solution, or not?

Once some initial experiments have uncovered a likely transformation path, it is time to test it. Committing to it right now could, if it is wrong, cause large problems and expense as the initiative continues.

You simply don't know enough to make a large commitment at this point. Any full commitment right now carries massive risk because switching to an alternative later will be very difficult. Adopting a solution you don't fully understand too early in the process compounds the risk, because you will continue to build further functionality on top of this solution.

- Hands-on work, rather than promises or explanations, is better for demonstrating value to skeptics.
- Changing early decisions is costly in the later stages of a migration project.

Therefore

Build a basic functional prototype to demonstrate the viability of a solution. Define the questions that need answers before starting the PoC and stop the work once the questions are answered.

- This should take a few days to a few weeks.
- Build the most primitive version you can get away with. Be ready to throw it away when you are finished. (This doesn't that mean you *must* throw it away, but often when initial quality is intentionally low, it's cheaper and easier to just scrap it and rebuild from scratch).
- Only work on hard issues related to the specific needs of the current project, and stop when the solution is clear.
- Try to demo something functional so you can collect business-related information regarding how this solution will impact future development.

Consequently

Risk is reduced for the overall project in the early stages of the migration. Critical knowledge and experience are gained during the experimentation process.

+ You have gained the knowledge and proved the solution works, and now understand how it fits into the overall project.

+ You now have reasonable confidence that this is the correct decision.

– Running PoCs carries cost. Every time you do it, you pay for it.

Common Pitfalls

Can be used to enforce existing beliefs (confirmation bias). This is how most PoCs are run, unfortunately—only one option is tested.

A team spends three days proving a concept and has the answer, but keeps going to reach a fully functional version. This is a waste of time. Once you understand it and the solution has proved viable, pull the plug and move on. Doing this is especially difficult for engineers.

You take the prototype to production, even though it was intended as a basic experiment.

Related Biases

Sunk-cost fallacy
> Once you've put this much effort into something, you just want to keep going even though you have your answer already.

Confirmation bias
> You think you already know the right answer so you embrace the information that supports your opinion (while ignoring any inconvenient facts that might disprove it).

Related Patterns

- Exploratory Experiments
- MVP
- Gradually Raising the Stakes
- No Regret Moves
- Options and Hedges
- Big Bet
- Objective Setting

Pattern: MVP Platform

Once Exploratory Experiments and PoCs have uncovered a probable path to success, build a simple version of a basic but fully functional and production-ready platform with one to three small applications running on it in production (Figure 8-19).

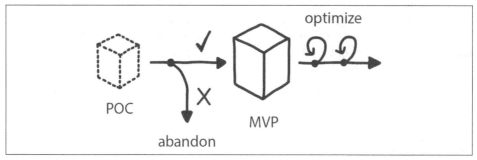

Figure 8-19. MVP Platform

The goal is clear, the tech is available, and knowledge is present, and all major questions are answered by a series of PoCs. Now is the time to build a real platform. Development teams are on hold and waiting for the new platform to start building new applications and refactoring old ones.

In This Context

Trying to add too many functions to the first release will make it very protracted and delay any release to production.

In the traditional Waterfall approach a new platform will be used in production only if it's fully finished and everything is ready. Building a fully featured cloud native platform may take up to three years, but since cloud native components work independently, the platform can be running apps in production even before it's completely built out. Not using the platform or any of its features until it is 100% complete would be a lost opportunity.

- Minimum basic functionality could be built in a fraction of the time it takes to build the full system.
- There is always something to remove from the list of critical features.
- Custom complex solutions are difficult to build and maintain.

Define and build a system with minimal useful—and production-ready—functionality on a quick timeline. It's important to release something quickly in order to start getting real feedback so you can then improve things based on that user response.

- "Minimal usefulness" can vary per company.
- Cloud native Platform MVP should take two to six months to produce.
- Build good basics and quality to reduce the need for user support, but don't go overboard.
- Extendability is critical.
- Plan additional two to three phases to bring the platform to full functionality.
- Use experiments and PoCs to define the MVP.
- Stress assumptions in real life—build a system that works with how people will need and want to use it.

The first MVP of the platform is ready and can be used by a small number of development teams to deliver a few apps to production. The Platform Team has a plan to expand the scale and functionality of the platform as it continues rolling it out to the rest of the organization.

+ Teams can begin learning the basics of using a cloud native platform even while the final production version is still being developed.

− The MVP represents 20%–40% of the final platform; further effort is still required to build out a complete, production-ready platform.

− Core team needs to do support for this version while continuing to develop the production platform that will eventually replace it.

Related Biases

Default effect
The Core Team will need to carefully configure the platform to be as optimal as possible before beginning to onboard the first teams. Users tend to simply accept the default options and settings provided to them as "the way to do things," and only an adventurous few will try changing or customizing them.

Related Patterns

- Exploratory Experiments
- Proof of Concept (PoC)

Pattern: Decide Closest to the Action

Those nearest to a change action get the first chance to make any decisions related to it (Figure 8-20).

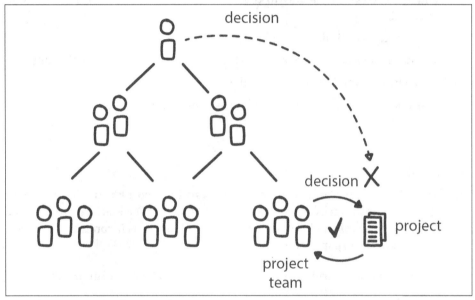

Figure 8-20. Decide Closest to the Action

Cloud native transformation is underway, and there is a lot of uncertainty. People are still learning about the tech, which itself is continually evolving, and the market is changing frequently and erratically. Each team is responsible for delivering its own microservice, and there are many moving pieces. Managers and lead architects have only a broad, high-level understanding of the product and little grasp of the technical details that underlie the actual development process.

In This Context

Decision making via chain of command is not sustainable in cloud native. Using hierarchy to resolve conflicts and agree on decisions takes too long, and solutions are limited to the capabilities of the managers making that level of decision. Engi-

neers might find a superior solution that never gets implemented because it takes too much time and effort to navigate the bureaucracy to get permission. So they will give up and just move on with whatever they have.

- Recent speed of technological change is growing exponentially.
- Market is now also changing frequently, with unexpected new competitors appearing.
- In traditional organizations, managers make all the decisions and give instructions to engineers.
- Further you go from the change, the slower the decision over time.

Push the decision power as close as possible to any change as it is happening. It is typically best if the dev team itself makes the decisions.

Because your team works as part of a bigger tribe of teams, sometimes your decision must involve others. For example, if you want to change APIs, you must inform those who use them—and they may object to the change. So whatever happens inside of a microservice is fully the domain of its development team, but anything going in/out is also the domain of the teams that consume them.

- Put in place security and regulation to make sure people are allowed to make these decisions.
- Complete separation of duties: execs in charge of strategy, managers in charge of setting objectives, engineers free to execute their work as they see best.
- Instill that it's OK to fail into the organization's values.
- Use hierarchical management for conflict resolution.

Executives delegate the power to create the vision and objectives to middle management, and middle managers delegate power over technical decisions to the execution teams.

+ Strong incentive to resolve conflicts first within team, then within tribe, only then go to management.

– Time and effort are required to coordinate with any teams who are consuming your particular service to make sure it works all around.

Common Pitfalls

Punishment for failure is the biggest mistake in most organizations. In cloud native, decision making happens fast and frequently, and mistakes are inevitable. Penalizing people when they make mistakes dramatically reduces their willingness to try new things, and they will move more slowly to avoid making errors. They will ask for permission, which will slow down or kill all innovation. If someone keeps failing in the same way, then there is need to intervene—but the company culture needs to allow failure without consequences.

Managers, especially executives, are used to being in charge and dictating solutions. In cloud native, leaders need to learn that teams often experiment their way to solutions and the path is not always clear. From the outside this can look like a lack of progress. It takes patience to let people make these decisions on their own, but higher-ups often feel frustrated and jump in to "fix" things too soon—thus derailing the team's progress and learning.

In this pitfall we find a CEO who is too impatient for results or middle managers who can't understand the strategy. In either situation the CEO feels compelled to step over the middle managers and micromanage the team. This sows confusion in the teams and undermines the middle managers, while dragging the CEO into a tactical hell.

Sometimes the executive team is too slow coming up with the strategy. In response, the rest of the company will usually just settle into the inertia or create their own guiding organizational strategy, which in turn is often shortsighted and causes more problems than it solves.

Related Biases

Law of the instrument
> An overreliance on familiar tools or methods, ignoring or undervaluing alternatives. "If all you have is a hammer, everything looks like a nail."

Related Patterns

- Communicate Through Tribes
- Dynamic Strategy
- Blameless Inquiry
- Research Through Action
- Value Hierarchy

Pattern: Productive Feedback

People are more engaged and creative when they feel comfortable receiving constructive information about their behavior and giving the same in return (Figure 8-21).

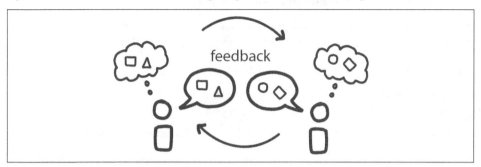

Figure 8-21. Productive Feedback

You have a team whose main responsibility requires creative or innovative work.

In This Context

People are often blind to their own biases and live in their own bubble without realizing it.

During a cloud native transformation, teams that have always worked in a proficient way now are tasked with innovation. They have no experience being creative, so they will keep using past solutions to attempt to solve new problems.

Lacking external perspective you will be blind to your own confirmation bias and interpret results to fit your preconceived notions, leading the project to very poor results. At the same time, other people within the organization can clearly see the problems before they happen.

- Judgmental tendencies are hardwired.
- Most people don't give positive feedback unless prompted to do so.
- Without empathy, feedback can be perceived as aggression or attack.
- For people who have never given feedback it can be difficult to start.
- An existing team has already solidified their relationships and will find it difficult to change their behavior.
- Significant feedback requires some level of personal relationship.

Create a safe environment and simplify ways for people to give feedback—positive, negative, even confrontational—in a constructive way.

Facilitate team activities to build personal connections between team members; this helps to create a sense of mutual trust that allows feedback to flow freely.

- Offer training or tools to teach people how to give constructive feedback.
- Create opportunities, such as one-on-one or group meetings or weekly email updates on the project, to exercise giving constructive feedback.
- If someone is doing something well, feel comfortable giving them praise.
- If you think someone is taking a wrong approach, tell them in a constructive way.
- Someone needs to act as leader to model how to do all this.
- Psychological safety is an essential prerequisite for Productive Feedback.

Consequently

Productivity goes up because people can learn and improve their work and behavior, and because they feel seen and appreciated.

– There are costs involved: honest and constructive feedback relies on personal relationships and psychological safety.

– High risk of personal conflict, but this is the chance you have to take if you really want to go fast. People will learn on their own without feedback, but it will take a lot longer, and some things they will never learn on their own.

Common Pitfalls

In a proficient delivery system Productive Feedback has little value because the process is algorithmic and innovation is not desired. Over time, the unspoken rule becomes "just shut up and do your own thing," and this becomes part of the culture in traditional companies. In the creative environment required for a cloud native transformation, however, Productive Feedback is essential. People don't really know how they are doing, and without feedback they can keep going in the wrong direction simply because it's their best guess and they have no other information. We see this all the time in big organizations building a new platform that works well for the team building it but does not fit what other stakeholders need. Since they never expose the work in progress to feedback, however, this problem emerges only at the very end.

Related Biases

Blind spot bias
> People can spot others' biases, but not their own.

Confirmation bias
> Seeking to "prove" your existing opinion, rather than genuinely exploring alternatives.

Related Patterns

- Psychological Safety
- Personalized Relationships for Co-Creativity
- Learning Organization
- Blameless Inquiry

Pattern: Psychological Safety

When team members feel they can speak up, express concern, and make mistakes without facing punishment or ridicule, they can think freely and creatively, and are open to taking risks (Figure 8-22).

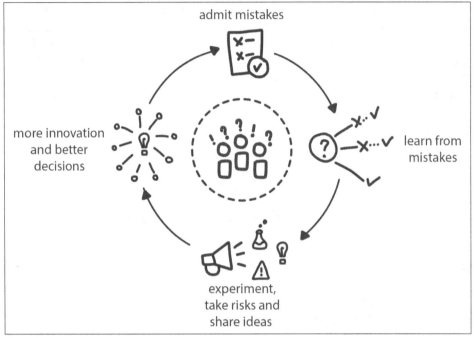

admit mistakes

more innovation and better decisions

learn from mistakes

experiment, take risks and share ideas

Figure 8-22. Psychological Safety

A company is about to embark on a complex journey toward cloud native. The path is uncertain and strewn with problems that the team has never encountered. The team needs to take a collaborative problem-solving approach, learn together, and push one another to think creatively.

In This Context

In traditional enterprises that are mostly designed to support stability, people fear exposing themselves by asking a "stupid" question, suggesting a "crazy" idea, or giving difficult feedback to a teammate, let alone a manager. All such actions typically are dismissed and ridiculed or, even worse, punished.

In such an environment people tend to keep their ideas to themselves until they're fairly certain they will be welcomed by others. That means the best and newest ideas might never have a chance of being adopted. And since many new ideas seem a bit crazy and risky in the beginning, the team never gets a chance to really innovate.

- Experimentation requires honest assessment.
- Fear of failure generates resistance to trying new tools or techniques.
- Many attempts to discover new things will fail.
- In hierarchical organizations, people at all levels tend to hide information that could be harmful for their own careers.
- If teams lack the ability to fail safely when experimenting, they must waste time analyzing all future outcomes to minimize exposing themselves to risk.

Therefore

Create the shared value that no group member will ever be punished or humiliated for speaking up with ideas, questions, concerns, or mistakes.

In the workplace, psychological safety among teams means that the members believe they can express ideas, concerns, or mistakes without being punished or humiliated for it. As a result, they are willing to express new or different ideas, even if they diverge from overall group opinion. When we feel safe, we become more open-minded, resilient, motivated, and persistent. A sense of humor is encouraged, as is solution-finding and divergent thinking—the cognitive process underlying creativity. This creates the confidence necessary for trying and failing and then trying again. It also shuts down time-wasting risk-avoidance behaviors like trying to find a solution that is absolutely going to work before you even start trying it out. In cloud native that solution does not even exist, anyway.

- Many discoveries look odd and "stupid" at first glance.
- In an environment with high trust, people will feel confident in speaking up.
- Creativity occurs much more often in high-trust environments.

Consequently

People can propose new methods or approaches knowing that their ideas will be treated respectfully.

+ Team members can put forward "wild and crazy" ideas without fear of shaming or embarrassment.

+ Even when experiments fail, learning from them via Blameless Inquiry feeds further improvements.

– Creating psychological safety in an organization requires intentional invest-ment of time and effort.

Related Patterns

- Productive Feedback
- Blameless Inquiry
- Learning Organization
- Manage for Creativity
- Personalized Relationships for Co-Creation

Pattern: Personalized Relationships for Co-Creation

Solutions to complex problems are best created collaboratively by teams with high levels of interpersonal connection (Figure 8-23).

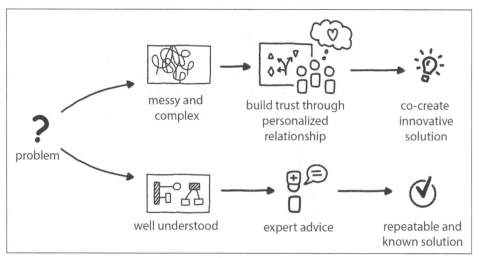

Figure 8-23. Personalized Relationships for Co-Creation

The team is working on the more creative part of the implementation and still is only partially knowledgeable about it. There are no immediate answers, and the future is not clear or predictable. Teams are based on personal expertise and have clear roles and responsibilities.

In uncertain environments, what worked in the past may not work here, so you need to invent rather than attempt to reuse existing solutions.

- Creativity requires trust and volunteering information.
- By default people will use existing knowledge to solve a problem.
- People will not volunteer information to an expert.
- They will only volunteer when there is trust and a personalized connection.
- New solutions are best achieved in highly collaborative, small creative teams.

Therefore

In complex environments where there is no clear path forward, a strong team needs personalized relationships to collaborate on creative solutions. Creativity is not the goal—co-creation is the goal. Creativity is open-ended and may not lead to anything, but co-creation generates results.

Cloud native is better suited to co-creative relationships where the team itself collaborates on the future solution with all team members participating. People are solving the problem together rather than relying on the expert advice of individual members.

Co-creation teams are significantly more innovative and creative because people are thinking together and drawing from group understanding and experience. They work by building mutual trust, volunteering extra information, and being willing to take risks as a group.

- To create closer relationships, literally reduce the physical distance between team members. Teams should share the same workspace whenever possible.
- Run trust-building experiences, bringing people together to build personal relationships.
- Encourage collaboration and co-creation by working in groups.

Consequently

The team has established trust and a relationship that helps people share information effectively, which leads to co-creating new solutions.

+ Each person on the team is helping to create solutions.
+ The team as a whole is more creative than each individual.

+ People have individual expertise, but they contribute it to the wider team objectives.

– Effort is required to bring people together for social events, extra activities, etc. Not just money and time, but also psychological safety and other organizational culture aspects that take investment.

Common Pitfalls

Assuming that just because people sit together, they are a team and will be effective working together. Thus not investing in any team-building programs or efforts, and then still expecting people to innovate.

Looking for a guru: When seeking solutions and figuring out requirements, a team can understandably turn to an individual with deeper knowledge or experience—an "expert relationship" delivering knowledge from above. Relying on the existing knowledge of individuals, even very knowledgeable ones, significantly hinders innovation and creative thinking. Once the knowledge is stable and well-understood, however, the expert relationship is useful in an economy of scale approach—it can be packaged in terms and names and executive strategy and rolled out to everyone.

Related Biases

Bystander effect
> The tendency to think that others will act in an emergency situation. This is very relevant for overlapping responsibilities. In a Waterfall organization, when a task doesn't officially belong to anyone, no one will volunteer to pick it up.

Law of the instrument
> An overreliance on familiar tools or methods, ignoring or undervaluing alternatives. "If all you have is a hammer, everything looks like a nail."

Authority bias
> The tendency to attribute greater accuracy to the opinion of an authority figure and be more influenced by that opinion. In this context, seeking an "expert relationship" is falling back on the desire for someone with more experience to tell you what they think the right solution would be.

Related Patterns

- Remote Teams
- Co-Located Teams
- Communicate Through Tribes

Pattern: Blameless Inquiry

When a problem occurs, focusing on the event instead of the people involved allows them to learn from mistakes without fear of punishment (Figure 8-24).

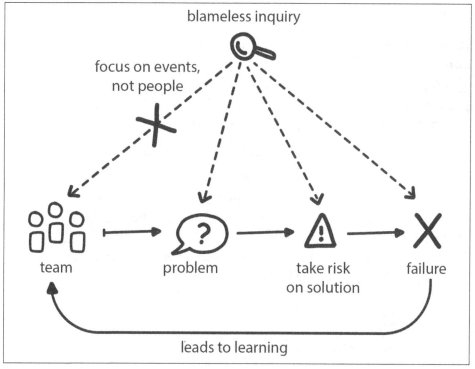

Figure 8-24. Blameless Inquiry

A company is proficiently delivering existing products or services while investing some resources into continued innovation. There is a lot of uncertainty, and experimentation is required for figuring out the tech and exploring new business opportunities. Naturally, many of the experiments lead to dead ends.

In This Context

When no inquiry is done after a problem occurs or an experiment fails, the team doesn't improve and is likely to keep making similar mistakes. In many organizations, fault-seeking occurs, and blame gets assigned to anyone involved with a problem. This leads to mediocre performance, since most innovative actions carry significant risk.

- Once punished for failure, people tend to avoid risks.

- Waterfall organizations tend to punish teams or individuals associated with problematic events to ensure stability; novelty is discouraged.
- There is no innovation without risk.

Therefore

Understand what went wrong by focusing on the problem instead of the people involved.

Talk about what went wrong and why, and how to avoid it in the future. Don't punish people for mistakes—encourage them to learn from the experience instead. This creates the psychological safety required for taking risks.

- Gather everyone involved and review what happened.
- Share the results with the rest of the team.
- Find possible solutions for avoiding similar problems in the future.
- Focus on the problem, not the people: don't ask who did what and never assign blame.
- If some mistakes occur repeatedly, find out who is involved and introduce personal commitment/responsibility.

Consequently

People have the autonomy and the confidence to try and fail, and try again.

+ Teams are always improving by learning how to find and avoid repeated mistakes.

+ Progress happens faster since people don't waste time and effort trying to find a solution that is "guaranteed to work" before they even risk trying it.

− If there are no consequences for failure, some people may fail due to not taking personal responsibility for solving problems as they arise.

Common Pitfalls

The nature of experiments is that some prove the point in question and some disprove it. The biggest pitfall in this context is to blame and punish the people running the experiment for a negative result. This leads to fear of failure and significantly reduces innovation, because most people who have experienced punishment will subsequently run experiments only when they are certain of the outcome.

Related Biases

Confirmation bias
> Picking test variables that will "prove" your existing opinion, rather than genuinely exploring alternatives.

Congruence bias
> If you have a preconceived outcome in mind and test results that confirm this, you stop testing instead of seeking further information.

Related Patterns

- Psychological Safety
- Learning Organization
- Manage for Creativity
- Manage for Proficiency

Summary

In this chapter we introduced patterns around organizational culture and structure. The intent is to first expose readers to the patterns themselves before applying them —fitting them together in the transformation design outlined in Chapter 11 and Chapter 12. There, we show how a company like WealthGrid can apply patterns step by step, from start to finish, as a transformation design. The design moves the company through four stages to emerge successfully transformed into a flexible, responsive, and above all confident organization, able to work both proficiently and innovatively as needed.

When working in a design context, this chapter—along with the other chapters presenting patterns for strategy, development, and infrastructure—functions as a more in-depth resource for referencing and working with particular patterns.

New cloud native patterns are emerging constantly. To continue sharing them and extending the cloud native pattern language we have established here, please visit www.CNpatterns.org.

This is where to find the latest pattern developments, but also an online community for discussing and creating new patterns. We are inviting people from across the industry, thought leaders and influencers but most importantly everyday engineers and managers— those out there working elbows-deep in cloud native code and architecture—to contribute and participate. Hope to see you there!

CHAPTER 9

Patterns for Development and Process

A cloud native transformation is an exciting time for an organization. Who doesn't want to work with the hottest new technologies using cutting-edge approaches? Introducing these new technologies and ways of working, however, can also knock you seriously off balance at first. You're not only changing everything you do, but how you go about doing it—which can create a whole slew of problems. These can include slow delivery, reduced product/service quality, and difficulties in both team and project management, not to mention any brand-new complications that may be unique to your own transformation circumstances.

Cloud native processes are still being fleshed out because cloud native itself is still so emergent. This is not yet a beaten path so much as one that's being actively created by the people walking it. What we do know, however, is that it's critical to make sure that the foundation is right and the system architecture can support future growth, extension, and constant change.

The patterns in this chapter address how to approach designing, building, and delivering your business's products or services in this new paradigm. This is where we look at the architecture and processes that support cloud native's fast, dynamic, and responsive delivery model: microservices, continuous integration, and other process-oriented tools and methods that empower teams to be independent, proactive, and self-sufficient while delivering rapid, iterative changes on a daily basis. They are not inherently superior to other ways of building software, either singly or when harnessed together. What they do represent is a better set of tactics and processes to deal with uncertain situations. What we are giving you here is a practical way to implement them.

The following patterns describe and address cloud native development and process. They are presented in an order that we believe will be useful or helpful for the reader, but there is no right (or wrong) order for approaching them: patterns are building blocks for a design and can be combined in different ways according to context.

This chapter is intended as an introduction to the patterns themselves, and there is intentionally little explanation relating them to each other at this point. When considering an individual pattern, the decision is not just where and when to apply it, but whether to apply it at all—not every pattern is going to apply in every transformation or organization. Once the concepts are introduced we will fit them together, in progressive order and in context, in Chapter 11 and Chapter 12 as a design that demonstrates how patterns are applied in a typical cloud native transformation.

- Open Source Internal Projects
- Distributed Systems
- Automated Testing
- Continuous Integration
- Reproducible Dev Environments
- No Long Tests in CI/CD
- Microservices Architecture
- Communicate Through APIs
- Reference Architecture
- Architecture Drawing
- Developer Starter Pack
- Demo Applications
- Secure System from the Start
- Strangle Monolithic Application
- Delayed Automation
- Avoid Reinventing the Wheel
- A/B Testing
- Serverless

Pattern: Open Source Internal Projects

Use open source solutions for any software need that is not directly related to the company's core business value (Figure 9-1).

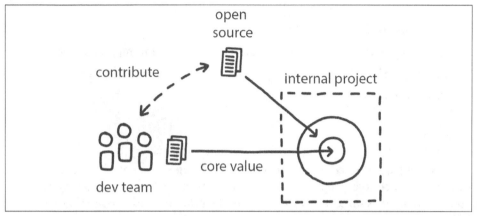

Figure 9-1. Open Source Internal Projects

The company is building a lot of software, but most of it covers generic needs—only a minor percentage is related to delivering the actual core business products/services.

In This Context

When a project is strictly internal, there is a tendency to cut corners to save time. Meanwhile, the open source community is constantly coming up with new tools to solve business use cases in the cloud native world.

Internal projects that are not in a company's core business area take time away from that essential work. Furthermore, they rarely get the priority to be built at the highest quality, and always get lowest priority for maintenance. Over time they become outdated and quality suffers, while innovation is limited or lost. Meanwhile, the rest of the market goes full-speed ahead.

- When something is invisible to the public, there are few incentives to make it nice.
- There are many other teams outside of the company having similar challenges.
- Good devs are attracted to interesting tech.
- Internal projects rarely get budget for cosmetic or procedural improvements.
- Many major cloud native tools are open source projects (Kubernetes!).

All software that does not address company core business ("secret sauce") can be open sourced from the start.

- Use open source software (OSS) whenever possible.
- New projects should be OSS by default.
- Use OSS governance and development practices even for internal projects.
- Always give back by contributing to the open source products you choose.
- Promote and market OSS projects.

If there is a gap in functionality, instead of building a new solution internally, use existing open source projects and contribute back to them. Alternatively, create your own open source solution and invite others to use, contribute to, and improve it.

+ Code quality is higher, as the project is more visible.

+ Contributions from other people help the project continually improve.

+ Contributing to OSS boosts the company's tech reputation.

− Lose some control.

− Competitors can use it too.

Common Pitfalls

Using existing open source projects, such as Kubernetes, Linux, and many others, without ever contributing back. Open source projects are the best when a variety of developers and companies embrace them and help to improve and extend them.

Related Patterns

- Avoid Reinventing the Wheel

Pattern: Distributed Systems

When software is built as a series of fully independent services, the resulting system is, by design, fast, resilient, and highly scalable (Figure 9-2).

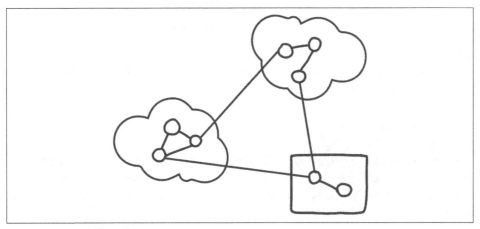

Figure 9-2. Distributed Systems

System complexity has grown beyond the capabilities of the key architects to understand it, but additional growth is still required.

In This Context

Once the system has grown beyond the capacity of a single architect/engineer to understand, it becomes difficult and time-consuming to add functionality. With the growth of the old software systems, more people join the team and the system constantly collects technical depth, which leads to fragility and unpredictable side effects that come with every change. This creates fear of adding new functionality and stagnates development.

- Human mental capacity for grasping complex systems is finite.
- Monolithic systems require someone with full understanding of the complex relationships among components to make/approve any changes to the system.
- Almost all software systems start out as small monoliths.

Therefore

Build the software system as a number of independent components (microservices) running on different computers and communicating through APIs. Develop-

ment, delivery, and scheduling of each component is completely independent, and any component can fail without affecting the others.

Distributed systems are much more complex to initially architect and implement, but once that initial work is invested they are much simpler to grow—and evolve with improvements, new features, and changes.

- Split the system into small pieces (microservices components).
- Define APIs.
- Use more, but simple, computers that are less expensive and easy/fast to provision. Public clouds are most effective.

Consequently

Higher complexity through many decoupled components makes a more resilient and scalable system. Each component can become more complex until it is divided into smaller independent pieces to allow the system to grow indefinitely in scale and complexity.

– At this level of complexity truly no one is capable of fully understanding the system, which makes it difficult to maintain.

+ High levels of automation and good observability help prevent problems.

Common Pitfalls

People fail to recognize cloud native as a true paradigm shift and attempt to treat the transition as simply a new installation of an Agile toolset. They try to implement cloud native using the ways they have always worked, so the new system—if they can even get it functioning—begins to resemble their existing monolith due to Conway's law.

Related Biases

Illusion of control
The tendency to overestimate one's degree of influence over other external events is common in very complex systems, like distributed systems, and especially so in the uncertain circumstances of a cloud migration. Engineers think they know how to build microservices, and managers think they know what it takes to do DevOps. But in reality it is only an illusion of control. Many complex and emergent processes are difficult to even steer, much less control. Sometimes we need to embrace some uncertainty to ultimately get results.

Related Patterns

- Architecture Drawing
- Reference Architecture
- Microservices Architecture
- Automated Infrastructure
- Serverless
- Strangle Monolithic Application

Pattern: Automated Testing

Shift responsibility for testing from humans (manual) to automated testing frameworks so the quality of the released products is consistent and continuously improving, allowing developers to deliver faster while spending more of their time improving features to meet customer needs (Figure 9-3).

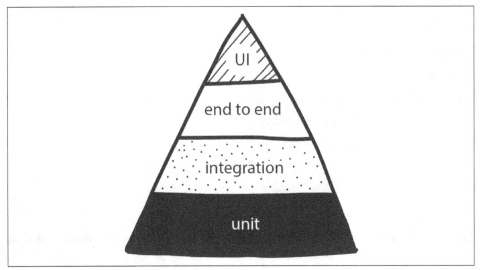

Figure 9-3. Automated Testing

CI and CD are in progress. Legacy code is being refactored to microservices, and the team is aiming to deliver changes a few times a day.

In This Context

Humans are too slow and inconsistent to be a blocking factor in the pipeline for deployment to production.

Any human handover or task performed by a human will significantly reduce the number of changes a team can deliver and increase the time required to deliver them.

- Humans can never be as fast as computers.
- Poor testing quality undermines trust in the delivery process, and testing is a waste of time.
- People tend to delay and combine changes if each delivery is risky.
- When tests are slow, people tend to avoid running them as frequently as they should.

Therefore

Automate all the testing required to take any product change to production.

Most functionality should be tested using fast and local unit tests, integration tests can ensure that components are working well together, and only a small portion of the test coverage needs to be on the system UI levels. All long-running and manual tests should be gradually refactored and automated, and they should not block consistent flow of changes to production.

- Use testing pyramid.
- Long tests should not block release.
- Manual and long-running processes happen only in background.
- Continuously add and change tests.
- Consider test-driven development.
- Add advanced in-product testing like A/B, canary, blue/green, etc.

Consequently

The team can trust that the delivery process will catch most issues and that changes will flow to production quickly.

+ The team is ready to deliver changes and take the risks.

+ Developers write tests, which gives deeper insight into the code.

− If there is a team in charge of manual testing, they may need to be retrained for new responsibilities.

Common Pitfalls

Automating everything except the actual release. Any manual step slows the process significantly, but some businesses (like finance/banking) are required by law to have a responsible administrator manually approve changes to go live. Where such manual approval is legally regulated, everything before and after the approval should still be fully automated.

Related Patterns

- No Long Tests in CI/CD
- Measure What Matters
- Observability
- A/B Testing
- Self-Service
- Build-Run Teams

Pattern: Continuous Integration

Frequent integration of small iterative changes speeds overall delivery and improves the quality of the code (Figure 9-4).

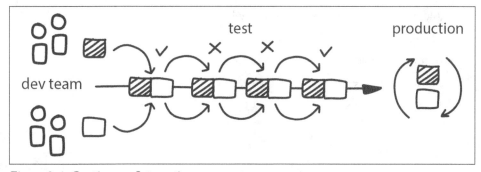

Figure 9-4. Continuous Integration

Many developers are working within the same codebase and need to integrate their changes.

In This Context

When a team of developers works on a set of features that integrates only when all features are finished, the integration process tends to be very complex. The code-

base change is large, and in the meantime other devs have integrated separate large changes that can further complicate the integration. To increase productivity, devs often delay interim integration—which leads to a single "big bang" integration just prior to release. A minor bug or conflict that could have been easily caught in an interim integration can now end up delaying the entire release.

- Memory of the change you made fades with time, so delayed integration can increase difficulties.
- Chance of conflicts is smaller when the change is small.
- Frequent execution of the same task creates incentives for automation.
- It is very easy to lose trust in the system if reports are not available.

Therefore

All developers integrate their changes at least once per day.

Integration of all changes is done on a main codebase for each microservice. Code differences are small, less than one day of work, which leads to simpler integration. The main codebase is continually rebuilt and tested to ensure that every developer has functioning and up-to-date code to work with, which minimizes unexpected conflicts with any other newly integrated code.

- Introduce test automation and unit tests.
- Build each change and test it immediately.
- Immediately fix any broken build.
- Commit to the same mainline on the codebase.
- Must have good reporting.
- Use feature toggling.

Consequently

Integration is a nonevent. Products are always in a releasable state.

+ Code is always good-quality, tested, and functional.

+ Collaboration is easier.

+ Minor bugs and conflicts are caught before they cause major problems.

− There is some overhead.

Common Pitfalls

Many teams consider having Jenkins or some other continuous integration build tool running and then doing a full product build upon every change as a fully functional continuous delivery (CD). In reality, this is just a single element of the proper CD setup. The main goal is to have all the changes integrate quickly and very close to the actual time when the change was introduced. This requires all the team members committing their code to the same branch, a good and reliable test suite, fast uncompromising response to any failures that arise in the CD build, and more. Full CD can significantly boost code quality and team agility, while partial implementation will typically provide only marginal real value while creating the illusion of success.

Related Patterns

- Continuous Delivery
- Continuous Deployment
- Decide Closest to the Action
- Build-Run Teams

Pattern: Reproducible Dev Environments

Developers need to test their daily work in an environment that is easy to spin up and that matches production tooling as closely as possible (Figure 9-5).

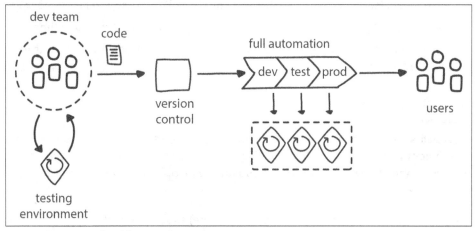

Figure 9-5. Reproducible Dev Environments

Developers are building containerized microservices and deploying them to the containerized platform. Each microservice is built by a team, and microservices are interpreted into the larger system. There are many devs on many teams.

In This Context

Shared environments and databases are difficult to keep in good shape and create dependencies that lead to delays.

When developers can't create their own test environments, they may avoid running proper tests before submitting the code or run them on shared environments that may affect the work of their teammates. This affects other developers by making interpretation more difficult.

Differences between development environments and the eventual production environment may lead to the introduction of bugs that happen only in production and are related to those differences.

In all of these scenarios, product quality and developer productivity suffer.

- Local testing reduces interpretation problems.
- If setup for the developer environment is too slow, devs will reuse the same environments.
- If not refreshed, local environments tend to undergo configuration drift.
- Shared environments create dependencies that lead to delays.
- Developers tend to create many test environments if it is easy and fast.
- Developers often have multiple changes that require testing at the same time.
- CI and CD are much more difficult to achieve without being able to test each change thoroughly.

Therefore

Establish a fully automated and fast process to create development environments where devs can test-run their apps. Each developer should be able to have their own environment, or multiple environments, that resemble the eventual production environment.

- Provide the same (or at least close to the same) tooling to deploy apps as in production.
- It is possible to do this on the cloud but will require cost management.

Each developer can run tests on their own without delays or disturbing the rest of the team.

+ Productivity and product quality are high.

− Could require a lot of hardware to create, at high cost.

− If on cloud, devs may forget to switch them off and accidentally create large use charges.

Related Biases

Bystander effect
Doing nothing while hoping someone else will solve the problem.

Related Patterns

- Containerized Apps
- Risk-Reducing Deployment Strategies
- Build-Run Teams
- No Long Tests in CI/CD
- Continuous Integration
- Continuous Delivery
- Decide Closest to the Action
- Self-Service

Pattern: No Long Tests in CI/CD

Execute non-critical long-running tests in the background so they don't block delivery to production (Figure 9-6).

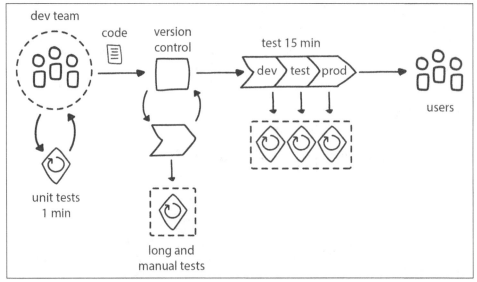

Figure 9-6. No Long Tests in CI/CD

CI/CD is in place, and most tests are automated. Some are taking hours or even longer, and others require manual execution.

In This Context

Delivering changes quickly is a major goal of the cloud native approach to delivering software.

Long-running performance tests, reliability tests, and manual and other types of full-system tests can take too long and delay delivery for hours—rendering CI/CD less valuable. Instead of dozens or even hundreds of times a day, delivery frequency gets reduced to just a few times per day. Similarly, fixing a bug or problem goes from taking a few minutes to instead requiring several hours.

- Manual intervention can create very long delays.
- Frequent integrations require a fast build/test cycle.

Run your fastest tests earliest in the process. Schedule all tests that are manual, or which take longer than a few minutes to run, outside of the normal delivery process. If you have a test that is critical for functionality, however, it should be run as a blocking test.

Mitigating risk is an equally important cloud native goal, which is why automated testing is a core tenet of the architecture. These two things need not conflict. There are strategies that allow adequate testing while enabling teams to still release quickly and constantly. Short-running tests can be incorporated into the pre-deployment process, while long-running tests can be executed in the background without blocking delivery to production.

- Run tests periodically post-delivery, and if a problem is found, either roll back the change or fix the problem and roll forward in a new release.
- Run long tests in parallel.
- Split the test automation into smaller test segments.

Testing does not delay or disturb delivery. Quality of the products is kept high by the right balance of ever-changing tests.

+ Non-blocking long-running tests reveal problems without slowing velocity.

+ Release is quick and easy.

+ Devs can deliver many times a day.

− Some issues can carry through to production.

− Requires strong roll back/roll forward protocol and procedures in place.

Related Patterns

- Continuous Integration
- Continuous Delivery
- Continuous Deployment
- Automated Testing
- Reproducible Dev Environments

Pattern: Microservices Architecture

To reduce the costs of coordination among teams delivering large monolithic applications, build the software as a suite of modular services that are built, deployed, and operated independently (Figure 9-7).

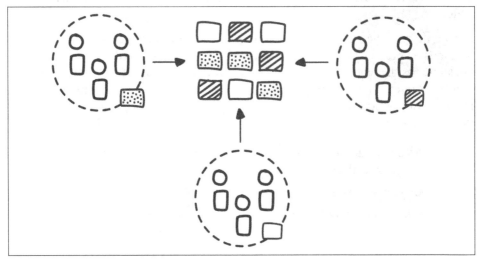

Figure 9-7. Microservices Architecture

A company has decided to move to cloud native and is looking at ways to speed up feature development and to optimize their use of cloud resources. The size of the development/engineering staff can range from a few tens, for a small to medium business, up to a few thousand for a large enterprise.

In This Context

Delivery of large monolithic applications developed by large teams require long and complex coordination and extensive testing, leading to longer TTM (Time to Market). Hardware use by such applications is inefficient, which leads to wasted resources.

- People tend to delay painful moments; since integration and delivery are typically painful, their frequency tends to decrease as system longevity increases.

- Larger monolithic systems are increasingly difficult to understand as they grow in size and complexity.

- Monoliths are easier to work with than modular applications as long as they are small enough to be understood by each developer.

- Tiny monoliths (not big ones) are often the quickest, simplest solution to relatively easy problems.
- Conway's law: architecture tends to resemble the organizational structure.

Split applications into smaller, loosely coupled microservices that can be built, tested, deployed, and run independently from other components.

- Small and independent teams work on separate modules and deliver them with only limited coordination across the teams.
- Independent components allow different teams to progress at their own pace.

New systems are created from many small and independently built components with a complex web of connections.

+ Faster-moving teams are not held back by slower ones.

+ Teams can choose the most appropriate tools for delivering their particular service.

− Independence and freedom of choice are achieved, but with the tradeoffs of reduced standardization and certain types of reusability.

Common Pitfalls

All-or-nothing thinking: trying to build all the components at once, instead of concentrating on getting one service working well before moving on to the next.

Moving to microservices first—before establishing containerization, automation, or CI/CD. So you get hundreds of mini monoliths running around that all need to be deployed manually.

Not restructuring how teams are organized, so you are still building all your microservices in single-delivery cadence.

Related Biases

Bandwagon effect
   The tendency to do something because many other people are doing it. When a hot technology is getting talked up at all the conferences or when Gartner puts

certain tech on its chart, everyone decides to adopt it even without understanding how it relates to their use case.

Pro-innovation bias
Having excessive optimism toward an innovation's usefulness and applicability because it is new and cutting edge, without understanding its limitations or implementation context.

Related Patterns

- Build-Run Teams
- Continuous Integration
- Continuous Deployment
- Avoid Reinventing the Wheel
- Communicate Through APIs
- Dynamic Scheduling

Pattern: Communicate Through APIs

In a highly distributed system, microservices must communicate with one another via stable and strongly segregated APIs (Figure 9-8).

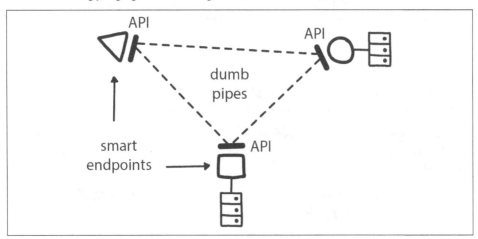

Figure 9-8. Communicate Through APIs

A company is building a microservices application. Some teams work on a single microservice, others on multiple microservices. Teams are independent and aim to reduce interteam dependencies on both technical and organizational levels.

If APIs among microservices are not well-defined and fully segregated, they will require tighter coupling in development and/or delivery. This in turn introduces dependency, both service-to-service and among teams on an organizational level. This process essentially undoes the move to decouple the monolithic app in the first place, as it leads to coordinated development for the delivery of multiple services and requires very tight collaboration across teams.

This reduces the speed and agility of the organization and effectively re-creates the original monolithic architecture and organizational structure.

- Tight coupling begins with a simple decision to share data directly.
- Conway's law: a software application's architecture will evolve to mirror the organizational structure of the company producing it.
- A single team working on multiple microservices may take shortcuts and introduce tight coupling.

Therefore

Microservices should communicate with one another only through the network, using simple, consistent, and stable APIs.

- Build stable APIs with backward compatibility.
- Place most of the service logic within the service itself, keeping the API simple and easily maintainable.
- Smart endpoints, dumb pipes (most of the business logic is in the microservices themselves and not in the APIs).
- Ensure each microservice has no direct access to data of other microservices.
- Make sure there is version control and version management for APIs.

Consequently

Microservices are kept decoupled and independent.

+ Old microservices can easily be replaced when needed as long as APIs are preserved.

− Communication through network can be slower and is more complex to architect.

Common Pitfalls

Some teams choose to do the quick and easy thing rather than the right thing at the beginning, thinking there will always be a chance to go back in later to refactor for APIs over a network. Even if this refactoring does eventually happen, which is not reliable, dependencies grow very quickly. It will be a time-consuming task to detangle such a mess, almost certainly more work than was saved by not doing well-defined, strongly segregated APIs in the first place.

Related Patterns

- Microservices Architecture

Pattern: Reference Architecture

Provide an easily accessible document laying out a standardized system architecture for all teams to use for building their applications/components. This ensures higher architectural consistency and lowers development costs via better reusability (Figure 9-9).

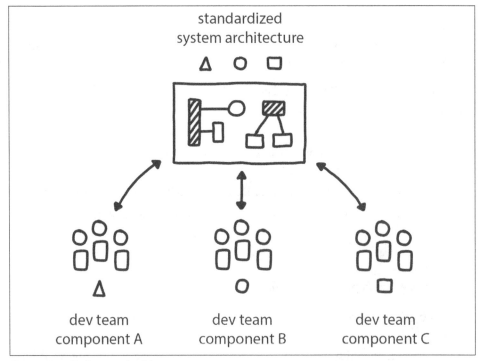

Figure 9-9. Reference Architecture

The Core Team is designing the setup of the initial platform and the migration of the first few applications that will test it. The rest of the teams will start migrating soon and will need to understand the platform architecture.

When moving to cloud native, teams have no experience and no clear reference on the right ways to architect cloud native systems. When a transformation proceeds without a proper plan for standardizing the platform, each team will likely choose very different architecture for the particular piece it is in charge of building.

This makes interpretation of components difficult and maintenance more complex, and will make it more difficult to move developers across teams due to steep learning curves among the different platforms. Furthermore, in the absence of both knowledge and easy solutions, teams may revert to well-known ways (biases) and significantly diminish the value of the transformation.

- It's easier to reuse existing architecture.
- Some teams would never extend the original version.
- Given full freedom, teams will come up with many different architectures.
- It's difficult to consider the whole system from within one team.

Document the architectural principles to be used in the company, educate the teams on the standardized way to build software in this system, and create an architecture review process to ensure consistency among teams.

Standardizing the architecture early on paves the way for more rapid adoption while preventing chaos. This is an extension of the Vision First pattern: rather than making a bunch of random decisions to move the initiative forward, people with an understanding of how to build distributed systems software have helped make proper technical decisions.

Providing good reference points coupled with clear architectural guidelines right from the start helps the teams to bootstrap the projects in better ways and may avoid costly mistakes.

- Make the architecture sufficiently high-level to allow flexibility for the teams to choose tools.
- Use demo apps as example implementations.
- Create a procedure to uniformly educate everyone who will be using the system.

- Review and help teams to improve their microservices to run optimally on the standardized platform.

- Include recommended languages and tools.

- Just because we are being creative and doing experiments doesn't mean we should not be doing architecture.

Components are consistent across all teams and projects. There is a clear understanding regarding the platform and agreement over preferred application architecture styles. The current state of the platform is known, and it is open for improvements.

+ Easier to improve and maintain.

+ Easier to onboard new devs.

− May limit freedom of choice.

Common Pitfalls

Teams will just accept the standardized platform, with default settings, as given and never work to improve or extend it to suit their particular work.

Related Biases

Default effect
When given a choice between several options, people will tend to favor whatever default is already in place. This is why solutions to problems have to consider the correct/optimal defaults, since those will be adopted more frequently than any customized option. This is true both for the tools built into cloud platforms like Amazon Web Services, Azure, etc., as well as internal tools provided to employees. It's why we have the Starter Pack pattern.

Related Patterns

- Vision First
- Architecture Drawing
- Communicate Through Tribes

Pattern: Architecture Drawing

A picture—or, in this case, a high-level outline sketch of your system's basic architecture —can replace a thousand words, save time, and prevent misunderstandings (Figure 9-10).

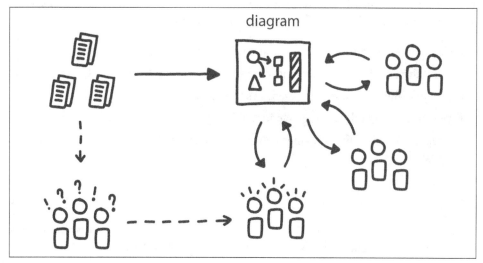

Figure 9-10. Architecture Drawing

The company is in the middle of cloud native adoption. Strategy is set, architecture defined. Now the company needs easy ways to discuss and improve the architecture.

In This Context

When architecture is very complex and difficult to replicate—or, if as sometimes happens, a piece is entirely missing—a team can struggle to have a quick and effective conversation about technical solutions. Describing complex technical discussions using words can be time-consuming and confusing, resulting in many misunderstandings later on. This may lead to deviations in implementation, which can harm product quality and make maintenance more difficult.

- Different people grasp information in different ways.
- Visualization helps people think more creatively.
- Common language (visual or verbal) helps save time and increase the volume of information during technical discussions.

Draw the high-level architecture on a whiteboard and teach all team members how to repeat the drawing.

Use the drawing consistently in team discussions and in all internal documents. Create similar drawings for each subcomponent recursively.

- Create simple elements that are easy to draw.
- Limit the drawing to 20 elements or so.
- Create a digital version that resembles the drawings.
- Use the same graphical language for subcomponents.
- Keep a version of the drawings centrally available for easy reference, and keep it updated.

Everyone in the team can draw parts of the architecture in seconds. There is a common visual language as a basis for improved collaboration.

+ Consistent visuals are used throughout the project.

+ Internalized understanding of the architecture's components and how they relate to each other.

− Standardized representation of the architecture can crimp creative thinking in the team and lead to conformity in early stages of the product development.

Common Pitfalls

Though this is a No Regret Move—easy and inexpensive yet extremely beneficial—few companies produce a single, unified official version of the architecture for circulation and reference. Instead, teams and individuals create their own versions, leading to a lot of confusion.

Another pitfall is when they do create one, but their visual representation of the architecture is so complex that no one on the team can understand it, much less replicate it.

Related Patterns

- Distributed Systems
- Design Thinking for Radical Innovation
- Internal Evangelism
- Periodic Checkups

Pattern: Developer Starter Pack

Provide a "starter kit" of materials, guides, and other resources to help new teams onboard to the new cloud native system quickly and with confidence (Figure 9-11).

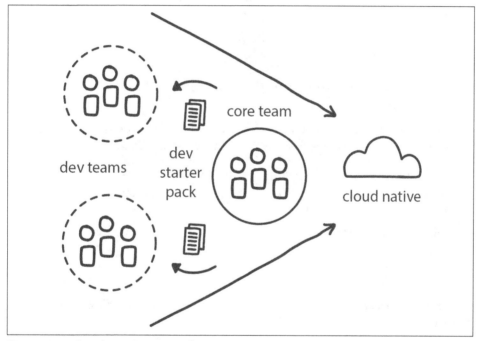

Figure 9-11. Developer Starter Pack

The new cloud native platform is approaching production-ready status, and it's time to begin onboarding teams.

Teams onboarding to cloud native don't know the tools or technologies and typically receive poor onboarding materials. At best, this leads to wasted time, and at worst, teams are forced to create their own cloud native practices, which are uninformed, not designed for this platform, and not uniform.

- There are limited publicly available materials.
- People will use known techniques if they are not provided with clear guidance to new ones.
- If teams are onboarded with insufficient training, they will overload the support team with requests for help.
- People tend to accept default choices, so giving them good defaults increases overall quality.

Provide developers onboarding to cloud native everything they need to start working immediately.

Optimally, new developers should be able to commit their first change and deploy it to the test environment on the first day following the onboarding.

- This cloud native "starter kit" of materials should include tool configurations, version control repository, CI/CD pipelines, demo applications for practice, target platform description, trainings, and more.
- All of this needs to be prepared before the next step of onboarding.

Cloud native practices are adopted as the Core Team has planned, and there is consistency.

+ Less work and fewer problems for the Core Team after onboarding, because the newly onboarded developers have the tools and confidence to solve their own problems.

– Less freedom for learning by doing for the dev teams.

Common Pitfalls

Teams will tend to anchor on using the provided starter pack as an ultimate solution instead of using this as a starting point and then innovating when better solutions are needed or become available. That is, they accept the starter pack as "this is just how you do it" and never explore alternatives.

Related Biases

Curse of knowledge bias
> The Core Team has been doing this for a while and has thus lost touch with being new to cloud native technologies and tools. They know exactly what to do and can't imagine why others don't also understand/have this knowledge.

Default bias
> When given multiple options, the tendency is to choose the provided default. People accept what is provided and do not seek to adjust or customize it. We can use this as a nudge toward optimal choices by providing excellent default options.

Related Patterns

- Gradual Onboarding
- Reference Architecture
- Demo Applications
- Full Production Readiness

Pattern: Demo Applications

Teams onboarded to the new cloud native system receive demo applications as an educational starting point for building their own cloud native applications (Figure 9-12).

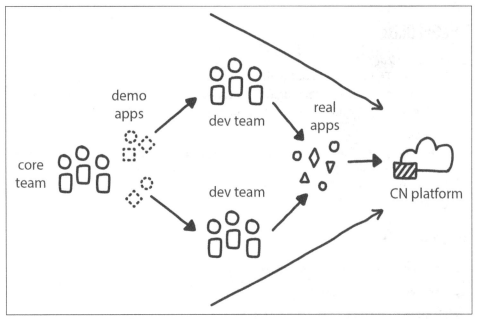

Figure 9-12. Demo Applications

The Core Team has built the initial platform and is ready to start onboarding the rest of the organization to cloud native. Developers have gone through platform trainings and soon need to start moving apps to cloud native. The level of cloud native experience is low.

In This Context

Teams newly onboarded to cloud native have limited knowledge and no experience creating cloud native applications. They will tend to apply established skills and approaches carried over from previous experience in non-cloud native systems. This will lead to re-creating tightly coupled, interdependent applications—suboptimal architecture that conflicts with cloud native. This reduces overall quality for the apps they deliver and fails to capture cloud native's development velocity benefits. Re-architecting apps later is much harder than building them the right way in the first place.

- People tend to use known methods to solve new problems.
- Much easier to start from something rather than nothing.
- People learn by doing and from experiencing examples.

Therefore

Build a number of simple, functional apps that fully fit cloud native practices.

Make those apps known and available to new teams as they join the cloud native setup. Keep the demo apps up to date and adjust them to the latest best practices developed by the Core Team.

- Applications are basic but fully functional with a UI and a database, and built on microservices architecture with services communicating via APIs.
- Continuously improving—as the teams learn, they can incorporate new tools and methods to expand the application.
- Emphasize clean and high-quality code.
- Tests need to be automated/built in.
- The apps are to be delivered using CI/CD, and the delivery scripts are part of the applications.
- Always up and running—practice Build-Run Teams delivery workflow.

Consequently

Teams moving to the new system have a way to practice their new skills and prepare to deliver a full enterprise application.

+ Devs can start from the right place.

+ Core team can apply their knowledge.

+ Architecture is more consistent.

− Demo apps could limit creativity (default effect).

− Core Team spends time on writing demo applications.

Common Pitfalls

Moving to cloud native and trying to deliver a distributed architecture application by using old techniques/processes. Most often we see an application architected as microservices, but these are tightly coupled and delivered all together at the same time, essentially delivering a monolith of microservices.

Related Biases

Law of the instrument
An overreliance on familiar tools or methods, ignoring or undervaluing alternatives. "If all you have is a hammer, everything looks like a nail."

Default effect
Whatever pre-selected options are given at the beginning tend to be kept as the default setting, instead of exploring better options.

Related Patterns

- Developer Starter Pack
- Gradual Onboarding
- Learning Organization
- Build-Run Teams

Pattern: Secure System from the Start

Build security into the platform beginning with the earliest versions to ensure your distributed system is unbreachable by design (Figure 9-13).

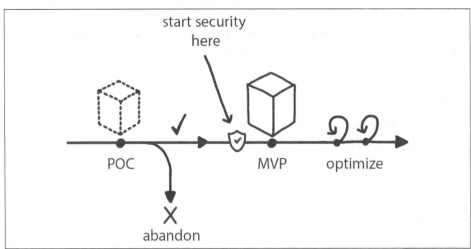

Figure 9-13. Secure System from the Start

The company is moving to cloud native and in the process of building an MVP platform and starting to set up cloud native organizational structure. Distributed Systems, Microservices Architecture, and CI/CD are being used. The MVP is planned to go into production in just a few months.

In This Context

Teams tend to delay setting up security until relatively late in a project. Cloud native, however, requires many new tools and security techniques, and teams are typically not proficient in working with distributed systems. Waiting to implement security features just before the platform is ready to go live leads to either poor security in production or significant delays while good security measures are finally taken.

- Security in distributed systems cannot be ensured by perimeter security.
- It is more difficult to add security after the fact.
- The cloud native world requires many new and unfamiliar tools and methods.

Therefore

Build the MVP as a highly secure system from Day One.

Embed security practices in the Startup Pack and the Demo Application and run security tests as an integral part of the testing suite during the CI/CD process. This will allow the needed time to create security practices and provide examples for the teams onboarding to the platform.

- Provide good-quality and ongoing security training.
- Ensure that automated security testing is in place.
- Review the security of every tool in your cloud native system.
- Use best practices to secure containers, clusters, APIs, access rights, etc.

Consequently

Security is a high priority from the start and baked in throughout the platform. The Build-Run teams and Platform Team have clear guiding principles for creating secure Distributed Systems.

+ There is no extra cost to add security from the start.

+ The team is proficient in distributed security.

Related Patterns

- Distributed Systems
- Automated Testing

Pattern: Strangle Monolithic Application

Gradually split pieces of the old monolithic application one by one, re-architect them into services, and move them over time to the new cloud native platform (Figure 9-14).

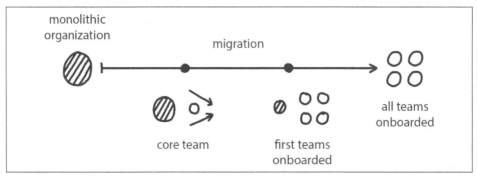

Figure 9-14. Strangle Monolithic Application

You have a monolith and are moving to microservices architecture. The new platform is ready or soon to be ready and you're preparing the strategy for splitting the monolith into microservices.

In This Context

Re-architecting a large monolith, built over many years or even decades, is a massive project that can take years. Some companies try to do it all at once, but rewriting a large monolithic application from scratch also carries great risk. You cannot start using the new system until it is developed and functioning as expected, but your company has little cloud native experience or knowledge to get this done. Building a new system from scratch will take a year or (likely) longer. While it is under construction there will be minimal enhancements or new features delivered on the current platform and so the business risks losing market share.

There is also a large risk of doing it all wrong in your first attempt. If the first project covers the entire application, then it will be very difficult to step back and start over due to sunk-cost fallacy—even if doing so is the best solution.

- Teams don't yet know how to split the monolith into microservices.

- The first time you do something you are going to make mistakes; it is a learning experience rather than an execution.
- Monoliths hide unexpected problems inside their huge size.
- A well-scoped migration can handle problems as they emerge, but if you are trying to do everything all at one time, they will cripple the initiative.
- 20/80 principle: it takes 20% of the time to get 80% finished, and then 80% of the time to finish the last 20% (and the last 1% will take as much time as the first 99%, so keep that 1% on the mainframe—see *Lift and Shift At the End*).

Therefore

Once the cloud native platform is ready, take small pieces of the monolithic application and, one at a time, re-architect them and then move them to the new platform.

The business value of new functionality is achieved much more quickly, and the cloud native architecture of loosely coupled services means future refactoring work will be simple. This is the cloud native version of Martin Fowler's classic strangler pattern.

- Going piece by piece and over an extended period of time is key.
- First have the final functional platform in place.
- Give priority to pieces that change frequently and those that are easy to extract.
- Create demo apps.
- Document a simple way for migrating pieces to the platform to make the process consistent, replicable, and as quick and effortless as possible.
- Leave the things that are running but not changing at all behind on the old system, and move them at the very end.

Consequently

There is a mixed environment of old and new applications working together. The team is getting better at re-architecting the pieces of the monolith.

+ A plan is in place for moving pieces over time.

− Some teams are still working in the old environment—the entire company is not all moving to Kubernetes on Day One.

− Two different operational models are in place, which can create its own set of problems.

Common Pitfalls

Trying to do it all at once as a single massive re-architecture project: regrooming the monolith into dozens or even hundreds of pieces.

Lifting and shifting the entire monolith at the beginning, instead of remnants at the end.

Related Biases

Pro-innovation bias
> The belief that new technology can fix all old problems.

Planning fallacy
> The human tendency to underestimate the time a project will require for completion. Especially operative in uncertain situations like moving to cloud native for the first time. We are eager to estimate the time and resources required, but we have no idea what it actually takes to move to cloud native. So some people estimate it as a few weeks of work when it often takes a year or longer.

Related Patterns

- Lift and Shift at the End
- Architecture Drawing
- Create Demo Apps
- Manage for Proficiency

Pattern: Delayed Automation

Automate processes only after a problem has been completely solved and the solution has been run manually a few times (Figure 9-15).

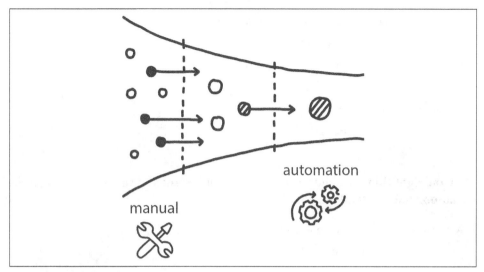

Figure 9-15. Delayed Automation

The team is building a complex system that needs to support stress and a large and fluctuating number of users. The problem and the domain are not fully known. The solution is new and not easily uncovered.

In This Context

Automation is essential for success in cloud native, but people tend to try to create a full and automated solution in the beginning before real pain points are uncovered (taking an academic approach rather than experimental). This leads to automation of the wrong thing when the problem is not fully understood. Or, paraphrasing Bill Gates, who describes this conundrum as "Crap in, crap out, only faster."

- Universities teach to solve the problem in the "right" way.
- Engineers prefer automation versus manual work.

Therefore

Understand the problem well, create a solution, make it work, and only then automate, scale, optimize, and improve.

Before automating anything, first solve the problem manually. The team needs to see the solution by doing it manually for a bit to experience and identify the pain points. Focus first on low-hanging fruit of automation (i.e., tasks that demand a lot of human time and are easy to automate).

- Run the process manually a few times.
- Create a blueprint (a document with steps).
- Do crude automation first (experiments, then an MVP version).
- Optimize and scale.
- Continually improve.

Only the right things get automated. All the important and time-consuming tasks get automated eventually.

+ Scaled work becomes a well-understood process.

− Process is manual for a while.

Related Biases

Bandwagon bias
Everyone says automation is important, so we'd better do it immediately!

Related Patterns

- Exploratory Experiments
- PoCs
- MVP
- Delayed Automation

Pattern: Avoid Reinventing the Wheel

When possible, use open source or purchase commercial solutions for any need that is not your actual core business instead of trying to custom-build perfect tools (Figure 9-16).

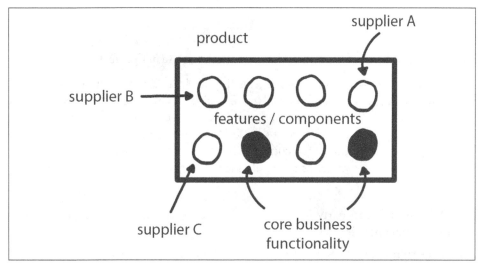

Figure 9-16. Avoid Reinventing the Wheel

A team is in the middle of a cloud native transition and missing some functionality. Out-of-the-box solutions are available on the market, although the team is capable of creating its own.

In This Context

Many development teams tend to create their own tools/solutions even when reasonable alternatives are available. Custom solutions are expensive and slow to build, difficult to maintain, and quick to become outdated. They don't take advantage of developments in the industry, and the eventual cost is high.

- Internal devs are most content to build core products.
- Tools that are not core business rarely get full attention.
- Everything that is not business logic or user interaction is not your core business.
- Every off-the-shelf product is a core business for the company or the community that makes it.
- Cloud native ecosystem is growing very fast.
- Many engineers think "they know better."
- Open source attracts many devs.

Use existing tools whenever possible, even when the fit isn't perfect.

Whether commercial or open source, existing products are typically better quality, better maintained, and more frequently extended than anything you can build yourself. Spend most of the development time on your core business functionality. This will significantly increase the time and effort available for investment into the core business parts that separate your company from the competition, while making sure that the rest of the components are easily maintainable and up to the latest industry standards.

- Make use of third-party libraries, off-the-shelf products, and existing architectures when possible.
- Focus your internal resources on delivering your core business.
- Build only if nothing else is available; give preference to an open source solution unless it's related to your core business.
- Seek the fullest possible solution; trying to fit together a variety of open source solutions, each addressing a separate business function, can lead to maintaining a complex environment of many moving parts.

The team can focus on core business.

+ New functionality is constantly introduced with third-party product releases.

+ Quality of off-the-shelf products is typically higher.

+ There is external product/user support.

+ Easier to hire people when using common tools.

− Some problems are too specific for any off-the-shelf solution to address.

− Third-party products are often expensive.

− Less control over functionality.

Common Pitfalls

Underestimating the cost of building and maintaining your own custom solutions. In the beginning it looks quick and easy, but developers are typically too optimistic in their estimates. Building your own tool always ends up being a long, difficult, and expensive initiative—much bigger than estimated in the beginning.

Related Biases

Illusion of control
> Engineers think they know best what the company needs and will be able to build a better solution than what is available from outside vendors.

Planning fallacy
> The human tendency to underestimate the time a project will require.

Related Patterns

- Open Source Internal Projects
- Exit Strategy Over Vendor Lock-in
- Public Cloud

Pattern: A/B Testing

Comparing multiple versions of something (a feature, new functionality, UI, etc.) under real customer use conditions quickly gives useful data about which performs better (Figure 9-17).

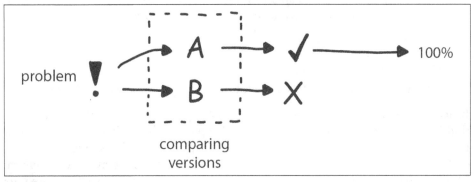

Figure 9-17. A/B Testing

A company has a working cloud native infrastructure in place and is aiming to deliver a lot of useful functionality to its customers. Teams are proficient, and all the tech and processes are in place.

In This Context

There is no practical way to predict how customers will respond to changes. In the absence of actual customer usage data, design and implementation decisions must

be based on guesswork and intuition. Since our intuition is not perfect and full of biases, we may not get the best possible results.

- People don't always know what they need/want.
- Delivering fast without adjusting the product based on measurement and feed-back will change nothing.
- It's impossible to make logical decisions in an unknown environment.
- There are unlimited variations and combinations of possible solutions.

Therefore

Prepare multiple versions of a solution to a challenge/problem and present them to randomized small portions of the client base. Measure the customer response in terms of value for them, and based on that choose the solution.

- Famous Google example of testing 41 shades of blue for its toolbar[1] to find which inspired the most consumer clicks—because, for Google, clicks equal revenue.
- The Obama campaign raised more money by using A/B testing to choose the most effective messaging.
- Need to provide businesspeople with the opportunity to run the A/B test experiments themselves, and an accessible way for them to do so.

Consequently

You now have an easy way to test assumptions live in a real-world environment.

Instead of making guesses or assumptions regarding which of two ideas, implementation strategies, etc., is better, a team can quickly put together a simple prototype with two or more versions and release them to small subsets of real customers. Based on customer response, the team can choose the more appropriate/preferred solution. This way many options could be tested while costs are ultimately saved because only the best option is ever fully implemented.

+ Customers see response to their needs.

+ If something doesn't work, you can easily roll back to previous version.

− Human insight might be sidelined when user response data is followed blindly.

---

1 Profile of Google engineer Marissa Mayer and her research-driven design decisions (*https://nyti.ms/34pOh3I*)

– Some innovative solutions take time to gain customer acceptance; A/B testing brings a risk of prematurely canceling such products.

Common Pitfalls

Taking a sequential approach by using an outcome as the basis for the next A/B test comparison. This "winner take all" approach risks premature elimination of the "'losing" variable, which could be the better choice in a different context. You can't know until you test this, of course! But by automatically rejecting the "losing" variable after each comparison, you lose the opportunity to experiment further with that variable. The solution is multivariate testing—instead of A/B comparisons, you have A/B/C or even A/B/C/D combinations of variables randomly exposed to different test groups.

Related Biases

Confirmation bias
Picking test variables that will "prove" your existing opinion, rather than genuinely exploring alternatives.

Congruence bias
If you have a preconceived outcome in mind and test results that confirm this, you stop testing instead of seeking further information.

Information bias
The tendency to seek information even when it cannot affect the outcome; in A/B testing this would lead to choosing meaningless variables to test.

Parkinson's law of triviality/"Bikeshedding"
Choosing something easy but unimportant to test and evaluate over something else that is complex and difficult but meaningful.

Related Patterns

- Measure What Matters
- Observability
- Feedback Loop
- Involve the Business

Pattern: Serverless

The soon-to-arrive future is event-driven, instantaneously scalable services (functions) on the cloud (Figure 9-18).

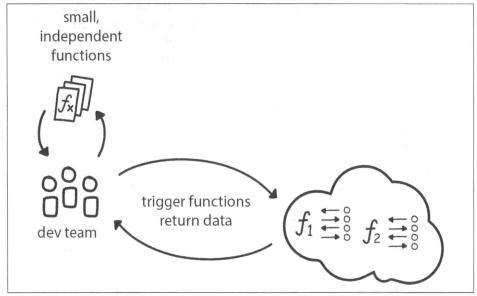

Figure 9-18. Serverless

The team is building a highly scalable system or using tools that require integration maintenance tasks. Tasks are well-defined and repeatable and may require aggressive scaling for short bursts.

In This Context

There are a lot of small tasks that can eat up a developer's time: writing boilerplate code, setting up infrastructure, and of course later maintaining everything they created. Meanwhile, it's very challenging to create scaling mechanisms that can respond in milliseconds. The first set of challenges leads to wasted developer effort plus extra costs related to setup and maintenance. The second typically results in over-provisioning of compute resources that have to be paid for whether they're used every day or only on Black Friday.

- Serverless is a recent and somewhat still emerging execution model for cloud computing.
- Some applications may change hardware requirements quickly and dramatically.

- Scaling up and down manually is difficult.

- Software components (microservices) become smaller all the time.

- Maintaining servers and/or container schedulers is an expensive task.

Package small pieces of code into fully independent executable functions that can be individually triggered on a serverless platform. Functions get one input source and return one output. Any number of functions can be executed in parallel. Functions are self-contained and repeatable.

Thought leaders and experts in distributed systems believe serverless technologies are the next evolution of application infrastructure—the horizon that lies beyond microservices. Serverless architecture is "serverless" in that users never need to take care of, or even ever really think about, individual machines: infrastructure is fully abstracted away. Instead, developers simply pick from a nearly limitless menu of compute, network, and storage resources via managed services from public cloud providers. Serverless is truly pay-as-you-go, calculated according to actual real-time consumption instead of pre-purchased services based on best guesswork. While this makes for cost-efficient application development, the true benefit is velocity: developers finally get to focus on writing code instead of managing servers or sharding databases.

Currently there are many challenges to serverless adoption, such as operational control, the introduction of even greater complexity into (already highly complex) distributed systems, and effective monitoring.

For now this falls under the H2/innovation and H3/research categories in the Three Horizons pattern, but some companies on the leading edge of cloud native have already embraced serverless. Those able to dedicate skilled engineers to conquering its current challenges are able to dramatically reduce operational overhead and streamline the DevOps cycle even further, while increasing scalability and resilience.

Think of Serverless as basically like cloud native, with superpowers.

- Functions only consume resources while running.

- Very short startup time.

- Highly scalable.

- Cheap to use.

Some software tasks can be executed very fast at any scale; the rest of the system is containerized.

+ Some tools/tasks are running in functions.

+ Running a function requires almost zero overhead.

+ Developers will never have to think about provisioning infrastructure ever again.

− Creating a full serverless app is difficult due to current architectural limitations.

Common Pitfalls

Trying to achieve an advanced, and still emerging, technology like serverless before you have even established an initial solid cloud native platform based on current tech that is well-supported. Get good at orchestrating containerized microservice applications first, then worry about next steps.

Related Biases

Bandwagon effect
The tendency to do something because many other people are doing it, and everybody is talking about serverless as the next hot thing these days. Ask for it by name, even if you aren't exactly sure what it does or whether it fits your use case!

Related Patterns

- Microservices Architecture
- Containerized Apps
- Distributed Systems
- Three Horizons
- Public Cloud

Summary

In this chapter we introduced patterns around cloud native development and processes. The intent is to first expose readers to the patterns themselves before applying them—fitting them together in the transformation design outlined in Chapter 11 and Chapter 12. There, we show how a company like WealthGrid can apply patterns step by step, from start to finish, as a transformation design. The design moves the company through four stages to emerge successfully transformed into a flexible, responsive, and above all confident organization, able to work both proficiently and innovatively as needed.

Once familiar with the patterns and ready to move on to applying them in a design, this chapter—along with the other chapters presenting patterns for strategy, organization/culture, and infrastructure—functions as a more in-depth resource for referencing and working with individual patterns.

CHAPTER 10

Patterns for Infrastructure and Cloud

Once upon a time (and not very long ago), infrastructure meant one thing: provisioning your own on-premise hardware. Cloud computing has radically expanded this definition. Today, enterprise market infrastructure can mean a public or private cloud, on- or off premises, utilizing virtualization, containerization, or serverless (functions as a service) computing—or any combination.

By comparison, legacy infrastructure has become akin to a physical anchor slowing you down and stopping your enterprise from changing. Buying servers, housing them, and configuring, provisioning, and maintaining them takes a great deal of time, attention, and money. For some companies there are still a few advantages to owning your own servers, but most are better off embracing the cloud. All the somewhat abstract changes you are making to your strategy, organization, culture, and processes to deliver software in a fast, responsive way, all the flexibility you are gaining, must be supported on a physical level by appropriately nimble infrastructure.

The entire point of going cloud native is gaining the ability to adjust course quickly. If you want to create stability in an increasingly uncertain environment, the best way to get it is to be able to respond to change quickly. That sounds like an oxymoron, but hear us out. Knowing that it will take you a long time to respond if a disruptor comes along in your market creates constant anxiety. But if you know you can react to meet a threat in a matter of months, it doesn't matter what the threat might look like—you are confident you can simply handle whatever comes. So the ability to stay steady in a fluctuating environment will create more stability, in the way that gyroscopes spin rapidly around a steady center.

It used to be companies could make a big, painful semi-risky move to new tech and then enjoy nice, stable quiet time for a decade, even two, before having to do it again. Those days are gone. The first iPhone was introduced in 2007; think about the things we take for granted now that were basically inconceivable just over ten years ago.

Think about all the human experiences that have been forever altered: communicating, navigating, shopping, taking a taxi. Innovation only keeps accelerating, and we can see that change is happening blindingly fast. We can't see what the change will be, but we can be ready for it.

Software tools inevitably change. So does infrastructure. The important thing is no longer where you build software, but how. In some ways, infrastructure is the most easily solvable of all the challenges embedded in a cloud native transition, and we have patterns to help you do just that. There are also unexpected pitfalls in the cloud to watch out for. Building custom tools instead of using what's already available. Major vendor commitments, significant contracts with suppliers: all of these things can be anchors as heavy as that on-premise data center, still blocking you from moving fast, just in a different way. We've got patterns to help you choose the right infrastructure, and avoid these pitfalls, too.

The following patterns describe and address cloud native development and process. They are presented in an order that we believe will be useful or helpful for the reader, but there is no right (or wrong) order for approaching them: Patterns are building blocks for a design and can be combined in different ways according to context.

This chapter is intended as an introduction to the patterns themselves, and there is intentionally little explanation relating them to each other at this point. When considering an individual pattern, the decision is not just where and when to apply it, but whether to apply it at all—not every pattern is going to apply in every transformation or organization. Once the concepts are introduced we will fit them together, in progressive order and in context, in Chapter 11 and Chapter 12 as a design that demonstrates how patterns are applied in a typical cloud native transformation.

- Private Cloud
- Public Cloud
- Automated Infrastructure
- Self-Service
- Dynamic Scheduling
- Containerized Apps
- Observability
- Continuous Delivery
- Continuous Deployment
- Full Production Readiness
- Risk-Reducing Deployment Strategies
- Lift and Shift at the End

Pattern: Private Cloud

A private cloud approach, operated either over the internet or on company-owned on-premises infrastructure, can offer the benefits of cloud computing services like AWS while restricting access to only select users (Figure 10-1).

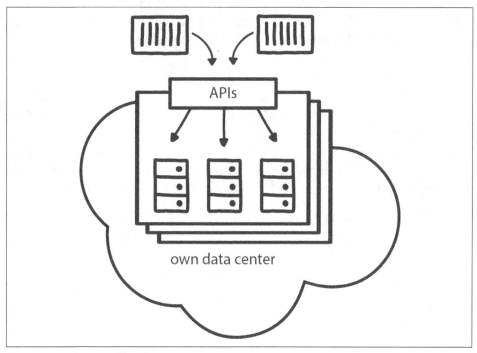

Figure 10-1. Private Cloud

A company in a highly regulated industry that is, by law, not allowed to use public cloud or a company in any sector that has recently made a major investment in new on-premises infrastructure. In the Private Cloud context, services are provisioned over private—though not necessarily on-premises—infrastructure for the dedicated use of a single organization and typically managed through internal resources.

In This Context

Connecting designated hardware to specific apps reduces their mobility and resilience. Building any kind of manual intervention by the Ops team into an application's life cycle will create long delays in deployment and reduce quality.

- There is a lot of fear around data on the public cloud.

- Public cloud vendors are very knowledgeable about, and experienced in, running large infrastructure.

- In much of the world, public cloud is allowed for almost all industries.

- A private cloud is under full control of the company, so you can optimize in different ways and customize different things that are not possible on public clouds.

- Proficient support is required to keep private clouds up and running, so you must have all that knowledge in your (typically limited) team.

Therefore

Decouple the setup of your physical infrastructure from the provisioning required for the application itself.

Treat all the servers and the rest of the infrastructure as a single large machine managed fully automatically through a set of APIs. Aim to use the same set of tools as would be required on at least one public cloud to ease any future migration.

- Fully automate everything related to running the application.

- Treat your on-premises infrastructure like a cloud; the hardware needs to be completely abstracted away from the users.

- Set up physical servers, network, storage, etc., all separately.

- Deploy and maintain applications through full APIs.

- Even if you need dedicated hardware, treat it as a part of the cloud so it is fully automated.

Consequently

The company enjoys the benefits of cloud native architecture with the additional control and security—but also expense—of hosting your own private cloud setup. Applications are running on the private cloud in exactly the same way as they would run on a public cloud.

+ Developers can get infrastructure on their own, and delivery is faster.

+ There is full control over the platform and data.

− Private clouds carry a high cost of ownership and quickly become outdated.

Common Pitfalls

If the private cloud is on premises, just like the old hardware was, it does not get treated as a true cloud platform. People try to build the new system using the techniques they always used on the previous on-premises infrastructure.

Related Patterns

- Public Cloud
- Automated Infrastructure
- Communicate Through APIs
- Distributed Systems
- Avoid Reinventing the Wheel

Pattern: Public Cloud

Instead of using your own hardware, rely on the hardware managed by public cloud vendors whenever possible (Figure 10-2).

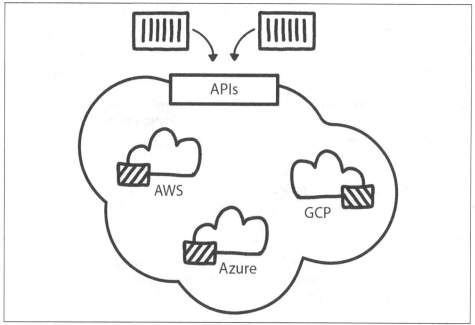

Figure 10-2. Public Cloud

You are moving to microservices, you are continuously growing your codebase, and teams now require automation for Continuous Delivery. The amount of manual work is going down, but the cost of maintaining hardware is going up.

In This Context

Procuring, installing, and maintaining hardware becomes a bottleneck that slows down the entire organization.

For most businesses, infrastructure and hardware are not their core business, so they do not invest heavily in maintaining and improving them. Public cloud vendors, however, invest a great deal of money and talent to optimize their services.

Furthermore, when you own the hardware, costs are typically higher: you need to overprovision for peak consumption. If Black Friday traffic is 10 times higher, then you must maintain that 10-times capacity the other 364 days of the year—there is no elastic capacity expansion.

- Private clouds quickly become outdated because they are not a high priority for the business.
- Never enough resources to make a private cloud as good as public cloud.
- In some business areas regulations may not allow use of public cloud due to security concerns and explicit data regulation.

Therefore

Hand over the management of hardware and rent capacity from public cloud vendors like Amazon, Microsoft, Google, and similar instead of owning, managing, and creating full automation for infrastructure.

- Rely on full automation.
- Use APIs to connect with public cloud.

Consequently

You rent fully automated, scalable, resilient infrastructure from a public cloud provider that can be increased and decreased on demand. You pay only for the resources you are actually using.

- Take advantage of integrated services.
- Public cloud vendors constantly upgrading to latest software and services.

- Built-in services like maintained databases, machine learning frameworks, and all kinds of SaaS continuously being built by the vendors.

Related Patterns

- Private Cloud
- Avoid Reinventing the Wheel
- Exit Strategy Over Vendor Lock-in
- Serverless
- Automated Infrastructure
- Dynamic Scheduling

Pattern: Automated Infrastructure

The absolute majority of operational tasks need to be automated. Automation reduces interteam dependencies, which allows faster experimentation and leads in turn to faster development (Figure 10-3).

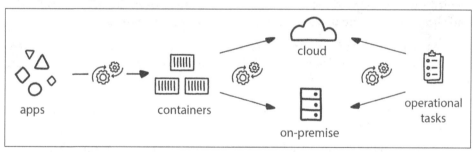

Figure 10-3. Automated Infrastructure

A company is moving to cloud native and adopting cloud native patterns such as Microservices Architecture, Continuous Delivery, and others. Teams are independent and require fast support services from the Platform Team. Most of the operational tasks are performed on demand by the Ops team.

Manual or semi-automatic provisioning of infrastructure leads to dependencies among the teams and to long waiting times for results, hindering experimentation and slowing development.

- Traditional operational teams don't have sufficient levels of automation and, due to high workload, no time to learn new technologies.

- Public clouds provide full automation of infrastructure resources.

- Manual requests and handover between development and operations teams is very slow.

- Number of operations engineers in manual systems must scale up proportionally to growth in infrastructure demands.

- Experimentation and research take longer and require more resources due to involvement of an already-busy operations department.

Therefore

Dedicate at least 50% of the Ops team's time to automating the operational tasks, and eliminate all manual infrastructure provisioning and maintenance tasks.

Any manual work that is required in between the changes committed by the developer and the delivery to production will significantly reduce the speed of delivery and introduce interteam dependencies.

- Treat infrastructure automation scripts with equal importance as the rest of the company codebase.

- Automate, fully and completely: compute, storage, networking, and other resources; patching and upgrading of operating systems; and deployment and maintenance of systems running on top of the infrastructure.

Developers spend less time waiting for infrastructure resources and can conduct quick experiments and scale running systems rapidly and easily.

+ Ops team spending significantly less time on repetitive support tasks and investing more time and resources in ongoing improvement of the system.

+ Full automation will allow the provisioning of exponentially more resources per member of operational staff.

Common Pitfalls

Understanding that everything needs to be automated, but deciding to "just do it later." It is difficult to improve something not built right in the first place. Your team gets locked into doing manual steps, it's a waste, but there is no time to improve it because they need to keep doing these manual steps to keep everything running.

Related Biases

Status quo bias
> We've always done manual provisioning, so let's just keep doing things that way. It might not be optimal, but we know it works (and changing something that works feels risky).

Related Patterns

- Dynamic Scheduling
- Platform Team
- Automated Testing
- Public Cloud
- Private Cloud
- Self-Service

Pattern: Self-Service

In cloud native everyone can do their own provisioning and deployment with no hand-offs between teams (Figure 10-4).

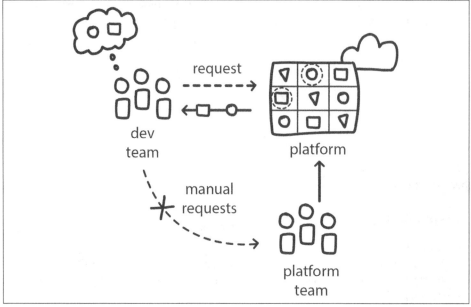

Figure 10-4. Self-Service

The company is moving from Waterfall/Agile and, within a structure of separate operations and development teams, is aiming to set up microservices, CD, and public (or private) cloud. Teams are running many experiments and PoCs and aiming to reduce the cost of experimentation.

In This Context

In traditional organizations, provisioning hardware or doing maintenance work requires filling out a form, sending it to Ops, and waiting for them to do it on your behalf. Each handover creates a delay of hours, days, even weeks, and this slows down the entire system. This process also discourages frequent releases from developers to production, and without that there is no Continuous Delivery (CD), no learning loop from delivering to customers and receiving feedback.

- Anything manual is, by definition, too slow for cloud native.
- People will do more of something if they can do it themselves.

- Premature optimization—automating the wrong thing—can be particularly bad in this context.

Across the company, everything related to software development should be self-service: everyone should be able to provision infrastructure or deploy their applications on their own without handoff to another team.

Self-Service is the requirement—Automate Everything is the way you achieve that.

- Create full automation around the platform. All manual or semi-manual processes must be fully automated.
- Create UIs and APIs so people can include this in their automation.
- Grant access to all developers (within reasonable security limits).
- Start during the MVP stage: Prerequisite is basically having the entire cloud native toolset.

Whenever anyone needs something done, they can do it on their own without handing off to Ops.

+ Reduced cost of experimentation because there is less waiting for results.

+ Reduced dependencies.

− Functional self-service needs a much higher-quality interface, which is a much higher cost.

− The system is automated to be bulletproof against wrong behavior by non-experts using it, which is valuable but also has cost. If you have experts working on infra, they don't need foolproof systems—but most people aren't experts.

Common Pitfalls

Automating things too early before it's fully understood what is going to happen, which leads to the biggest pitfall we see in this context: self-service for things you don't actually need to do. Aim for automation in the long term but don't take immediate action too early—you can automate the wrong things, which is a huge waste of time and money.

Automating self service on the legacy system. In many cases this is too difficult and too expensive and takes the focus away from the new infrastructure. It's often better to keep using manual procedures if they are well-rehearsed and easy to execute.

Related Biases

Pro-innovation bias
"Automation is good, so let's automate all the things!" Yes, automation is good, but automating the wrong things is not good.

Related Patterns

- Delayed Automation
- MVP
- Observability
- Dynamic Scheduling
- Build-Run Teams
- Automated Testing

Pattern: Dynamic Scheduling

An orchestrator (typically Kubernetes) is needed to organize the deployment and management of microservices in a distributed container-based application to assign them across random machines at the instant of execution (Figure 10-5).

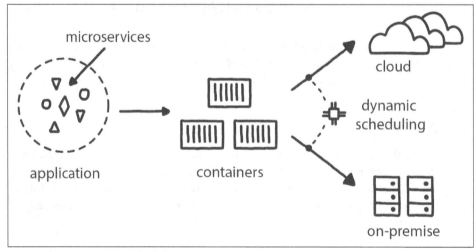

Figure 10-5. Dynamic Scheduling

An application has dozens of independent microservices, and the development teams want to deploy each of them multiple times a day on a variety of private and public cloud platforms.

The traditional hardware approach assumes "This app runs on this server"— which is not practical in a distributed system running on the cloud. Attaching specific microservices to specific pieces of hardware significantly compromises the stability and resilience of the system and leads to poor use of the hardware. Every time you want to improve something you need someone to understand how it is all related, so they can safely make the change.

The market demands that companies deliver value to clients very quickly, in a matter of hours or even minutes. However, the traditional deployment of applications to specified static servers using manual or semi-automatic procedures cannot support the growing demands of the development teams to deploy each component separately on multiple environments once, or even more times, per day.

- Software systems become more distributed overall and are required to run on many platforms.

- Dynamic scheduling tools (i.e. container orchestrators like Kubernetes, Nomad, and Docker Swarm, among others) are becoming mature and available for general use.

- Small pieces of applications can fail at random times.

- Advanced technology companies deploy thousands of times a day to large and varied array of development, testing, and production environments.

- In a system with hundreds of components, designating where each one runs increases complexity in the code because this must be specified in the build and is impractical.

- Predicting how a distributed system will behave in runtime is practically impossible.

- All major public clouds have managed dynamic scheduling as a service.

All application scheduling needs to be done using an orchestration system in a fully automatic way.

Dynamic schedulers function as container management, in the form of a platform for automating deployment, scaling, and operations of application containers across clusters of hosts. This helps to achieve much more efficient hardware use as the scheduler understands the latest state of the system and can squeeze many components to the same piece of hardware. It also helps to achieve much higher resilience by adding health checks and elements of self-healing and abstracts away the target hardware to simplify the development.

- Cross-functional teams need to understand how to use such tools effectively, and they need to become part of the standard development process.

- Dynamic scheduling also handles stability and resilience by autoscaling and restarting failing applications.

Developers build distributed systems and define how components will run and communicate with one another once they are deployed.

+ Applications can scale up and down.

+ Non-functional parts can be restarted and healed automatically.

– In a distributed system you invest in mechanisms for disaster recovery and disaster maintenance, which carry a high cost.

– Maintenance is more complex.

– Even when letting the public cloud handle it for you, Dynamic Scheduling is still exponentially more complex than running a single server.

Common Pitfalls

Trying to put Kubernetes (or any other orchestration tool) in place before making sure that all other pieces of the architecture are completely in place: containers, microservices, CI/CD, full monitoring. Trying to use a dynamic scheduler on its own will significantly increase the complexity and maintenance cost of the infrastructure while producing minimal value.

Related Biases

Bandwagon effect
    The tendency to do something because many other people are doing it, and everybody is talking about Kubernetes these days. Ask for it by name, even if you aren't exactly sure what it does or if it fits your use case!

Pro-innovation bias

Having excessive optimism toward an innovation's usefulness and applicability because it is new and cutting edge, without understanding its limitations or implementation context. Basically, thinking that Kubernetes is going to solve all of your scheduling problems for you.

Related Patterns

- Microservices Architecture
- Distributed Systems
- Containerized Apps
- Platform Team
- Build-Run Teams

Pattern: Containerized Apps

When an application is packaged in a container with all its necessary dependencies, it does not rely on the underlying runtime environment and so can run agnostically on any platform (Figure 10-6).

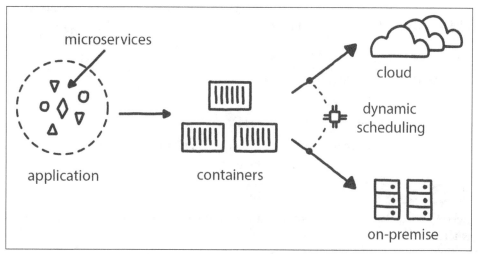

Figure 10-6. Containerized Apps

The team is building a distribution app that can scale up and down. Separate teams are meanwhile building microservices, and they need to take them quickly through a variety of dev and test environments all the way to production. There are a variety of different runtime environments, such as personal laptops, during development and different private and public clouds for testing, integration, and production.

In This Context

Speed of delivery can be slow if an app depends on uniformity among different environments. Maintaining consistency of different tools and their versions on many machines across many on-premises and/or public clouds is difficult, time-consuming, and risky.

- All stable environments tend to drift eventually.
- It's impossible to manage thousands of machines manually.
- Differences in environment are difficult to find and to fix.

Therefore

Package up an application's code and everything it needs to run (all its dependencies, runtime, system tools, libraries, and settings) as a consistent unit so the application can be distributed to start up quickly and run reliably in any computing environment.

This minimizes dependency on the runtime environment. Build once, run everywhere, and distribute quickly and easily.

- Use industry standards like Docker.
- Ensure proper versioning and simple and quick distribution.
- All dependencies included.
- All environments use the same basic tooling.
- Ensure that containers can run on local or any other environment.

Consequently

Every part of the app is packaged in a container and can be easily started anywhere.

+ Container tools like Docker improve efficiency.
− Large numbers of separate containers increase system complexity.
− Managing container images requires extra effort.

Common Pitfalls

Building or managing container images manually, or not managing the versions on the released container images. This can lead to differences in different environments during the development of the runtime, which will introduce instability and lower the quality of the application.

Related Patterns

- Microservices Architecture
- Reproducible Dev Environments
- Distributed Systems

Pattern: Observability

Cloud native distributed systems require constant insight into the behavior of all running services in order to understand the system's behavior and to predict potential problems or incidents (Figure 10-7).

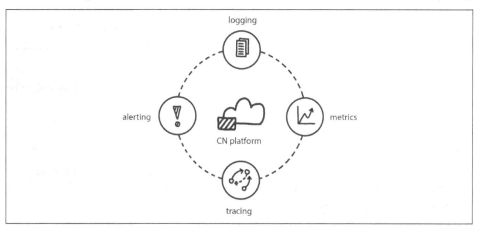

Figure 10-7. Observability

Teams are moving to microservices, and there are more and more pieces—the number of components is growing. Traditional responsive monitoring cannot recognize service failures.

Traditional systems practice assumes the goal is for every system to be 100% up and running, so monitoring is reactive—i.e., aiming to ensure nothing has hap-

pened to any of these components. It alerts when a problem occurs. In traditional monitoring if a server fails, you will have an event; response, even if automatic, is manually triggered. This assumption is not valid for distributed systems.

- A distributed system is by definition not 100% stable—when you have so many pieces, some of them will go up and down at random times.
- Resilience is built into the system to handle the assumption that eventually everything in the system will go down at some point.
- The number of components is always increasing while the number of people working on the application remains reasonably stable.
- Always a cost: if you get something, you must pay for it in some way. Here it is complexity, and you must manage it.
- Manual response is never fast enough in a cloud native system.

Therefore

Put in logging, tracing, alerting, and metrics to always collect information about all the running services in a system.

- Switch from a centrally planned system to distributed self-governing system.
- Continually analyze availability of services and behavioral trends of the individual services and entire system.
- Instead of focusing on specific pieces of hardware, focus on functional behavior of components.
- Consistently collect as many metrics as possible.
- Analyze the trends.
- Create an interface to make system state accessible to all stakeholders: anyone involved in system maintenance or development who needs to understand the system at any given time must be able to observe the system's behavior.

Consequently

There is a continuous overview of the state of the system, visible to anyone for whom this is relevant information.

+ Analytics and proactive monitoring can be used to discover trends, which can be used to predict failure.

− Any response to a single specific failure is extremely difficult.

Common Pitfalls

Lack of standardization through allowing multiple teams to do things how they like, so 10 different teams get to production in 10 different ways. Trying to create observability in this situation—to record, analyze, and reconcile behavior insights in a meaningful way from so many sources—is basically impossible.

Related Patterns

- Measure What Matters
- Avoid Reinventing the Wheel
- Public Cloud
- Full Production Readiness
- Learning Loop

Pattern: Continuous Delivery

Keeping a short build/test/deliver cycle means code is always ready for production and features can be immediately released to customers—and their feedback quickly returned to developers (Figure 10-8).

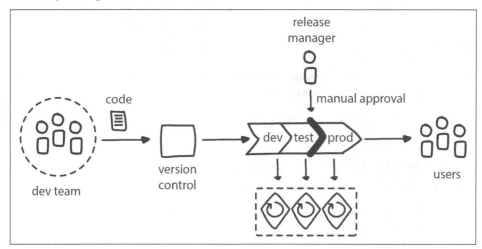

Figure 10-8. Continuous Delivery

Teams are doing Continuous Integration, so each change is automatically built and tested separately in a very short time. Developers commit changes at least once a day. Teams are building distributed systems using microservices architecture.

A full quality test of a distributed system can be done only when the entire system is fully deployed and used. Teams try to reduce complexity and increase quality through infrequent and coordinated multiple-team deployments to the test environment, and then handing off to the operations team for more extensive testing and, finally, delivery.

Large-scale deployments at long intervals are usually difficult and time-consuming, so teams tend to minimize their number. This leads to painful integrations between services, reduced independence of teams, slower time to market, and—eventually—lower quality and higher costs for building the product or service.

- There is more incentive to automate an operation if it happens more frequently (if something is painful do it more often).
- Some issues cannot be caught by automation.
- People gain trust in an action when it's executed frequently and rarely fails.
- People lose trust quickly if quality is low or reporting unreliable.
- Small changes delivered by the teams themselves are easy to fix or revert.
- Recent changes are still fresh in developers' minds.

Therefore

Deliver every change to a production-like environment where all the services are delivered continuously and independently.

Reduce the pain by using full automation coupled with increased speed and frequency of releases.

- No manual handovers on the way to deployment.
- Full automation is now in place.
- Test automation is now in place.
- Products are always in a releasable state.
- Experiments are more effective, as getting feedback from real customers is fast and painless.

Consequently

The business can release to customers anytime.

\+ A feature can be tested very quickly with customers.

– Some failures will sneak in through automation.

– Very high level of automation is critical; any manual steps slow the process and introduce problems.

Related Patterns

- Continuous Integration
- Continuous Deployment
- Learning Loop
- Build-Run Teams
- Automated Testing
- No Long Tests in CI/CD

Pattern: Continuous Deployment

Continuous Deployment automatically and seamlessly pushes code that has been accepted in the Continuous Integration/Continuous Delivery cycle into the production environment (Figure 10-9).

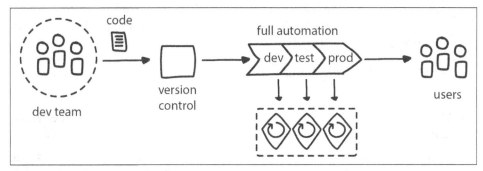

Figure 10-9. Continuous Deployment

The team is using Continuous Delivery and building a distributed system using microservices. There is no regulation nor any other restriction on fully automated delivery.

Changes are frequently delivered to a production-like environment in a quick and automated way, but then they get stuck there.

Many teams using CI/CD still have a human gate at the end, meaning that before changes can go live they may need to wait for the Ops team to do extensive testing, whether automated or manual, and/or wait for manual deployment. This means changes are not tested in a real live environment and carry high deployment risk due to potential differences in tools and processes. Time to market is slower; release manager delays releases due to risk and complexity.

- Any handover point slows down the process and introduces risk.
- Some industries have regulations that define roles during development and deployment (for example, release must be manually approved by a designated person of responsibility, as is common in financial sector regs).
- Frequent delivery better helps perceive customer needs.

Therefore

Create a fully automated deployment process to take all changes to production all of the time. Use gradual deployment strategies and prepare for failure mitigation.

Every change committed to the source code repository needs to be tested and ready for delivery to production at any given moment based on business needs and according to the relevant regulations.

- Build in full automation throughout system.
- No team or service dependencies are allowed.
- Make sure there is very good overview of the content and risks to the release manager.
- In case of regulatory restrictions that require a manual delivery step, automate everything before and after the release review point and make the release point as simple as pressing a button. Provide sufficient information to the release manager to allow fast and sound decisions.

Consequently

Speed of delivery to customers is very high, and the changes are flowing to the customers daily or even hourly. Products or services are continuously providing

higher value to the customers while allowing the developers to get real live feedback very quickly and learn and improve the products even further.

+ Experiments can be done quickly and changes rolled back if necessary.

– Some issues can still sneak in.

– You have less control over feature release cadence.

Common Pitfalls

Attempting Continuous Deployment without an adequate level of automation. Every
manual step or handoff inserts a significant speed bump in the process.

Related Patterns

- Continuous Integration
- Continuous Delivery
- Automated Testing
- Learning Loop

Pattern: Full Production Readiness

Make sure your platform is fully provisioned with CI/CD, security, monitoring, observa-
bility, and other features essential to production readiness before you try to take it live
(Figure 10-10).

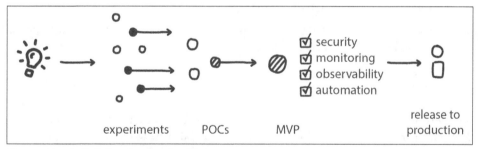

Figure 10-10. Full Production Readiness

Core Team is stepping up the cloud native platform. The new platform and the first
few applications moving over to it are scheduled for full production delivery very
soon.

Too many companies try to rush their newly built cloud native platform into production before it is really ready. Typically the container scheduling platform is installed, but it's still missing essential automation elements around maintenance and software delivery. This leads to poor quality of the running system and necessitates long delivery cycles. Many times the platform vendor will confirm production readiness of their tool—but without considering the whole system of delivery and maintenance cycles that are an equally crucial part of production.

- Typical cloud native platforms today include only a partial platform and require significant additional configuration and automation.
- A typical full cloud native platform includes 10 to 20 tools.
- Once the main platform is fully running, there is pressure to deliver.
- In case of poor maintenance automation, platform teams could be overloaded with support tasks as teams onboard.

Therefore

Before going to production all major elements of the platform, as well as those of any applications initially migrating to it, need to be in place. This includes having a scheduler, observability, security, networking, storage, and CI/CD. Also, at least basic maintenance automation must be in place.

- System is automated.
- Maintenance is automated or at least documented.
- A bare and basic MVP version of a platform is not enough: there must also be observability, CI/CD, security, etc.

Consequently

The new platform is functional and maintainable, and major tasks are automated. The Platform Team can continue extending the platform while providing satisfactory support for the development teams using it.

+ All major elements of the platform are in place.

− May delay release to production.

Common Pitfalls

The most common pitfall is going to production without having a fully functional and automated CI/CD setup. This often happens because the Platform Team is pressured to deliver to production by the management, so they make a plan to go live and then complete the CI/CD setup when they have a bit of free time. Unfortunately, as we all know, that bit of free time will never materialize; the pressure will stay high and will only grow after the users are exposed to the new system. Further, the lack of CI/CD automation will be the biggest time consumer, demanding most of the Platform Team's time as the Build-Run development teams introduce more applications. This leads to a vicious circle of not having enough time to automate delivery because we're too busy deploying applications manually.

Related Patterns

- MVP
- Observability
- Secure System from the Start
- Automated Testing

Pattern: Risk-Reducing Deployment Strategies

Employ release tactics to decrease the chance of problems happening when changes are introduced into the production system (Figure 10-11).

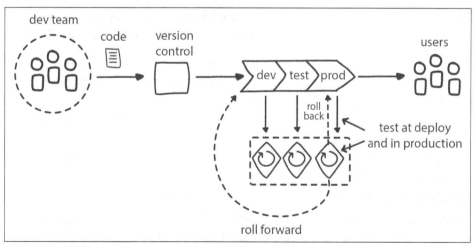

Figure 10-11. Risk-reducing Deployment Strategies

You have a cloud native system with high availability requirements. Teams are building microservices and releasing them independently and often.

Deployment is like a plane taking off: it's the most dangerous part of flying. System failures typically don't happen during normal operation but rather during maintenance and updating. This is because change always carries risk, and these are times when you are introducing change into the system.

Deployments are the most frequent and common type of change, and if not treated carefully can introduce a lot of instability. In cloud native, deployment happens *very* frequently, so this is an important area of concern.

- Maintenance tasks are risk points.
- Deployment frequency in cloud native is high.
- Impact of changes to a complex distributed system is impossible to predict and can lead to cascading errors.
- Modern web users expect 100% availability and high levels of system responsiveness.

Therefore

Use a variety of advanced release strategies to reduce the impact to end users when deployments occur.

There are multiple ways to more safely release a new version of an application to production, and the choice is driven by business needs and budget. Options that work well for cloud native are:

- **Re-create**: First the existing version A is terminated, then new version B is rolled out.
- **Ramped** (also known as rolling-update or incremental): Version B is slowly rolled out and gradually replaces version A.
- **Blue/Green**: Version B is released alongside version A, then the traffic is switched to version B.
- **Canary**: Version B is released to a subset of users, then proceeds to a full rollout.
- **Shadow**: Version B receives real-world traffic alongside version A until stability and performance are demonstrated, and then all traffic shifts to B.

When releasing to development/staging environments, either a re-create or a ramped deployment is usually a good choice. If releasing directly to production, a ramped or blue/green deployment is a good potential fit but proper testing of the new platform is necessary. Blue/green and shadow strategies require double resource capacity and so are more expensive, but reduce the risk of user impact. If an application has not been thoroughly tested or if confidence is lacking in the software's ability to carry a production load, then a canary or shadow release should be used.

Shadow release is the most complex, especially when calling external dependencies with mutable actions (messaging, banking, etc.). But it is particularly useful in common cloud native situations like migrating to a new database technology due to the ability to monitor live system performance under load while maintaining 100% availability.

(If your business requires testing of a new feature against a specific demographic filtered by parameters like geolocation, language, device platform, or browser features, then you may want to use the A/B testing technique. See the *A/B Testing* pattern.)

- Dynamic scheduling used in conjunction with other technologies supports a variety of deployment strategies to make sure infrastructure remains reliable during an application update.
- Use redundancy and gradual rollout to reduce risk.
- Limit the blast radius by deploying small parts of the system independently.

Consequently

Risks to the system during deployment/maintenance are anticipated and managed.

+ Deployments are frequent, and the Dev teams are confident.

+ Users get high availability and seamless responsiveness.

− These setups are complex, and cost can be high.

− The complex nature of these techniques can introduce new risks.

Related Patterns

- Dynamic Scheduling
- A/B Testing
- No Long Tests in CI/CD
- Reproducible Dev Environments

Pattern: Lift and Shift at the End

It's important not to approach a cloud native transformation by simply attempting a full "lift and shift" of your existing system onto the cloud. But it can be smart to move some intact pieces of it at the very end (Figure 10-12).

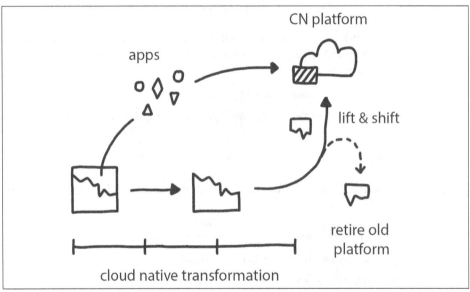

Figure 10-12. Lift and Shift at the End

Most of your existing apps have been re-architectured and moved to the new platform. Some old stuff remains, but it is stable and doesn't change too often.

In This Context

Companies often first approach a cloud native transformation with the belief that it simply means migrating their existing system and processes onto the cloud. This is so common that it's earned the name "lift and shift" and it categorically does

not work if you try to do this at the beginning of a transformation. An organization has to change not only its technology but also its structure, processes, and culture in order to succeed with cloud native.

When organizations do a lift and shift at the very beginning, they expect it will be a quick and easy project to execute, since the applications themselves do not change significantly. In most cases, however, it ends up being a large and expensive initiative requiring triple the anticipated time and budget. This is due both to the complexity related to the underlying platform and the new knowledge required for operating on the cloud. Such a painful experience may lead to delays or even total cancellation of the following refactoring initiatives.

- An expensive project to rebuild/refactor an app may prevent further improvements on app.
- "Moving to cloud" may look like a quick win.
- Public cloud vendors may offer incentives for you to move—lift and shift—inappropriately early in the transformation initiative.

Therefore

Move functioning and stable legacy apps as-is from data centers to the new cloud native platform without re-architecture at the very end of the initiative.

An organization has to change not only its technology but also its structure, processes, and culture in order to succeed with cloud native. Once the cloud native transformation is close to the end, however, it could be valuable to move any remaining parts of the old system to the new platform. This avoids the extra cost of supporting the legacy platform as well as gaining at least some benefits of the new platform for the old applications.

At the end of a successful refactoring, when the last few, rarely changing applications remain, the team continues to refactor them all, ignoring the piling costs and few benefits coming from such refactoring.

- Keep old tech like VMS and monoliths intact on the new platform.
- Spend minimal effort.
- Create easy ways to strangle remaining old apps.
- Lift and shift only apps that almost never change but cannot be retired easily.

You can retire the old platform, shut down the servers, and end the datacenter contracts.

+ Benefits are gained from some features on new platform.

− But this is a missed opportunity to update/re-architect these legacy apps/services, which will likely remain the same forever.

− Some teams are stuck with old tech.

Common Pitfalls

By far the most common is to try to move the entire existing system exactly as it is onto AWS or some other cloud provider. All your processes and procedures remain exactly the same, only now they're on cloud-based infrastructure instead of on premises. This kind of "lift and shift in the beginning" is a large effort that typically requires far more expense and effort than originally estimated. Furthermore, though there are always plans to continue refactoring to improve and update the new system, the team feels fatigue from change and becomes apprehensive of starting any other major refactoring project on the same set of applications.

Another, less common, pitfall is to insist on keeping two different platforms for years just to run a few remaining old applications that were never refactored in cloud native.

Related Biases

Status quo bias
　　If this way of doing things has always worked for us, why change anything now?

Default effect
　　When lifting and shifting an entire system onto a new public cloud platform, simply accepting the tools and options as packaged/configured by the provider instead of finding the best ones for your specific needs and circumstances.

Bandwagon effect
　　Rushing to move operations to the cloud because other companies in your sector are doing it and you want to do it too.

Related Patterns

- Strangle Monolithic Application

- Lean for Optimization
- Architecture Drawing

Summary

In this chapter we introduced patterns around cloud native infrastructure. The intent is to first expose readers to the patterns themselves before applying them—fitting them together in the transformation design outlined in Chapter 11 and Chapter 12. There we show how a company like WealthGrid can apply patterns step by step, from start to finish, as a transformation design. The design moves the company through four stages to emerge successfully transformed into a flexible, responsive, and above all confident organization, able to work both proficiently and innovatively as needed.

Once familiar with the patterns and ready to move on to applying them in a design, this chapter—along with the other chapters presenting patterns for strategy, organization/culture, and development/processes—functions as a more in-depth resource for referencing and working with individual patterns.

New cloud native patterns are emerging constantly. To continue sharing them and extending the cloud native pattern language we have established here, please visit www.CNpatterns.org.

This is where to find the latest pattern developments, but also an online community for discussing and creating new patterns. We are inviting people from across the industry, thought leaders and influencers but most importantly everyday engineers and managers—those out there working elbows-deep in cloud native code and architecture—to contribute and participate. Hope to see you there!

CHAPTER 11

Applying the Patterns: A Transformation Design Story, Part 1

This is a detailed design for a cloud native transformation. Here we will lay out patterns from start to finish, explaining the order and reason for the choices as we go along. It's a lengthy and involved process, so we have divided it into two chapters. This one covers the period from pre-initiative prep through the point where we have researched, experimented, and prototyped until successfully uncovering the likely best transformation path. Part 2 picks up with verifying the path and beginning to build a production-ready cloud native platform, carries through onboarding everyone onto the new system with a new way of working, and then moves to shutting down the old one.

For several chapters now we have watched WealthGrid struggle with multiple attempts at a cloud native transformation, only to fail each time. The story we are going to tell now is how to do it right—in other words, what WealthGrid would have done, had they known better. We will be using patterns to show the way, so that now *you* will know better.

First, let's take a quick review of the story thus far.

WealthGrid's first erroneous attempt to move to cloud native is an extremely common strategy: treating the transformation as only a minor technology shift. Many companies try exactly this, and equally many fail at it. The technology is new and rests upon a complex distributed architecture, so right away you have two things nobody at WealthGrid (or pretty much anybody at any other company, aside from a handful of tech giants) really understands or has any experience with. Setting a small team with no background in the tech to deliver a full transformation as a side project while also doing their usual work on the existing system? We saw how well that worked for WealthGrid—or, rather, didn't work.

WealthGrid's people, Jenny and Steve, as well as others, saw it too. And they did try to correct course. For their second attempt they tried going all in, assigning a big team (and big budget) to bringing the whole organization onto the cloud. Unfortunately, this all-hands-on-deck approach did not work any better. First, too many teams tried too many experiments and came up with too many possible solutions, none of which fitted together. Six months into the initiative—their original deadline—they were no closer to having a working cloud native platform than they had been at the start.

Again, they tried to adjust. They tried to clean up the too-many-platforms mess by calling in a systems architect (with zero experience in Kubernetes) to design a unified approach. He came up with an impressive diagram that, unfortunately, got it all wrong. Even more unfortunately, there was still not enough understanding of how cloud native works, within WealthGrid's ranks—from corner office to middle management to engineers—for anyone to see how wrong it was. Thus everyone set to work trying to implement the new but still nonfunctional architecture. Again, everyone worked hard. Six more months passed. Again, nothing was delivered.

Meanwhile, the skeleton crew of engineers maintaining the original system was able to keep everything working, but they weren't able to deliver new features. The team was understaffed. And besides, why invest in new functionality on the old system when it was about to be replaced? Initially nobody worried about this, because the new cloud native system would have such velocity that WealthGrid's feature debt would surely be paid back in very short time. But then the promised six-month delivery time turned into a year, and still the new platform was nowhere near ready.

This meant a year of no new features or other meaningful improvements for Wealth-Grid's customers—and a very real risk of losing market share. The sales and marketing teams got the ear of the CFO, who talked to the CEO and the board, who finally laid down an ultimatum: Here are five new features that we need, and fast. We don't care about which platform we use. *Just deliver them.*

Now what does WealthGrid do?

PHASE 1: THINK

Phase 1 of the transformation design is called "Think," because it's all about ideas, strategy, and objectives.

Most companies are going to enter this phase at a very similar standpoint: they are using Waterfall to Agile-ish delivery methods focused on very high proficiency. This means that most of the talent and resources in the company are dedicated to delivering a very stable core business product or service. There might be a bit of experimenting going on here and there, but it is definitely not an internal priority. There's probably no team dedicated to innovation, or any programs designed to inject creativity into the existing system. In short, this is very likely a company that has forgotten how to be creative.

To put some numbers on this, at this point the distribution of investment between delivery, innovation, and research is 95/5/0. The vast majority of focus, 95%, is on delivering the core product as efficiently as possible. A small amount, 5%, is left over for any innovation going on. Whatever this is, it's targeted mainly at improving systems around the core product, and expected to be useful or pay off very soon. Zero research is going into any kind of crazy ideas that might—or might not—pay off big someday.

It is against this backdrop that the first stirrings toward transformation take place. Our first set of patterns addresses getting the process started: first, effective strategic thinking and decision making from the organization's leaders. And then converting this strategy into vision and objectives to move the process to the next phase, execution.

Enter the Champion

Any significant innovation always begins in the same place, or rather with the same person: the Transformation Champion.

A large, established system in motion is usually slow to change direction: see Newton's First Law of Physics, also known as the law of inertia. And WealthGrid, like any other sizable and successful company, has invested a lot of time—years, if not decades—in streamlining its core business processes to be as proficient as possible.

The problem with achieving this impressively high proficiency, as we saw in Chapter 7, tends to be a corresponding decline in the ability to innovate. Every successful company was once a startup, and startups are all about creativity. Its ultimate goal, though, is to get to proficient, even algorithmic, delivery of their product or service, because that is where the profits lie. Once they make it, successful enterprises typically focus almost exclusively on operating as lean as possible. This is fine, good even, except that when they focus entirely on proficiency, they forget to keep a piece of creativity alive.

So when any company similar to WealthGrid decides to change course—i.e., innovate—even when it's in response to an undeniable threat to its bottom line, it must overcome a fair amount of resistance. Just as a catalyst like a disruptive stranger coming to your town is needed to stimulate the change, a corresponding force—a metaphorical town mayor—is needed to manage the community's response. In a cloud native transformation, this person is the Transformation Champion and the whole thing starts with them. There has to be trust in their leadership and willingness to follow their guidance.

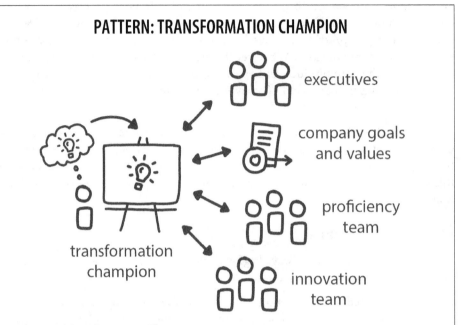

PATTERN: TRANSFORMATION CHAMPION

Figure 11-1. Transformation Champion

The Transformation Champion is a person (or sometimes a small team) who understands both the transformation and the company objectives, is well connected within the organization, and is highly motivated to promote the transformation. Unless they are recognized by the company's leaders and given authority, however, they will be unable to stimulate effective change across the organization.

Every company has some of these people. They see the future more clearly than most, and as a result they always want to change something. This is the hallmark of a true champion: they don't just have ideas; they try to take action. Champions are good at promoting a new idea while making sure it is a proper fit for the company's goals and values. Such people need to be identified, nurtured, and trained in general, but when it comes time to undertake a major initiative that will terraform the entire organization, they are critical for its success.

The trick is recognizing the champions in your midst, because this first pattern is not about *creating* a Transformation Champion—it's about *discovering* the one(s) you already have. These people tend to be self-selecting, and quite often they are the trigger for the whole thing.

So, look around! In every company we visit to consult about cloud native, there is one person super excited we are there. This is often the person who asked us to come in the first place.

Once we take on the client, our first question is, will that person lead the initiative, or will they name a different leader? This can be tricky. Not everyone is cut out to manage a large transition project. But in general this self-selected evangelist is going to be the right person to lead yours, and so it's important to appoint someone else only if there is a truly compelling reason to do so. (Said compelling reasons, FYI, do not include "In our company senior managers always lead large projects." Trust us on this. You're going cloud native now and it's time to do things differently.)

If you seek your champion, you will find them. Somebody inspired this whole transformation thing, and this person could be anyone anywhere in the company, engineer or manager or CEO. Finding this person is not the problem—they exist. The true problem is that, usually, they just don't have the power to get things done right. Fortunately, the simple fix is simply to empower them and then get out of the way!

So, once you find them and anoint them as the authorized Transition Champion, let this be known far and wide. Send a clear message that this transformation is an initiative supported by the company—not just a side project by a few motivated employees—and that participation is not only appreciated but expected. This is absolutely crucial. A champion can tell everyone the absolutely right thing to do as their part of the migration, but unless they are fully supported by the executive team (or are themselves very senior) people can ignore them and do nothing, or even block their efforts.

WealthGrid's Transformation Champion is Jenny, by the way. She is a classic example: Jenny saw what her company needed to do in order to be ready for the ways the market is permanently changing. And then she stepped up to make it happen.

You may rightfully wonder why, if Transformation Champion is an essential pattern and Jenny is a good example, did WealthGrid's efforts then fail not once but three times? After all, Jenny knew what needed to happen: the company had to go cloud native in order to remain competitive. She even, eventually, had the full confidence and backing of the CEO and board to do a full-on initiative, not to mention hands-on help from much of the company's engineering staff. What was missing?

The missing piece was Dynamic Strategy.

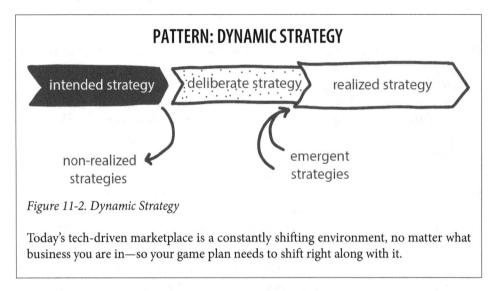

PATTERN: DYNAMIC STRATEGY

intended strategy → deliberate strategy → realized strategy

non-realized strategies

emergent strategies

Figure 11-2. Dynamic Strategy

Today's tech-driven marketplace is a constantly shifting environment, no matter what business you are in—so your game plan needs to shift right along with it.

WealthGrid's first transformation attempt, with Jenny's team trying to do it as a side project, did not have any real strategy at all. In the second attempt, though, everyone got on board, a strategy was created, and things still went sideways. Had the Dynamic Strategy pattern been applied, however, the story would have made the same missteps, only much more quickly. Instead of wasting a year to figure that things were simply not working, they could have moved through the process in two months. It would still have been painful, but at least it would have been quick.

Dynamic Strategy is essential for doing cloud native right, from inception to completion. This is actually a super pattern, one so essential that it overlays all the other patterns in our transformation design from the very beginning, and stays forever. Let's look at the next set of patterns now to learn more specific steps for getting a transformation off to the right start.

Ready to Commit

Even though it's time for enterprises to learn how to navigate this new paradigm, we aren't saying to forget the past. We learned a lot from WealthGrid's experience thus far, and we need to use it. The first lesson being, don't continue something from the past just because your organization started it. That is classic sunk cost fallacy, or irrational escalation: the phenomenon where people justify increased investment in a decision, based on the cumulative prior investment, despite new evidence suggesting that the decision was probably wrong. This unfortunately is a very frequent phenomenon in companies moving to cloud native. People routinely push forward with projects that are obviously not going to bring any value, just because they've already invested so much in the mess.

So let's use Dynamic Strategy to pause and reevaluate here at the very start, and make sure we are not going into sunk cost. Now is the time to ask, *Do we even need this thing?* using the Business Case pattern.

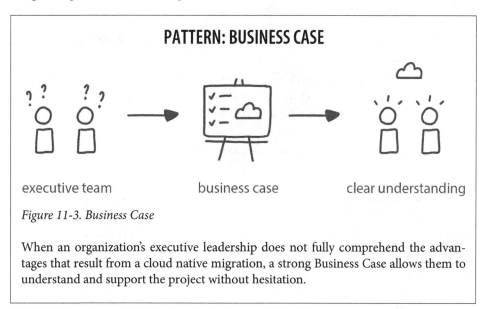

PATTERN: BUSINESS CASE

executive team   business case   clear understanding

Figure 11-3. Business Case

When an organization's executive leadership does not fully comprehend the advantages that result from a cloud native migration, a strong Business Case allows them to understand and support the project without hesitation.

Sometimes Business Case can be a tough sell even when a cloud native transformation is clearly the right response to an existential threat. The traditional model is for organizations to be massively risk averse, which means minimizing uncertainty at all costs. This is why it takes forever to plan anything in Waterfall—the process is designed to identify and mitigate every conceivable problem in advance. So pitching a cloud migration to a change-averse culture that avoids new technologies or experimental approaches can be challenging. Cloud native is complex, and the benefits are not easily visible, especially at first. So, for all these reasons, some companies are simply going to avoid talking about the risks and advantages. In these situations, Business Case facilitates the conversation in a factual, objective, and non-threatening way.

For most, though, Business Case is a valuable reality check before diving into an initiative they are already inclined to take on. Too many organizations jump on the cloud native bandwagon without doing a true cost/benefit analysis. (In fact, the cognitive bias known as the "bandwagon effect" exactly describes how companies caught in the hype of the cloud conversation make decisions without understanding exactly how a transformation fits with their business needs and goals.) Thus, evaluating the Business Case should involve business stakeholders, information-gathering interviews with internal and external subject matter experts, and a clear vision for where the organization is headed.

This may reveal that going cloud native is not actually the right thing for a company to do, at least not right now. There are a few times when cloud native likely would not be the right move, and an organization working through Business Case needs to be aware of them even if they're uncommon.

- When a company is struggling for survival and has no budget or time to allocate to the transformation.
- If there is an immediate crisis that cannot be solved with cloud native. This is a case of "right move, just not now." Cloud native will have no appropriate priority in this case, but once the situation has resolved, Dynamic Strategy tells us to revisit the decision.
- Maybe in a very stable market where nothing changes. But these markets are very few, and becoming fewer all the time, so this is a high-risk decision.

The best reason not to do cloud native at all is when the software part of the business is really simple and limited, and cloud native will overcomplicate things without adding significant value. But this mainly applies to smaller companies, since any large enterprise should have substantial IT that will benefit from a migration.

Everyone else should start investing in cloud native. The only question is pace: some can do it slowly, while others—for example, anyone in a stranger-danger situation—should do it with higher urgency.

Keep in mind the difference between cloud computing and cloud native. Namely, the cloud refers to on-demand delivery of virtual infrastructure (hardware/servers), storage, databases, etc., while cloud native is an architectural approach—a methodology. Even monoliths can benefit from taking advantage of the automation, ability to pay only for resources consumed, and other niceties built into public cloud platforms. Any enterprise running a highly stable monolith on a legacy codebase that requires very little change or updating ever needs to take a very hard look at the Business Case for regrooming that monolith into microservices. (Don't stop reading, though. There are many more patterns to help you move your functional monolith onto the cloud!)

Business Case in hand, the next step in our transformation design is the Executive Commitment pattern.

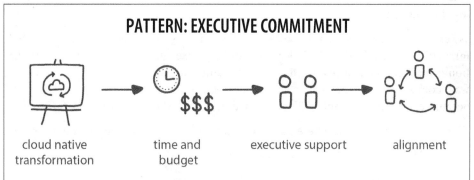

PATTERN: EXECUTIVE COMMITMENT

cloud native transformation → time and budget → executive support → alignment

Figure 11-4. Executive Commitment

To ensure allocation of sufficient resources and reasonable delivery time frames, large-scale projects such as a cloud native transformation require strong Executive Commitment.

This function of this pattern is to establish the cloud native transformation as a high-priority strategic initiative with explicit support from the company's executive management. Public announcement of the cloud native transformation as a key strategic initiative creates company-wide alignment and awareness, while also setting the expectation of collaboration from all departments within the organization.

It might seem that Executive Commitment for a transformation should go without saying, but it's an important moment in a migration. It establishes that this is not some small engineering project driven by a handful of motivated employees but a full-company effort, and the senior leaders are standing behind it. This is needed for a number of reasons. First and most obvious is that commitment from the company's most senior leaders makes sure the project gets an appropriate level of resources and budget allocated. Less obvious but equally important is that announcing their full support makes it known across the organization that change is coming, and that the cloud native transformation is an official part of the company's value hierarchy. Maybe the project doesn't need to be *the* top priority, but it is indeed a real one.

WealthGrid's first attempt failed in part due to a lack of Executive Commitment. Though Jenny got permission from upper management, she didn't get support. No extra budget or resources were given to the project, and it remained a small, localized effort that most people in the company had no idea was even happening. This is exactly the reason why it all gets spelled out as a pattern: Such commitment from the management needs to include preparation of a Transformation Strategy (pattern coming up), public announcement of the project, and the allocation of adequate resources and budget. Again, had Jenny gotten full Executive Commitment for her first try, it would have gone quite differently. It may still have failed, but it would have failed much faster and according to an actual strategy—which could then be refactored for lessons learned.

When an organization stands poised at the first step of a migration journey, it is important that the leaders, well, lead the way. Because when the cloud native destination is reached, the company will not be the same company. It will build in a different way, compete in a different way, generally behave in a completely new way. And because change is scary, the CEO and board need to lead the way with confidence.

That is why the moment where Executive Commitment is achieved is the moment a transformation truly begins.

Vision and Core Team

Having named a Transformation Champion (fortunately, WealthGrid was smart enough to officially name Jenny to the role she had been filling all along), established the compelling need for cloud native with Business Case, and achieved Executive Commitment for making it actually happen, it's now time to plan the actual transition.

Two things need to happen now: we need to create a proper migration strategy and pick the team to deliver it. In its first attempt to go cloud native, WealthGrid had neither. Not on purpose, but because it simply made the same mistake most companies do when launching a transformation: simply adding the transformation to the usual Agile backlog of tasks. Functionally, this means tasking an existing team with building the new system while still being responsible for their regular duties, too. Jenny's team never had the chance to build much of anything at all. But even when a team does get more time to work on it than they did, or has simply a long timeframe to do it in, they still won't be able to deliver. Limited experience coupled with a lack of space and flexibility for research leads to pursuing cloud native implementation using "well-known ways"—that is, trying to deliver cloud native using incompatible approaches from Waterfall, Agile, or a combination of the two. As we have seen, the initiative falters.

Two cognitive bias factors influencing things here are the ambiguity effect, where people facing a situation with a lot of unknowns will fall back on simply doing what they already know how to do, using methods that have worked in the past. Similarly, law of the instrument leads them to choose tools that they know, rather than seeking the right ones for the job. When there is time pressure and little or no opportunity to explore new tools and techniques, guess what is going to happen? Yes, people will pick up their comfortable tools without even thinking.

Furthermore, without an overall consistent vision and a core team in charge of delivering it, different teams will make independent and frequently conflicting architectural decisions. This is exactly what we saw happen with WealthGrid's second attempt.

To avoid both of these problems, we use the Vision First, Objective Setting, and Core Team patterns to set the correct path right away. These mark a gradual shift away from abstract strategy toward concrete execution, which moves down the chain to middle management and the tech teams. But first, before we leave Steve and the rest of WealthGrid's C-suite execs, we have one more pattern for them: Decide Closest to the Action.

Delegating Power

Traditional organizations are all about delegating responsibility, but not authority. Important execution decisions are rarely if ever delegated to those actually in charge of carrying them out. This pattern is about putting the decision close to where the change is happening, and doing this is key to successfully evolving to a cloud native culture.

In the past, the flow went: strategy -> vision -> execution. All planning happened at the first step and almost always at the top of the chain of hierarchy. Once you moved on to vision, planning was done; strategy was set and execution was to follow. Static strategy doesn't work in cloud native, as we have seen with the Dynamic Strategy pattern.

In a way, the Decide Closest to the Action pattern is about dynamic planning and delegation. The simple (but not easy) idea behind it is for decisions to be made at the point of action by the person who's going to be doing the action. So, if your team is responsible for delivering a particular microservice, it is your responsibility to do the planning around that microservice. Not your boss, not the project manager, not the systems architect, certainly not the folks several flights up in the nice offices. *You.*

This is where this pattern perhaps gets a bit tricky to implement. In traditional organizations, managers typically do the vast majority of planning and decision making. Then they hand down a set of pre-specified tasks to the engineering teams to execute. Cloud native velocity, however, depends on teams being able to make fast decisions regarding whatever task they are working on, without needing to consult the boss. The managers have to be willing to give up their traditional position of control in order for this to happen.

This is important so we will say it again: in cloud native, the engineers get to plan and to make decisions regarding what they're working on. They don't get handed a set of marching orders from a project manager to fulfill exactly as specified. They don't need to seek permission to try something different if they spot a better way to go. In cloud native, the power to decide rests with the person doing the job.

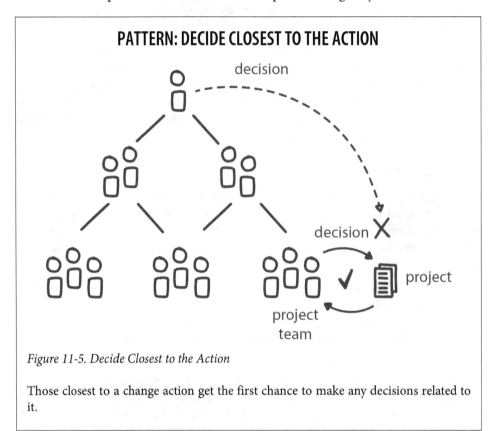

PATTERN: DECIDE CLOSEST TO THE ACTION

Figure 11-5. Decide Closest to the Action

Those closest to a change action get the first chance to make any decisions related to it.

Like Dynamic Strategy, Decide Closest to the Action is a super pattern that applies not just in every phase of the transformation but permanently across the entire organization. Paired closely with Decide Closest to the Action is another super pattern, Psychological Safety. This addresses the need for people throughout the organization to feel they can express ideas, concerns, or mistakes without being punished or humiliated for speaking up.

In a work environment that lacks Psychological Safety, team members hesitate to offer new or different ideas, especially when these may diverge from the overall group opinion, and will generally act in risk-averse ways. Since cloud native depends on teams collaborating to come up with innovative solutions through independent, divergent thinking, Psychological Safety is essential for creating an environment that makes this kind of co-creative work possible.

If teams lack the ability to fail safely when experimenting, they waste time exhaustively analyzing all future outcomes to minimize exposing themselves to risk, effectively killing both creativity and velocity. In a psychologically safe work environment, though, people are willing and even excited to try, possibly fail, and then try again as they strive to come up with the next idea (which might be wild, but also possibly game-changing). And they will be able to make decisions with confidence, knowing that their team will tell them—honestly yet constructively—when they might be making the wrong one.

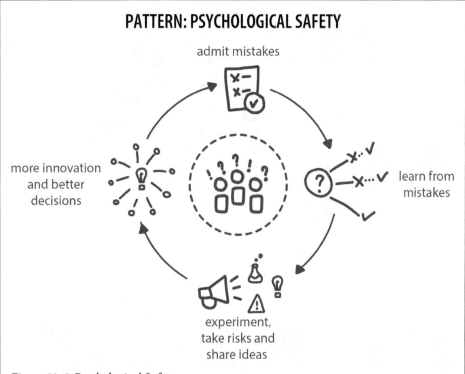

PATTERN: PSYCHOLOGICAL SAFETY

admit mistakes

more innovation and better decisions

learn from mistakes

experiment, take risks and share ideas

Figure 11-6. Psychological Safety

When team members feel they can speak up, express concern, and make mistakes without facing punishment or ridicule, they are able to think freely and creatively, and to be open to taking risks.

Once these innovation-empowering cultural patterns are put in place, the company is now ready to take its first concrete step toward the cloud native transformation: naming the Core Team.

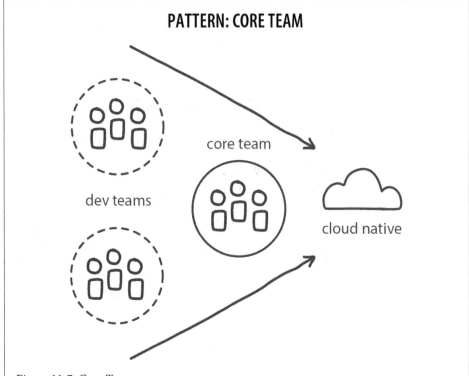

PATTERN: CORE TEAM

core team

dev teams

cloud native

Figure 11-7. Core Team

A dedicated team of engineers and architects, constantly diving deeper into technical challenges, will reduce the risk of the transformation. The team members gain experience that will help onboard the remaining teams more quickly and effectively.

Creating the Core Team means handpicking a relatively small team to drive the overall innovation and, especially, take charge of the initial stages.

What does a Core Team look like? Well, it's compact—typically, five to eight engineers (including software architects, if you've got them to draw from). Team responsibilities will include ownership of the technical vision and architecture, de-risking the transformation by running a series of Proofs of Concepts (PoCs), creation of a Minimum Viable Product (MVP) version of the platform, and later onboarding and guiding other teams. (No worries, we've got patterns coming for all these.)

Essentially, the Core Team rapidly iterates through the most challenging parts of the transformation. They begin by establishing a high-level vision and then translating the vision into concrete, executable objectives. They use research and experimentation to build their own knowledge and experience in the cloud native paradigm—using the knowledge they gain to adjust the transformation vision and architecture as they go. Later, the Core Team's first-hand understanding helps them to onboard other teams to the new way of working. Their knowledge paves the path for the rest of the company for a seamless and successful cloud native adoption.

The team often stays together even once the transformation is done, because they have effectively become the main repository for the organization's cloud native knowledge. Sometimes the Core Team, or perhaps a portion of the team, forms the Platform Team (more on that soon). Or, once the new system is running fully in production mode, they may remain in charge of continually improving the platform—remaining in an innovation-and-research mode to help the company stay ready for whatever future comes next.

Once chosen, the Core Team's very first task is Vision First, outlining a high-level transformation plan.

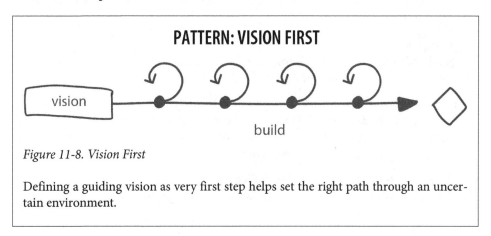

PATTERN: VISION FIRST

Figure 11-8. Vision First

Defining a guiding vision as very first step helps set the right path through an uncertain environment.

In Vision First, the Core Team needs to define a clear and achievable vision that can be translated into specific executable steps. This vision defines and visualizes the architecture of the whole system up front. Since the Core Team is likely still themselves early in the cloud native learning curve, this vision can be created with the help of external resources, such as consultants. This will definitely help the vision stage move quickly.

If time allows, the Core Team can work to find their own way, uncovering the vision/design through a series of small research and prototyping projects, ranging from a few hours to a few days each. This DIY approach is ideal, since it hastens the learning that the Core Team needs to undergo anyway, but it can make this initial phase of the transformation take longer to complete. An experienced consultant can help jump-start that learning, though, while steering things in the right direction, so perhaps a combination of the two is the best of both worlds.

No matter which way you get there, Vision First outlines the technical and organizational roadmap for the company for the next year or two. As the team members work to create this vision, they need to remember that this is not carved in stone—vision needs to be dynamic, just like strategy. At this point, they don't have the full picture of what they are trying to achieve and the initial vision is just their best guess at the very beginning. Don't get stuck on this early idea, because it needs to evolve as the transformation progresses and new information is uncovered.

The question to answer is, essentially, *Where are we going?* It's important to keep the answers high level enough to allow freedom of choice during implementation (in other words, don't start choosing tools just yet). At the same time, though, things need to be detailed enough to provide clear guidance, which will help avoid common pitfalls.

The practical implementation of creating a cloud native transformation vision is, *do* name names—of architectural elements. *Don't* start choosing specific tools or service providers at this stage.

Good things to include
Semi-technical terms describing broad concepts, such as "microservices" and "containerized platform in the cloud."

Things to avoid:
Committing to any specific tool or tech, no matter what kind of great things you've heard about it. (Don't worry, we will be getting to that very soon, and by way of applying patterns to help make sure your choices are the right ones.)

Once the Core Team lays out the Vision First pattern, it moves quickly and directly to translate it into concrete objectives. This is where we begin to create specific architecture and a series of steps to move toward the Maturity Matrix cloud native standard (see Chapter 5).

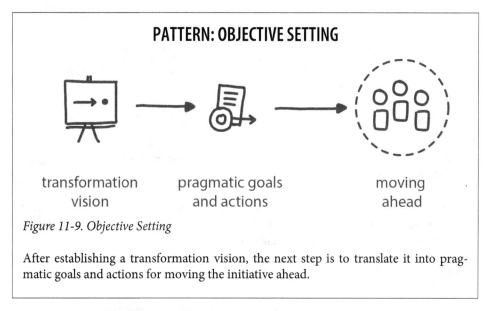

PATTERN: OBJECTIVE SETTING

transformation
vision

pragmatic goals
and actions

moving
ahead

Figure 11-9. Objective Setting

After establishing a transformation vision, the next step is to translate it into pragmatic goals and actions for moving the initiative ahead.

The Objective Setting pattern marks a pivotal point, because this is where we move from theoretical strategic planning to defining concrete, pragmatic, and above all executable steps toward the cloud native goal line.

The whole thing began with a strategic, executive decision-making phase, which—aside from the Transformation Champion, who can come from any part of the organization—was chiefly in the hands of the company's senior leaders, CEO, and board. The journey there was abstract, moving through establishing a case for and then committing to a transformation initiative. The key outcome was to make a firm decision: *We want to be cloud native and we are willing to provide the resources to make it happen.*

The Core Team was then created to begin turning strategy into reality. First, defining the vision—the high-level roadmap for the transformation—and then translating that into an architecture and a set of achievable objectives: *We want DevOps teams structure, need to refactor into containers and microservices, and want to install an orchestration platform to manage everything.*

The time has come for creating the steps that will pragmatically achieve these objectives: A framework of tasks to achieve specific goals—first we need a basic platform, so we will do experiments, try some PoC—that becomes execution. Figure 11-10 shows the patterns that we've followed thus far.

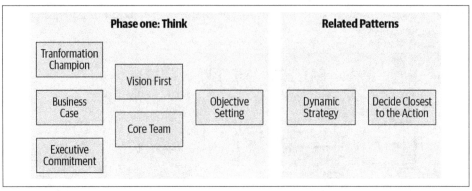

Figure 11-10. Phase 1: Think, the first step in our cloud native transformation design, covers strategy and objective setting.

Thus have we progressed from idea to strategy to objectives, which brings us to the end of Phase 1. It's time to move into Phase 2: Design, where we begin to identify the elements for constructing our cloud native platform.

PHASE 2: DESIGN

Phase 1 gave us a first, rudimentary roadmap for finding our way to the cloud: a high-level vision of Microservices Architecture delivering Containerized Apps in the cloud by Build-Run Teams. Wait, what are all those things?! Don't panic: these are all patterns that, along with others, will carry us from vision to delivery. Let's take a look.

The pivot point between Phase 1 and Phase 2 consists of splitting the organization, at least temporarily. The Core Team is setting off to design and build the new platform, while the rest of the company carries on with business as usual for the time being.

These two paths require separate sets of patterns and separate approaches. The Core Team is managed as a creative team, given a purpose and the freedom to experiment and research their way to answers. The rest of the teams still keep building the value in the existing system, until the new platform is ready. They are managed for proficiency.

Not to give short shrift to the proficiency teams—they are busy making money for the company while the Core Team innovates—but they only get one pattern for the time being. Most teams will eventually need to evolve to cloud native's more flexible, intuitive, and problem-solving way of working. During the transition, however, it's important to keep the proficient teams proficient and run them as they have always been run, not changing to cloud native techniques yet. Since they aren't changing much (yet—their time is coming soon!) the only thing to discuss right now is how best to manage them in the interim.

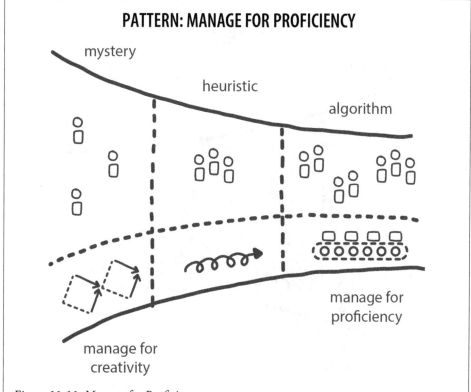

Figure 11-11. Manage for Proficiency

Teams delivering stable and highly repetitive or algorithmic work should be managed for high quality and optimal efficiency.

We have named this the Design phase, but it could just as easily be called the Exploration or Innovation phase. Now is the time that the Core Team delves into creative research, and they need to be appropriately managed for producing innovation.

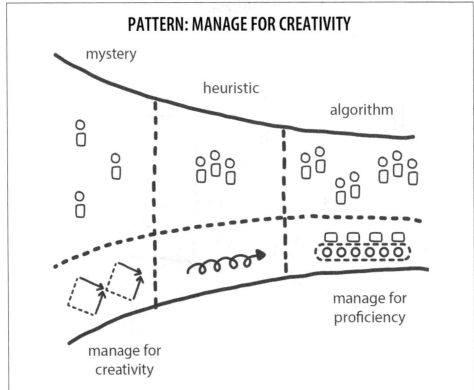

PATTERN: MANAGE FOR CREATIVITY

Figure 11-12. Manage for Creativity

Teams charged with innovation need the open-ended freedom to experiment their way to solutions without pressure for delivering specific results on a set schedule—and the freedom to sometimes fail along the way.

In their first attempt to go cloud native, WealthGrid made the extremely common mistake of having an existing team work on building the new system while still responsible for their regular duties, too. The obvious problem is that urgent issues on the existing system—the one that is making money for the company—will always take priority over building something new that isn't going to add value for who knows how long. For that reason it makes sense that the Core Team should do nothing but focus on the transformation. It also makes sense that this team is going to need some intense time investment for learning and experimentation, so they shouldn't be distracted by unrelated work.

The most important reason that the Core Team needs to stand alone, however, is because they are breaking away from a longstanding way of doing things in order to do something completely new and different. This means that the team needs to work, and be managed in their work, in a completely new and different way.

Remember Chapter 7 and all that talk about proficiency vs. creativity? The Core Team needs open-ended time to work, and this can be a challenge for others in the organization. Managers are used to overseeing responsibilities you can, well, manage, in a predictable, top-down, hands-on way. Managing for creativity is more about facilitating innovation: providing the opportunity for innovation to incubate by defining the goal, providing the proper circumstances, and then stepping back. You cannot manage facilitation.

Practically speaking, how does the Core Team start to make smart design choices for this new cloud native system while minimizing risk? Gradually Raising the Stakes.

PATTERN: GRADUALLY RAISING THE STAKES

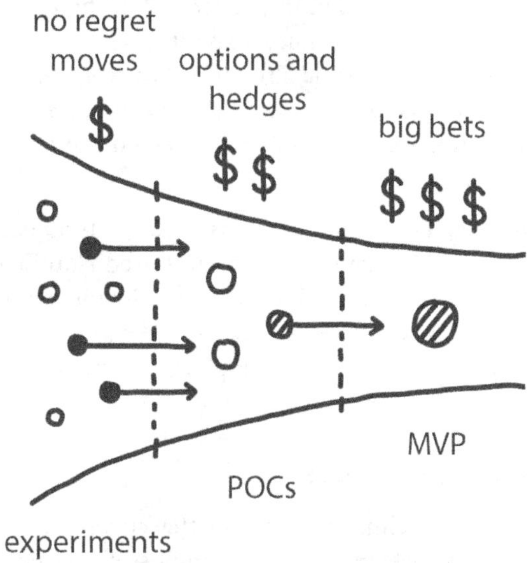

Figure 11-13. Gradually Raising the Stakes

In an uncertain environment, slowly increase investment into learning and information-gathering actions; eventually you uncover enough information to reduce risk and make better-informed decisions.

Related sub-patterns: No Regret Moves, Options and Hedges, Big Bet

In the predictive world of Waterfall, when you launch a big project, you can typically make big decisions right away. The project itself might be new, but it's almost certainly going to be a lot like previous initiatives. Now, however, the Core Team is feeling their way onto the cloud with only a very basic map. The next move is far from clear because they are still early in the process of building their own cloud native knowledge, and low-certainty projects carry extremely high risk. Any decision made early on in this uncertain environment is highly likely to turn out to have been a wrong choice.

Gradually Raising the Stakes is a super pattern and a general strategy for cloud native risk management that is critically applicable to this pivotal point in a transformation. This pattern gives us the tools to address uncertainty by moving step by logical next step. The way it works is through three graduated levels of risk taking: little risk, moderate risk, high risk. In terms of pure strategy formation these are the sub-patterns No Regret Moves, Options & Hedges, and Big Bet. There is a lot more about the Gradually Raising the Stakes super pattern and its sub-patterns in Chapter 5.

When it comes to creating a transformation design, however, these patterns correlate with three technical patterns. Applied in proper order, these are practical steps for reducing transformation risk: Exploratory Experiments, PoCs (Proof of Concepts), and Platform MVP (Minimum Viable Product). We will encounter these patterns now, along with other patterns that are important at this stage of the initiative. These are mainly around adopting new, cloud native-oriented ways of thinking and doing things.

The gateway to these is the Distributed Systems super pattern, because the rest of the transformation is essentially implementing an optimized cloud native version of distributed systems architecture. The Exploratory Experiments pattern, to establish the initial framework for our cloud native explorations. We then unpack Distributed Systems super pattern and all the related pattern puzzle pieces the Core Team will get to play with.

Distributed Systems and Friends

Welcome back to the most technical subject matter covered in this book: the broad technologies and methodologies that together compose cloud native architecture. The Core Team is experimenting to find the best implementation of each pattern for their particular transformation initiative—a level of technical detail we are saving for the sequel to this book—but the pillars are unchanging. It all begins with Distributed Systems.

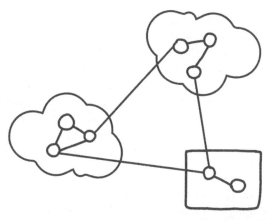

PATTERN: DISTRIBUTED SYSTEMS

Figure 11-14. Distributed Systems

When software is built as a series of fully independent, loosely coupled services, the resulting system is, by design, very fast, resilient, and highly scalable.

The development of a monolithic software system is limited by its sheer complexity, which only a few top-level architects and managers may be able to comprehend (but even this is not guaranteed). Indeed, it is tempting to start a new software project as a monolith to get things started quickly, since the architecture is simple, and the few components share resources in a single codebase.

As the system expands, however, the size and complexity of its major components keep growing. Over time, this causes a variety of bottlenecks to develop, mainly in the form of dependencies on all different levels: data sharing, calling functions from other components, and teams being held up by other teams. All this leads to an increasing level of coordination required to produce any change, to the point where the overhead of coordination becomes larger than the work itself. We have seen systems that require three days and seven different teams to release a single small change that took three hours to create.

All of this eventually makes further system growth functionally impossible. The main, maybe only, fix would be to scale the whole system, even though only a small part of it is running out of resources—which requires buying very expensive hardware. (And then, over time, the same problems would simply re-emerge anyway.)

Distributed systems are much more complex to initially architect and implement, but once that initial work is invested they are much simpler to grow and evolve forward with improvements, new features, and changes. This is due to a much lower level of coordination overhead. That same three-hour code change task can simply proceed to production in 10 minutes without any human involvement at all.

A distributed system is any system whose components are executing independently, communicating and coordinating their actions by passing messages to one another. Historically these were on-prem servers, but systems began moving to the cloud. Cloud native then emerged as a software development approach that makes full and optimal use of the cloud computing model. Cloud native applications are built with modular service components—microservices—that communicate through APIs and get packaged in containers. The containers themselves are managed via an orchestrator (Kubernetes) and dynamically deployed on an elastic cloud infrastructure through Agile DevOps processes and continuous integration/continuous delivery (CI/CD) workflows.

OK, so that was a lot. Don't worry, it's only the general concepts we need to worry about right now—the high-level master blueprint for the system under construction. This leads us, aptly enough, to literally drawing one up.

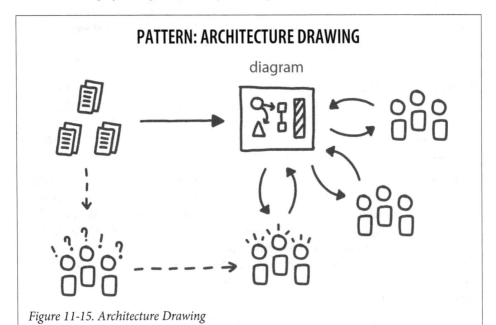

PATTERN: ARCHITECTURE DRAWING

diagram

Figure 11-15. Architecture Drawing

A picture—or, in this case, a high-level outline sketch of your system's basic architecture—can replace a thousand words, save time, and prevent misunderstandings.

Distributed systems are inherently complex, which makes them difficult to visualize and describe, much less discuss. The Architecture Drawing is a classic No Regret Move, easy and inexpensive yet extremely beneficial. It's also, thankfully, straightforward to do: produce a single, unified, and official version of the new cloud native system's architecture for circulation and reference. This creates a simple and consistent visual that everyone on the Core Team should be able to draw, from memory, in less than 30 seconds.

A huge benefit to the Architecture Drawing is that it helps all stakeholders internalize a deep understanding of the architecture's components and how they relate to each other. It also provides consistency of thought and makes discussion vastly easier.

With this clear blueprint of our distributed cloud native system in hand, let's look at the patterns that comprise it. Figure 11-16 shows the technical, structural, and process-oriented patterns that go into designing cloud native distributed systems and underlie the Distributed Systems pattern:

- Microservices Architecture and Containerized Apps are fundamental pillars of cloud native architecture.
- Dynamic Scheduling, Automated Infrastructure, Automated Testing, and Observability describe these core technical aspects of a cloud native system.
- Continuous Integration (CI) and Continuous Delivery (CD) are the processes for implementing them.
- Secure From the Start Systems addresses how to keep everything safe.
- Reproducible Development Environment describes the workspace necessary for the Core Team to assemble all these pieces.

Thumbnail versions of all these patterns are available in Appendix A: Library of Patterns, which will direct readers to the full versions of each pattern in Chapter 9, Patterns for Development & Process, and Chapter 10, Patterns for Infrastructure & Cloud. Since we have discussed all of these technical aspects, particularly microservices, containers, and dynamic scheduling (a.k.a. Kubernetes), throughout the first part of this book, let's leave the nitty-gritty details to the Core Team and keep the transformation design moving along at the level of architecture rather than detailed execution.

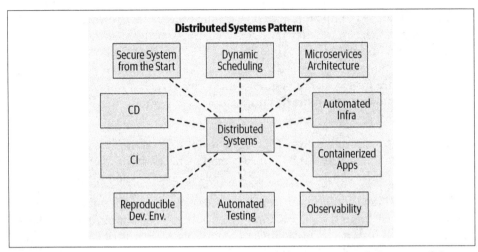

Figure 11-16. The Distributed Systems pattern unpacks into essential elements of the cloud native architecture and development process.

Exploratory Experiments

This is the practical first step in an organization's technical transformation. At this point, the Core Team doesn't yet have enough cloud native knowledge to identify the most general direction to head in—you can't research unknown unknowns. So they begin by doing theoretical research: reading what others have done, case studies, white papers. Certainly doing No Regret Moves like trainings and other learning opportunities. There is no clear solution available because this is a complex problem and you cannot simply Google it—there are many solutions out there that sound great but simply don't fit your particular use case.

The scope of the transformation is very wide. You need to collect many different puzzle pieces to create a consistent platform, and right now you don't even know enough to understand what the right pieces even look like.

How do you find the right pieces? By doing experiments. Small, quick, low-cost investigations into different tools, techniques, and architectural combinations just to see what works and, more to the point, what does not. Core Team members learn enormously as they do this, building their understanding and skills. After a relatively short time, usually a month or two, this new knowledge and the experimentation process helps the team narrow down the field of options and uncover likely best-fit directions for meeting the transformation objectives.

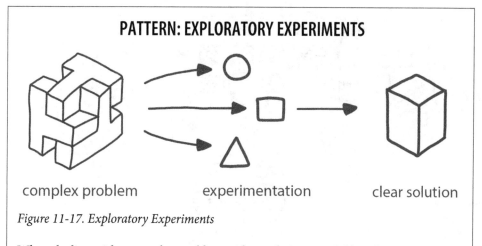

PATTERN: EXPLORATORY EXPERIMENTS

complex problem   experimentation   clear solution

Figure 11-17. Exploratory Experiments

When dealing with a complex problem with no obvious available solution, run a series of small experiments to evaluate the possible alternatives and learn by doing.

This is the time of working with the fundamental building blocks of cloud native: Microservices Architecture, Containerized Apps, Continuous Integration, Continuous Delivery, and different types of automation. We will start with Microservices Architecture, because that drives everything else.

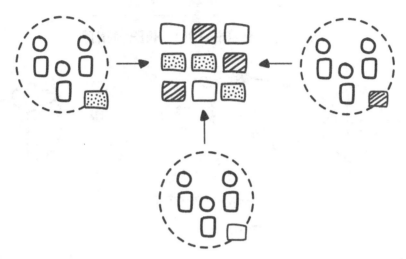

PATTERN: MICROSERVICES ARCHITECTURE

Figure 11-18. Microservices Architecture

To reduce the costs of coordination between teams delivering large monolithic applications, design software as a suite of modular services that are built, deployed, and operated independently.

Microservices are an implementation of distributed-systems architecture where an application is delivered as a set of small, modular components that are completely independent from each other and communicate via APIs. This is an extremely flexible, resilient, and scalable way to build software, but also a very complicated one. In the cloud native way of working, a team is responsible for delivering one service, from design to delivery, and then supporting it as it runs even as they iterate forward with small improvements.

To run the application, all of its microservices get packaged into a container. Containers are lightweight, standalone executable software packages that include everything required to run an application: code, runtime, system tools, libraries, and settings.

They are a sort of "standard unit" of software that packages up the code with all its dependencies so it can run anywhere, in any computing environment.

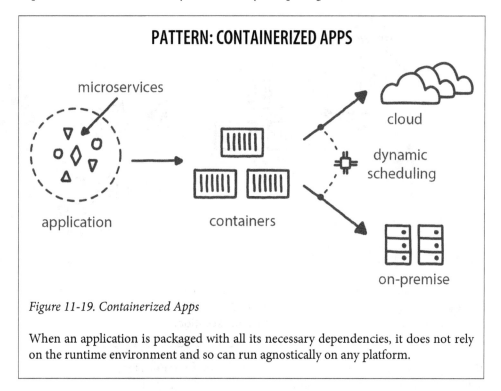

PATTERN: CONTAINERIZED APPS

Figure 11-19. Containerized Apps

When an application is packaged with all its necessary dependencies, it does not rely on the runtime environment and so can run agnostically on any platform.

To run in the cloud, whether public or private, the containerized microservices need to be organized, managed, and told when and where to run. This is the job of the Dynamic Scheduler, or orchestrator (Kubernetes is by far the most well known and widely used but is far from the only orchestration option out there).

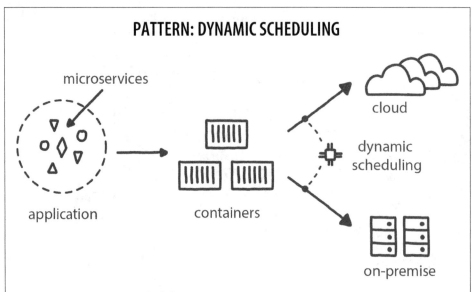

Figure 11-20. Dynamic Scheduling

An orchestrator (typically Kubernetes) is needed to organize the deployment and management of microservices in a distributed, container-based application to assign them across random machines at the instant of execution.

Building software that is optimized for the cloud is complicated, but it does come with a few helpful advantages. Since there are so many moving pieces now, far more than humans can manage or keep up with, cloud native computing requires full automation. Automated Infrastructure handles server provisioning, configuration management, builds, and deployments and monitoring at top speed and without the need for manual intervention. Similarly, Automated Testing ensures that all the testing required to take any product change to production is built into the development process.

PATTERN: AUTOMATED INFRASTRUCTURE

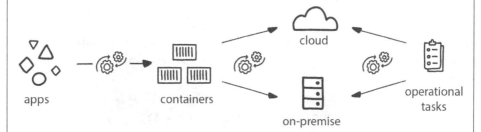

Figure 11-21. Automated Infrastructure

The absolute majority of operational tasks need to be automated. Automation reduces inter-team dependencies, which allows faster experimentation and leads in turn to higher development velocity.aut

PATTERN: AUTOMATED TESTING

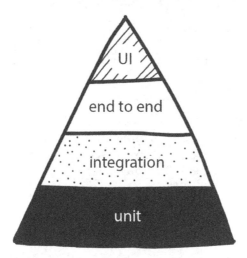

Figure 11-22. Automated Testing

Shift responsibility for testing from humans (manual) to an automated testing framework so developers can deliver faster and have more time to focus on improving features to meet customer needs.

To make the most of automation, the Core Team must adopt Continuous Integration and Continuous Delivery as their workflow.

Continuous Integration (CI) is a coding philosophy and set of practices that drive development teams to implement small changes and check in code to version-control repositories frequently. The technical goal of CI is to establish a consistent and automated way to build, package, and test applications that are always highest quality, and always ready to be released.

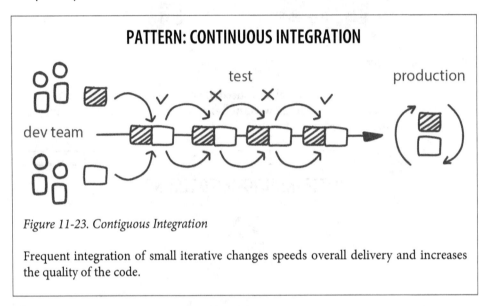

PATTERN: CONTINUOUS INTEGRATION

Figure 11-23. Contiguous Integration

Frequent integration of small iterative changes speeds overall delivery and increases the quality of the code.

Continuous Delivery(CD) starts where Continuous Integration ends. CD automates the delivery of applications to selected infrastructure environments. Most teams work with multiple environments outside the production pipeline, such as development and testing environments, and CD ensures there is an automated way to push code changes to them. CD automation then performs any necessary service calls to web servers and databases, and executes procedures when applications are deployed.

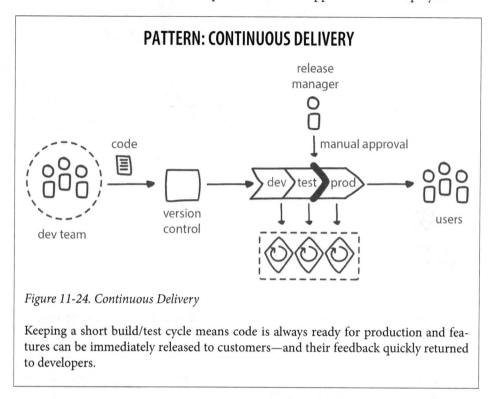

PATTERN: CONTINUOUS DELIVERY

Figure 11-24. Continuous Delivery

Keeping a short build/test cycle means code is always ready for production and features can be immediately released to customers—and their feedback quickly returned to developers.

Better together: Continuous Integration and Continuous Delivery are so integral both to each other and to the cloud native approach that they are usually used as a single term. CI/CD used together make it possible to implement continuous deployment, where application changes run through the CI/CD pipeline. Builds that pass Automated Testing get deployed directly to production environments with Automated Infrastructure. This happens frequently, on a daily—or even hourly—schedule.

CI and CD are difficult to achieve, however, unless developers are able to test each change thoroughly. The Reproducible Dev Environment pattern defines the conditions for where the Core Team can practice all of these brand new tools and techniques while applying CI/CD processes.

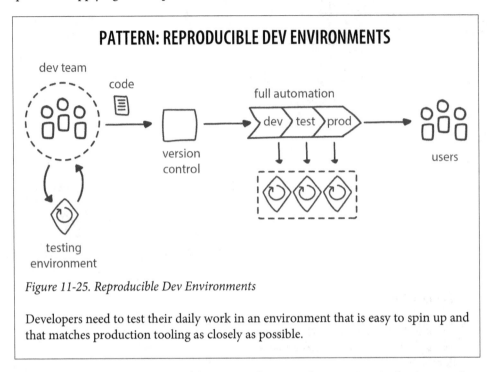

PATTERN: REPRODUCIBLE DEV ENVIRONMENTS

Figure 11-25. Reproducible Dev Environments

Developers need to test their daily work in an environment that is easy to spin up and that matches production tooling as closely as possible.

The Core Team has now learned how to orchestrate the containerized microservices they've been experimenting with, using automation and cloud native methodologies. What comes next?

Proof of Concept

So, great! Your research has given you a better understanding of what is going on, but there is still fairly high risk involved in making decisions at this point. How do you know when it's time to stop Exploratory Experiments and take the next step?

The trick is to look at it as a balance situation. You are weighing the need for more certainty against the need to move things forward. The moment of truth comes when a few likely looking paths begin to stand out from the cloud native wilderness of choices. You still need to gather more information—a lot more—but you have achieved the milestone of identifying some promising areas where you need your information to be deeper.

At this point it's time to move to the next stage of the process: deepening understanding of the most promising areas. It's time for the Proof of Concept (PoC) pattern.

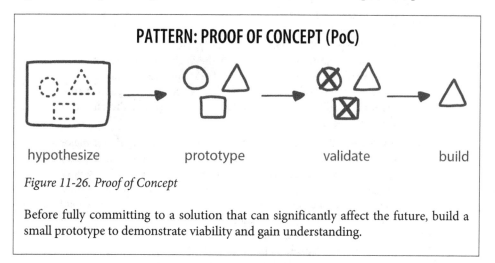

PATTERN: PROOF OF CONCEPT (PoC)

hypothesize   prototype   validate   build

Figure 11-26. Proof of Concept

Before fully committing to a solution that can significantly affect the future, build a small prototype to demonstrate viability and gain understanding.

You still don't know enough to make any kind of large commitment at this point, whether to a vendor or an open-source solution. Any decision right now carries massive risk because full commitment to one path means you will continue to build further functionality on top of this solution. The further you go, the harder it becomes to change course.

You have, however, narrowed the field to a few potential transformation paths that appear promising. It is time to investigate these different options for architecture and toolsets through deeper, though still not prohibitively difficult, Proof of Concept exercises. The stakes are a little higher now: PoCs are more complicated than the simple experiments the Core Team has been running thus far, so costs and time investment do go up. Thus, if your best-guess PoC fails there is some pain, but it's not a terrible tragedy. You can revert if needed (not to mention gain valuable insight into what doesn't work).

PoCs are fun! A real chance for the engineers to roll up their sleeves and play with these cool cloud native toys by choosing one of the potential solutions the Core Team has identified through experiments and building a basic prototype to demonstrate viability—or lack thereof. Remember that it's still OK to fail.

PoCs: Eliminating Weak Options

Something to keep in mind during the PoCs phase is how young the cloud native ecosystem still is. Even now there is still a lot of uncertainty and knowledge to be gained, and there are also still significant gaps in the toolset. Cloud native right now is similar to the birth of the automotive industry at the beginning of the 20th century, when there were more than 100 automobile manufacturers in the United States alone. Now there are fewer than 20 major manufacturers worldwide, and who has heard of most of the ones that dropped away?

So, there will be shakeout and consolidation. Every month major new tools get introduced into the cloud native ecosystem, and they don't always fit each other well. The entire point of PoCs is to choose 10 to 20 of those tools and try to see how they work together. Among the safest bets to choose from are in the Cloud Native Computing Foundation's *"Graduated Projects"* (*https://www.cncf.io/projects/*). These are well-established tools like Kubernetes, which are likely to be around for the long run, and there are many related/supporting tools and resources built around them.

Quick and dirty is the theme with PoCs, which should take a few days to a few weeks at most to build the most primitive version you can get away with. Focus only on hard issues related to the specific needs of the current project, and stop when the solution is clear—don't worry about creating a nice UX, just make the darn thing work. If possible, try to actually demonstrate something functional so you can collect information about how this solution will affect the business.

But, most of all, be ready to throw it away when you are finished proving your point. This doesn't mean that you must absolutely trash all your hard work. But you probably should. Very often when initial quality is intentionally low, it's cheaper and easier to just scrap it and rebuild. This way you get a clean slate and the chance to do things right, applying all those hard-earned PoC lessons you just learned. Otherwise, you will probably have to spend a lot of time fixing all the stuff you did wrong before you can even start building anything new on top.

Figure 11-27 shows the map of patterns we've covered in Phase 2: Design, from the point where the Core Team began researching the best possible design for the company's cloud native transformation. The team members are being managed for creativity, with freedom to experiment and fail if necessary, while the rest of the company keeps on delivering on the existing system. The Core Team does Exploratory Experiments to investigate all the aspects of Distributed Systems that will go into the new cloud native platform, until their learning curve has flattened and they've identified some good candidates for more in-depth investigation through PoCs.

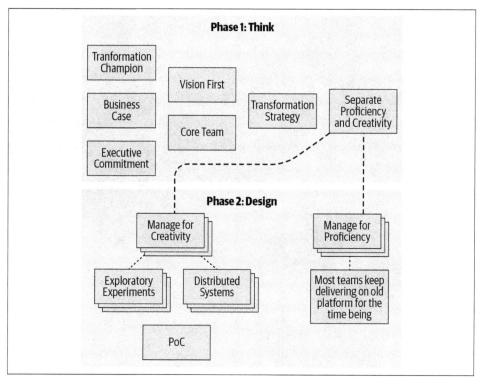

Figure 11-27. Phase 2: Design cloud native transformation design patterns

Because once you've picked a clear winner—once the PoC process has mapped the likely right transformation path—it's time to get ready to build for real!

So far in our design for a cloud native transformation, we have covered getting ready for the transition (including figuring out if you really even need to do one in the first place!). Next we had a detailed look at how to de-risk the transformation by experimenting your way to the right path, using a gradual and iterative approach. Now that PoCs have revealed the likely best platform, we will move on to Part 2 for applying patterns to do the actual implementation.

CHAPTER 12

Applying the Patterns: A Cloud Native Transformation Design, Part 2

Welcome to the second half of our detailed design pattern for a cloud native transformation. Here we will lay out patterns from start to finish, explaining the order and reason for the choices as we go along. It's a lengthy and involved process, so we have divided it into two chapters. Part 1 covered the period from pre-initiative prep through the point where we have researched, experimented, and prototyped our way to uncovering the likely best transformation path. In Part 2 we begin verifying the path by building a production-ready cloud native platform, move through onboarding everyone onto the new system with a new way of working, and then finish by shutting down the old one.

PHASE 3: BUILD

Phase 2, the Design stage, concludes with a major turning point in the transformation: the goal is clear, the tech is available, substantial knowledge has been gained, and all major questions are answered, thanks to a series of PoCs. Now is the time to build a real platform. Development teams are on hold and waiting for the new platform to start building new applications and refactoring old ones.

The MVP Platform pattern is the bridge between designing the new cloud native system and then actually building a functional, production-ready version. It's the final test of whichever winning candidate emerged from your PoCs.

This is also a pivotal moment for the Core Team, because this is the point where the team often divides and multiplies. Frequently, several members split off to form the Platform Team, while the remaining Core Team members focus on getting the first test application ready and preparing materials for eventually onboarding all the rest of the teams in the company. (Remember them, off to one side, keeping the old system running? We told you their turn would come, and it's almost here!)

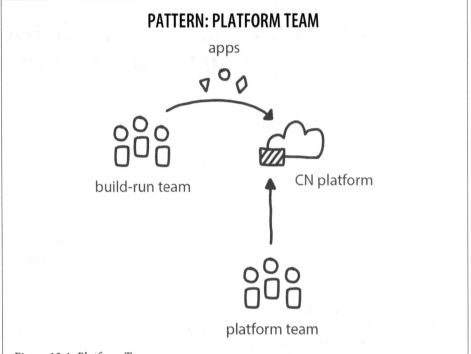

PATTERN: PLATFORM TEAM

apps

build-run team

CN platform

platform team

Figure 12-1. Platform Team

Create a team to oversee architecting, building, and running a single, consistent, and stable cloud native platform for use by the entire organization, so that developers can focus on building applications instead of configuring infrastructure.

The Platform Team is an essential component of cloud native systems' architecture. It is also separate, by design, from all the other engineering teams in an organization.

Cloud native developers know how to build for distributed systems. They know how to build in network and security and all other necessities so all parts of the distributed system become part of the application. However, these applications still need to deploy somewhere. A common mistake companies make is expecting their developers to not just build applications but also take charge of the platform they run on, all in the name of DevOps. This is detrimental in many ways, but there is one problem to rule them all: if there is not one standard, unified platform in place, each application team will build their own version.

This is how you end up with seven different systems deployed in different ways with different tools—even running on different clouds. Everything is random, and it's impossible to refactor these to a standardized platform for production. This is exactly what we saw happen during WealthGrid's second transformation attempt.

To prevent this all too common problem from ever arising in the first place, we have the Platform Team pattern. A platform team sits off to one side from the rest of the engineering teams and is fully invested in designing and maintaining the platform to make sure it is stable and provides all needed functionality. Devs don't need to worry about provisioning or any other infrastructure details, they just deploy to the platform. Platform people handle Kubernetes and below, while the devs work on top of Kubernetes with APIs. This line of separation may move as the emerging serverless and service-mesh paradigm becomes increasingly adopted into the cloud native stack and change the balance.

Emerging Pattern: Service Mesh

A service mesh is a dedicated infrastructure layer built right into an application to govern service-to-service communication, and one of cloud native's most recent forward iterations. It is perhaps a bit too early to write a full Service Mesh pattern, but it's definitely an emerging innovation to watch closely.

While Docker and Kubernetes reduce the operational burden on deployments by standardizing packaging and deployment, they do not address runtime. But what happens once the application is running? Even fully independent and autonomous microservices need to align with some kind of organizational standards to work together efficiently. The service mesh paradigm has risen to address this gap and standardize the runtime operations of microservices applications in the same way that Docker and Kubernetes standardized deployments.

(Service Mesh is also of service in deployment, too, where it serves as more intelligent and adaptive networking. Without something like a service mesh, you may need to add what is effectively networking or deployment knowledge into your microservice code.)

The service mesh is emerging as a potent new component of the cloud native stack. High-traffic companies like Netflix, Google, and Ticketmaster have added a service mesh to their production applications (Google in fact created Istio, an open source service mesh tool). Gartner and other industry research firms advise that in less than two years, a service mesh will simply be a requirement for any organization running microservices in production.

The technology is not quite ready for us to include in our current transformation design. It's not mature enough for a company like WealthGrid to embrace at this time. But we predict that very soon people will be talking about Istio and Linkerd with the same excitement and reverence currently used for discussing Kubernetes. This is a prime example of how fast things are evolving and it is why we emphasize over and over that the core of cloud native is *how* we create and deliver software, not where.

When the Platform Team does its job well, standardization and developer freedom are both in place. Strong standardization is a good thing in that it limits support and maintenance costs and increases development velocity across the organization by providing a consistent set of tools and shared expectations. Too much standardization, however, shuts down any ability for devs to experiment with new tools and approaches.

The trick is finding the balance between freedom and separation: you want to standardize for economy of scale, but a fundamental principle of microservice architecture is choosing the best tool for the job. Thus the Platform Team's prime directive is to optimize standardization while building a platform that allows developers to choose the best and most appropriate tools for their jobs.

The first job of the Platform Team is to create a minimum viable product version of the platform. Given that many if not all the team members came through the PoC process as part of the Core Team, they should be pretty well acquainted with the ins and outs of whatever candidates have been identified to go into the cloud native platform stack. This is where the MVP Platform pattern enters our transformation design.

PATTERN: MVP PLATFORM

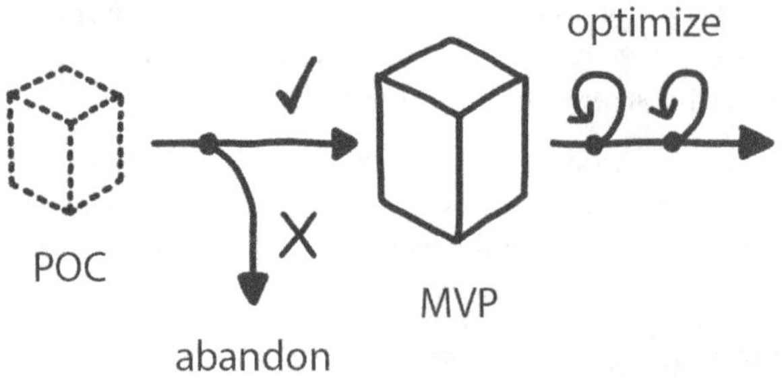

Figure 12-2. MVP Platform

Once Exploratory Experiments and PoCs have uncovered a probable path to success, build a simple version of a basic but fully functional and production-ready platform with one to three small application running on it.

The MVP is a bare-bones system, built to have minimal yet useful functionality and in a very short period of time. Quick turnaround is key, because it's important to get the platform in front of users as fast as possible to get feedback and make improvements. "Minimal usefulness" can vary according to your company's needs, but it should serve at least some actual business functions. Extendability is critical. Even if this version does not ultimately go into production, you still need to understand how to continue expanding platform capabilities and capacity.

Don't confuse the MVP with your final-version platform—we aren't there yet! The MVP is meant only as a very basic thing that can be done in a few months by a few people, meant to serve as the basis for future development. It does need to be production ready. The point is to test the architecture in real-world conditions—but only on a small scale, with a small number of users. Yes, it runs, but running is not the same thing as ready to go into full production (though it is definitely a major step in the right direction). The MVP is far from feature complete; though it has security, monitoring, and observability in place, these are only rudimentary versions.

Doing all this should take two to six months to produce the first basic, bare-bones version, with Continuous Integration and Continuous Delivery in place from the very start. After that, definitely plan for an additional two to three phases to bring the platform to full functionality, refining as you go based on user response. Two important aspects of this full functionality to include in the MVP are Observability and Secure System from the Start.

As organizations move towards containerized workloads and dynamic microservice architectures, monitoring after the fact no longer suffices. Observability must be built in to give better insight into an application's performance.

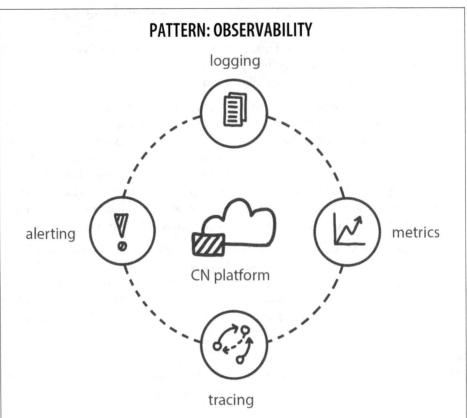

PATTERN: OBSERVABILITY

logging

alerting

CN platform

metrics

tracing

Figure 12-3. Observability

Cloud native distributed systems require constant insight into the behavior of all running services in order to understand the system's behavior and to predict potential problems or incidents.

In cloud native you must observe the system to see what is going on. Monitoring is how we see this information, but Observability is the property we architect into a system so that we are able to discern internal states through monitoring external outputs. Furthermore, you have built resilience into the system because you are working from an assumption that any single component of MVP system may go down at some point. So you optimize by understanding things on a system level, rather than trying to track each separate component.

In a 100-container system, if one container fails, it's nothing. A non-event. Kubernetes will restart it. But you do want to record that it happened in order to analyze trends in the system's behavior.

Observability is one of the key elements of microservices architecture. Well-engineered services expose metrics that both allow efficient system monitoring and trace each interaction the customer has with it. Observability gives engineers the information they need to adapt systems and application architectures to be more stable and resilient. This, in turn, provides a feedback loop to developers that allows for fast iteration and adaptation to changing market conditions and customer needs.

Like Observability, security also needs to be baked directly into the platform from the very start. Perimeter security measures simply do not work in distributed systems. Unfortunately, transition teams tend to delay setting up security until the relatively late stages of a project and then attempt to bolt something on at the end.

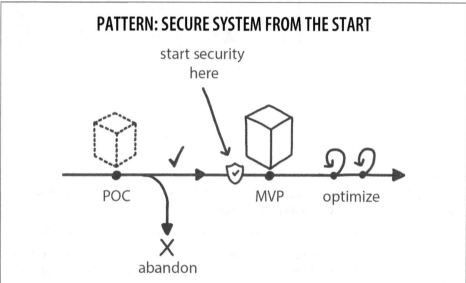

PATTERN: SECURE SYSTEM FROM THE START

Figure 12-4. Secure System from the Start

Build security into the platform beginning with the earliest versions to ensure your distributed system is unbreachable by design.

The only way to handle a cloud native system's complex security requirements is to build the MVP as a highly secure system from day one. This means providing in-depth security training for teams; choosing tools carefully and reviewing how they work together to check for gaps; using best practices to secure containers, clusters, APIs, access rights, etc. and ensuring that automated security testing is part of your workflow.

While considering the needs that must be fulfilled in the final version of the system, we have some good news: you certainly don't have to custom-build every piece.

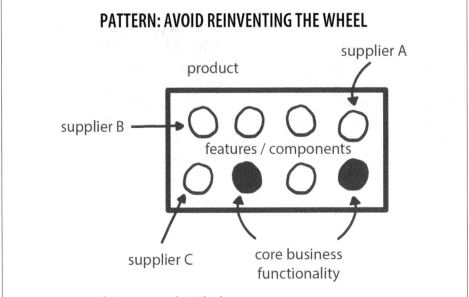

PATTERN: AVOID REINVENTING THE WHEEL

Figure 12-5. Avoid Reinventing the Wheel

When possible, purchase solutions for any need that is not your actual core business instead of trying to custom-build perfect tools.

Not every single piece of your platform needs to be custom built—cloud native is new, but it's not *that* new. There are plenty of existing tools and services available for purchase to run as, for example, Software-as-a-Service. When assembling your platform, use existing tools when possible, especially for functionalities that aren't part of your core business. Choose these even if the fit isn't exactly perfect: Whether commercial or open source, third-party products are typically better quality, better maintained, and more frequently extended than anything you can build yourself.

Whew! Fully building out even a basic MVP, and even with some purchased pieces, is a pretty big achievement. Significant investments of budget, time, and work have now been invested in building and improving it. Once the MVP platform is ready, it's time to pause and review the current transformation strategy to make sure it's still valid before we move even further with extending MVP functionality. It could be painful now if, for some reason, it still turns out to be the wrong direction for the company; it will be painful indeed to abandon it and begin again. Better to find out now, though, than many months down the road.

Prepare for Onboarding

Achieving the MVP is big news, and a major transformation milestone: You now have a few apps in production on a real cloud native platform! This is a good time for celebration and even more evangelism.

The Platform Team will continue working to prepare the MVP for full production. Meanwhile, we've still got all those proficient teams working on the legacy products and delivering value to the customer in existing ways. Mostly they still need to keep doing what they're doing; however, once we get close to achieving an MVP platform, it's time to start preparing teams that will be gradually onboarding. Let's go now to check in on the Core Team, which has been preparing the way for onboarding the rest of the organization onto the new system.

Prepare for onboarding means more than educating teams and moving them onto the new system, though. Now is the time where organizational culture also begins to shift in a broad and permanent way to reflect the company's new cloud native approach. Pay attention now, because this is actually the most important part of the whole transformation. It's where we begin the long, slow process of strangling both the technical and organizational monoliths.

At this point, word has almost certainly spread through the company that there is a big change coming. People are likely feeling anxiety that their work is going to change. They need to know when and how. When there is little available information, negative attribution bias leads people to assume the change is not going to be good for them. Actually, the majority of cognitive biases all rise from a lack of information one way or another, so preparation during the pre-onboarding period is all about reducing anxiety by sharing an abundance of information.

It's important to give people opportunities to learn but equally important to make sure they understand that this is a gradual and long-term process. If you start sharing information about the transformation initiative from the Executive Commitment stage onward, by the time teams are actually scheduled to onboard, it will be a trivial procedure with little resistance. Indeed, if the groundwork is laid properly, they will be excited and ready for the change.

Internal Evangelism is the key to managing the pre-onboarding process, which should begin months before the actual onboarding itself. Starting up Internal Evangelism at the same time the MVP phase begins is a good move.

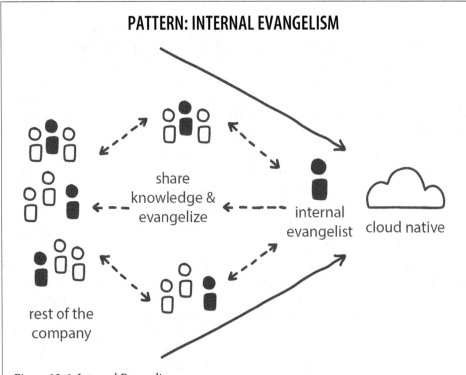

PATTERN: INTERNAL EVANGELISM

share knowledge & evangelize

internal evangelist

cloud native

rest of the company

Figure 12-6. Internal Evangelism

Provide plenty of information about the transformation across the entire company right from the start to create understanding, acceptance of, and support for the initiative.

For the first six to 12 months of the initiative, only the Core Team has much active involvement in the transformation. With proper evangelism, however, people are excited and want to help, to be involved. Use this excitement to engage people: raise the level of general cloud native knowledge across the organization.

The Transformation Champion is often the person in charge of Internal Evangelism, organizing events like lunch and learns—"Come eat pizza and learn about microservices!"—to start building general knowledge across the organization. At this time, the emphasis is on basic education over dedicated training: how containers work, what Kubernetes does. Regular open sessions that anyone can join should be part of Internal Evangelism. Slowly the knowledge builds up so when the actual onboarding comes there is a feeling of familiarity and comfort with the concepts.

Meanwhile, the Transformation Champion is also directing internal marketing efforts to promote awareness of and engagement with the cloud native initiative across the entire organization, for example, sponsoring internal newsletters, hackathons, and regular demo sessions to show the platform development's current status keep everyone informed and engaged. (Incidentally, these same tactics can, and really should, also be extended externally. This is a great opportunity to evangelize outside of the organization to start building a better technological reputation for the company. This will make the company more attractive for good engineers looking for interesting and challenging jobs.)

The lack of internal evangelism certainly damaged WealthGrid's second transformation attempt. Even when they were throwing most of the engineering teams at the transformation effort, the rest of the organization had no insight into what was happening. The sales and marketing teams could only see that the company's offerings were not being improved while their competitors were introducing new customer features, and there was a lot of frustration because no one thought to Involve the Business (see pattern). Finally, since there was no internal evangelism happening around the transformation, biases were likely at work—status quo bias, hostile attribution bias—creating internal resistance to the transformation and further causing it to lag or fail.

Internal events are opportunities to prevent all of that from happening in the first place. Talking about the plan, and the schedule for when the time does come for onboarding everyone onto the new system, makes sure everyone is informed, engaged, and has appropriate expectations. Don't worry about predicting exact timeframes: People don't mind if the transition gets delayed when they know that it is certain to happen.

Onboarding the Right Way, at the Right Time

When the MVP platform is nearing full production readiness, we have reached another pivotal moment in the transformation process: it's time to begin actively moving the proficient teams onto the new system and thoroughly educating them in using it.

It is important to approach onboarding in not just the right way, but also at the right time. Formal onboarding is the time where teams are slowly restructured into cloud native Build-Run teams, and taught to work in the new way, and it should only begin when the actual migration is very close to starting. This is a very important period for the teams—literally, their own moment of cloud native transformation—and requires an appropriate level of time and attention invested in moving them through it properly.

Only the teams specifically scheduled for onboarding (and only a few teams at a time) are actively engaged in the process; all others remain exactly as they are until their turn arrives. This is important because if you teach people new skills, they are excited to use them. If they have to wait six months or a year before they can apply their new knowledge, they are really frustrated—and, without use, these skills quickly erode anyway.

Again we have a super pattern, Gradual Onboarding, to get this evolution underway through application of its constituent sub-patterns.

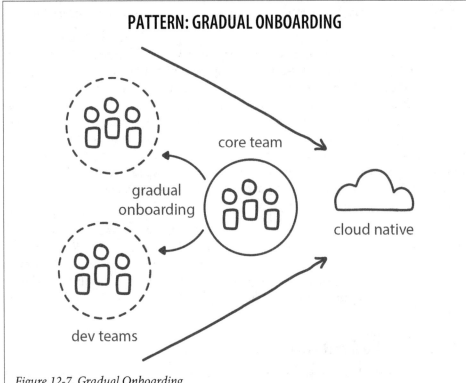

PATTERN: GRADUAL ONBOARDING

Figure 12-7. Gradual Onboarding

One to three months before the new platform goes live, begin training a couple of teams at a time, with a pause between each cohort to incorporate feedback and improve the process/materials.

The main goal of the Gradual Onboarding pattern is to start small organizational changes early in the cloud native transformation and keep them growing slowly and steadily. The teams working on the legacy software are slowly introduced to the new platform, given access to education, training materials, and experiences—described in the Dev Starter Pack pattern—and begin to build skills by working on practice projects as laid out in the Demo Applications pattern.

This whole process happens very gradually, as in only two to three teams at a time. This gives time for the Core Team to work with the new groups in depth and fully support them in completing their new cloud native knowledge and skills without rushing.

The creative team also takes breaks in between onboarding cohorts in order to use their feedback to improve the platform and onboarding materials. Remember Reference Architecture, from our earlier pattern? That is going to come in handy here, too.

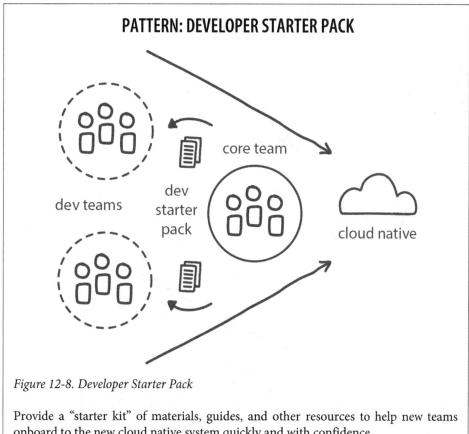

PATTERN: DEVELOPER STARTER PACK

dev teams

dev starter pack

core team

cloud native

Figure 12-8. Developer Starter Pack

Provide a "starter kit" of materials, guides, and other resources to help new teams onboard to the new cloud native system quickly and with confidence.

Teams onboarding to cloud native don't know the tools or technologies and are typically provided with very poor onboarding materials. Time is wasted while they try to figure things out on their own. Worse, if the onboarding resources are truly lacking, they might be forced to create their own cloud native practices. Inevitably these will be uninformed and unlikely to fit properly with the platform. Since each team will have to figure these out on their own, there will be variation in practices between teams.

Provide developers onboarding to cloud native everything they need to start working immediately.

This cloud native "starter kit" of materials should include tool configurations, version-control repository, CI/CD pipelines, example applications for practice, target platform description, trainings, and more. This Developer Starter Kit should include a Demo Application to practice on.

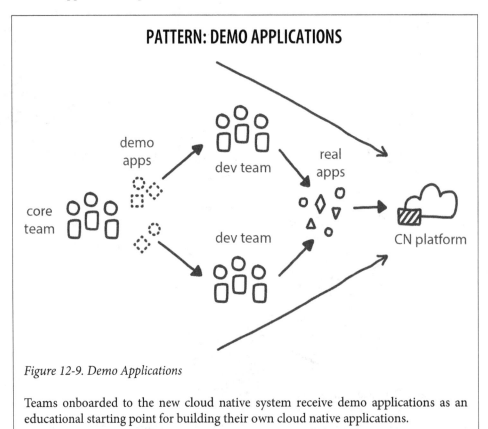

PATTERN: DEMO APPLICATIONS

Figure 12-9. Demo Applications

Teams onboarded to the new cloud native system receive demo applications as an educational starting point for building their own cloud native applications.

These are very helpful tools for making onboarding an easy and effective process. As mentioned earlier, though, a crucial part of this phase is also shifting the organizational culture from traditional to cloud native. This means that, even as you are training the teams in the new cloud native tools and techniques, you are also teaching them a new way of working. You're refactoring them structurally and culturally to fit with these very different processes and methodologies, and even introducing new ways of thinking that may at first seem totally opposite to the world they worked in before.

"Gradual" is the important word here. Iterative education is the foundation of the Prepare for Onboarding pattern and progresses over time, from very general background exposure to cloud native concepts to advanced training. It is important that the education provided is appropriate to the stage of onboarding; if a team is not scheduled to be on the new platform for six more months, basic introduction to concepts like microservices, Docker containers, and Kubernetes is good. But they don't need advanced training yet—save the hands-on learning for when they are actively moving onto the new system.

This gradual education process shapes and drives the essential cultural shift that developers must undergo as part of the move to cloud native: the transformation into Build-Run Teams.

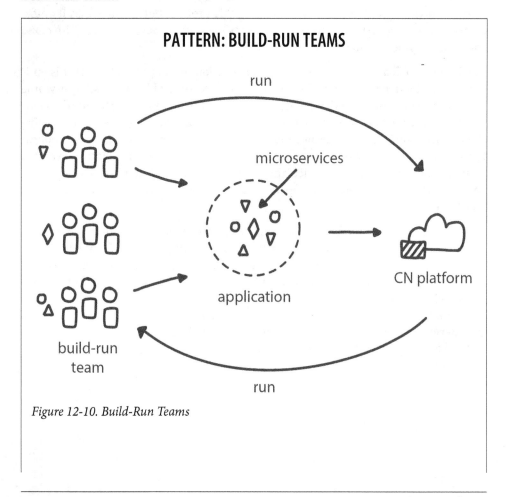

Figure 12-10. Build-Run Teams

> Dev teams have full authority over the services they build, not only creating but also deploying and supporting them.

In traditional software development, developer teams rely on the Ops team to deploy artifacts to production. This handover kills production speed and agility. However, trying to fix that by putting an Ops person on each developer team is how you end up with 10 different irreconcilable platforms. Conway's law shows us that software architecture will come to resemble the organization's structure. So if we want the platform to be independent, then the teams developing an application need to be separate from the team running the production platform.

Most teams onboarding to a new cloud native system will be coming from a Waterfall approach, where specialist teams hand off artifacts by essentially tossing them over the wall to the next team. Agile invented cross-functional teams, removing the wall between developers and testers, but there is still a handoff to Ops for deployment. DevOps further tore down the walls dividing this process, but the model as it's most commonly understood and implemented needs to evolve to align properly with cloud native development practices.

The Build-Run Team pattern is a specific formulation for a DevOps team that is optimized for cloud native. This team should be able to build (and test) everything needed to deploy their service to production and then support it afterward. Build-Run teams are the definition of "you build it, you run it" when it comes to developing cloud native applications. (But not the platform or infrastructure that those applications run upon.) Build-Run teams have full responsibility and control over the requirements for the microservice they are building. They don't just design and deploy, but also participate in the operational side of whatever service or component they build.

In traditional organizations, provisioning hardware typically requires filling out a form, sending it to ops, and waiting for them to do it on your behalf. Each handover creates a delay of hours, days, even weeks, and this reduces velocity for the entire system. Needless to say, this approach is eradicated in cloud native Build-Run teams, so the Self-Service pattern is an essential partner to the Build-Run teams pattern. Self-Service emphasizes the full automation of any manual or semi-manual practices, so that developers can provision infrastructure and deploy their own applications without handing off to anyone else.

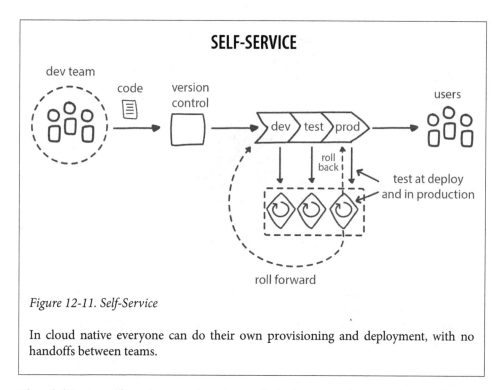

Figure 12-11. Self-Service

In cloud native everyone can do their own provisioning and deployment, with no handoffs between teams.

The ability to self-service provisioning and deployment also encourages frequent releases from developers to production. Without it there is no Continuous Delivery, and no Learning Loop from delivering to customers and then incorporating user feedback to create improvements.

Self-Service is the final piece in the metamorphosis of teams from traditional software development processes into cloud native ninjas. Figure 12-12 shows the patterns that go into this crucial Gradual Onboarding stage of the transformation.

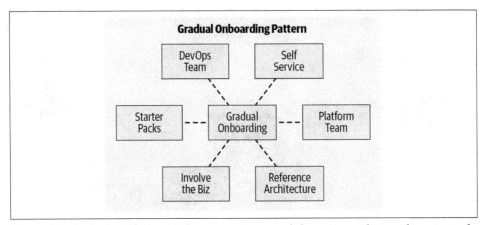

Figure 12-12. Gradual Onboarding super pattern and the patterns that apply as part of it

And this brings us to the end of Phase 3: Build. We have our functional MVP being extended into a fully production-ready platform by the Platform Team, while the Core Team takes care of the Prepare for Onboarding activities and then, when the time is right, begins the Gradual Onboarding process. Figure 12-13 shows our progress thus far, and opens the door to Production Readiness and entering Phase 4: Run.

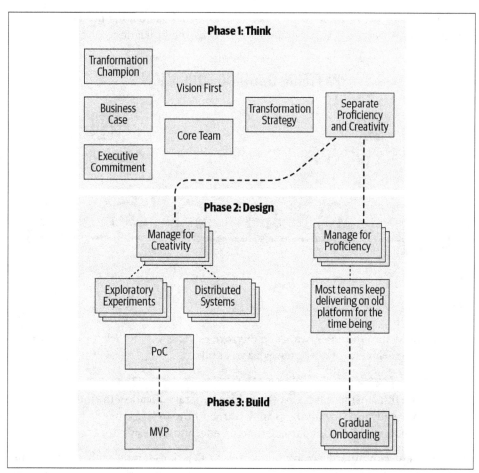

Figure 12-13. The transformation journey thus far—phases 1 through 3, shown in patterns

PHASE 4: RUN

The platform is completed and ready for production. Onboarding is in full swing. What happens now?

Well, here is one pattern that we have already applied, back during pre-boarding, but that is a prime directive going forward as well: Ongoing Education.

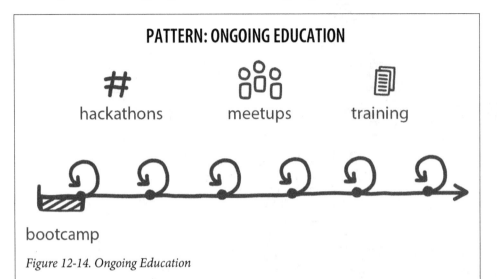

Figure 12-14. Ongoing Education

Continuously introduce new ways and improve existing ones to help teams continually develop their cloud native knowledge and skills.

Earlier in the transformation teams were given general education in cloud native topics, then more advanced training as they learned how to work hands-on in the new system. Once successfully onboarded, though, education doesn't stop!

Unfortunately, continual learning often falls to the side—along with creativity and innovation—as teams get comfortable in their new way of working and the company steers its major focus back to proficient delivery. Companies are used to the way things worked in the past, when they bought a big new tool: everyone took two days of massive training and a couple weeks on a learning curve to adapt to it. After that, everyone knew the tool and could forget about education.

Cloud native never rests, however. Ongoing Education assures your teams are always learning, building upon the core of what is to constantly improve, update, and iterate forward.

As the teams delve into their Developer Starter Kits and practice with Demo Applications, they are building confidence in their work on the new platform. One way to keep a positive upward spiral going is to Involve the Business and ensure that Feedback Loops are in place.

Both of these patterns address the challenge of incorporating business needs into the company's new way of working. When developers are running quick iterations without involving their customer-facing colleagues, the features they come up with could be limited to tech solutions only. Businesspeople, however, can't run full tech experiments to investigate ideas they might have for adding customer value to the company's core products/services. To close the learning loop, experiments and changes need to include everyone, from developer to customer and back. The results can then be used to define and drive the next change.

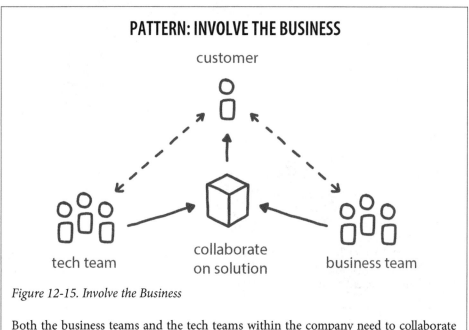

PATTERN: INVOLVE THE BUSINESS

Figure 12-15. Involve the Business

Both the business teams and the tech teams within the company need to collaborate to create an effective customer feedback loop that drives product improvement.

Doing this requires close collaboration between dev teams and people from the business side to define experiments for testing new customer value and quickly executing them. The Involve the Business pattern describes practical ways to make sure this happens. Dev teams need to embed measurement of customer feedback into products so the business teams gets insight, and the business teams in turn need to work with devs to define what is most valuable to deliver. The practical way to incorporate this insight into future features or improvements to existing ones is the Learning Loop pattern.

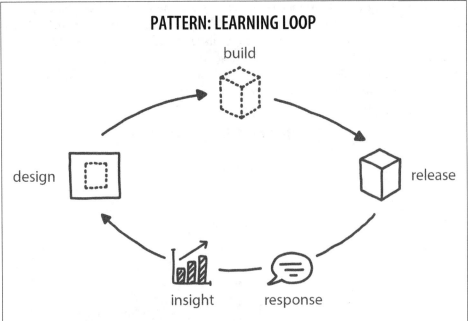

PATTERN: LEARNING LOOP

build

design

release

insight   response

Figure 12-16. Learning Loop

Building feedback collection into the delivery process closes the loop between engineers and the people who use their products, putting the customer at the center of the product development cycle.

Strangle All the Old Things

Things are going pretty well! The new cloud native platform is up and running, and most teams are trained, or well into the process of training, to deliver on it. It's time to migrate the legacy business applications. (Won't the proficient teams left behind to babysit the old system be happy to hear this!)

Re-architecting a large monolith that's been around, and slowly but inexorably growing for years and years, is a massive project. Some companies try to do it all at once, by simply trying to re-create the functionalities in a brand new codebase on the brand new platform. This makes a certain amount of intuitive sense, because a clean slate is very appealing, but rewriting a large monolithic application from scratch also carries a large amount of risk.

You cannot start using the new system until it is developed and functioning as expected, but of course our company has little cloud native experience or knowledge to actually pull this off. As we saw in the story of WealthGrid, building a new system from scratch will take a year or longer, and during this time there will be minimal enhancements or new features delivered on the current platform, so the business risks losing market share.

WealthGrid, and everyone else, should never attempt to re-create their monolith on the cloud, for all kinds of reasons. The solution is to instead slowly dismantle it. This avoids the significant risks embedded in the greenfield approach of rewriting the entire application all at once, since you re-create functionalities step by step while appropriately re-architecting them (and your culture) for the cloud. This way, the business value of new functionality is achieved much more quickly, and a cloud native architecture of loosely coupled services means future refactoring work will be simple.

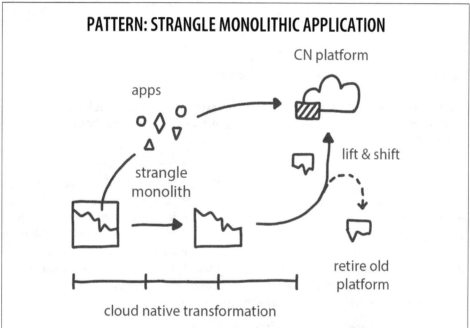

PATTERN: STRANGLE MONOLITHIC APPLICATION

Figure 12-17. Strangle Monolithic Application

Gradually split pieces of the old monolithic application one by one, re-architect them into services, and move them over time to the new cloud native platform.

Naturally, the Strangle Monolithic Organization pattern complements Strangle Monolithic Applications.

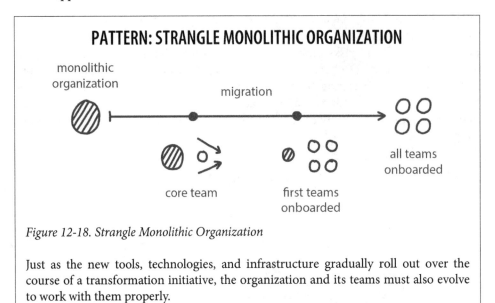

PATTERN: STRANGLE MONOLITHIC ORGANIZATION

Figure 12-18. Strangle Monolithic Organization

Just as the new tools, technologies, and infrastructure gradually roll out over the course of a transformation initiative, the organization and its teams must also evolve to work with them properly.

Migrating an existing company to the cloud can take years if done the right way, which is slowly and gradually. Instead, though, many companies commonly make the unfortunate choice to move everyone over at once. It's hard to do good training in that scenario; without a solid background in the new tech, teams will be slow to become productive on the new system. There will be huge pressure on the Core Team to help solve all their problems. Or, instead of seeking help from the overloaded support team, some people will attempt to hack their own best-guess solutions or fall back on old habits that don't work well in cloud native.

This is what happens when the cultural and organizational changes necessary in a cloud native transformation are not supported to evolve equally along with the technology. We can simply avoid creating the problem in the first place by following the patterns from the pre-onboarding and Gradual Onboarding phases.

Don't Create "Second Class" Engineers

There is a second bad move that is less common, but we still see it often enough to make note of the phenomenon. This happens if a company has a significant legacy codebase that is going to remain relatively intact. It will be ported over to and deployed from the cloud but otherwise remain unchanged. This legacy core will require engineers to maintain and look after it.

In this case, companies create a dual culture by simply leaving one part of the organization in legacy while everyone else moves to cloud native. This divides the company into a second-class citizen scenario, where the teams who will never get moved to cloud native are simply stalled professionally. They'll never get to play with the cool new tech and build modern developer skills if they are left behind to babysit the legacy system. This, naturally, leads to frustration, resentment, and reduced motivation, not to mention difficulty retaining engineers.

These earlier patterns lay the groundwork for new team structures and ways of working before the teams are actively trying to deliver on the new platform. With these in place, the natural next step is then to slowly strangle the process and cultural relics like specialized teams, along with the monolith itself.

The two systems, old and new, can coexist very well during the transformation process. Once the migration is complete, any remaining pieces of the legacy system can be ported over to the new cloud native platform using the Lift & Shift at the End pattern, and gradually refactored into microservices until the old monolith is no more. Then the legacy system maintainers—the very last of the proficiency teams—are the final cohort to be onboarded to the new system.

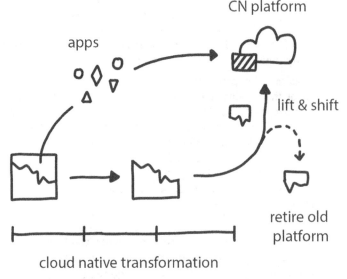

PATTERN: LIFT & SHIFT AT THE END

Figure 12-19. Lift and Shift at the End

It's important not to approach a cloud native transformation by simply attempting a full "lift and shift" of your existing system onto the cloud. But it can be smart to move some intact pieces of it at the very end.

Lift and shift is a bad move if done at the beginning of a transformation, but at the very end it can actually be a very good move. Sometimes, after everything else has been moved over, we find that there is still a functional piece of the original codebase, or even more than one, that would be prohibitively difficult to refactor to fit the cloud native platform. If this is a strong system that is functioning, stable, and requires few changes, just keep it. Package it so that it sits on one server and works forever, and create the new pieces needed to talk to the old piece. This could be a one or more microservices that essentially serve as an interface to the old system by talking directly to the old database or, even better, to the old APIs.

Keeping Creativity Alive

The new system is fully up and running, and all the teams are working well using their new-found skills to deliver new features and improvements quickly and iteratively. This is actually a dangerous time due to the temptation to fall back into full proficiency mode. By which we mean focusing almost exclusively on delivering your product or service, while slowly but inevitably forgetting about innovation and creativity.

At this stage the Core Team has successfully delivered a new system and helped everyone onboard onto it. They are the ideal candidates to stay at the forefront of innovation efforts, to be in charge of keeping creativity alive in the company. How does this work in the real world?

In Chapter 6, Tools for Understanding and Applying Cloud Native Patterns, we introduced the Three Horizons model for balancing proficient delivery with ongoing innovation. It's so important to cloud native that it becomes a pattern in its own right.

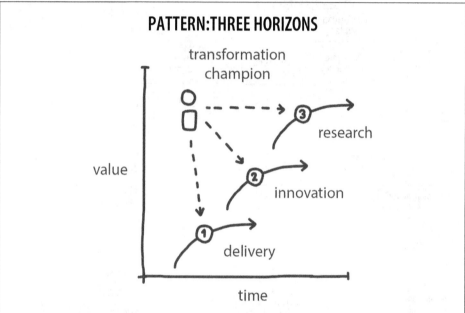

Figure 12-20. Three Horizons

Dynamically distributing resources between delivery, innovation, and research makes an organization responsive to change while reliably delivering core business value.

The Core Team now invests their well-practiced creative abilities to H2 and H3, innovation and pure research. They work on identifying and trying out next-generation technologies and methodologies that might interest the company a few years down the road. Everyone else, the majority of teams working in the new system, do indeed stay focused on delivery and so remain in H1—most of the time.

The beauty of the Three Horizons model is its ability to rebalance responsively when circumstances change. The distribution of investment between delivery, innovation, and research can simply be shifted as needed. Figure 12-21 shows how this dynamic distribution changes through the course of a cloud native transformation initiative to reflect varying levels of investment in creative innovation and research, versus proficient delivery.

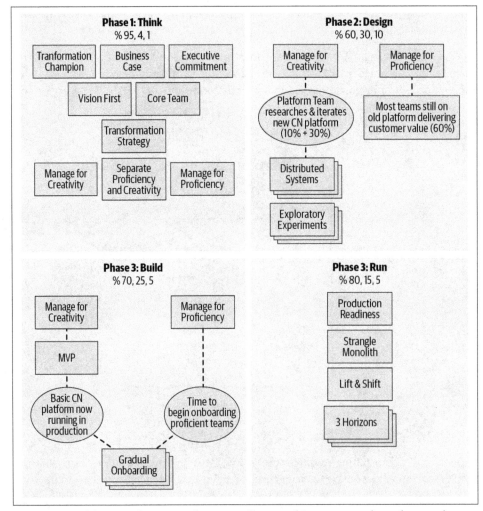

Figure 12-21. The transformation design, as illustrated in patterns, shows how each phase recalibrates the distribution of investment between delivery, innovation, and research.

This varying relationship is demonstrated throughout our transformation design. Before beginning, we had a company that has been putting probably close to 100 percent of its focus into delivery and only a token amount, if anything, into innovation or research for quite some time. It had functionally forgotten how to be creative.

WealthGrid is our fictional example, but this accurately describes a great many real-world companies, too. So, right now the numbers invested in delivery, innovation, and research would be essentially 100, zero, and zero, respectively.

Early in the transformation we begin applying Phase 1 "Think" patterns to investigate the Business Case and gain Executive Commitment for a cloud native initiative, along with other establishing patterns. The numbers shift only a small amount to 95/4/1[1] during this stage because most of the organization is focused on delivering value on the old system while the company leaders and then a small Core Team begins planning and designing the transformation.

As the transformation moves forward, however, more investment flows into the initiative, and people from all across the organization start to become involved. At the height of the transformation, Phase 2,"Design" and Phase 3, "Build," a larger proportion of the company is involved in H2, innovation mode, because people are being trained how to not just work differently but also think differently as they move to the cloud native system. Phase 2 also has a relatively high H3 number—60/30/10—because so much research and experimentation are being invested in identifying the best migration path. This is an innovative time across the board because the company is dedicating itself to undergoing intentional change, meaning the focus has shifted, very temporarily, from pure delivery.

Once the MVP is production ready, things begin to rebalance once again in the direction of a higher percentage in H1/proficiency. Most of the teams return to steady delivery mode, but a respectable amount of attention is being paid to innovation and research. The H2 efforts are directed toward realistic improvements that could become money-making (or -saving) projects in the next year or so. They are practical explorations of all kinds of things to continuously improve the future of the products, such as maybe adopting serverless, or building A/B testing. H3 is mostly pure research, maintaining awareness of things that may be several years out in terms of technological readiness but that might be valuable eventually.

Right around this 80/15/5 distribution is the sweet spot for cloud native companies to strive for: most of the focus (80%) is on delivering the products or services that drive the company's profits, but a respectable amount of investment still goes into innovation (15%) and pure research (5%). Keeping an eye on the balance is key, and for this we apply the Periodic Checkups pattern to maintain situational awareness and use

---

1 These numbers are hypothetical for this fictional example, but based on our observation of how client companies and other organizations the authors have encountered have allocated their resources. Ratios will of course vary from org to org.

Dynamic Strategy to adjust the ratio between proficient delivery versus investment in innovation and research as needed.

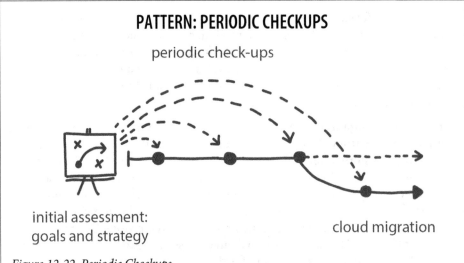

PATTERN: PERIODIC CHECKUPS

periodic check-ups

initial assessment:
goals and strategy

cloud migration

Figure 12-22. Periodic Checkups

Frequently reassess vision and objectives to ensure these remain the correct direction to proceed as the business environment shifts.

There are other patterns for fostering creativity to apply at this point, if they have not already emerged organically during the transformation process. Either way, these carry forward in the life of the company, even after the transformation is complete. They are additional supports for creativity and keeping innovation alive across an entire organization, even as the new system swings into mainly proficient operation mode. Two of these patterns are Reduce Cost of Experimentation and Personalized Relationships for Co-Creation.

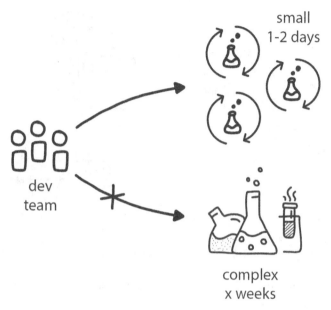

PATTERN: REDUCE COST OF EXPERIMENTATION

small
1-2 days

dev
team

complex
x weeks

Figure 12-23. Reduce Cost of Experimentation

When someone has an idea that requires validation, the costs of doing experiments around it need to be as low as possible.

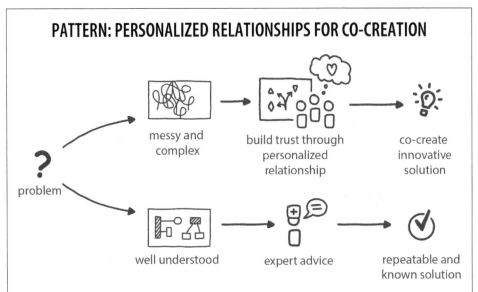

PATTERN: PERSONALIZED RELATIONSHIPS FOR CO-CREATION

Figure 12-24. Personalized Relationships for Co-Creation

Solutions to complex problems are best co-created by teams with high levels of interpersonal connection.

The End?

All the teams are onboarded onto the new system and working in a cloud native way —Build-Run Teams doing CI/CD and other cloud native methods to rapidly develop new features and deliver quick, incremental improvements. There is a focus on delivery, but also meaningful investment in ongoing innovation, with teams dedicated to more pure creativity. Everything is working well, and everyone is feeling confident. It is time to shut down the old data centers. Congratulations, you have reached the end of your transformation journey!

Definitely pause for a well-earned celebration and to appreciate how far you have come. But also please be aware that the end is only the beginning. You have finished the transformation, but this is merely a milestone in a longer journey. The cloud native road goes on.

And here is where we let you in on the secret at last. Cloud native transformation is never just about microservices and Core Teams and Kubernetes, or even about evolving from Waterfall/Agile. The true metamorphosis was from being an organization that rarely faced change, and that probably even feared it, to an adaptive organization that can change direction as needed, quickly and confidently.

You've got the tools now, and we don't mean Kubernetes. We mean you can now use this same framework of patterns to do anything you like. Whether you just want to create a new product or embrace whatever new tech comes next, you'll still just apply your new process: Start with a Business Case, define a Core Team, experiment your way to an MVP, and so on to completion.

You are ready for the world of cloud native but—even better—you are ready for whatever comes after that!

CHAPTER 13

Common Transformation Challenges

Now it is time to look at some typical cloud native transformation challenges and scenarios. These are situations commonly found when a migration initiative has stalled or otherwise gone wrong. In fact we find these same situations so often, and across so many different types and sizes of enterprises, that we developed profiles to speed up analysis and enhance understanding. It is important to note that every organization has its own unique set of needs and circumstances, such that every transformation path differs in the details. Thus, these scenarios represent broader "big-picture" profiles, not analysis on a granular level.

Each scenario contains sample a Cloud Native Maturity Matrix graph representing how results would typically look when that situation is found. Remember Chapter 6, where we introduced the matrix as a tool for assessing organizational state and readiness for migration? If you have been playing along to assess and graph your own status, you can compare your results to the scenarios described in this chapter. Really, though, you would only find a match if you're reading this book to find out why your cloud migration initiative is not going as planned. If you are at the beginning of the process, let this be a lesson in "what *not* to do when planning a cloud native transformation."

 After we explore each problem, we name a set of patterns that can be applied as part of a design solution. Bear in mind that these address only this specific problem at this specific stage. The set of patterns we describe then fits into an overall design—a larger set of patterns that holistically addresses the entire process and serves as the transformation design. See Chapter 11 and Chapter 12 for a start-to-finish roadmap.

Too-Early "Lift & Shift" Move

When we see the "lift and shift" mistake, the enterprise suffering the consequences is almost always taking a traditional Waterfall approach to software development (a company very much like WealthGrid, in other words). The organization may have adopted some Agile processes, such as work sprints, but the hierarchy and bureaucratic way of doing things that become ingrained in large companies are still in charge.

Companies like this tend to be comfortable with large initiatives and making big bets, once identified as a proper strategic goal for the business. They are willing to invest the resources to make a cloud native transition happen, but they are operating under the mistaken belief that it simply means migrating their existing system and processes onto the cloud. Unfortunately, there is little cloud native understanding or experience inside the company to guide more informed decision making. This is so common that it's earned the name "lift and shift" and it categorically does not work if you try to do this at the beginning of a transformation. An organization has to change not only its technology but also its structure, processes, and culture in order to succeed with cloud native.

The "lift and shift" decision can come from the company's engineers, who have been to some conferences and are eager to try out this cloud native stuff. They likely have set up an account on one of the big cloud providers—after all, it's free to get started! —and have played around with setting up a container or two. From there they may have even built a small experimental app. It all goes pretty well, so they are confident they can manage a full-scale transition. Based on this, the engineers seek and get approval from management to move forward with a full-fledged cloud migration. (Sound familiar? This was exactly how WealthGrid undertook its first failed transformation attempt.) They'll move to cloud infrastructure and split their existing monolith into some (but not too many—typically, four to six) components so that they can justify playing with Kubernetes.

As previously discussed in Chapter 1, companies with existing cloud native expertise or who have hired outside guidance for their transformation have gained real advantage from moving a monolithic system or application to the cloud first, before re-architecting everything to optimize for the cloud. The intent behind such a move, however, is to jump-start your journey to cloud native as a starting point for further transformation such as moving to a true microservices architecture. Yes, you get to shut down your on-premises data centers. But there is still serious work to be done in terms of evolving your processes, organizational structure, and culture to suit your new cloud platform.

The point is, the situations where lift and shift works are when it is done as a tactical move, not a strategic one. For example, sometimes a lift and shift could be exactly the right thing to do as an experiment, on a small scale, to understand more about the way a cloud vendor works. It's not automatically a wrong move, it's just wrong as a goal or an end move. Intent is key: lift and shift should not be a strategic direction, done at the very start as the core of your transformation strategy.

Or, alternatively, perhaps the transformation drive comes from the top down, when the CEO and board decide the company needs to go cloud native and hand it off to the middle managers as a large but not particularly difficult technical upgrade. The mistaken expectation in this case is that the company can throw money at the project and simply purchase a full solution from a major cloud vendor. After all, that was how it always worked in the past when it came time for a technology overhaul. It'll be a rough two weeks while everything gets installed and people get used to the new tools, but after that smooth sailing.

Both of these scenarios are based on the same understandable but fundamentally flawed assumption: Since their current system works well, they should just be able to re-create it on the cloud, right? (Vendors may even be promising that this indeed how the process will go. More or less. Emphasis on the less, but please sign here, thanks!)

In both cases the migration plan is essentially to take the old system (the "lift") and move everything onto the cloud more or less intact (the "shift").

In both cases, everything else, however—organizational and cultural aspects such as planning, design, development processes, etc.—remain unchanged. The technology goes cloud native, but the company itself is the same as it ever was.

In both cases, after struggling for months to move the old system—and, possibly, a couple million dollars or pounds or Euros later—the company is baffled to realize that, yes, they've got Kubernetes and cloud infrastructure...and nothing works. Or maybe things are even mostly sort of working, but not any faster or better than they did before.

Take a look at Figure 13-1 to see how this plays out when graphed on the Maturity Matrix.

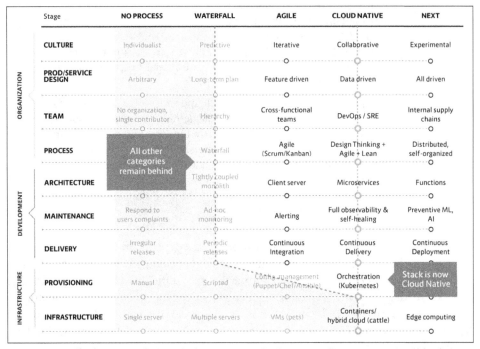

Stage	NO PROCESS	WATERFALL	AGILE	CLOUD NATIVE	NEXT
CULTURE	Individualist	Predictive	Iterative	Collaborative	Experimental
PROD/SERVICE DESIGN	Arbitrary	Long-term plan	Feature driven	Data driven	All driven
TEAM	No organization, single contributor	Hierarchy	Cross-functional teams	DevOps / SRE	Internal supply chains
PROCESS	All other categories remain behind	Waterfall	Agile (Scrum/Kanban)	Design Thinking + Agile + Lean	Distributed, self-organized
ARCHITECTURE		Tightly coupled monolith	Client server	Microservices	Functions
MAINTENANCE	Respond to users complaints	Ad-hoc monitoring	Alerting	Full observability & self-healing	Preventive ML, AI
DELIVERY	Irregular releases	Periodic releases	Continuous Integration	Continuous Delivery	Continuous Deployment
PROVISIONING	Manual	Scripted	Config management (Puppet/Chef/Ansible)	Orchestration (Kubernetes)	Stack is now Cloud Native
INFRASTRUCTURE	Single server	Multiple servers	VMs (pets)	Containers/ hybrid cloud (cattle)	Edge computing

Figure 13-1. "Lift and Shift the whole system at the beginning" scenario as graphed on the Maturity Matrix

In this scenario we see: A company with Waterfall or Agile culture, architecture, design, and processes that has attempted a "lift and shift" strategy for moving their current system (and comfortable way of doing things) onto the cloud. On the Maturity Matrix, Infrastructure has moved all the way to Containers/Hybrid Cloud while all other categories remain rooted around Waterfall/Agile status.

What will happen: Operating costs will go up. Few, if any, benefits will be gained. Time and money will be wasted: you now have a bunch of expensive complex tools on top of the same system you always had—but you are not faster or cheaper. Worse, you have missed the opportunity to use this motivation and momentum to make real, lasting changes to truly transform your organization and its processes.

A better approach: Focus on progressing all the points toward their respective cloud native states. For most organizations this likely means starting with Architecture and Process while simultaneously working to gradually evolve Culture.

So, again, doing a lift and shift is itself not a completely flawed approach. Early on, pursued as an open-eyed tactic rather than a strategy, it can have value. But doing a lift and shift as your *entire* transformation strategy is setting the stage for later disaster. In many migrations—toward the end, once the new platform is working in production—there may be parts of the original system that are still necessary and in place. If these legacy components are stable and seldom changed, they can indeed be moved to the cloud using lift and shift at the *end* of the initiative. See "Lift and Shift at the End" in the Appendix A patterns library.

Practical patterns solution: An honest and thorough assessment of your current state is essential before moving forward in any aspect of a cloud migration. Once that is in hand, start with Vision First. (Presumably you already have buy-in and support from the CEO/board, but if not, do the Business Case and Executive Commitment patterns first). Next, name your Core Team. You will emerge from this initial set of patterns with a clear vision, a high-level architectural direction, and a team that is equipped to implement both.

Treating Cloud Native as Simply an Extension of Agile

Changing your software development practices from Waterfall to Agile is a huge paradigm shift. Most companies understand that to remake themselves as truly Agile organization, they would need to alter a lot of the ways they do go about developing and delivering software, from building processes all the way down to where people sit. Unfortunately, they don't extend this same understanding when it comes to moving the company from Agile to cloud native practices.

This particular scenario happens when a company that did a reasonably good job of transforming between Waterfall and Agile practices fails to recognize that moving to cloud native is a second true paradigm shift. Instead, they believe cloud native to be "just a new way to do Agile."

Instead of being treated as a major and serious change in its own right, the cloud native transformation is treated as just a bunch of tech-related tasks that get added to the existing development backlog. As we saw in WealthGrid's first failed attempt to deliver a new cloud native system, this approach doesn't work.

This is similar to the Lift and Shift scenario, but not identical. In this scenario the organization makes more real progress toward building a cloud native platform but is still not able to deliver software on it. Worst case, pretty much nothing works well at all. Best case, things are basically working, but the real value isn't there—the company isn't getting the product velocity and data-driven design they just spent all that money to create. The overall feeling is that the new system is not much better or even worse than the old one. (And then they say, having no idea how much they have just missed out on, "Those containers aren't such a great idea as we were thinking in the beginning.")

Figure 13-2 nicely illustrates the somewhat subtle but significant difference between attempting "Lift and Shift" and treating your cloud native transformation as though it is just another technical upgrade.

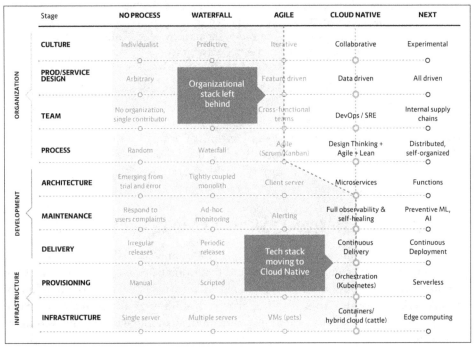

Stage	NO PROCESS	WATERFALL	AGILE	CLOUD NATIVE	NEXT
CULTURE	Individualist	Predictive	Iterative	Collaborative	Experimental
PROD/SERVICE DESIGN	Arbitrary	Organizational stack left behind	Feature driven	Data driven	All driven
TEAM	No organization, single contributor		Cross-functional teams	DevOps / SRE	Internal supply chains
PROCESS	Random	Waterfall	Agile (Scrum/Kanban)	Design Thinking + Agile + Lean	Distributed, self-organized
ARCHITECTURE	Emerging from trial and error	Tightly coupled monolith	Client server	Microservices	Functions
MAINTENANCE	Respond to users complaints	Ad-hoc monitoring	Alerting	Full observability & self-healing	Preventive ML, AI
DELIVERY	Irregular releases	Periodic releases	Tech stack moving to Cloud Native	Continuous Delivery	Continuous Deployment
PROVISIONING	Manual	Scripted		Orchestration (Kubernetes)	Serverless
INFRASTRUCTURE	Single server	Multiple servers	VMs (pets)	Containers/ hybrid cloud (cattle)	Edge computing

ORGANIZATION spans CULTURE, PROD/SERVICE DESIGN, TEAM. *DEVELOPMENT* spans PROCESS, ARCHITECTURE, MAINTENANCE. *INFRASTRUCTURE* spans DELIVERY, PROVISIONING, INFRASTRUCTURE.

Figure 13-2. This is what it looks like when a system moves ahead of the people who must work within it

In this scenario we see: The cloud native portion of the transition gets placed within the scope of Agile coaches and thus gets led by them. This is a genuine paradigm shift, but Agile sees it as only a simple platform iteration. Install Kubernetes, two sprints, done!

What will happen: This results in cloud native tools such as Kubernetes, CI/CD (Continuous Integration and Continuous Delivery), and Microservices being treated simply as normal extensions of the Agile approach, which they are not. You may be building small pieces faster, but if you are still releasing them all at the same time every six months as part of a tightly coupled monolithic app, you are completely missing the point of cloud native.

Waterfall's predictive culture dictates long-term planning, where you don't take steps unless you understand exactly where you are going: this is how you avoid risk. Com-

---

panies that have adopted Agile manage risk by delivering more frequently and reducing the risk of failure to smaller pieces of work. However, even though you are now creating it faster, you are still creating something very predictable—from within a hierarchical organizational structure, with all of its bureaucracy and handoffs.

This is why Agile processes and culture are still not fast enough, nor responsive and flexible enough, to take best advantage of cloud computing. If Agile was able to do this, we would not have needed to invent a new/different approach through cloud native practices!

A better approach: This is a major shift for a culture used to a tightly coupled approach where everything is developed in parallel for delivery all on the same day. Doing a contained experiment first helps teams coming from an Agile background understand how they will need to think, and work, differently once they are no longer operating within a hierarchy-driven monolith. It then helps them evolve into a collaborative and distributed cloud native way of working.

Practical patterns solution: Start with *Vision First*. Name a *Core Team* and a *Platform Team*. Take small steps for a gradual transformation, starting by working on one small contained side experiment that may be very basic but encompasses the major elements of cloud native (*Exploratory Experiments; PoCs; MVP)*. The culture of the platform team likely will begin naturally evolving to reflect the new platform, but this needs to be ensured.

"Spiking" Cloud Native Transformation via Unbalanced Approach

This is actually the most common scenario we see—or, rather, the same situation caused by one of three factors. An unbalanced approach can happen at any point on the Maturity Matrix. When we are called in to help with a migration gone wrong, however, we typically find an organization that has moved significantly forward in only one of three areas—Microservices, Orchestration/Kubernetes, or DevOps—without also moving forward in the other related areas crucial for keeping a cloud native transformation on track.

In this scenario, when you draw the Maturity Matrix line connecting all the axes, we find a single sharp "spike" in an otherwise uniform line. The particular problematic "spike" area can vary, but the final outcome is the same: the migration will bog down and is likely to ultimately fail.

This almost always happens when the initiative is started in, and driven from, a single faction in the company. No other groups are participating, and so the migration progresses happens only in the area that affects the originating group. The members of that faction unilaterally proceed with the migration, doing only what is important from their point of view—without taking into consideration any other stakeholders or the role of every other division in the organization.

If the transition is top-down, with the CEO and board deciding the company must go cloud native, you are going to see teams moving to DevOps. Adopting a DevOps approach is a good thing, but in this case they don't really understand what it means. Management will simply restructure things to add Ops people to the Dev teams and be done with it. Other than the seating assignments, nothing else really changes—process, delivery, and product/service design practices continue as of old. And once this one arbitrary idea has been enacted, they have no strategy for the future...and still no idea what a cloud native transformation means or how to get there. Figure 13-3 illustrates this.

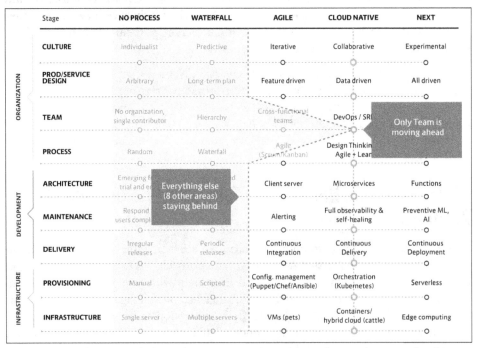

Figure 13-3. When an unbalanced migration is driven from the top down, and only concerning organizational structure, the Teams are told to start doing DevOps while everything else stays unchanged

If the move to cloud native is being driven by developers, however, Figure 13-4 shows that we see a surge ahead to Microservices while the rest of the company stays behind.

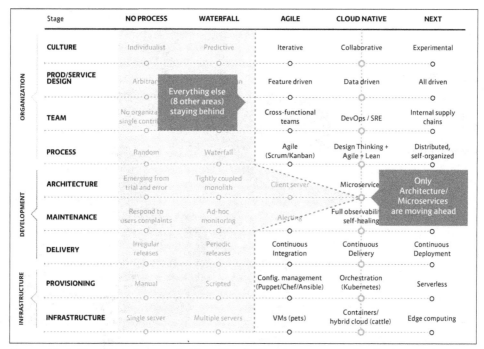

Stage	NO PROCESS	WATERFALL	AGILE	CLOUD NATIVE	NEXT
CULTURE	Individualist	Predictive	Iterative	Collaborative	Experimental
PROD/SERVICE DESIGN	Arbitrary	*Everything else (8 other areas) staying behind*	Feature driven	Data driven	All driven
TEAM	No organization, single contributor		Cross-functional teams	DevOps / SRE	Internal supply chains
PROCESS	Random	Waterfall	Agile (Scrum/Kanban)	Design Thinking + Agile + Lean	Distributed, self-organized
ARCHITECTURE	Emerging from trial and error	Tightly coupled monolith	Client server	Microservice	*Only Architecture/ Microservices are moving ahead*
MAINTENANCE	Respond to users complaints	Ad-hoc monitoring	Alerting	Full observability self-healing	
DELIVERY	Irregular releases	Periodic releases	Continuous Integration	Continuous Delivery	Continuous Deployment
PROVISIONING	Manual	Scripted	Config. management (Puppet/Chef/Ansible)	Orchestration (Kubernetes)	Serverless
INFRASTRUCTURE	Single server	Multiple servers	VMs (pets)	Containers/ hybrid cloud (cattle)	Edge computing

Figure 13-4. If a migration gets initiated by the developer teams, the devs surge ahead to building with microservices architecture while all the areas that need to support them remain unchanged

If that group is Ops, they say, "We need Kubernetes" and the Provisioning/Orchestration axis leaps ahead of where the whole rest of the company finds itself left behind on the Maturity Matrix, as seen in Figure 13-5.

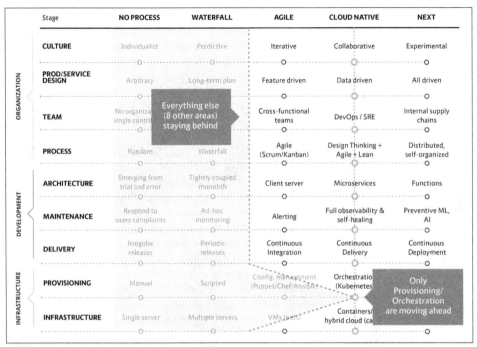

Stage	NO PROCESS	WATERFALL	AGILE	CLOUD NATIVE	NEXT
CULTURE	Individualist	Predictive	Iterative	Collaborative	Experimental
PROD/SERVICE DESIGN	Arbitrary	Long-term plan	Feature driven	Data driven	All driven
TEAM	No organiza, single contri	Everything else (8 other areas) staying behind	Cross-functional teams	DevOps / SRE	Internal supply chains
PROCESS	Random	Waterfall	Agile (Scrum/Kanban)	Design Thinking + Agile + Lean	Distributed, self-organized
ARCHITECTURE	Emerging from trial and error	Tightly coupled monolith	Client server	Microservices	Functions
MAINTENANCE	Respond to users complaints	Ad-hoc monitoring	Alerting	Full observability & self-healing	Preventive ML, AI
DELIVERY	Irregular releases	Periodic releases	Continuous Integration	Continuous Delivery	Continuous Deployment
PROVISIONING	Manual	Scripted	Config. management (Puppet/Chef/Ansible)	Orchestratio (Kubernetes	Only Provisioning/ Orchestration are moving ahead
INFRASTRUCTURE	Single server	Multiple servers	VMs (pets)	Containers/ hybrid cloud (ca	

Figure 13-5. When an unbalanced migration is driven initially by the Ops team, they embrace Kubernetes while the rest of the company keeps on building the way they always have

Even when the isolated initiative in question is actually going well, this is still a problematic scenario. For example, consider a situation where the development teams decide to try out microservices without engaging or even informing other important stakeholders, like the operations part of the company. Things eventually become problematic because, while the engineering team may understand microservices and are implementing them properly in their own limited setting, the rest of the organization is not involved. And the engineers don't know enough about cloud native architecture to consider the impact of doing microservices on the rest of the organization.

What they fail to consider is that they will have nowhere to deploy those microservices. Since they were operating in isolation, there are no Ops teams deploying and maintaining the target clusters. So, either it will stall or the devs will provision poorly configured clusters without talking to Ops. No one will be able to maintain such a mess.

The main problem, though, applies no matter who causes the imbalance: If there is no reorganization, then Conway's law dictates that the way microservices get divided up will inevitably come to mirror the company's organizational structure. Which will lead to the eventual and wholly unintentional re-creation of a monolith exactly like the one they have abandoned.

In this scenario we see: A company has decided to move onto the cloud and adopts one new practice or technology (Microservices, DevOps, Kubernetes) without considering the impact upon all other areas in the organization. This one area looks like a spike on an otherwise uniform matrix line.

What will happen: These initiatives rarely lead to success because teams very quickly run into all kinds of problems they never considered. Gridlock ensues: the teams know they have a problem, but they don't know enough to even begin to understand what to do about it.

A better approach: Senior managers or executive/board leadership needs to intervene and define the cloud native transformation as a company-wide priority. Bringing all branches on board to work simultaneously on migrating their particular area of responsibility.

Practical patterns solution: The first need is to establish full support for the transformation, including dedicated resources, a defined vision, and a (high-level, not too detailed at first) plan for proceeding, so turn to the *Executive Commitment*, *Vision First*, and *Reference Architecture* patterns, plus the *Core Team* to execute everything. From there, we apply patterns for establishing the architecture and all major design decisions: *Exploratory Experiments, PoCs, MVP*. The neglected stakeholders also need to be engaged, so this calls for the *Involve the Business, Transformation Champion* and *Internal Evangelist* patterns.

New System, Old Structure

Sometimes a company tries to go cloud native in every area except Team. We mean "Team" in the Maturity Matrix sense: how responsibilities are assigned within your organization and how communication and collaboration happen—or maybe don't. Unfortunately, scoring even eight out of nine on matrix axes achieved is not a passing grade when it comes to a cloud transformation.

This particular challenge arises when, during the transition, your culture fails to evolve along with your new cloud technology. Typically it happens in one of two ways, both of which are artifacts of Waterfall culture wrongfully kept in place. Either you are retaining a very strong organizational hierarchy or keeping your teams specialized—grouped by skill instead of according to which piece of the system they deliver. Cloud native requires restructuring teams to become cross-functional, "you build it, you run it" groups capable of developing, delivering, and supporting a service from creation to production. In other words, capable of building microservices-based applications, and also defining infrastructure needed for those microservices in the process. (Think of it as microservices and infrastructure as code.)

You can have all the other areas in place and running smoothly, even the previous scenario's problem areas of Microservices, Kubernetes, and DevOps. Unfortunately, no matter how well the rest of the system has been built, you are holding onto the mistaken belief that you can completely modernize your tech stack on the cloud, yet still produce things exactly the same way you've been doing for decades.

This scenario is the inverse of the previous one. Here we see a kind of "reverse spike" where all areas of the company have moved forward in the cloud native transformation process except for one single area, Team, remaining stubbornly behind. Figure 13-6 shows how striking this looks.

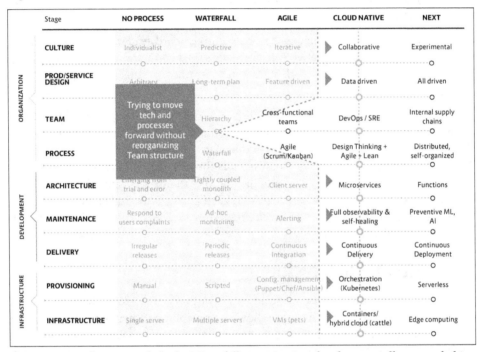

Figure 13-6. A "reverse spike" of a Waterfall organization that has actually succeeded in moving toward cloud native in every area except how their people actually work to build things: Team.

If your matrix graph looks like this, it means either you are attempting to deliver microservices using a fully hierarchical Waterfall process or that your process still requires handoff between specialized teams rather than each team delivering fully and independently.

Attempting to apply microservices (also true of DevOps) in a hierarchy might actually look like it's working at first. After all, you are probably successfully delivering something on the new system. But all you're really doing is streamlining a sub-process! You have in no way shortened the end-to-end release cycle, and you are definitely not delivering faster to the customer. Attempting this is an example of siloed thinking, a mistaken belief that optimizing the parts automatically means optimizing the whole. But your enterprise won't find transformative business value unless you optimize *all* the areas on the Maturity Matrix.

Likewise, keeping your teams highly specialised—divided by skills like database administrators, QA, backend, front end, etc.—creates dependencies during the delivery stage. So attempting to build a distributed system of many small independent services using highly interdependent teams of specialists, none of which can deliver without handoffs to all the *other* specialist teams, goes completely against cloud native principles.

Unless that is you actually want to harness the advantages of this cloud computing system you just spent so much time and effort to create, in which case you're going to need to restructure your teams.

In this scenario we see: Classic Conway's law in action, i.e., the principle that system architecture will come to resemble the structure of the organization that contains it. In other words, Conway's law describes how your system architecture will eventually and inexorably come to resemble your org chart: if the teams are organized based upon their specialized functions, eventually some sort of layered (and likely hierarchical, to boot) structure will emerge.

What this means is, if you attempt to introduce microservices without changing the organizational structure, over time the microservices will tend to drift together. Inevitably tight coupling will be introduced in one (or more) of the develop, build, or deploy stages. This will lead to more coordination and reduce the independence of the teams and—hey, look, a monolith!

What will happen: Basically you just re-created your previous monolith, only now on the cloud. Yes, it has microservices and containers and Kubernetes, but you used them to build a hierarchical system with very strong dependencies at the lower levels, single-specialty teams, and potential bottlenecks at each point in the process. There must be a handoff at each stage of progress, slowing things down even more.

A better approach: If you're going to go cloud native, it means completely restructuring your codependent, highly specialized Waterfall teams into collaborative DevOps teams. Each fully functional team includes planning, architecture, testing, development, and operations capabilities for whatever service it builds. It does not mean that they are responsible for the cloud native platform itself—that, of course, is built and run by your platform team.

Practical patterns solution: Apply the Build-Run Teams ("cloud native DevOps") pattern. This ensures that each team has its own planning, architecture, testing, development, and operations capabilities and that there is collaboration both within the same team and across multiple teams. Most importantly, there needs to be a Platform Team building the platform to run microservices and containers, and separate teams of developers building the application(s). This way, Devs can deploy directly and automatically to the platform without any need for handover to Ops.

These teams will also work best when they have Personalized Relationships for Co-Creation and the patterns for managing Co-Located Teams (or at least how to optimize Remote Teams) are applied to make this happen.

Wrong Order of Implementation

Waterfall organizations are pretty good with order of implementation in general, in large part due to their predictive culture. Unfortunately, many enterprises moving to the cloud don't consider the interactivity between cloud native elements—again, they don't know what they don't know! What they *do* know is they want microservices and so they move ahead on that sole axis, unaware of the havoc this can bring when implemented without also doing containerization, orchestration, automation, etc.

This can happen in a number of different ways, but the most common ones we see—as well as the most damaging—are when microservice architecture is launched either before CI/CD (Continuous Integration and Continuous Delivery) are in place or when companies try to run microservices without packaging them in containers.

When this happens, the result is literally hundreds of mini-monoliths running simultaneously—all of which need to be deployed manually. A nightmare, basically, which is happening because once again a monolithic team structure is expressing itself, via Conway's Law, as a large number of strong inter-team dependencies. Figure 13-7 does not fully depict the chaos.

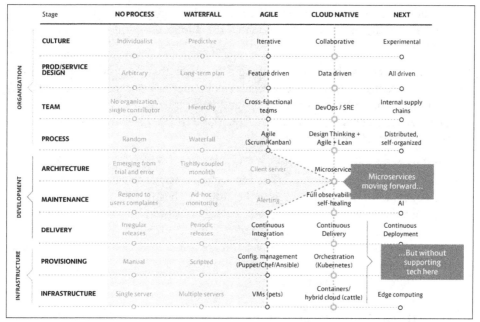

Stage	NO PROCESS	WATERFALL	AGILE	CLOUD NATIVE	NEXT
CULTURE	Individualist	Predictive	Iterative	Collaborative	Experimental
PROD/SERVICE DESIGN	Arbitrary	Long-term plan	Feature driven	Data driven	All driven
TEAM	No organization, single contributor	Hierarchy	Cross-functional teams	DevOps / SRE	Internal supply chains
PROCESS	Random	Waterfall	Agile (Scrum/Kanban)	Design Thinking + Agile + Lean	Distributed, self-organized
ARCHITECTURE	Emerging from trial and error	Tightly coupled monolith	Client server	Microservice	Microservices moving forward...
MAINTENANCE	Respond to users complaints	Ad-hoc monitoring	Alerting	Full observability self-healing	AI
DELIVERY	Irregular releases	Periodic releases	Continuous Integration	Continuous Delivery	Continuous Deployment
PROVISIONING	Manual	Scripted	Config. management (Puppet/Chef/Ansible)	Orchestration (Kubernetes)	...But without supporting tech here
INFRASTRUCTURE	Single server	Multiple servers	VMs (pets)	Containers/ hybrid cloud (cattle)	Edge computing

Figure 13-7. What happens when you try to implement cloud native application architecture without also adding cloud native tools, technologies, process, and culture

In this scenario we see: A typical non-cloud native company struggles to deliver a few components to production every few months, or maybe every few weeks if they have been moving toward Agile. They decide to move to microservices without ever considering the need to have other cloud native components in place to manage or run them.

What will happen: The number of components (microservices) goes up dramatically (from 5–10 to 100–300). The time required for delivering them, meanwhile, drops dramatically (down from months or weeks to days—or even hours). Juggling this many components in a greatly reduced timeframe means both quality and system stability are significantly affected. Trying to fit hundreds of microservices to a non-containerized platform without a high level of automation will be at best highly inefficient, and at worst possibly even disastrous.

The main result is that releases will inevitably end up becoming coordinated and scheduled as a natural consequence of needing to manage this myriad of microservices. Then, as the delivery process grows ever more painful and unwieldy, these coordinated and scheduled deliveries will start to happen at longer and longer intervals. First you just release at the end of the day, to keep things tidy; then, once a week because interdependencies seem to be growing and those take time to sort, and then even less frequently. This utterly defeats the purpose of cloud native, namely, reducing dependencies to go faster. Effectively, without the ability to deliver each microservice independently, quickly, and frequently, the application will over time develop into a monolith.

A better approach: With so many moving parts, reducing dependency on the infrastructure is essential. In such circumstances containerized packaging is essential, as well as implementing full automation around it. Simultaneously you need to cleave any dependencies between teams so that each one is able to move to delivery independently as soon as their code is ready.

Practical patterns solution: Choose one small application as an experiment (*Proof of Concept*). Assign a *Core Team* to do the research necessary (*Exploratory Experiments, Research by Action*) to steadily progress the entire application across every axis of the Maturity Matrix. Not just Architecture/Microservices, but also putting in place containers, orchestration, CI/CD, and the kind of non-hierarchical *Build-Run Teams* culture that supports working in such a vertical environment. After establishing these, you should be in good shape to step back into a typical transformation design as outlined in Chapter 11 and Chapter 12.

Platform Not Ready for Production; Going to Production Anyway

Public cloud platforms like AWS and Azure, as well as on-premises platforms like OpenShift, are presented as full end-to-end solutions, but beware: they are far from plug-and-play. Companies used to the full functionality of VMware (or any other fully mature tech solution) are unpleasantly surprised to find that configuration is partially manual, and not all the necessary pieces are even present.

Recall our metaphor from Chapter 1 where you buy a TV, bring it home, and open the box to find there are no cables, no power cord, no remote. None of the peripherals that are essential for operating the television set: it's literally just a screen. You grab the directions only to read steps like, "Now go buy this piece here, that piece there, and assemble your TV—eventually, it will be fine!" So it is with cloud platforms: they claim to be full solutions, but half of the necessary stuff is missing. Because you believed your vendor that its platform was a full solution, you haven't allocated people or budget or time to build or buy the missing or incomplete pieces.

The worst example of this scenario is when teams get ready to run microservices in production—or even already have them in production—but fail to prioritize strong observability and monitoring. They likely have some sort of event-based alerting set up, because that is how things have always worked before. In the past, when things went down, people would go into the servers to fix it locally. Once you move to MS and containers, however, you no longer have access to local storage. Containers go up and down in seconds, leaving no trace of themselves. Now you need dynamic monitoring with anomaly detection. If you are relying on traditional alerting triggered only when an actual problem occurs, by the time you log in, there will be zero evidence of what just happened.

Microservices, which run as many independent units, in particular must be well monitored and fully logged. Manual maintenance of microservices is costly and deeply impractical and of course you're not going to do it. However, configuring your out-of-the-box platform to take care of maintenance tasks for you automatically is complex and beyond the abilities of inexperienced engineers.

Figure 13-8 is a bit bare, but this is for a reason: no matter what the rest of your matrix looks like, if there is a gap in platform quality, your cloud native system is not going to launch.

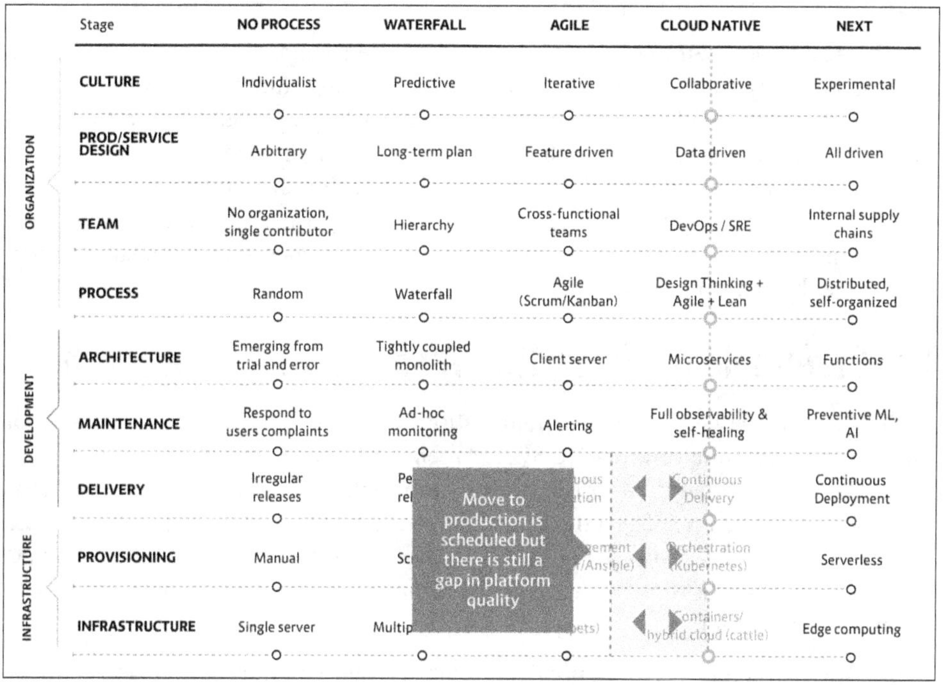

Stage	NO PROCESS	WATERFALL	AGILE	CLOUD NATIVE	NEXT
CULTURE	Individualist	Predictive	Iterative	Collaborative	Experimental
PROD/SERVICE DESIGN	Arbitrary	Long-term plan	Feature driven	Data driven	All driven
TEAM	No organization, single contributor	Hierarchy	Cross-functional teams	DevOps / SRE	Internal supply chains
PROCESS	Random	Waterfall	Agile (Scrum/Kanban)	Design Thinking + Agile + Lean	Distributed, self-organized
ARCHITECTURE	Emerging from trial and error	Tightly coupled monolith	Client server	Microservices	Functions
MAINTENANCE	Respond to users complaints	Ad-hoc monitoring	Alerting	Full observability & self-healing	Preventive ML, AI
DELIVERY	Irregular releases	Pe… rel…	…uous …tion	Continuous Delivery	Continuous Deployment
PROVISIONING	Manual	Sc…	…ement /Ansible)	Orchestration (Kubernetes)	Serverless
INFRASTRUCTURE	Single server	Multip…	…ets)	Containers/ hybrid cloud (cattle)	Edge computing

Left-side vertical group labels: ORGANIZATION (Culture, Prod/Service Design, Team), DEVELOPMENT (Process, Architecture, Maintenance), INFRASTRUCTURE (Delivery, Provisioning, Infrastructure).

Overlay box: *Move to production is scheduled but there is still a gap in platform quality*

Figure 13-8. Build your system all the way to completion before you try to run it, OK?

In this scenario we see: You have a bare platform with limited monitoring, security, storage, networking, etc., that is not ready for production. Or, interestingly, we also sometimes find that a company does install the proper tools—but then never checks to see if they work. The real truth is that nobody cares about monitoring until two days before going live with production. It's the same with security and other functional requirements.

What will happen: Things go wrong. Many, many things. No one has any understanding what happened, or why. In many cases an automated response to a detected anomaly gets executed before the system's human handlers are alerted, making it even harder to track down what went wrong.

A better approach: Harden your tools. Build in dynamic monitoring and anomaly detection—not just event alerting—from the beginning. Do a security review and implement load testing. Create full observability, including collection of all logs in a fully accessible central repository and status dashboards visible to everyone. Take advantage of cloud native's "self-healing" abilities, with constant health checks offering auto-restart in the event of failure. MONITOR. ALL. THE. THINGS.

Practical patterns solution: Bring the platform to a stable and production-ready stage in one complete prototype before full rollout to the entire organization.

The approach we recommend is to have a dedicated *Platform Team* that builds an *MVP* first, incorporating all major components at a basic functional level. Once the platform is ready, then it is time for *Gradual Onboarding* of a couple (literally, one or two) advance teams and improve the system based on their experience to build your *Developer Starter Pack*. The final step is to gradually roll it out to the entire organization while running an extensive educational program to make sure that developers can use the toolset effectively—and incorporating feedback as they learn so as to further refine the platform for long term use.

The Greenfield Myth, or, the "All or Nothing" Approach

In this scenario we see a Waterfall organization with a deep legacy codebase—say, for example, a mainframe running COBOL. An enormous amount of work and organizational change are required to refactor any monolithic system into a flexible, functional cloud native one. The understandable temptation is to simply scrap the old system completely in favor of building a brand new one from scratch. A complete greenfield project must be cheaper, faster, and more efficient than trying to work with the existing one, right?

The COBOL example is a bit dramatic, though we have certainly seen it. The point is, though, that lots of people think this way. There is also talk of having a cloud native greenfield advantage being the reason that disruptor companies are so successful, so fast, when they pop up.

There are multiple problems with this "all or nothing" approach. Your legacy codebase does not automatically need to be abandoned. Yes, maybe it's slow, changes are slow, the code itself is slow, and it definitely needs to be replaced someday—but so long as it is in place and working, *you should not touch it*.

This was exactly the mistake that WealthGrid made in their second attempt to go cloud native: setting aside the old system, essentially leaving it on life support with a skeleton crew keeping it alive while everyone else scrambled to build the new cloud native platform.

However, as WealthGrid discovered, in order to shut down the old system, the new one must first be working perfectly while re-creating 100% of the functionality provided by the existing one—all before you can ever begin rolling out new features. We have over and over seen real-world companies that, like WealthGrid, attempt to re-architect their monolith into 20 microservices and attempt to deliver them in a completely new greenfield system. Of course they built no connections to the old monolith—that is about to be abandoned. Of course they invest no effort, over the year or longer that this new platform takes to be built, to extend or upgrade the old one.

What they eventually realize is that this means they must build all 20 pieces and have them fully cross-functional, talking to each other and working together perfectly, before they can ever put the new system into production. This will rarely happen.

Figure 13-9 shows how an "all or nothing" approach can lead to a disorganized and uneven migration attempt.

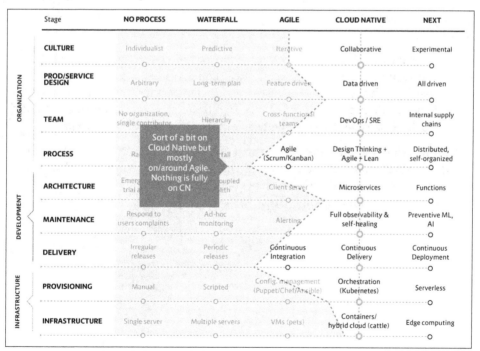

Figure 13-9. Note how the initiative's progress line is all over the place, indicating an uncoordinated transformation with multiple bottlenecks.

An "all or nothing" attempt—rebuilding a monolith into microservices from scratch —is not categorically a bad move. Greenfield can be a great way to go but only *if* you know what you are doing. Most companies don't. Cloud native is simply too new.

This is actually a nice illustration of the Pareto principle, which states that the first 80 percent of a project is pretty simple and will take 20 percent of the total time to achieve. Unfortunately, the last 20 percent is the most difficult and complicated, so finishing takes the other 80 percent of the time. In our scenario what the Pareto principle is saying is that the delivery of microservices to the new platform will be delayed for a very long time.

In this scenario we see: Companies with a large, venerable codebase that decide it's time to scrap that and just build a brand new cloud native system. After six months to a year of dedicated all-or-nothing effort, all they have is a stalled attempt to build a completely new system. None of it is ready to run anything. Meanwhile there has been no development at all on the old system.

What will happen: Confusion, chaos, and a deeply frustrated and unhappy team. You can't just go all in, assign all your COBOL engineers to shift to Kubernetes, and expect it to work out. You may as well ask them to fly your mainframe to the moon. It'll be just as effective.

A better approach: You did read the transformation design in Chapter 11 and Chapter 12, didn't you?

Practical patterns solution: First of all, if any part of your existing legacy system is stable and requires few or no changes, just keep it. At least a first, anyway. In many cases it isn't worth moving to microservices or cloud native in general as the value might be very low and the cost of change significant. A prime example of "if it ain't broke, don't fix it." We even have a pattern for this: *Lift and Shift at the End.*

Meanwhile, you can follow the transformation design we outlined in Chapter 8, starting with a small dedicated *Core Team* in charge of building your new cloud native platform while the rest of the engineers continue delivering on the existing system until the new one is production ready.

If It Ain't Broke...Build a Bridge

An important note: if you do have a deep legacy system that does what it needs to do, rarely needs fixing or changing, and is completely stable—don't try to rebuild it. There could be five to six million lines of code in the old system, produced over years if not decades of work. You can't rebuild that. You probably shouldn't even try. It's expensive and unnecessary to rebuild from scratch an entire monolith that is actually working pretty well for you, just because you bought into the greenfield myth. Rather than starting over, why not keep the legacy codebase in place and build a custom bridge to the cloud? It's cheaper, it's faster, and it's much, much easier.

The goal of a migration is to increase the speed and frequency of delivering value to the customers—*not* to have all the code in microservices. Therefore you want to focus on the parts of the system that are changing the most and where most of the engineering effort will be focused. This gets that boost in productivity without a massive, and not very necessary, rewrite of any stable and functional legacy parts of the original codebase.

So, package that piece (or pieces) so that it sits on one server and works forever. After that, you can design and then create brand new segments that talk to the old code. Build a tiny greenfield platform and then slowly move one piece over at a time, refactoring and rebuilding your platform as you go. It's a very slow, iterative long-term process, not a lift and shift of your whole legacy system to the cloud. But it will get you there.

Lack of Platform Team

It is extremely common, especially in larger companies, to find that before an "official" cloud native initiative is ever launched multiple teams have gone off on their own to experiment. This happens when they come back from tech conferences all excited about trying out cloud native tools and approaches. The company IT team has nothing to offer, so they go off to the side and start trying things on their own. This is such a common phenomenon that it even has its own name: shadow IT. This is all too easy because all you need is a credit card to be up and running on AWS or Google Cloud Services or Microsoft Azure in a basic way. At this stage, though, this is a good thing to happen. Teams are learning by doing, and the cost of experimentation is greatly reduced because they are not waiting for permission.

Eventually, though, if no organized company-wide initiative takes over, you end up with too much of a good thing. Seven different teams have each proudly produced their own version of a cloud native platform—but you can't maintain seven different platforms. It is too expensive and makes no sense. The teams will still struggle to make it work, but thanks to a hierarchical organizational structure and the fact that each team has its own specialty, they don't really know each other. They have no process for working together, or even talking with each other, for trying to figure out an effective solution (not that one exists). Often they are completely unaware that anyone else in the company was doing the same thing they were. All of that means that the organization has no way to capture or learn from the experience these separate teams gained.

This unfortunately is a pretty difficult problem to solve. You need to find a balance between flexibility and standardization. Strong standardization is great because you limit the support and maintenance costs, but this dramatically limits experimentation and research, which are crucial aspects of cloud native. Unfortunately, going fully in the direction of flexibility means you can't support all the varied and random things everyone comes up with. So a good organization finds a way to standardize to a certain extent while still enabling experimentation and research into new things.

In this scenario we see: A company where multiple DevOps teams have separate, non-standardized setups, possibly on the same public cloud or (worse) multiple clouds. So now there are, say, seven different systems, all built and deployed in different ways, using different tools. Everything is random. Not much harm done—yet.

What will happen: If any of these independent projects goes to production with their custom setup, which was created without appropriate knowledge, and without involving other stakeholders, it will be difficult to refactor it to a consistent setup with proper consideration of operational, security, compliance, usability, and other concerns.

If that is difficult with just one rogue platform, consider trying to reconcile seven different versions to run on a single system. It is basically impossible to refactor these to all work on a standardized platform for production; such a platform simply does not exist. And of course each one of these teams believes their approach is the best, the one the company should adopt.

A better approach: In properly implemented cloud native architecture, the platform team is permanent. This is because its work does not end with the successful creation of the initial platform—that was simply its first task. Once the major parts of the transformation are up and running, the team continues to work on improvements to refine and optimize the platform. Only a dedicated and constantly improving team can consistently dive deeper into technical challenges.

The practical solution: Assign an official *Platform Team* of five to eight engineers and architects. This team is dedicated to building the platform and are given sufficient resources to research, experiment, and implement the technology. Meanwhile, *Internal Evangelism* alerts the rest of the organization that a unified platform is being developed. Any teams who have built their own skunkworks platform on the side are invited to share their experience and contribute to the new platform if possible through applying the *Learning Organization* and *Communicate Through Tribes* patterns.

Lack of Education and Onboarding Plan

Sometimes an organization starts out the right way with their cloud migration: they name a small transformation team to learn cloud native by experimenting and building PoCs and eventually an MVP. This *Core Team* then uses their new skills to expand the platform, get it production ready, and evangelize the transformation to the rest of the company.

Everyone is excited and ready to launch. The only problem being there is no plan for educating and onboarding the other 300 developers who are about to be working in the shiny new cloud native system. Many of them were unaware that it was even on the way!

This sounds implausibly short-sighted, but we actually see this happen shockingly often. So much focus is placed upon getting the new system designed and built that no thought is given to how it will actually be put into use once it's in place and ready. Many times this happens because the transformation is led by engineers with a narrow focus on their own work and simply do not think in terms of the strategic company vision (which is exactly why the Dedicated Strategist pattern arose).

Unfortunately, the fix for this is not an easy matter of, "Here's a wiki and some docs; see you in Kubernetes on Monday!" Preparing developers for working in a cloud native style in your new cloud native system carries a steep learning curve. Getting them properly onboarded requires dedicated training and proactive education that begins long before the platform is even fully built.

Lack of adequate education leads, as a start, to inefficient use of the platform and the tools, among other problems. (Another problem: unhappy developers feeling blindsided by this huge change.) Failing to adequately prepare and educate the developers who will be using the new system will dramatically reduce the overall value produced by doing the transformation in the first place.

In this scenario we see: Realizing a week before going into actual production that there are 300 engineers who don't know how to do the work. That is when managers start frantically Googling "cloud native team training." Consultants *looooove* to get exactly this type of desperate phone call.

What will happen: Either the go-live date gets pushed back to create a training window or the project proceeds with undereducated engineers who don't know the best way to operate within the new system. Unfortunately this second outcome is what usually happens, because delaying the release date will harm the platform owner's reputation.

Many mistakes get made as everyone scrambles to adapt to a steep learning curve for the new tech, the new processes, and the new platform all at the same time. They will make decisions based on their current knowledge and experience, because without good education or onboarding that is mainly what they've got to go on. This not only reduces the value the company will get from this transformation but eventually will start re-introducing monoliths, manual testing, delayed deliveries, etc.

A better approach: Prioritize a training plan as part of the migration strategy from the beginning. Gradual onboarding of teams means earlier adopters can help train later teams. Timing is important; obviously, waiting until the last minute to train can be disastrous. But training too early is also bad. It's demotivating to get educated and then have nowhere to apply your new knowledge for a long time. Newly learned skills fade quickly if not put into practice.

It is important to say here that education is not just for onboarding, but needs to continue long after the platform and the apps are in production. Education is an ongoing and never-ending process that, once you start it, requires intentional support, organization, and planning to make sure your team's skills stay current.

The practical solution: WealthGrid's transformation design in Chapter 8 shows how, optimally, training begins during the middle stages of a migration. First, the *Platform Team* gets the training necessary to begin the initial design and build. It takes four to six months to build a platform and get it fully operational. This is the point to begin *Gradual Onboarding* to train the first few teams onto the platform. This is not just functional "how to" training, but full onboarding with architectural principles and culture, including examples and tutorials in the *Developer Starter Pack*. Once this first wave of teams is fully grounded they can help the next teams to come. *Ongoing Education* ensures that teams keep their skills refreshed and current even once they've been successfully crossed over the new system. And all the while the *Dedicated Strategist* helps keep everything on track.

Summary

You may have noticed a lot of repetition in the patterns presented for solving each of these commonly occurring problems. Here is another Leo Tolstoy quote to help explain this phenomenon:

> "All happy families are alike; each unhappy family is unhappy in its own way."

Tolstoy was talking about how unhappy families seem to take the same basic set of existential building blocks everyone gets, only they assemble these in a skewed way to create their own particular family fortress of misery and dysfunction. Meanwhile, happy families are all kinds of uniform in their contentment.

It works the same way with cloud native transformations. We witness the nine common challenges we describe in this chapter happen all the time, even as part of unique migration projects in very different kinds of companies. And yet when it comes to handling these challenges we keep showing you the same patterns again and again—*because they work.*

Fortunately, if you come to this book early enough in your own transformation journey, you will be equipped with the patterns (and context for when and how to apply them) to make sure your company's migration story has a reasonably happy ending. Chapter 8 is your main map, though this chapter is still worth your time since it's always worthwhile to see examples of what not to do.

And if not, well, late is better than never. Forget the sunk cost and use everything you've learned to rethink your strategy. We can't resist a second quote here, this time a Chinese proverb, because it captures this perfectly: "The best time to plant a tree is twenty years ago. The second best time is now."

So: If you are here because you're stuck in the middle of a migration gone awry, we hope that you recognize yourself in one, or even more, of these scenarios, and use the suggested patterns—repetitive as they may be—as a way to find your way back on course.

CHAPTER 14

Building a Bank in a Year: Starling Bank Case Study

By Greg Hawkins

Greg Hawkins is an independent consultant on tech, fintech, cloud, and DevOps. He was CTO of Starling Bank, the UK mobile-only challenger bank from 2016–2018, during which the fintech start-up acquired a banking license and went from zero to smashing through the 100K download mark on both mobile platforms. He remains a senior advisor to Starling Bank today. Starling built full-stack banking systems from scratch, became the first UK current account available to the general public to be deployed entirely in the cloud. Voted the best bank in Britain in 2018—and again in 2019—in a survey of more than 27,000 consumers, Starling beat out High Street mainstay banks with hundreds of years of experience behind them a mere year after its launch.

As a startup Starling was able to do cloud native from the start, while most companies are looking to migrate existing operations to the cloud. It's a complex and challenging process no matter where you're starting from! We are including Starling's story in part to illustrate what building a greenfield cloud native system looks like, but mainly how the same patterns can be used to compose many different kinds of transformation designs.

Greg Hawkins oversaw the creation of the cloud native platform as Starling's CTO. He remains involved as a senior advisor, helping the bank grow and shape its cutting-edge services as it continues to disrupt the financial services industry. This is the story of how Greg and the Starling tech team built a cloud native bank in a year.

So this is the tale of how we took advantage of our small scale to build a bank in a year, completely from scratch, completely cloud native. OK, so to be fair, before that year of intense building we did have a couple of prior years to lay the groundwork, mainly preparing the application for a banking license and getting the business side in place. There had also been a couple of technological false starts, meaning that when I joined Starling to begin building the tech stack in the beginning of 2016, we already had an idea of what didn't work for us, which was helpful. And of course we didn't stop after a year—many of the features that make Starling great today came later; the work is never done. But from a standing start we had a real live UK current account with payments and cards in place in a year, and we built it cloud native.

It was a bit nerve-wracking that, as we got started, we were having lots of meetings with regulators about how and why a bank should be allowed to deploy entirely in the cloud—it was far from certain that it would be allowed at all. We were right in there at the dawn of cloud banking in the UK, building all the software from scratch, before we knew it was even legal to operate as a cloud bank at all.

To a degree, the tight build period was actually imposed on us by regulation. In the UK once you have been granted your provisional banking license (or banking license with restriction, as it's called) you have precisely one year to sign up your first customer, or else lose your license and have to start all over. So there was that driver behind our timeline, as well as competitive disadvantages that would arise from delay.

Even though cloud banking was in the process of being invented as we (and also a few other challenger banks starting up around the same time) went along, building for the cloud was already fairly well-understood. Primitives like auto-scaling groups were well known, and the associated architectural patterns were well-established by companies like Netflix. Kubernetes and Terraform were pretty new at the time. After some bad experiences we judged them too immature for our purposes back then, and so we built directly using a handful of Infrastructure-as-a-Service primitives—building blocks that Amazon Web Services (AWS) rests many of its other services upon. These were services like Elastic Compute Cloud (EC2) and CloudFormation that allowed us to build a collection of related AWS resources and provision them in an orderly and predictable fashion.

Fortunately, we were a well-funded startup, so we were able to make sure our devs had everything they needed instead of trying to keep costs down and save on the AWS bill. We kept an eye on costs but didn't manage them too closely. The first decision was architecture, with a goal of building in such a way that we would be able to change quickly and remain resilient as the startup evolved.

In Starling's case, cloud native was a core part of their business plan. But in any organization it is essential to have Executive Commitment for the project to be successful, and Dynamic Strategy for adjusting plans and tactics in response to changing business conditions.

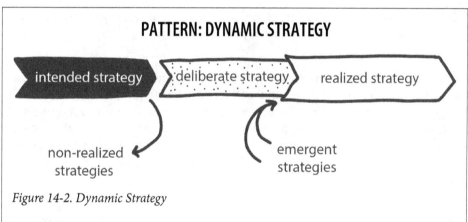

PATTERN: EXECUTIVE COMMITMENT

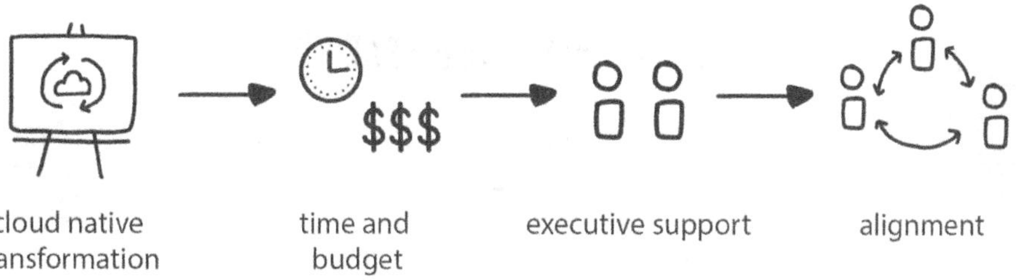

cloud native
transformation

time and
budget

executive support

alignment

Figure 14-1. Executive Commitment

To ensure allocation of sufficient resources and reasonable delivery time frames, large-scale projects such as cloud native transformation require strong Executive Commitment.

PATTERN: DYNAMIC STRATEGY

intended strategy

deliberate strategy

realized strategy

non-realized
strategies

emergent
strategies

Figure 14-2. Dynamic Strategy

Today's tech-driven marketplace is a constantly shifting environment, no matter what business you are in—so your game plan needs to shift right along with it.

Acing the Architecture

A key value hierarchy that guided our choices was security over resilience over scale. In reality, these values entangle and overlap, but having a clear hierarchy allowed us to make concrete decisions about how to proceed. Without some recognition of what's important to you it's hard to make the decisions that allow you to move forward in a complex and fast-changing environment. Then a secondary value hierarchy of velocity over economy further guided the decisions we made. We needed an approach around not just software architecture but also the organization itself that prioritized pace. And that is why in various areas we deliberately tempered our microservice architecture with some pretty monolithic practices.

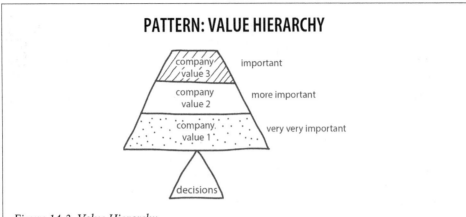

PATTERN: VALUE HIERARCHY

Figure 14-3. Value Hierarchy

When an organization's values are clearly stated and prioritized, day-to-day decisions can be made without seeking consent or permission/approval.

A monolith lets you go very quickly to start with, because you don't have to manage all the interrelationships between all the different microservices and all the common things that they need to share. The problem is that monoliths slow down over time—a lot. Everyone's all working on the same thing and stepping on each other's toes; it becomes harder and harder to change anything in a tightly coupled system that has a lot of stakeholders. And on top of that it's frighteningly easy for small errors to have enormous implications.

By contrast, microservices are very slow at the start because of all the complexity, but then you do get faster as you get more proficient at managing things. And you don't slow down so much from the effect of everyone stepping on each other's toes in the same codebase. So my plan, my big idea—though it's probably everyone in the world's big idea—was to try and get the best of both worlds. To start fast and stay fast.

Our approach to capture the benefits of both was to follow a sort of microservices, or maybe miniservices, architecture but to behave monolithically in many ways. For instance, even though we have something like 30 microservices, we tend to release them all at the same time rather than having separate release cycles for all of them. That will change over time, but we're still working this way almost three years later, to be honest and just looking to kind of break it, round about now actually, when we've got 60 to 70 developers.

This might just be the inflection point where a microservices-style organizational structure becomes easier, more sustainable. And this makes sense because microservices solve the problems of large organizations quite elegantly. But when you are a startup, if you were to introduce all the necessary overhead of that when you have a team of two to five developers, then you just hurt yourself with no benefit. And that is just where we were, at the time: we started out with just two engineers. The team grew, of course—by the time we went live we were up to 20 or so—but during those earliest days we were in the low single digits.

PATTERN: CORE TEAM

This is an absolutely perfect illustration of the Core Team pattern in action: never doubt that you can build a cloud-native platform with a small team of five to eight engineers—Starling did!

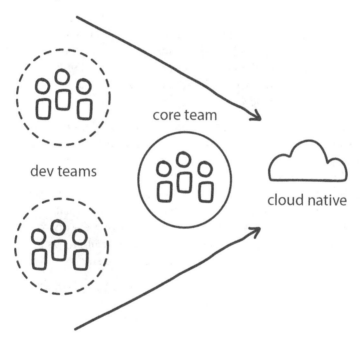

Figure 14-4. Core Team

Dedicate a team of engineers and architects to the task of uncovering the best transformation path and implementing it along the way. This reduces risk embedded in the transformation while the team gains experience helpful for onboarding the remaining teams later.

Although we were too small to organize ourselves along the same lines as a distributed microservice architecture, the idea was still to try and build in the ability to eventually make the organization more, well, microservice-y. So we architected for change. We decided we would build separate services that could be deployed independently and managed independently, but then for convenience, at least at first, we would behave monolithically—we would release them all together. That way you get the simplicity of a monolith in early days and the ability to move to independent management of microservices as the organization grows or as circumstances change or as the structure of the organization becomes clearer over time. The risk, of course, is that unexercised muscles atrophy, and so if you're not actually releasing these things independently, how do you really know anymore that you could? These sorts of trade-offs are the bread and butter of delivering big projects like Starling. While this approach helped us to move fast at first, my definite concern was to stave off the sort of stagnation, or even eventual paralysis, that results if you go on long enough delivering a monolith.

In cloud native, microservices helps you stave off that paralysis by allowing different parts of your organization to act independently without being bottlenecked by others. It's also fosters resilience: if all your services can tolerate the failure of all the others—if they can all live or die independently—then you've by default built in a lot of fault tolerance and natural resilience.

Microservices also give you tremendous flexibility to be compliant with Conway's law, which states that software structure will come to reflect the organizational structure of the company building it. It's easy to adjust service ownership to ensure that the system architecture is consistent with and reflects the structure of your organization. Unfortunately for a small startup growing at explosive rates, the structure of your organization is only half-formed, and probably extremely volatile. I often say that Conway's law is a bit of a mess with startups. So devoting energy to complying with Conway's law is best deferred by maintaining as much flexibility as possible and worrying about it later as the organization's mature structure emerges.

So much of my decision-making was guided by trading off flexibility and simplicity against each other.

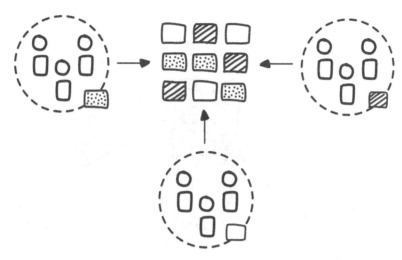

Figure 14-5. Microservices Architecture

To reduce the costs of coordination between teams delivering large monolithic applications, build the software as a suite of modular services that are built, deployed, and operated independently.

These were the principles I followed while architecting for change—for that point at which different teams are going to take ownership or responsibility for different components, going from the point where you have fairly few developers, they're kind of all able to work on everything, and no one's specialized around a single service because you need that flexibility. As the company becomes larger and split across different floors or different locations, etc., then you're in a different world. The goal is that you've architected such that it becomes a case of just taking ownership rather than re-architecting the software to support the communication structure of your new organization.

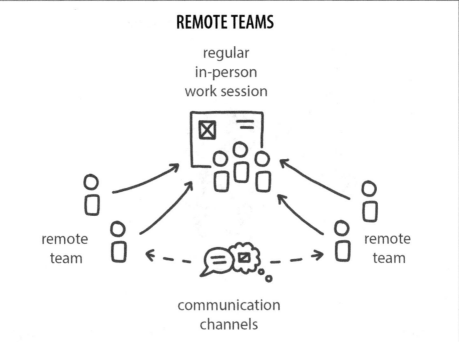

REMOTE TEAMS

regular
in-person
work session

remote
team

remote
team

communication
channels

Figure 14-6. Remote Teams

If teams must be distributed, whether across an office building, a city, or the globe, build in regular in-person retreats/work sessions as well as robust channels for close and freely flowing communication.

How we built is the important thing. *What* we built, our tech stack, is rather beside the point, because things are changing so much and so fast and every company is different. The whole idea with cloud native truly is how you build, not with what, and so the architecture is what truly matters. But for those with a technical bent, we built Java services in Docker images, which we deployed 1:1 onto EC2 instances running CoreOS, along with sidecars for log shipping and metrics publishing. We used many cloud services like GitHub, Quay.io, Artifactory, and Slack. We used Circle and then TeamCity for CI/CD. Our infrastructure code was CloudFormation and our rolling deployment tooling was our own.

Building the Apps

Once the initial platform architecture was decided, it was time to figure out what exactly we would run on it. As a mobile-only bank, this was our sole customer interface, and quite critical. We chose to have two mobile apps, one for the iPhone and one for Android.

We made no attempts to share code, for two reasons: one, we inevitably need quite deep native access to the hardware, and, secondly, we believe the best people to be writing for iPhones are those who eat, drink, sleep iPhones, love iPhones, and write in Swift for iPhones. Similarly with Android. Various technologies try to target both platforms, none of which super hot groups of engineers really love. So we've got two separate codebases there and we think it was the right decision.

That determined, we built our bank according to five principles I felt were important for cloud-native optimization.

No IT Department

At Starling, we wanted to be the first bank with no IT department. A lot of the people who came together to join Starling had a lot of experience of how banking traditionally delivers software, which is very badly. The main problem is the business/IT distinction: typically, you'll get businesspeople writing specs; these get thrown over the wall to IT, who tries to translate them and deliver, and then throws it back over the wall to business, who will do some sort of acceptance testing, find they didn't get what they want, have a bit of a moan, and the whole cycle goes round again.

We see all sorts of problems with this, not least efficiency, and we didn't want to build our organization that way. We think of ourselves as a tech company with a banking license, not a bank that needs to try to do technology.

Some of the smarter incumbent banks have tried to fix this, but not very well. They see an Agile transformation as simply an IT initiative, which is merely tolerated by the business. So you might reorganize teams so they aren't strictly specialized—instead of layers like a Unix team and a firewall team, you might have product- or feature-centric teams—but ultimately they're still not with the core business. Communication with the business still has to be mediated by people who used to be called business analysts, who now might be called product owners. This still has many of the same problems as before.

Cloud native represents a genuine paradigm shift in modern software development and delivery. Previously most companies understood that, in order to remake themselves as a truly Agile organization, they would need to alter a lot of the ways they do go about developing and delivering software, from building processes all the way down to where people sit and the way they talk to each other. Unfortunately, most don't extend this same understanding to moving from Agile to cloud native practices.

This particular scenario can happen any time in any organization, but most often arises when a company that has adopted Agile practices fails to recognize that moving to cloud native a second true paradigm shift. Instead, they believe cloud native to be "just a new way to do Agile"—seeing it as a technical, not pan-organizational, change. (See "Treating Cloud Native as Simply an Extension of Agile" on page 399.)

Instead of being treated as a major and serious change in its own right, the cloud native transformation is treated as just a bunch of tech-related tasks that get added to the existing development backlog. As we saw in WealthGrid's first failed attempt to deliver a new cloud native system, it simply doesn't work. And now Starling Bank confirms the same phenomenon, which they successfully avoided by observing what *didn't* work when traditional banks tried to go cloud native.

So we went a completely different way.

We structured Starling so that our delivery teams, the people actually delivering new features and parts of the bank, were largely engineering and engineering-led but also contained members from what you'd normally regard as "the business" end of the company. So our cross-functional teams were truly cross functional. We would have infrastructure expertise, Java expertise, iPhone expertise, Android expertise, possibly UX, UI, and product expertise as well, and then non-tech people as well, to keep us grounded in building for customer needs. At one point, for instance, one of our delivery teams had the CFO on it!

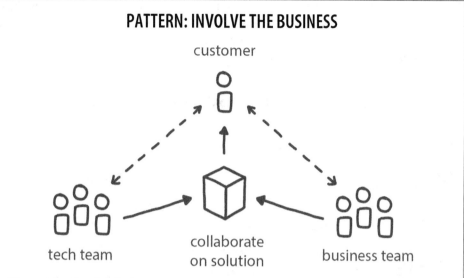

PATTERN: INVOLVE THE BUSINESS

customer

tech team

collaborate on solution

business team

Figure 14-7. Involve the Business

The business teams and the tech teams need to collaborate to create an effective customer-feedback loop that drives product improvement.

Not only are those mixed teams working together on the same goals, many things that they are doing come directly from those people in the business. If someone in payment operations is having difficulty administering some direct debits or there's been a problem with a direct debit run the night before, there's no one at any sort of high level making a decision whether that needs fixing. It gets fixed because the engineer's sitting right next to the person who's actually seeing the problem and just takes care of it. Ultimately, of course, the big priorities are set by the executive committee. But there's quite a lot of latitude for the engineers in the delivery teams to set their own priorities and to manage their own backlogs.

Thus the distance between business and IT is dissolved to a very high degree. As far as possible, we try to have teams that focus on products, not projects—nothing that will be important one year and not the next. That way we don't end up with all sorts of sins bequeathed unto the next generation. And this naturally means that teams are doing a lot of stuff, because not only are they delivering new things, but they're also responsible for running all the old things.

You Build It, You Run It

Which leads to our next guiding principle: You build it, you run it, the true meaning of DevOps, but even more than that. Being an engineer at Starling isn't easy: you conceive and you design it, you build it, you run it, you support it, you fix it, you enhance it, you work out how it's being used, how it's being abused, how to sunset it, how it's going to be reported on, how the auditors are going to approach it—every aspect of it, because you are truly accountable and an owner of the system that you're working on.

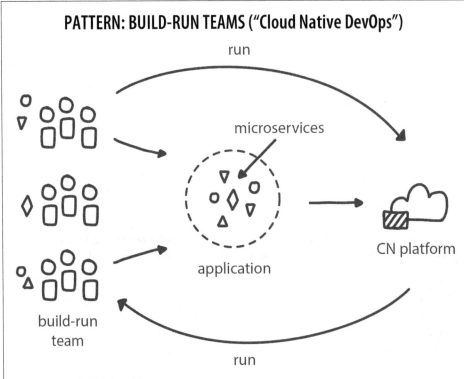

Figure 14-8. Build-Run Teams

Dev teams have full authority over the services they build, not only creating but also deploying and supporting them.

The real point here is accountability: our engineers are on the front line of incident response. In traditional incumbent banks, you normally have no view of what's happening in production. You might deliver something and maybe two months later it will go into production, but you've got no idea whether it's working—you never see any of the logs. In the pre-cloud-native approach, where you just send it off to the QA department, you have very little incentive to take it seriously to the degree you're going to deliver quality, supportable code. Whereas in the cloud-native way, you're the one watching the metrics, you're watching the logs, you're going to make very sure it's supportable—that you're not going to be woken up at 4 a.m. by something crazy going on. So the level of accountability we require from our engineers is, I think, a key part of how we deliver so well at speed.

Continuous Delivery

I think CD is probably the most important of the principles that we built Starling Bank around, but it might be the least important to talk about, because I think it's comparatively well-understood. But it's worth pointing out that we release pretty fast. Not as fast as Amazon, but nonetheless, we release and deploy our entire backend between one and five times every day. Every day we'll also make at least that many infrastructure changes as well, so AWS CloudFormation-type changes. The mobile apps we release every one to two weeks.

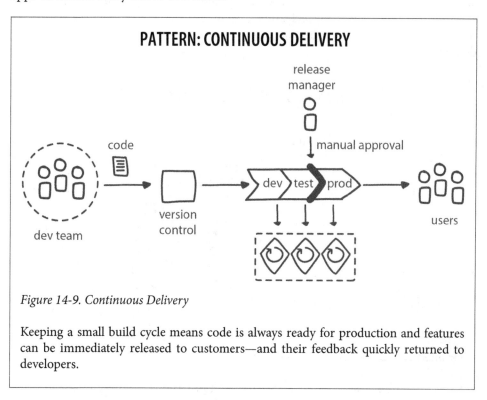

PATTERN: CONTINUOUS DELIVERY

Figure 14-9. Continuous Delivery

Keeping a small build cycle means code is always ready for production and features can be immediately released to customers—and their feedback quickly returned to developers.

More important than the actual rates, though, is this point: if a single day passes without a release, we're already worried. This is a big red flag for us, for a lot of reasons. A day without a release is a day that we haven't practiced one of the most critical functions in our business. Therefore it's a day that we're less sure that we can do it. It's an extra day accumulating risk for the next release. All of our software processes are built around minimizing risk of release by keeping those releases small, minimizing risk of changes themselves by keeping changes small and incremental. If we can't do a release, we're building up more and more changes that are going to result in a riskier release, and we hate that.

A day without a release is also a lost opportunity. We frequently use releases to get extra diagnostics or things into production to gain insight into what's happening in areas that we don't understand. It's one day potentially more vulnerable to out-of-date dependencies, because every time we do a build we use the latest versions of our Docker image dependencies and all that sort of stuff.

Finally, it's a clear red flag that something somewhere is broken, because otherwise why aren't we releasing? It suggests that we've got a paralyzed process somewhere and that we have a degraded incident-response capability. One of the great things about all this automation is that we can get to 4 a.m. and we see a bug and we don't have to do a rollback. We can actually wake up a couple more developers, do a fix, and roll it out, and go through all our automated QA and be confident by 5 a.m. that what we're doing is right.

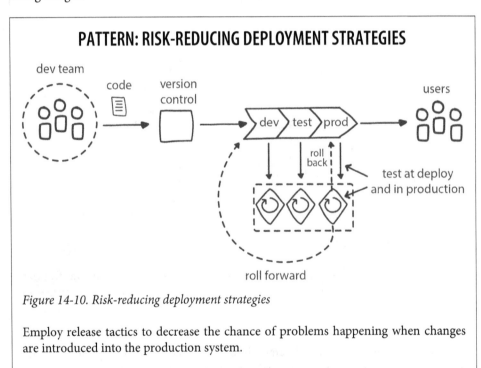

Figure 14-10. Risk-reducing deployment strategies

Employ release tactics to decrease the chance of problems happening when changes are introduced into the production system.

One interesting thing we do at Starling is the take-ownership ceremony we do in the engineering Slack channel when changes are going out. According to continuous delivery, this should be theoretically pointless, right? If all your tests have gone green and you've got signoffs, then you should be good to go, right? There shouldn't be anything else. But we make this ceremony out of it anyway, because this is really about ownership. A way of publicly saying, "OK, we've gone through all this automation now, guys, and everything sounds good, but who's really responsible for this? It's me and it's you, and it's you. Are we all good?" And everyone involved saying, "Yes, we're good." And then the button gets pressed and, just for fun, the actual release is announced by animated gif on Slack. It can be anything on the theme of "rolling" and some are quite creative—parrots on roller skates, famous cartoon characters. You can sometimes tell just by a quick look at the channel who's doing a release because people have their favorite images dancing around.

PATTERN: AUTOMATED TESTING

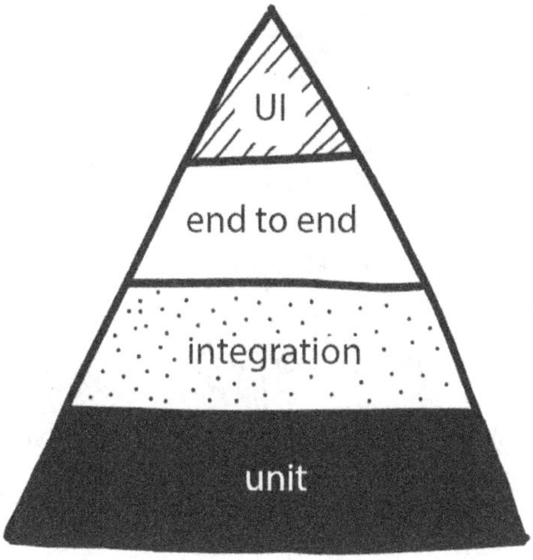

Figure 14-11. Automated Testing

Shift responsibility for testing from humans (manual) to an automated testing framework so developers can deliver faster and have more time to focus on improving features to meet customer needs.

Whimsy aside, what is really important about this ceremony is commitment. In an incumbent bank you would have no idea when your code is finally going out the door, so what sense of ownership can you possibly have? None. With this, your code goes into production and on the way home from work you're going through a turnstile station in the Tube, seeing someone use their Starling card, and knowing that your code has just gone into that—it's very motivational.

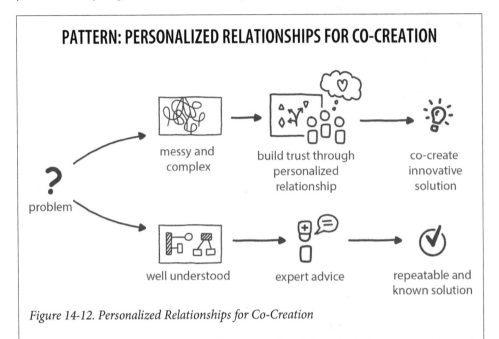

PATTERN: PERSONALIZED RELATIONSHIPS FOR CO-CREATION

Figure 14-12. Personalized Relationships for Co-Creation

Solutions to complex problems are best created collaboratively by teams with high levels of interpersonal connection.

Cloud Everything

When I say Starling is a cloud bank, I mean it. All our processing is in the cloud, all our balances, accounts, services, APIs, everything. Initially this was purely AWS, but we are becoming increasingly cloud-neutral as we mature to address some of the regulatory and commercial challenges we face. By building portably and making use of open source technologies, it's possible to remain largely vendor neutral, and even in advance of running redundantly across more than one cloud provider, we maintain AWS exit plans.

Only when we are absolutely forced to host a physical piece of hardware (like a Hardware Security Module for instance) do we use space in traditional data centers.

As well as our core services, a lot of our tooling consists of cloud services. We have over 100 SaaS [Software-as-a-Service] services in use, outsourcing as much non-core business functionality as we can: many of our customer support capabilities and items like SMS delivery rely on cloud integrations to some degree. This is great for all sorts of reasons. Not having to run them is really important. (Side note: this does complicate some of our disaster-recovery planning, because if we've lost AWS, it is likely we've lost half of the tooling that we use to actually deliver our software. Imagine a world where *every* service dependent on AWS has instantaneously and irrevocably disappeared, and suppose that's a world in which you're trying to rebuild a bank. Yep—that's a disaster. We have to consider it.)

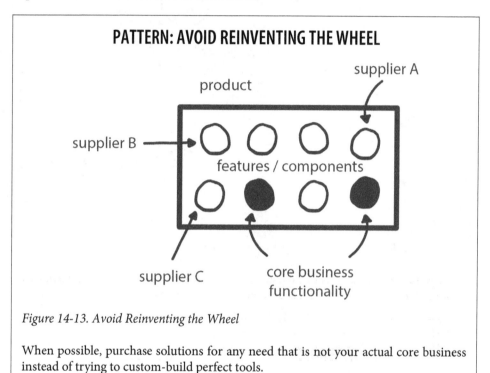

Figure 14-13. Avoid Reinventing the Wheel

When possible, purchase solutions for any need that is not your actual core business instead of trying to custom-build perfect tools.

Most of these cloud benefits are pretty well-known, but one benefit that I don't think gets enough appreciation from companies considering a cloud migration is the ability to experiment. If you're in AWS and you want to try something out with a hundred servers, then you try it out for an hour, and if it's rubbish, you stop. Who cares? No cost. You can't do that sort of thing with on-prem infrastructure!

PATTERN: REDUCE THE COST OF EXPERIMENTATION

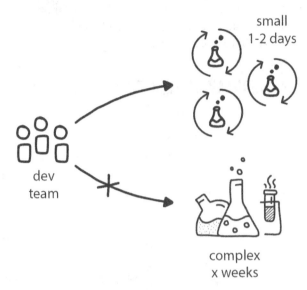

Figure 14-14. Reduce the Cost of Experimentation

When someone has an idea to validate, the costs (both financial and organizational) of doing experiments around it needs to be as low as possible.

PATTERN: EXPLORATORY EXPERIMENTS

complex problem   experimentation   clear solution

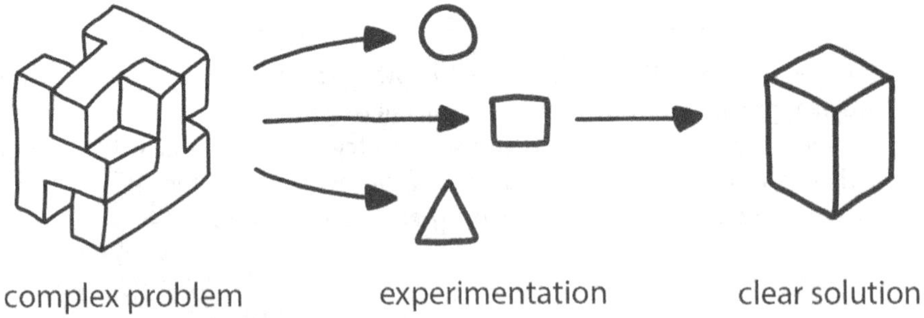

Figure 14-15. Exploratory Experiments

When dealing with a complex problem with no obvious available solution, run a series of small experiments to evaluate the possible alternatives and learn by doing.

Resilient Architecture

This last principle does get a bit techie but summarizes what was important to us as we built for resilience: self-contained systems [SCS]. This is a distributed system architecture approach, or manifesto, I guess, which is broadly the same as microservices. In fact SCS was a bigger influence on our architecture than the microservices movement. The SCS approach shares a lot of concepts with microservices: isolated, independently deployable units, the lack of centralized infrastructure—there is no getting away from distributed systems in cloud native!—and the ability to make technology choices. But there is less of an emphasis on size (the "micro" bit) leaving more of the emphasis on the independence.

PATTERN: DISTRIBUTED SYSTEM

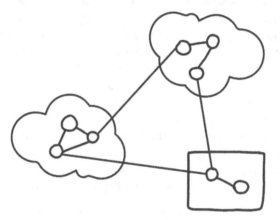

Figure 14-16. Distributed Systems

When software is built as a series of fully independent, loosely coupled services, the resulting system is, by design, very fast, resilient, and highly scalable.

SCS inspired our approach to our services, which, really, I should call miniservices rather than microservices, because they're not that small. We've got about 30. There are organizations out there, even small ones, running thousands of microservices That's a very different architecture. I often think that, as well as our motivations, they've started out from a point of view that regards many of the in-language facilities for segregation and abstraction as somehow bankrupt or passé. Well, we don't accept that. We don't write that way. Our SCS services are larger and fewer in number than microservices. But they are each strongly autonomous, independently deployable, they each have their own database, they don't share any infrastructure. They don't even have a Kubernetes cluster or a data layer in common.

What SCS means is splitting an application into its required functionalities and making each one of these a standalone system. The overall app becomes essentially a collaboration of many smaller self-contained software systems, all delivered independently via the cloud. Each SCS is an autonomous web application that can fulfill its primary use cases on its own, without having to rely on other systems being available. The SCS approach fits with our "Conwayization" trajectory quite well. The fewer, larger components make things simpler, and in many cases we can avail ourselves of the facilities offered by the language or the database where they might not be available with a more fine-grained microservices architecture, while hopefully avoiding the problem of a large monolith that eventually becomes unsustainable. But this is some fairly subtle cloud-native architecture philosophy that could be a book on its own, so let's talk about immutable infrastructure and chaos instead!

Immutable infrastructure to us means crash-safe architecture where we can kill any of our servers at any point and it doesn't matter. There is no state or configuration on any of our servers that cannot be automatically reproduced from scratch in a minute or two. We can blow away servers at will and other identical ones rise in their place. We have our own chaos demon that sits there and kills four or five servers a day in production just to make sure that we can. For us, killing a production server is considered a safe operation. Occasionally we will do more targeted tests as well to prove database failover and suchlike, and there are times you have to be creative to do this. We also use synthetic load in production when it makes sense. There was a time where we didn't have enough card traffic to really be confident that our services would scale up, so we were running a hundred thousand fake card authorizations in our infrastructure every day just to make sure that it was all there. If we had a sudden surge, we could dial back the fake load to allow space for real load.

We do zero-downtime releases and because we've got immutable infrastructure, we can do this mainly just by killing servers. So we update some settings somewhere, then we kill servers one by one, and then they come back at the newer versions and it's all very nice.

We designed our architecture to be resilient but at the end of the day we know it is resilient, because we are continually beating it up ourselves.

We have diverged from pure SCS architecture in some ways to suit our own business needs, and eventually we coined the name DITTO[1] for our homegrown approach to architecture. DITTO: do idempotent things to others. Basically, this is taking self-contained systems, which gives us our sort of microservices—our independent autonomously running, independently deployable services—and governing how they

---

1 In fact, credit for this must go to Adrian Cockcroft who was none too impressed with my previous acronym LOASCTDITTEO (Lots of Autonomous Services Continually Trying To Do Idempotent Things To Each Other). I'm still rather fond of the old version.

interact. It covers how we keep things operationally simple (no buses or external caches, just a "bag of services") while still ensuring loose coupling (async over HTTP via "202 Accepted," DNS for service discovery) and resilience (idempotence and pervasive retry processing).

Again this is just a principled selection of trade-offs: we accept some complexity of development, for instance, building some capability directly into our services rather than offloading it to specialized external components, in return for a system that has some nice operational characteristics, chief amongst them resilience and simplicity and portability of deployment.

And, Really, That's It

So no radical new secrets revealed here, just a lot of careful thinking about what Starling needed and how to architect this entirely on the cloud for optimal pace and resilience. Our original motivation for going cloud native was because we believed that it would help us move faster. We believed that by using Infrastructure-as-a-Service, DevOps, and continuous delivery, we would organically grow an innovation culture in our tech teams.

Where we ended up: CD and DevOps plus DITTO architecture gave us a super-resilient system, even in the face of bugs and human failure, both of which are inevitable.

All of which enables us to move fast enough to deliver plenty of UK banking firsts: first to deliver in-app provisioning of both Google Pay and Apple Pay. First current account available to the UK public entirely on the cloud. And so on.

Architecture brought us here. Chaos keeps us honest.

CHAPTER 15

Welcome to the Jungle: Adidas Cloud Native Transformation Case Study

By Daniel Eichten

Adidas is the largest sportswear manufacturer in Europe and the second largest in the world. With an ambitious plan to not just retain its significant share of a fast-paced, highly competitive market but continue growing it even further, the company turned to cloud-native technology to help hone its competitive edge.

Daniel Eichten, senior director for platform engineering at Adidas, helped lead the company's successful journey through what he calls "the IT jungle" and onto the cloud.

Welcome to the Jungle

We knew we needed a platform that would help us gain speed. For us, this really means speed of development of our products, but also speed of delivering our solutions for internal IT. So the goal was speed all over the place, wherever it makes sense.

The metaphor I use to explain IT at Adidas is to think of it as a jungle. Nowadays IT departments are not only the people who are building a lot of things but also the guides who help you through the IT jungle. We see ourselves more as partners for the business side to help orient them in the jungle and make sure they don't get lost. Being in a real jungle can be exciting but also quite dangerous, and it's the same with an IT jungle. Very exciting when you do all of the crazy stuff with AR [augmented reality], VR [virtual reality], blockchain, containers, and so on—or, for my team, cloud native and serverless—but it can also sometimes be very, very dangerous for a company if you take the wrong assumptions or simply turn the wrong direction.

Of course, you have animals living in the jungle, and one of the animals in the Adidas IT jungle is the elephant, our traditional core IT systems. This is the stuff that we develop ourselves, the enterprise Java applications, so a couple of hundred thousand lines or even sometimes a couple million lines of code. We call them elephants because they are quite heavy and they take a lot of time to develop. So if you want to create a new elephant, usually it's a period of two years until this elephant comes to life. It's a long project. Controlling these elephants and keeping them alive also requires a special handler, trained in taking proper care of them.

There are good things about elephants: they can get a lot of work done, and they can move really big things. They are very robust creatures. But they are cumbersome, very slow, and they are hard to train to do new things.

At the other end of the animal kingdom, then, you have the tiniest of creatures, the ants. These are the microservices, which can also do a lot of things and get a great deal of work done because there are so very many of them, all very busy at the same time. These tiny creatures are not very smart one by one, but all together they can accomplish amazing tasks. They can actually move the same load an elephant can, but by working in a completely different manner: they cut it into a million tiny pieces, and each ant takes one piece. The challenge is how to control them and direct them. In nature ants communicate via pheromones; IT ants, microservices, are controlled by systems that give all the little creatures direction and coordinate them.

In between you have carnivores, your crocodiles and jaguars. At Adidas crocodiles are our SAP systems, our enterprise resource planning and data processing software. They look the same as 200 million years ago. And then the newest visitor to the IT jungle is the jaguar, or Salesforce, our software as a service customer-relationship platform. These are both dangerous creatures because you don't see them much; they mostly stay out of sight—but they are eating all of your budget. Both are quite expensive, for the licenses and usage.

Our goal then was to tame the IT jungle. To build a cloud native platform that could be as reliable as an elephant, as fast and as efficient as a colony of ants, and to also take on the work of the crocodile and jaguar.

A Playground for Kubernetes

That's when our Day Zero came, when we said, "OK, we have to do things differently. What should this new world look like, what do we need it to contain?" We sat together and collected some requirements: it should work on-premise. It has to be open source. We don't want to have any vendor lock-in. It should be operable, it should be observable, it should be elastic, it should be resilient, it should be agile, and so on. And when we looked at the last five points, this is exactly what the Cloud Native Foundation came up with as their definition for cloud native. Everything embedded into CNCF also checked against these five items. So for us it was pretty clear that everything we were looking for could be found in cloud native.

And we looked a little bit around and then we found something like Figure 15-1, which is not the map of some city transportation system, but the structure of the API for Kubernetes.

What it really looked like, to us, was the map out of the IT jungle: something that made containers and microservices understandable and controllable, that could harness all those ants to move the big things we needed. But what we also saw was complexity. In Kubernetes we found something that made impossible things possible but easy things rather complicated. Knowing that there were a lot of unknowns, we understood that this was nothing we could run on our own. We needed a guide, a partner who could really help us to get that pretty map up and running all of the different clouds, in our data center and so on. We found that partner in Giant Swarm. They were the only company willing to not just give us the product, but take the operations, give us consulting, and do that in all of the environments we needed to cover. No one else was, at least in 2016, really willing to go that far. All of the other companies were trying to sell their products, but they did not have the guide service we needed. They would do their demos, and then I would say, "OK, it's all nice, I can install it on AWS and on-prem, but whom do I call if something breaks?" And then they really had to admit, "Yeah, sorry, we don't do that kind of support."

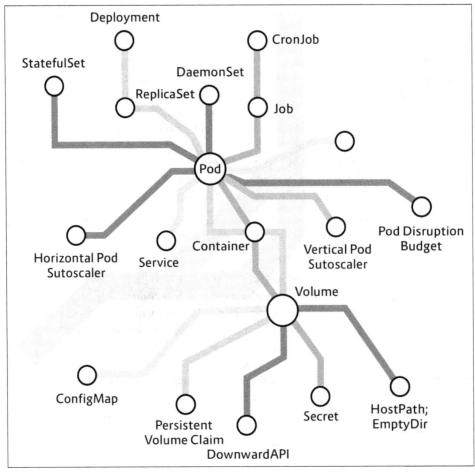

Figure 15-1. Map of the Kubernetes API (image courtesy of Adidas)

What Giant Swarm did for us was to provide a consistent toolset around Kubernetes, essentially a Kubernetes distribution, and help us to implement it successfully. Our Day 1 still didn't come for a while, even after we found Giant Swarm, because enterprise processes always take a little bit longer than expected. It was not until 2017 that we were able to begin building.

Giant Swarm started us off with a Kubernetes playground cluster that they provided in their environment. This is a very good way to begin: learning by doing, exploring. You install, you de-install, you run stuff and see what happens. After some time we had created multiple namespaces. *[Note: A Kubernetes namespace provides the scope for container pods, services, and deployments in a given cluster.]* So I forcibly deleted all namespaces and our cluster made "boom" and exploded, and nothing was working anymore. Pure panic in the entire team! But it was a good learning experience.

More importantly, it was also a clear indicator that the tools that we had always used before for CI/CD, for building stuff, for compiling stuff, for testing stuff, even for running and monitoring stuff—these were not the tools that would help us in the future.

Because we were shifting really from storing, MSIs and JARs and NPMs, to storing containers, we needed a new toolset around CI/CD, around our code repositories. We needed new monitoring (Microsoft SCOM proposed by the infrastructure department were definitely not working like a charm in a container environment). And we also had to rethink security, obviously. But where to get started? How to know the right tools to pick?

We got in touch with the Cloud Native Computing Foundation, which at that point in time, 2016, was very helpful because you could ask, "Hey, what do you have in the area of XYZ?" and the answer was very simple. The original landscape map had only a few things. For each area you picked that tool from the shelf, you used it, and it was fine. The landscape started with Kubernetes. Then Prometheus for monitoring, which we also use, and they added Envoy as a proxy, which we use implicitly through Istio but not explicitly.

Fast travel to 2019, though, and the CNCF landscape map now has over 1,000 tools and options. So currently the ecosystem is kind of a mess, and a problem for anyone trying to build a proper platform toolset now. In some cases it's easy: if you just look at container runtimes you have a couple of options, which are official CNCF-incubated or even graduated projects. For other use cases, though, it's really, really, really hard to pick. So many options now, and how to know which ones will endure?

Fortunately, we did not have so many choices at the time, and the ones available worked out well for us. So we got started running with Kubernetes and Prometheus, producing and operating a full environment until we felt confident we were ready to move on to Day 2 and put something into actual live production on our new cloud-native platform. But what would we try first?

Day 2

It had to be something meaningful. No one is giving us applause or any great feedback or additional money for further projects if we play it safe now and, say, move some of our HR department's request forms from an external SaaS service to an internal cluster. That would be useful but not a big change for the company. A really big change that we did need was the thing that was becoming our biggest retail door: our e-commerce store. That was a big reach, risky to get wrong. But we decided only with great risk do you get great rewards—and more project funding, right?

PATTERN: GRADUALLY RAISING THE STAKES

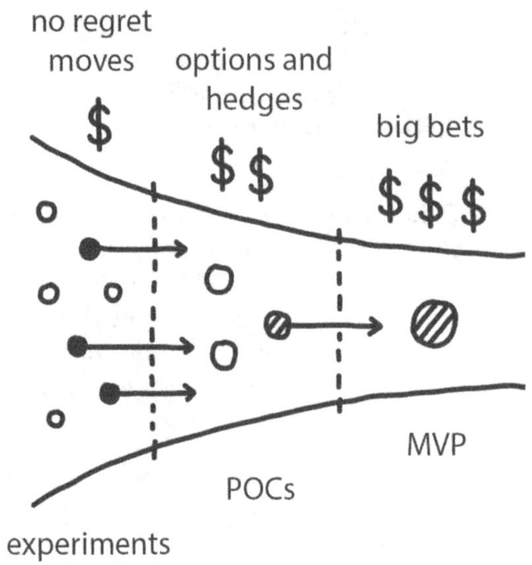

Figure 15-2. Gradually Raising the Stakes

In an uncertain environment, slowly increase investment into learning and information-gathering; eventually you uncover enough information to reduce risk and make better-informed decisions.

See also the related next-step patterns No Regret Moves, Options & Hedges, and Big Bet.

To keep the risk contained somewhat we started with migrating just our Finland e-commerce platform; there's not too much volume on that one. When we did the first small tests we started easy, like opening a faucet very slowly. We opened up the valves a little bit and everything was working like a charm, and the website was fast and responding great, and it was pretty cool. So then we increased the throughput a little bit more, expecting that to also go very smoothly, but it turned into the cluster being on fire. Panic all over again! But after breathing into some paper bags to relax, we set out to figure out what went wrong. Again, the cluster was fine, but there was a cluster performance load-testing tool that we were still learning. It turns out there is a setting applicable to single nodes but that we thought was applicable all over the cluster, so when we spun it up we accidentally tested 100 times the amount of throughput we had intended.

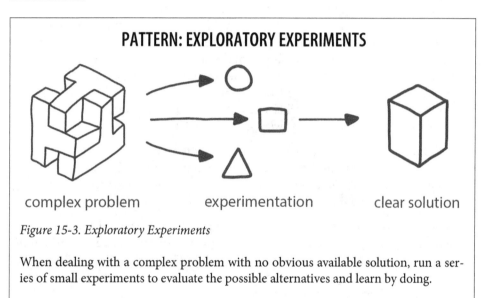

PATTERN: EXPLORATORY EXPERIMENTS

complex problem   experimentation   clear solution

Figure 15-3. Exploratory Experiments

When dealing with a complex problem with no obvious available solution, run a series of small experiments to evaluate the possible alternatives and learn by doing.

We were a bit guilty of trying to solve imaginary scaling issues, which taught us another very important lesson: when you pick a new tool set, you can't expect to immediately be the master of it. And you have to be open-minded to working differently than you always did before. Because of my experience before cloud native, when the cluster was on fire I thought it had to be a cluster issue, something wrong with the cluster itself. It took some time to realize the cluster was fine—we were actually testing the wrong thing.

There are some very technical details here, beyond the scope of the patterns we've presented. They're included to bring a deeper insight into this use case. The story itself is what's important here, and even non-technical readers can understand what happened even if the more technical terms are unfamiliar.

At this point, we were still Day 2, but I would say around lunchtime. It was October 2017, approaching the period where holiday sales start and we have e-commerce traffic spikes for Black Friday, Cyber Monday, and so on. By now we already migrated most of the countries to the cloud data center in preparation, and we had an unexpected opportunity to test on a global scale. Adidas introduced a special edition shoe designed by Pharrell Williams that suddenly went through the roof. People were going crazy, hammering the servers and the systems, trying to grab a pair of these shoes. The cluster was on fire and went down. We investigated and found the cluster running the e-com app was actually OK—instead, the application itself was not responding anymore. It turns out our e-com application was fighting with our ingress controller for resources, and apparently the application won. So whenever the ingress controller was forwarding a request to the application, the application was eating so much CPU that the ingress controller was not even able to respond anymore to handshake, and this is when Kubernetes went in and killed it.

What did we do wrong? Well, we completely forgot that we had to put some reservations there for core components. So, again the iterative approach—failure, and what do you learn from it? We actually were happy it had happened with just this one item, because we got to learn that lesson before Black Friday.

So we learned from it and we prepared for the next big sale event. We scaled everything up, everyone was dialed into a war room, a virtual one, we sat ready and waiting … and then none of the countries showed up. What? No traffic?! This time it was because of some caching feature implemented on our CDN [content delivery network] level, which was not letting any traffic through to the cluster.

This brings us to the practice of outage-driven infrastructure. Because, to be honest, similar situations happened a few more times, and we aren't the only ones. Other platform engineers I talk to say it is the same for them, to the point where there is a nice GitHub repository from Zalando, another European e-commerce retail site, sharing their and other production screw-up stories and all the different ways they have killed their clusters. In the meantime this turned into a whole website, *https://k8s.af/*. Our count isn't quite there yet. But it was good to be able to show that repo to management to show that this learning curve is normal, and it is steep, and we aren't the only ones who have to go through it.

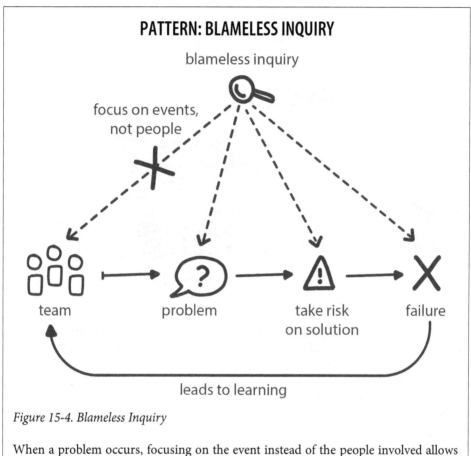

PATTERN: BLAMELESS INQUIRY

blameless inquiry

focus on events, not people

team   problem   take risk on solution   failure

leads to learning

Figure 15-4. Blameless Inquiry

When a problem occurs, focusing on the event instead of the people involved allows them to learn from mistakes without fear of punishment.

To help guide our learning curve, we use a product pyramid to help guide decision making on how we're developing our e-commerce application for resilience, speed, and every other metric, including not blowing up. Figure 15-5 shows the one the Adidas cloud platform team uses.

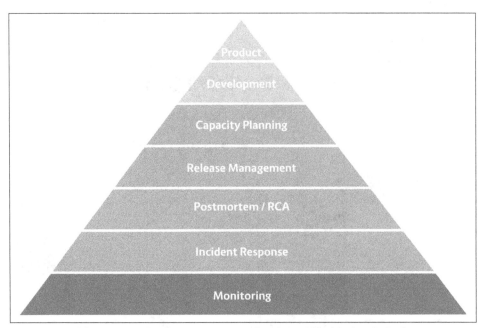

Figure 15-5. The product development pyramid tool used by the cloud platform team at Adidas

This pyramid helps us prioritize and think through: how do we do release management? How do we do incident management? After we had these kind of events, though, we realized there were gaps in our pyramid. These gaps included doing proper postmortems, which was only partially missing—we did it for the big ones, and we learned from it, so that's great. But there were plenty of smaller events where we didn't do postmortems, and then sometimes running multiple times into the same problem.

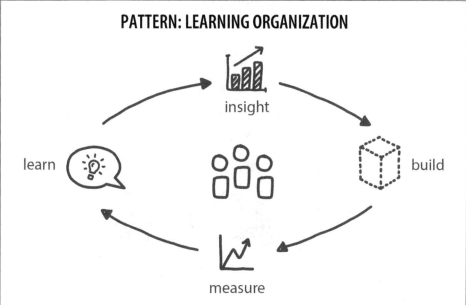

Figure 15-6. *Learning Organization*

An organization skilled at acquiring information, creating insight, and transferring knowledge can tolerate risk with confidence and solve difficult problems through experimentation and innovation.

Another gap we needed to address in our Day 2 platform version was proper capacity planning. And there I don't mean infrastructure so much as how we can develop to make the best use of the resources we already have. Another very important missing piece—so important that it's on the bottom holding up everything else—is monitoring, or the better word is observability. This is something that we worked on heavily all over the place and constantly; now, for us, everything begins with observability.

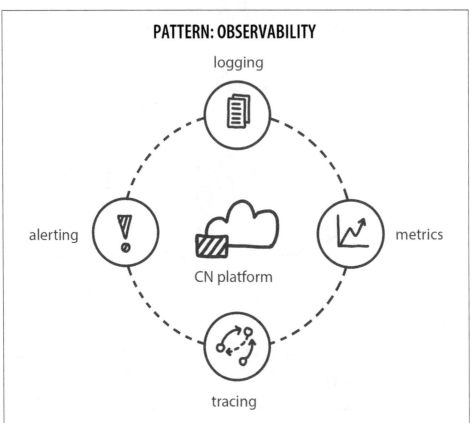

PATTERN: OBSERVABILITY

Figure 15-7. Observability

Cloud native distributed systems require constant insight into the behavior of all running services in order to understand the system's behavior and to predict potential problems or incidents.

Speaking of beginning. If there is one thing I wish I had known when we started, it would be that, with cloud native, sometimes decisions don't stay decided for very long. And that this is actually OK. This is now reflected in our cloud strategy, to constantly revise what we do.

PATTERN: DYNAMIC STRATEGY

intended strategy → deliberate strategy → realized strategy

non-realized strategies

emergent strategies

Figure 15-8. Dynamic Strategy

Today's tech-driven marketplace is a constantly shifting environment, no matter what business you are in—so your game plan needs to shift right along with it.

There was another decision which we made early on, when we didn't know enough to be making such big commitments, that slowed us down quite a bit. This was the assumption that, in order to be as agnostic as we can possibly be, everything had to work and feel on-prem exactly as it is in the cloud. This assumption was already wrong as soon as we made it because the engineers working on applications that are running on-prem are so different in their mindset and in the solutions they develop. They don't have to think about the crazy scaling patterns like you have sometimes in the cloud.

So now we have to go back and revise the results of this early decision. I think we could have saved a lot of time and a lot of manual work if we had not reinvented the wheel to make sure our cloud also worked on-prem. If we just would have said from Minute One, "OK, it's one cloud vendor, and we use the highest-level services we can find on them. And only if there's a good reason do we go down and build it ourselves." I think that's the one thing I would say which would have sped up the process quite heavily.

PATTERN: EXIT STRATEGY OVER VENDOR LOCK-IN

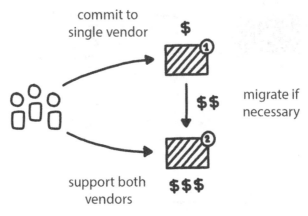

Figure 15-9. Exit Strategy Over Vendor Lock-In

Public cloud vendors can handle all aspects of building and operating a cloud native platform, and their tools are often excellent—but when committing to a vendor/technology/platform, it's important to identify an alternate solution and any costs associated with switching over.

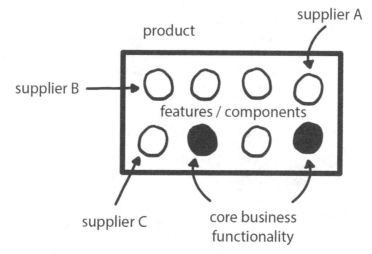

Figure 15-10. *Avoid Reinventing the Wheel*

When possible, purchase solutions for any need that is not your actual core business instead of trying to custom-build perfect tools.

Ultimately, building so much custom to make sure everything worked on-premises as well as in the cloud is nothing I regret, even though it slowed us down. It's always good to know how things work and the insights gained are valuable. Like now I can buy a managed Kubernetes and I still would know how things would work underneath. That's always a good thing, right?

Day 2 Afternoon in Cloud City

And that leads us up to now, which we can say is afternoon on Day 2 in the city that we have grown.

From one cluster and a single e-commerce application, we have now grown to five global locations with, in some cases, more than one production cluster each. We are in China, we are on-premise, we are in Singapore, we have clusters in Ireland, we have clusters in Oregon. And when I say clusters, that's always Kubernetes. In each location we have Kafka clusters next to it [*Author's note: Apache Kafka is a high-throughput distributed messaging system used to facilitate scalable data collection.*] and all the infrastructure necessary to also get all the monitoring and observability tools, plus also our CI/CD processes. So, each of these production clusters goes from core to content.

This story tells our engineering technology journey. What I did not realize when we started was how it would also become an engineering team journey. Four years ago the engineering team was a handful of people, heads down, trying to work the best we can, unfortunately not talking much to each other because we were really spread across the organization—there was no one uniformed engineering department. Turn the clock forward to now, when our most recent companywide engineering day was 600 people, not only engineers but also service managers, ops people, architects, and even some business product owners.

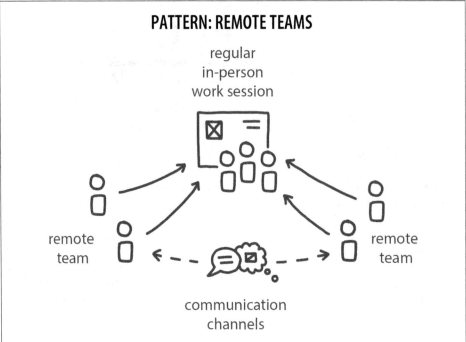

PATTERN: REMOTE TEAMS

Figure 15-11. Remote Teams

If teams must be distributed, whether across an office building, a city, or a continent, build in regular in-person retreats/work sessions as well as robust channels for close and freely flowing communication.

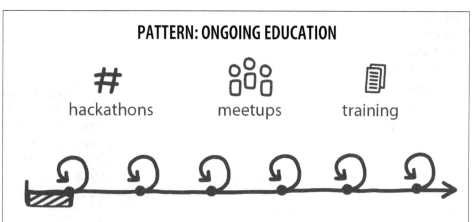

PATTERN: ONGOING EDUCATION

hackathons　　　meetups　　　training

bootcamp

Figure 15-12. Ongoing Education

Prioritize ways to help teams continually develop their cloud native knowledge and skills.

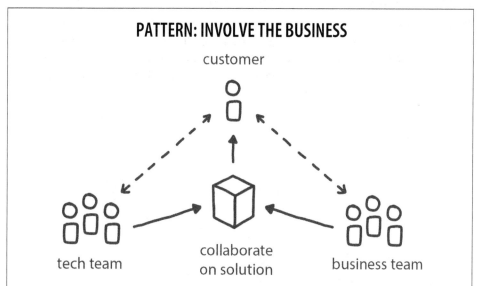

PATTERN: INVOLVE THE BUSINESS

customer

tech team

collaborate
on solution

business team

Figure 15-13. Involve the Business

A company's business teams and the tech teams need to collaborate to create an effective customer-feedback loop that drives product improvement.

Numbers wise, now we have 300-plus internal engineers. We're still working heavily with extra partners, too, so that gives us up to 2000+ Bitbucket accounts. (One of these partners is Container Solutions, who we originally brought in to create ongoing cloud native education programs, trainings, hackathons, etc.)

Our CI/CD system does roughly 100,000 builds per month. Every week we gather 25 terabytes of metrics on our central logging infrastructure. The data lake is over 750 terabytes as of today. Beyond 10 million Kafka messages and it's constantly growing because we now include more and more systems. We have nearly 4,000 Kubernetes pods across all of our clusters and the code base in Bitbucket recently crossed the border of 100 million lines of code. We also make heavy use of all the tools available on the AWS platform, 28 of those at last count, including Amazon E2, ECS, CloudWatch, Elasticsearch, and Amazon API Gateway.

These numbers are always changing, too, and what that says is this is not simply a new technology that you get installed and then it's done. In the same way you can't say, "We are training now everyone on Agile, and therefore we are an Agile organization!" It simply doesn't work that way; there's no "set it and forget it." All of these things have to be in place and working in tandem. The processes have to go hand in hand with the technology, and both must be hand in hand with the culture: from the top down the management style and the organization itself has to change.

This is truly the most important lesson of all, the number one thing to know about succeeding with cloud native: If you don't have all three of these things evolving together, your tech, your processes, and your people, well. I don't want to say your transformation is headed for certain failure, but you will have to hit some hard boundaries and some hard rocks before you really can get through.

Epilogue

We have reached a point that would usually count as the finish line for a story: the happy ending.

It is time to go back for a final visit with WealthGrid, where they have been working through exactly the transformation design that we explored in Chapter 11 and Chapter 12. The third time was the charm in terms of migration attempts: By applying the correct patterns in the proper order at the right times, the company was able to complete the first phase of the full transformation process. A transformation is not truly done until any remaining monoliths are re-architectured, a gradual process that will probably take another year or two to accomplish. The truly major milestone that WealthGrid has achieved, however, is that they've gained the ability, understanding, and awareness to do this as a natural course of business. The company is confident that they can continue to evolve; meanwhile, they can clearly see the results, and rewards, of all the progress they've made.

WealthGrid's senior executives took a great deal more care to be involved with creating strategy for this third attempt, but to their credit they also recognized when it was time to get out of the way and let the middle managers and engineers take over executing the transition details. Jenny, the program manager who had catalyzed the company to go cloud native in the first place, was named Transformation Champion in recognition of her initiative and the knowledge she and her team had gained through their first two attempts. Both these efforts failed, and in very different ways, but were valuable learning experiences nonetheless.

Jenny led the Core Team and helped choose its members. They were able to work off to one side in creative mode to find a transformation path that *would* work for WealthGrid, while the rest of the company's engineers focused on proficiently delivering features on the existing platform to keep customer value high in the meantime. Within three months, the Core Team was able to uncover the best approach for a new cloud native system through Exploratory Experiments and PoCs. At that point, a Platform Team was formed by splitting off several Core Team members; they were joined by a few more engineers who had shown particular ability during the organization's failed "Let's let everyone build a platform and see what happens!" over-investment in creativity during the first part of attempt number 2.

The Platform Team delivered a solid production-ready cloud native platform in under six months. Meanwhile, Jenny and the remaining Core Team members focused on developing some simple microservices applications both to test the new platform and create processes around developing on it. The Core Team was also preparing to onboard the remaining teams. They created excellent Dev Starter Pack materials, trainings, and Demo Apps while evangelizing the soon-to-come system across the organization, building excitement and buy-in. When the platform was ready, the development teams were incrementally onboarded onto the new system. Very quickly, WealthGrid was delivering new features and functionality for its products working entirely on the new cloud native platform (and using a newly evolved cloud-optimized delivery approach).

The entire company has gradually evolved to be working in the cloud native way: Build-Run Teams doing CI/CD and other cloud native methods to rapidly develop new features and deliver quick, incremental improvements—which the business teams are delighted to be included in planning. CEO Steve and the executive teams have embraced Dynamic Strategy. Throughout the entire organization there is a focus on delivery, but now there is also continued and meaningful investment in ongoing innovation. Even some pure research into emerging new technologies—Jenny has been named Designated Strategist and is now directing research, as well as shepherding innovation through all areas of the company. Everything is working well, and everyone is feeling confident. Once any remaining "Lift and Shift at the End" monoliths have been re-architected it will be time to shut down the old data centers for good. WealthGrid is well on its way to being a fully cloud native company.

What's Next?

The next steps for WealthGrid are the same next steps for any company completing a cloud native transformation: keeping the balance between proficiency and creativity that current conditions dictate. The entire story of WealthGrid's transformation journey can be shown as this fluctuating balance, graphed in Figure E-1, according to the different stages and the different ways they tried to reach the cloud.

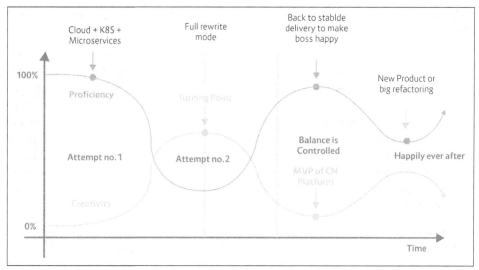

Figure E-1. The relationship between proficiency and creativity at different points along WealthGrid's transformation journey

Attempt number 1 is where WealthGrid does not treat the transformation as a full initiative and remains in primarily proficient mode while Jenny's small team tries to implement a new cloud native platform as a side project while also still responsible for their regular tasks. Proficiency is very high, and creativity almost zero.

This didn't work, so the company tried to swing the other way. There was Executive Commitment this time: a big budget allocated and most of the people moved to work on the initiative. Unfortunately, they were still using proficient management and Waterfall team structure—and still treating the transformation as a normal project that is supposed to have predictable results. Thus, the process and the culture did not change to match the new tech. Meanwhile there was so much investment in the new platform that the current platform—the one still in production and delivering the business value to the customers, not to mention earning money—was almost ignored. As a result, the numbers were out of whack again. They were working at perhaps 10 percent investment in delivery, while most of the rest of the company was experimenting all over the place. They were being creative, but in a very disorganized way that generated more problems than it solved.

Once WealthGrid finally stepped back, reassessed, and then came back for their third try, they had a much more balanced approach. By using a Dynamic Strategy, Gradually Raising the Stakes, and in general evolving their processes, management, and culture to be appropriately cloud native they were finally set up for success. A small portion of the engineers formed the Core Team and Platform Team to uncover and then build an MVP version of the new cloud native platform, so creativity swung back to an effective but reasonable level while the remaining team members kept building the functionality customers needed.

At the end, with the new platform in place and all teams onboarded, WealthGrid could rebalance again for optimal efficiency: 80/15/5. Most of the focus (80 percent) returns to delivery, using the Manage for Proficiency approach with the majority of teams to efficiently deliver core business value. However, some teams remain in innovation mode, where Manage for Creativity keeps them effective at innovation—incorporating new tools and methods to significantly improve existing products—while a small percentage does continual research. Research means checking out new technologies that may or may not pan out, but it's important to understand how they work. Some of these may be useful in a year or two when they become more stable and/or more relevant for the business.

This is how WealthGrid handled things, but it works the same way for everyone. This balance is under your control. You can play with it as needed. You can decide to invest in a big refactoring or to build a new product and pull people into that project for the duration, temporarily placing a significant portion of your team on more creative and innovative tasks. During that time these people need to be managed in a different way, with more open-ended autonomy to create new things. Eventually, however, the problem is solved or the change is achieved, and things rebalance once more toward an emphasis on stable and efficient delivery. Until the next time.

Jedi Powers Unlocked

Ultimately this book, all these patterns, were never intended to teach you how to do a cloud native transformation (though it is certainly a helpful byproduct). We wrote this book to help you become comfortable with transformation as a process, so you can move forth confidently as an adaptive, responsive, aware organization ready for any stranger that comes your way.

You have now unlocked your power to deal with uncertainty—*any* uncertainty. That is the essential Jedi mind trick necessary for surviving and thriving in these ever-changing times. In the early days of software development, and up until very recently, everything was very segregated and competition was basically limited by geography. Now everything is fast and global: you are no longer competing only with your neighbors. You are competing with the world. To put it in disruptive stranger-danger terms, in the past you might encounter one stranger in your town every five to ten years. Now, you meet ten on the street every day.

Fundamentally, then, cloud native is *not* about speed, scale, or margin (though these are all terrific side benefits!). Yes, you can now vary your company's products or services in a cloud native pipeline with the same ease and speed you might update your website using a content management system. The point is not the speed itself, though, but your ability to move at that speed. *Cloud native is about building an organization that can transform and adapt far faster by removing the technical risks associated with change.* With the tools we have outlined throughout this book, using these strategies and methods and patterns, you can handle any change that comes.

At its best, a cloud native approach is as much about de-risking as it is about accelerating change, allowing companies to become more responsive. It's extremely powerful, yes—but unfortunately "low risk" does not mean "low effort." Now that you know what you are doing, you still need to do the work. After reading this book you know how to structure your transformation, but you still have to go through a year or two of actually doing it. We can give you the knowledge and tools, but we can't save you the journey.

The transformation process isn't free, and it isn't easy. But what we can tell you is that it's imperative, in an existential threat sort of way, and absolutely worth it.

And the risk of undertaking it has never been lower.

Library of Patterns
(Thumbnail Reference Versions)

New cloud native patterns are emerging constantly. To continue sharing them and extending the cloud native pattern language we have established here, please visit www.CNpatterns.org.

This is where to find the latest pattern developments, but also an online community for discussing and creating new patterns. We are inviting people from across the industry, thought leaders and influencers but most importantly everyday engineers and managers—those out there working elbows-deep in cloud native code and architecture—to contribute and participate. Hope to see you there!

A/B TESTING

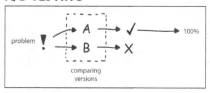

Comparing multiple versions of something (a feature, new functionality, UI, etc.) under real customer use conditions quickly gives useful data about which performs better.
See Chapter 9: Patterns for Development and Process for full version.

AGILE FOR NEW DEVELOPMENT

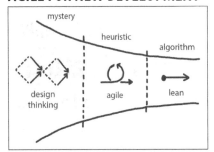

Balance proficiency and innovation by building a separate time for each into your development cycle.
See Chapter 8: Patterns for Organization and Culture for full version.

ARCHITECTURE DRAWING

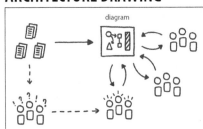

A picture—or, in this case, a high-level outline sketch of your system's basic architecture—can replace a thousand words, save time, and prevent misunderstandings.
See Chapter 9: Patterns for Development and Process for full version.

AUTOMATED INFRASTRUCTURE

The absolute majority of operational tasks need to be automated. Automation reduces interteam dependencies, which allows faster experimentation and leads in turn to faster development.
See Chapter 10: Patterns for Infrastructure and Cloud for full version.

AUTOMATED TESTING

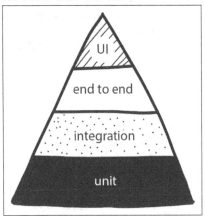

Shift responsibility for testing from humans (manual) to an automated testing framework so the quality of the released products is consistent and continuously improving, allowing developers to deliver faster while spending more of their time improving features to meet customer needs.
See Chapter 9: Patterns for Development and Process for full version.

AVOID REINVENTING THE WHEEL

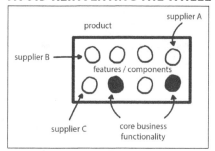

When possible, purchase solutions for any need that is not your actual core business instead of trying to custom-build perfect tools.
See Chapter 9: Patterns for Development and Process for full version.

BIG BET

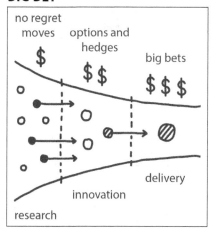

When enough information is available, commit to a significant solution for moving the cloud migration forward. Focus on execution rather than research.
See Chapter 7: Patterns for Strategy and Risk Management for full version.

BLAMELESS INQUIRY

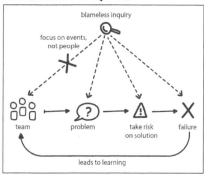

When a problem occurs, focusing on the event instead of the people involved allows them to learn from mistakes without fear of punishment.
See Chapter 8: Patterns for Organization and Culture for full version.

BUILD-RUN TEAMS ("CN DevOps")

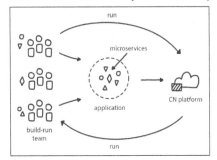

Dev teams have full authority over the services they build, not only creating but also deploying and supporting them.
See Chapter 8: Patterns for Organization and Culture for full version.

BUSINESS CASE

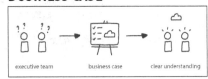

Before launching a cloud native transformation, an enterprise's leadership must make sure the initiative is needed and that the benefits will justify the investment.
See Chapter 7: Patterns for Strategy and Risk Management for full version.

CO-LOCATED TEAMS

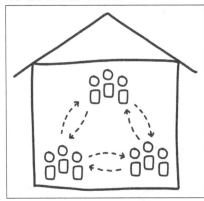

Teams that work together in person develop naturally closer relationships and better collaborative problem-solving abilities, which in turn nurtures greater innovation.
See Chapter 8: Patterns for Organization and Culture for full version.

COMMUNICATE THROUGH APIS

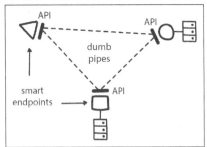

In a highly distributed system, microservices must communicate with one another via stable and strongly segregated APIs.
See Chapter 9: Patterns for Development and Process for full version.

COMMUNICATE THROUGH TRIBES

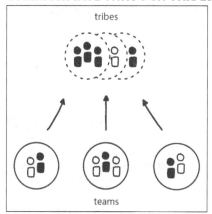

Create groups of people who have similar skills but are on different teams to cross-pollinate ideas across the company and provide valuable whole-organization perspective.
See Chapter 8: Patterns for Organization and Culture for full version.

CONTAINERIZED APPS

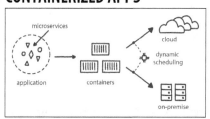

When an application is packaged in a container with all its necessary dependencies, it does not rely on the underlying runtime environment and so can run agnostically on any platform.
See Chapter 10: Patterns for Infrastructure and Cloud for full version.

CONTINUOUS DELIVERY

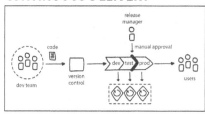

Keeping a short build/test/deliver cycle means code is always ready for production and features can be immediately released to customers—and their feedback quickly returned to developers.
See Chapter 10: Patterns for Infrastructure and Cloud for full version.

CONTINUOUS DEPLOYMENT

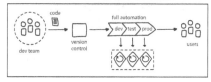

Continuous deployment automatically and seamlessly pushes code that has been accepted in the continuous integration/continuous delivery cycle into the production environment.
See Chapter 10: Patterns for Infrastructure and Cloud for full version.

CONTINUOUS INTEGRATION

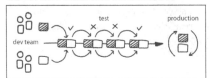

Frequent integration of small iterative changes speeds overall delivery and improves the quality of the code.
See Chapter 9: Patterns for Development and Process for full version.

CORE TEAM

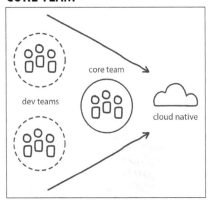

Dedicate a team of engineers and architects to the task of uncovering the best transformation path and implementing it along the way. This reduces risk embedded in the transformation while the team gains experience helpful for onboarding the remaining teams later.
See Chapter 8: Patterns for Organization and Culture for full version.

DATA-DRIVEN DECISION MAKING

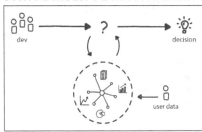

Collect data, extract patterns and facts, and use them to make inferences to drive objective decision making.
See Chapter 7: Patterns for Strategy and Risk Management for full version.

DECIDE CLOSEST TO THE ACTION

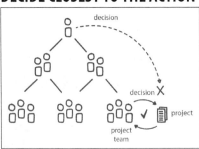

Those nearest to a change action get the first chance to make any decisions related to it.
See Chapter 8: Patterns for Organization and Culture for full version.

DELAYED AUTOMATION

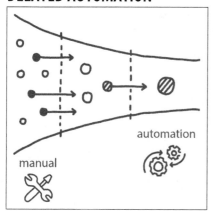

Automate processes only after a problem has been completely solved and the solution has been run manually a few times.
See Chapter 9: Patterns for Development and Process for full version.

DEMO APPLICATIONS

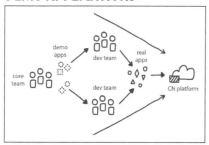

Teams onboarded to the new cloud native system receive demo applications as an educational starting point for building their own cloud native applications.
See Chapter 9: Patterns for Development and Process for full version.

DESIGN THINKING FOR RADICAL INNOVATION

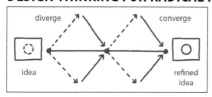

Whether faced with a radical new idea or a big problem, Design Thinking can be used as a process for first brainstorming a robust list of solutions and then narrowing it down to the best possibilities for actual exploration.
See Chapter 8: Patterns for Organization and Culture for full version.

DESIGNATED STRATEGIST

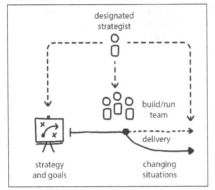

When you're running forward as fast as you can, it's difficult to look around you—so appoint one person within the organization to be in charge of situational awareness.

See Chapter 7: Patterns for Strategy and Risk Management for full version.

DEVELOPER STARTER PACK

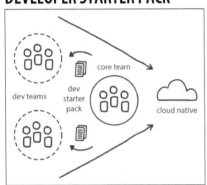

Provide a "starter kit" of materials, guides, and other resources to help new teams onboard to the new cloud native system quickly and with confidence.

See Chapter 9: Patterns for Development and Process for full version.

DISTRIBUTED SYSTEMS

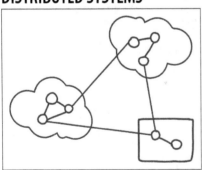

When software is built as a series of fully independent, loosely coupled services, the resulting system is, by design, fast, resilient, and highly scalable.

See Chapter 9: Patterns for Development and Process for full version.

DYNAMIC SCHEDULING

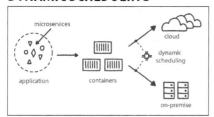

An orchestrator (typically Kubernetes) is needed to organize the deployment and management of microservices in a distributed container-based application to assign them across random machines at the instant of execution.
See Chapter 9: Patterns for Development and Process for full version.

DYNAMIC STRATEGY

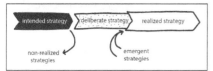

Today's tech-driven marketplace is a constantly shifting environment, no matter what business you are in—so your game plan needs to shift right along with it.
See Chapter 7: Patterns for Strategy and Risk Management for full version.

EXECUTIVE COMMITMENT

To ensure allocation of sufficient resources and reasonable delivery time frames, large-scale projects such as cloud native transformation require strong commitment from the top executive team.
See Chapter 7: Patterns for Strategy and Risk Management for full version.

EXIT STRATEGY OVER VENDOR LOCK-IN

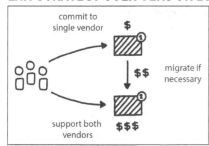

Public cloud vendors can handle all aspects of building and operating a cloud native platform, and their tools are often excellent—but when committing to a vendor/technology/platform it's important to identify an alternative solution and any costs associated with switching over.
See Chapter 7: Patterns for Strategy and Risk Management for full version.

EXPLORATORY EXPERIMENTS

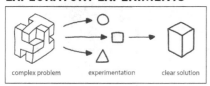

When dealing with a complex problem with no obvious available solution, run a series of small experiments to evaluate the possible alternatives and learn by doing.
See Chapter 8: Patterns for Organization and Culture for full version.

FULL PRODUCTION READINESS

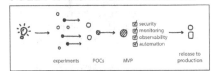

Make sure your platform is fully provisioned with CI/CD, security, monitoring, observability, and other features essential to production readiness before you try to take it live.
See Chapter 10: Patterns for Infrastructure and Cloud for full version.

GRADUAL ONBOARDING

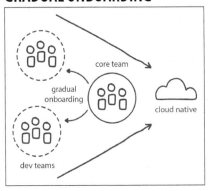

One to three months before the new platform goes live, begin training a couple of teams at a time with a pause between each cohort to incorporate feedback and improve the process/materials.
See Chapter 8: Patterns for Organization and Culture for full version.

GRADUALLY RAISING THE STAKES

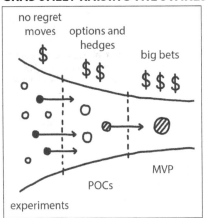

In an uncertain environment, slowly increase investment in learning and information gathering; eventually you uncover enough information to reduce risk and make better-informed decisions.
See Chapter 7: Patterns for Strategy and Risk Management for full version.

INTERNAL EVANGELISM

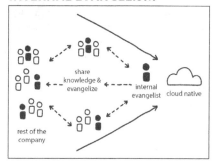

Provide plenty of information about the transformation across the entire company right from the start to create understanding, acceptance of, and support for the initiative.
See Chapter 8: Patterns for Organization and Culture for full version.

INVOLVE THE BUSINESS

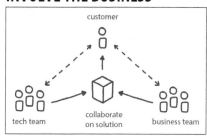

The business teams and the tech teams need to collaborate to create an effective customer-feedback loop that drives product improvement.
See Chapter 7: Patterns for Strategy and Risk Management for full version.

LEAN FOR OPTIMIZATION

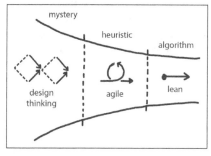

When a stable system delivers the value that's intended and is not a target for technical innovation, focus on improving the system by continuously and incrementally improving delivery and maintenance processes with emphasis on repeatability.
See Chapter 8: Patterns for Organization and Culture for full version.

LEARNING LOOP

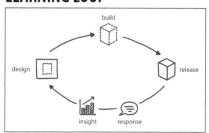

Building feedback collection into the delivery process closes the loop between engineers and the people who use their products, putting the customer at the center of the product development cycle.
See Chapter 7: Patterns for Strategy and Risk Management for full version.

LEARNING ORGANIZATION

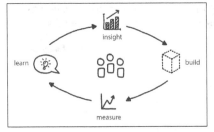

An organization skilled at acquiring information, creating insight, and transferring knowledge can tolerate risk with confidence and solve difficult problems through experimentation and innovation.
See Chapter 7: Patterns for Strategy and Risk Management for full version.

LIFT AND SHIFT AT THE END

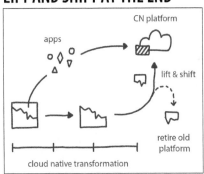

It's important not to approach a cloud native transformation by simply attempting a full "lift and shift" of your existing system onto the cloud. But it *can* be smart to move some intact pieces of it at the very end.
See Chapter 10: Patterns for Infrastructure and Cloud for full version.

MANAGE FOR CREATIVITY

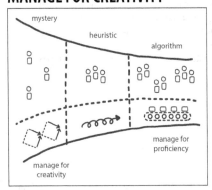

Teams charged with innovation need the open-ended freedom to experiment their way to solutions without pressure for delivering specific results on a set schedule—and the freedom to sometimes fail along the way.
See Chapter 8: Patterns for Organization and Culture for full version.

MANAGE FOR PROFICIENCY

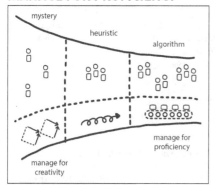

Teams delivering stable and highly repetitive or algorithmic work should be managed for high quality and optimal efficiency.
See Chapter 8: Patterns for Organization and Culture for full version.

MEASURE WHAT MATTERS

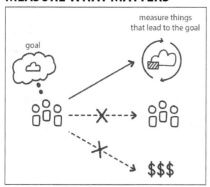

People optimize their actions based on how their work is measured. Assessing the wrong things leads people to optimize for the wrong goals.
See Chapter 7: Patterns for Strategy and Risk Management for full version.

MICROSERVICES ARCHITECTURE

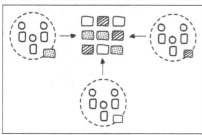

To reduce the costs of coordination among teams delivering large monolithic applications, build the software as a suite of modular services that are built, deployed, and operated independently.
See Chapter 9: Patterns for Development and Process for full version.

MVP (PLATFORM)

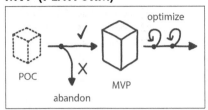

Once Exploratory Experiments and PoCs have uncovered a probable path to success, build a simple version of a basic but fully functional and production-ready platform with one to three small applications running on it in production.
See Chapter 8: Patterns for Organization and Culture for full version.

NO LONG TESTS IN CI/CD

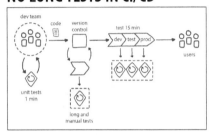

Execute non-critical long running tests in the background so they don't block delivery to production.
See Chapter 9: Patterns for Development and Process for full version.

NO REGRET MOVES

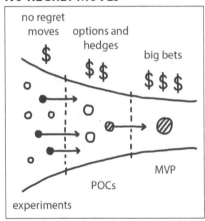

Small, quick actions that require little investment of time and money but increase knowledge, reduce risk, and benefit the entire organization—inside or outside of a transformation scenario.
See Chapter 7: Patterns for Strategy and Risk Management for full version.

OBJECTIVE SETTING

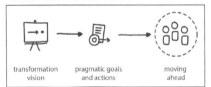

After establishing a transformation vision, the next step is to translate it into pragmatic goals and actions for moving the initiative ahead.
See Chapter 7: Patterns for Strategy and Risk Management for full version.

OBSERVABILITY

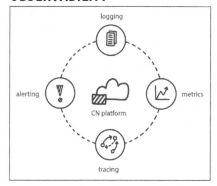

Cloud native distributed systems require constant insight into the behavior of all running services in order to understand the system's behavior and to predict potential problems or incidents.
See Chapter 10: Patterns for Infrastructure and Cloud for full version.

ONGOING EDUCATION

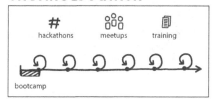

Continuously introduce new ways and improve existing ones to help teams continually develop their cloud native knowledge and skills.
See Chapter 8: Patterns for Organization and Culture for full version.

OPEN SOURCE INTERNAL PROJECTS

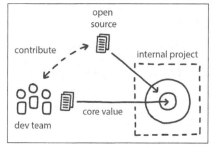

Use open source solutions for any software need that is not directly related to the company's core business value.
See Chapter 9: Patterns for Development and Process for full version.

OPTIONS AND HEDGES

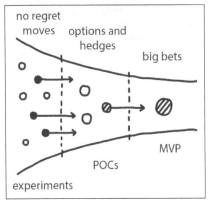

Research has created deeper understanding, and a few potentially promising transformation paths have begun to emerge. Continue reducing the risk by focusing on the most promising options and developing them further.

See Chapter 7: Patterns for Strategy and Risk Management for full version.

PERIODIC CHECK-UPS

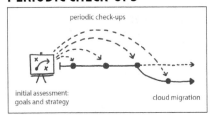

Frequently reassess vision and objectives to ensure these remain the correct direction to proceed as the business environment shifts.

See Chapter 7: Patterns for Strategy and Risk Management for full version.

PERSONALIZED RELATIONSHIPS FOR CO-CREATION

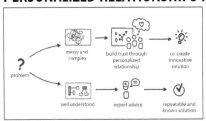

Solutions to complex problems are best created collaboratively by teams with high levels of interpersonal connection.

See Chapter 8: Patterns for Organization and Culture for full version.

PLATFORM TEAM

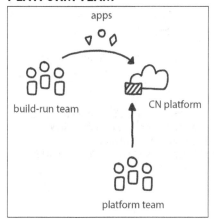

Create a team to be in charge of architecting, building, and running a single, consistent, and stable cloud native platform for use by the entire organization so that developers can focus on building applications instead of configuring infrastructure.
See Chapter 8: Patterns for Organization and Culture for full version.

PRIVATE CLOUD

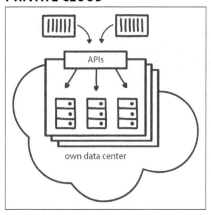

A private cloud approach, operated either over the internet or on company-owned on-premises infrastructure, can offer the benefits of cloud computing services like AWS while restricting access to only select users.
See Chapter 10: Patterns for Infrastructure and Cloud for full version.

PRODUCTIVE FEEDBACK

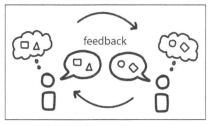

People are more engaged and creative when they feel comfortable receiving constructive information about their behavior and giving the same in return.
See Chapter 8: Patterns for Organization and Culture for full version.

PROOF OF CONCEPT (PoC)

Before fully committing to a solution that can significantly affect the future, build a small prototype to demonstrate viability and gain better understanding.
See Chapter 8: Patterns for Organization and Culture for full version.

PSYCHOLOGICAL SAFETY

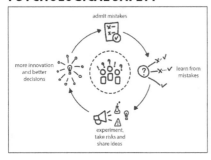

When team members feel they can speak up, express concern, and make mistakes without facing punishment or ridicule, they can think freely and creatively and are open to taking risks.
See Chapter 8: Patterns for Organization and Culture for full version.

PUBLIC CLOUD

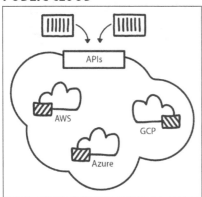

Instead of using your own hardware, rely on the hardware managed by public cloud vendors whenever possible.
See Chapter 10: Patterns for Infrastructure & Cloud for full version.

REDUCE COST OF EXPERIMENTATION

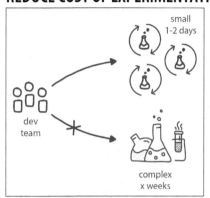

When someone has an idea that requires validation, the costs of doing experiments around it needs to be as low as possible.
See Chapter 9: Patterns for Development and Process for full version.

REFERENCE ARCHITECTURE

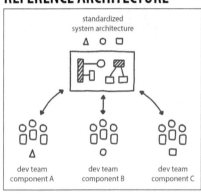

Provide an easily accessible document laying out a standardized system architecture for all teams to use for building their applications/components. This ensures higher architectural consistency and lowers development costs via better reusability.
See Chapter 9: Patterns for Development and Process for full version.

REFLECTIVE BREAKS

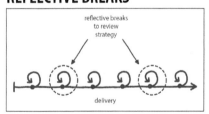

Build periodic times into the business delivery cycle dedicated to reviewing current strategy in light of shifting market conditions or other new information.
See Chapter 7: Patterns for Strategy & Risk Management for full version.

REMOTE TEAMS

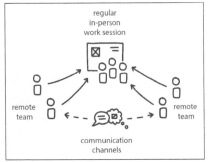

If teams must be distributed, whether across a city or a continent, build in regular in-person retreats/work sessions as well as robust channels for close and free-flowing communication.
See Chapter 8: Patterns for Organization and Culture for full version.

REPRODUCIBLE DEV ENVIRONMENT

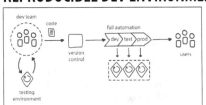

Developers need to test their daily work in an environment that is easy to spin up and that matches production tooling as closely as possible.
See Chapter 9: Patterns for Development and Process for full version.

RESEARCH THROUGH ACTION

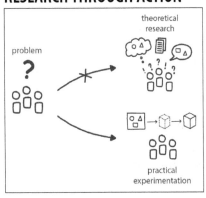

People can sometimes use research as a way to avoid making decisions, so hands-on learning through small experiments builds confidence and jump-starts progress.
See Chapter 7: Patterns for Strategy and Risk Management for full version.

RISK-REDUCING DEPLOYMENT STRATEGIES

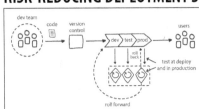

Employ release tactics to decrease the chance of problems happening when changes are introduced into the production system.
See Chapter 10: Patterns for Infrastructure and Cloud for full version.

SECURE SYSTEM FROM THE START

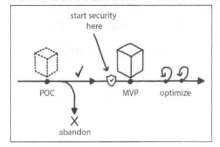

Build security into the platform beginning with the earliest versions to ensure your distributed system is unbreachable by design.
See Chapter 9: Patterns for Development and Process for full version.

SELF-SERVICE

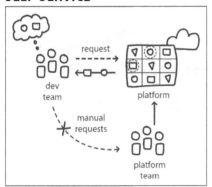

In cloud native everyone can do their own provisioning and deployment with no handoffs between teams.
See Chapter 10: Patterns for Infrastructure and Cloud for full version.

SERVERLESS

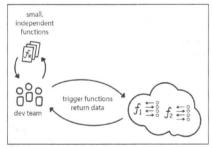

The soon-to-arrive future is event-driven, instantaneously scalable services (functions) on the cloud.
See Chapter 9: Patterns for Development and Process for full version.

SRE TEAM

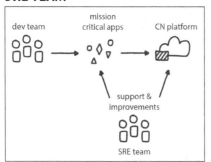

The SRE (Site Reliability Engineering) team helps the development teams to maintain and improve the application (not the platform or infrastructure).
See Chapter 8: Patterns for Organization and Culture for full version.

STRANGLE MONOLITHIC APPLICATION

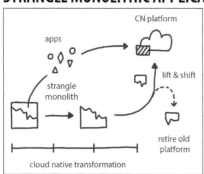

Gradually split pieces of the old monolithic application one by one, re-archtect them into services, and move them over time to the new CN platform.
See Chapter 8: Patterns for Organization and Culture for full version.

STRANGLE MONOLITHIC ORGANIZATION

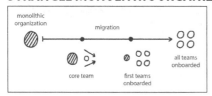

Just as the new tools, technologies, and infrastructure gradually roll out over the course of a transformation initiative, the organization and its teams must also evolve to work with them properly.
See Chapter 8: Patterns for Organization and Culture for full version.

THREE HORIZONS

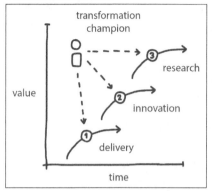

Proportional allocation of resources among delivery, innovation, and research makes an organization responsive to change while reliably delivering core business value.
See Chapter 7: Patterns for Strategy and Risk Management for full version.

TRANSFORMATION CHAMPION

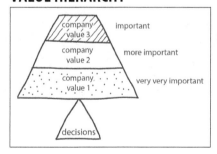

When a person is promoting a good new idea that can take the company's goals and values into the future, recognize and empower them to lead the action.
See Chapter 7: Patterns for Strategy and Risk Management for full version.

VALUE HIERARCHY

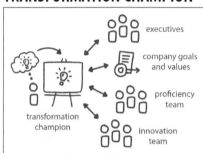

When an organization's values are clearly stated and prioritized, as well as fully internalized across the company, people have the basis for making day-to-day decisions without needing to seek consent or permission/approval. When an organization's values are clearly stated and prioritized, day-to-day decisions can be made without seeking consent or permission/approval.
See Chapter 7: Patterns for Strategy and Risk Management for full version.

VISION FIRST

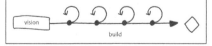

Defining a high-level transformation path as the very first step helps set the right course through an uncertain environment.
See Chapter 7: Patterns for Strategy and Risk Management for full version.

Index

About the Authors

Pini Reznik is CTO and cofounder of Container Solutions, a consultancy that is helping companies to successfully adopt cloud native technologies and practices.

In the five years of existence of Container Solutions, they've participated and led dozens of cloud native transformations and collected extensive hands-on experience in both technical and organizational aspects of the transformation.

Jamie Dobson is cofounder and CEO of Container Solutions, a professional services consultancy specializing in cloud migration. A first encounter with a BBC computer and BASIC at the age of nine launched a lifelong passion for programming and software development. He eventually developed a matching passion for coaching and organizational strategy to help humans work effectively and beneficially with the technology that increasingly drives our lives.

Michelle Gienow is a web developer, JAMstack evangelist, and former journalist whose clients include The New Stack, Linux Foundation, New York Times, and Discovery Channel, among many. She is happiest when working amid the fascinating confluence of technology and writing, whether it's JavaScript code or cloud native principles.

Colophon

The animal on the cover of *Cloud Native Transformation* is the Blue Clipper butterfly (*Parthenos sylvia*). It lives in the rainforests of India, Sri Lanka, Bangladesh, Myanmar, Papua New Guinea, and most of Southeast Asia. Its large (four inch) wingspan and beautiful colors wings make it a favorite of photographers and butterfly conservatories.

The name of the species means "virgin of the forest" in Greek. The English name refers to the 18th century clipper ships whose billowing sails the butterfly's white wing patches resemble. The wings' background color may be orange, green, or brown instead of blue.

The Blue Clipper is a fast, powerful flier, flapping its wings stiffly and keeping them mostly horizontal as well as gliding. The male is smaller than the female and flies closer to the ground, taking water from puddles. Both sexes also feed on nectar, often from lantana flowers. Larvae feed on tropical plants such as the passionflower and moonseed.

Many of the animals on O'Reilly covers are endangered; all of them are important to the world.

The cover illustration is by Karen Montgomery, based on a black and white engraving from *Encyclopedie D'Histoire Naturelle*. The cover fonts are Gilroy Semibold and Guardian Sans. The text font is Adobe Minion Pro; the heading font is Adobe Myriad Condensed; and the code font is Dalton Maag's Ubuntu Mono.

O'REILLY®

There's much more where this came from.

Experience books, videos, live online training courses, and more from O'Reilly and our 200+ partners—all in one place.

Learn more at oreilly.com/online-learning

CPSIA information can be obtained
at www.ICGtesting.com
Printed in the USA
JSHW040932220322
24091JS00004B/102